PROPHETS MALE AND FEMALE

Society of Biblical Literature

Ancient Israel and Its Literature

Thomas C. Römer, General Editor

Editorial Board

Suzanne Boorer
Victor H. Matthews
Benjamin D. Sommer
Nili Wazana

Number 15

PROPHETS MALE AND FEMALE

Gender and Prophecy in the Hebrew Bible, the
Eastern Mediterranean, and the Ancient Near East

PROPHETS MALE AND FEMALE

GENDER AND PROPHECY IN THE HEBREW BIBLE, THE EASTERN MEDITERRANEAN, AND THE ANCIENT NEAR EAST

Edited by
Jonathan Stökl and Corrine L. Carvalho

Society of Biblical Literature
Atlanta

PROPHETS MALE AND FEMALE
Gender and Prophecy in the Hebrew Bible, the
Eastern Mediterranean, and the Ancient Near East

Copyright © 2013 by the Society of Biblical Literature

All rights reserved. No part of this work may be reproduced or transmitted in any form or by any means, electronic or mechanical, including photocopying and recording, or by means of any information storage or retrieval system, except as may be expressly permitted by the 1976 Copyright Act or in writing from the publisher. Requests for permission should be addressed in writing to the Rights and Permissions Office, Society of Biblical Literature, 825 Houston Mill Road, Atlanta, GA 30329 USA.

Library of Congress Cataloging-in-Publication Data

Prophets male and female : gender and prophecy in the Hebrew Bible, the Eastern Mediterranean, and the ancient Near East / edited by Jonathan Stökl and Corrine L. Carvalho.
    p. cm. — (Society of Biblical Literature ancient Israel and its literature ; 15)
  Includes bibliographical references and indexes.
  ISBN 978-1-58983-776-8 (paper binding : alk. paper) — ISBN 978-1-58983-777-5 (electronic format) — ISBN 978-1-58983-773-7 (hardcover binding : alk. paper)
  1. Prophets. 2. Prophecy. 3. Sex role—Biblical teaching. 4. Bible. O.T.—Criticism, interpretation, etc. 5. Middle East—Religion. I. Stökl, Jonathan, 1977- II. Carvalho, Corrine L..
  BS1198.P758 2013
  224'.06081—dc23   2013004359

Printed on acid-free, recycled paper conforming to
ANSI/NISO Z39.48-1992 (R1997) and ISO 9706:1994
standards for paper permanence.

To Martti Nissinen,

whose scholarship, leadership, and warmth

has benefited us as colleagues and friends

Contents

Abbreviations ix

Introduction
    Corrine Carvalho and Jonathan Stökl 1

PART 1: PROPHECY IN THE ANCIENT NEAR EAST AND GREECE

"Her Outdoors": An Anthropological Perspective on Female
    Prophets and Prophecy
    Lester L. Grabbe 11

Gender and Prophetic Agency in the Ancient Near East and in Greece
    Martti Nissinen 27

Gender "Ambiguity" in Ancient Near Eastern Prophecy?
    A Reassessment of the Data behind a Popular Theory
    Jonathan Stökl 59

The Misconstrued Role of the *Assinnu* in Ancient Near
    Eastern Prophecy
    Ilona Zsolnay 81

The Role of the Female Seer/Prophet in Ancient Greece
    Anselm C. Hagedorn 101

Female Prophets among Montanists
    Antti Marjanen 127

PART 2: PROPHECY IN BIBLICAL TEXTS

Speaking in Dreams: The Figure of Miriam and Prophecy
    Hanna Tervanotko 147

Childless Female Diviners in the Bible and Beyond
  Esther J. Hamori 169

"Misogyny" in Service of Theocentricity: Legitimate or Not?
  Dale Launderville 193

Spermatic Spluttering Pens: Concerning the Construction and
  Breakdown of Prophetic Masculinity
  Roland Boer 215

Sex and the Single Prophet: Marital Status and Gender in
  Jeremiah and Ezekiel
  Corrine L. Carvalho 237

Bibliography 269
Contributors 315
Index of Primary Texts 319
    Old Testament   319
    Deuterocanonical Works   324
    Pseudepigrapha   324
    Dead Sea Scrolls   325
    New Testament   326
    West-Semitic   326
    Rabbinic Literature   326
    Jewish Authors   327
    Cuneiform Texts   327
    Hittite/Luwian   330
    Egyptian   330
    Greek and Latin Texts   330
    Greek Epigraphy   335
Index of Modern Authors 336
Concordance of Text Numbers 344

Abbreviations

AB	Anchor Bible
ABD	*Anchor Bible Dictionary*. Edited by David Noel Freedman. 6 vols. New York: Doubleday, 1992.
ABRL	Anchor Bible Reference Library
AGJU	Arbeiten zur Geschichte des antiken Judentums und des Urchristentums
AnOr	Analecta orientalia
AOAT	Alter Orient und Altes Testament
ARM	Archives royales de Mari
AS	Assyriological Studies
ATD	Das Alte Testament Deutsch
AYBRL	Anchor Yale Bible Reference Library
BA	*Biblical Archaeologist*
BBB	Bonner biblische Beiträge
BDB	Brown, Francis, S. R. Driver, and Charles A. Briggs, *A Hebrew and English Lexicon of the Old Testament*. Oxford: Clarendon, 1907.
BEATAJ	Beiträge zur Erforschung des Alten Testaments und des antiken Judentum
BETL	Bibliotheca ephemeridum theologicarum lovaniensium
Bib	*Biblica*
BibInt	*Biblical Interpretation*
BibOr	Biblica et orientalia
BiSe	Biblical Seminar
BIS	Biblical Interpretation Series
BJS	Brown Judaic Studies
BKAT	Biblischer Kommentar, Altes Testament
BM	Tablets in the collection of the British Museum
BMW	The Bible in the Modern World
BiOr	*Bibliotheca orientalis*

BRev	*Bible Review*
BZ	*Biblische Zeitschrift*
BZAW	Beiträge zur Zeitschrift für die alttestamentliche Wissenschaft
BZNW	Beiträge zur Zeitschrift für die neutestamentliche Wissenschaft
CAD	*The Assyrian Dictionary of the Oriental Institute of the University of Chicago.* Edited by Ignace J. Gelb et al. 21 vols. in 26. Chicago: University of Chicago Press, 1956–2011.
CANE	*Civilizations of the Ancient Near East.* Edited by Jack Sasson. 4 vols. New York: Scribner, 1995.
CBQ	*Catholic Biblical Quarterly*
CHANE	Culture and History of the Ancient Near East
CC	Continental Commentaries
CDLI Bulletin	*Cuneiform Digital Library Initiative Bulletin*
CM	Cuneiform Monographs
CQ	*Classical Quarterly*
CRRAI	Compte rendu, Rencontre Assyriologique Internationale
CT	*Cuneiform Texts from Babylonian Tablets in the British Museum.* London: Trustees of the British Museum, 1896–.
DJD	Discoveries in the Judaean Desert
DMOA	Documenta et monumenta orientis antiqui
DSD	*Dead Sea Discoveries*
DSSR	*The Dead Sea Scrolls Reader.* Edited by Donald W. Parry and Emanuel Tov. 6 vols. Leiden, 2004–2005
DSSSE	*The Dead Sea Scrolls Study Edition.* Edited by Florentino García Martínez and Eibert J. C. Tigchelaar. 2 vols. Leiden: Brill, 1997–1998.
ET	English translation
ETCSL	Electronic Text Corpus of Sumerian Literature
EvT	*Evangelische Theologie*
f.	feminine
FAT	Forschungen zum Alten Testament
FCB	Feminist Companion to the Bible
FGH	*Die Fragmente der griechischen Historiker.* Edited by Felix Jacoby. Leiden: Brill, 1954–1964.
FOTL	Forms of the Old Testament Literature
FRLANT	Forschungen zur Religion und Literatur des Alten und Neuen Testaments

GAG	Wolfram von Soden, with Werner R. Mayer, *Grundriss der akkadischen Grammatik*. 3rd ed. AnOr 33. Rome: Pontifical Biblical Institute, 1995.
GAS	Gender and Archaeology Series
GBS	Guides to Biblical Studies
GCT	Gender, Culture, Theory
HALOT	Köhler, Ludwig, Walter Baumgartner, and Johann Jakob Stamm. *The Hebrew and Aramaic Lexicon of the Old Testament*. Translated and edited under the supervision of M. E. J. Richardson. 5 vols. Leiden: Brill, 1994–2000.
HBM	Hebrew Bible Monographs
HBS	Herders biblische Studien
HBT	*Horizons in Biblical Theology*
Heb.	Hebrew
HellSt	Hellenic Studies
HM	Historical Materialism
HSM	Harvard Semitic Monographs
HSS	Harvard Semitic Studies
HTKAT	Herders theologischer Kommentar zum Alten Testament
HTS	Harvard Theological Studies
HUCA	*Hebrew Union College Annual*
IBC	Interpretation: A Bible Commentary for Teaching and Preaching
ICC	International Critical Commentary
IDB	*The Interpreter's Dictionary of the Bible*. Edited by George A. Buttrick. 4 vols. Nashville: Abingdon, 1962.
IDBSup	*Interpreter's Dictionary of the Bible: Supplementary Volume*. Edited by Keith Crim. Nashville, 1976.
IG	*Inscriptiones graecae*. Editio minor. Berlin, 1924–
IGR	*Inscriptiones Graecae ad res Romanas pertinentes*. Ed. René Cagnat et al. 5 vols. Paris: Leroux, 1911–1927.
Int	*Interpretation*
JAOS	*Journal of the American Oriental Society*
JBL	*Journal for Biblical Literature*
JCS	*Journal of Cuneiform Studies*
JETS	*Journal of the Evangelical Theological Society*
JHNES	Johns Hopkins Near Eastern Studies
JJS	*Journal of Jewish Studies*
JNES	*Journal of Near Eastern Studies*

JPSTC	Jewish Publication Society Torah Commentary
JQR	*Jewish Quarterly Review*
JR	*Journal of Religion*
JSHRZ	Jüdische Schriften aus hellenistisch-römischer Zeit
JSJSup	Journal for the Study of Judaism in Persian, Hellenistic, and Roman Periods Supplement Series
JSOT	*Journal for the Study of the Old Testament*
JSOTSup	Journal for the Study of the Old Testament Supplement Series
JSP	*Journal for the Study of the Pseudepigrapha*
JSPSup	Journal for the Study of the Pseudepigrapha Supplement Series
JSQ	*Jewish Studies Quarterly*
JSS	*Journal of Semitic Studies*
JQR	*Jewish Quarterly Review*
KAV	Keilschrifttexte aus Assur verschiedenen Inhalts
KJV	King James Version
KTU	*Die keilalphabetischen Texte aus Ugarit*. Edited by Manfried Dietrich, Oswald Loretz, and J. Sanmartín. AOAT 24. Neukirchen-Vluyn: Neukirchener, 1976.
LCL	Loeb Classical Library
LHBOTS	Library of Hebrew Bible/Old Testament Studies
m.	masculine
MARI	*Mari: Annales de recherches interdisciplinaires*
MC	Mesopotamian Civilizations
MDP	Mémoires de la Délégation en Perse
MSL	Materialien zum sumerischen Lexikon. Edited by Benno Landsberger.
NABU	*Nouvelles assyriologiques breves et utilitaires*
NIB	New Interpreter's Bible. Edited by Leander E. Keck. 12 vols. plus index volume. Nashville: Abingdon, 1994–2004.
NICOT	New International Commentary on the Old Testament
Nin	*Nin: Journal of Gender Studies in Antiquity*
NovTSup	Supplements to Novum Testamentum
NRSV	New Revised Standard Version
OBO	Orbis biblicus et orientalis
OIS	Oriental Institute Seminars
Or	*Orientalia*
OTL	Old Testament Library

OTP	*The Old Testament Pseudepigrapha*. Edited by James H. Charlesworth. 2 vols. New York: Doubleday, 1983–1985.
OTS	Old Testament Studies
OtSt	*Oudtestamentische Studiën*
PMS	Patristic Monograph Series
PNA	*The Prosopography of the Neo-Assyrian Empire*. Edited by Simo Parpola et al. 3 vols. Helsinki: Neo-Assyrian Text Corpus Project, 1998–2011.
PRSt	*Perspectives in Religious Studies*
PrTMS	Princeton Theological Monograph Series
RA	*Revue d'assyriologie et d'archéologie orientale*
RB	*Revue biblique*
RevQ	*Revue de Qumran*
RGRW	Religions in the Graeco-Roman World
RIME	The Royal Inscriptions of Mesopotamia, Early Periods
RINAP	Royal Inscriptions of the Neo-Assyrian Period
RSV	Revised Standard Version
SAA	State Archives of Assyria
SAAB	*State Archives of Assyria Bulletin*
SAAS	State Archives of Assyria Studies
SAC	Studies in Antiquity and Christianity
SAOC	Studies in Ancient Oriental Civilizations
SBH	George Andrew Reisner, *Sumerisch-babylonische Hymnen nach Thontafeln griechischer Zeit*. Berlin: Spemann, 1896.
SBL	Society of Biblical Literature
SBLAIL	Society of Biblical Literature Ancient Israel and Its Literature
SBLDS	Society of Biblical Literature Dissertation Series
SBLEJL	Society of Biblical Literature Early Judaism and Its Literature
SBLMS	Society of Biblical Literature Monograph Series
SBLRBS	Society of Biblical Literature Resources for Biblical Study
SBLSCS	Society of Biblical Literature Septuagint and Cognate Studies
SBLSymS	Society of Biblical Literature Symposium Series
SBLWAW	Society of Biblical Literature Writings from the Ancient World
SC	Sources Chrétiennes. Paris: Cerf, 1943–
SecCent	*Second Century*

SEG	Supplementum epigraphicum graecum
SemeiaSt	Semeia Studies
SHBC	Smyth & Helwys Bible Commentary
SHCANE	Studies in the History and Culture of the Ancient Near East
SJOT	*Scandinavian Journal of the Old Testament*
SOTSMS	Society for Old Testament Studies Monograph Series
StBL	Studies in Biblical Literature
STDJ	*Studies on the Texts of the Desert of Judah*
StP	Studia Pohl
StPatr	Studia patristica
STT	Oliver R. Gurney, Jacob Joel Finkelstein, and P. Hulin, eds. *The Sultantepe Tablets*. 2 vols. London: British Institute of Archaeology at Ankara, 1957–1964.
StudOr	Studia Orientalia
SVTP	Studia in Veteris Testamenti pseudepigrapha
TCL	Textes cunéiformes. Musée du Louvre
TDOT	*Theological Dictionary of the Old Testament*. Edited by G. Johannes Botterweck, Helmer Ringgren, and Heinz-Josef Fabry. Translated by John T. Willis, Geoffrey W. Bromiley, and David E. Green. 15 vols. Grand Rapids: Eerdmans, 1974–2006.
UC	siglum of the Petrie Museum, University College London
UF	*Ugarit-Forschungen*
USQR	*Union Seminary Quarterly Review*
VAS	Vorderasiatische Schriftdenkmäler
VAT	Vorderasiatische Abteilung Tontafel. Vorderasiatisches Museum, Berlin
VCSup	Supplements to Vigiliae christianae
VT	*Vetus Testamentum*
VTSup	Supplements to Vetus Testamentum
WBC	Word Biblical Commentary
WO	*Die Welt des Orients*
WVDOG	Wissenschaftliche Veröffentlichungen der deutschen Orientgesellschaft
WW	*Word and World*
ZA	*Zeitschrift für Assyriologie und vorderasiatische Archäologie*
ZAW	*Zeitschrift für die alttestamentliche Wissenschaft*

Introduction

Corrine Carvalho and Jonathan Stökl

The essays for this volume come out of the Prophetic Texts in Their Ancient Context section of the Society of Biblical Literature in Boston (2009) and New Orleans (2010). This section studies prophetic texts from the Hebrew Bible and other ancient Near Eastern corpora within their respective ancient contexts. Over the course of two years, this section focused on the intersection of gender and prophecy. Because of the nature of the section, all of the essays rely on textual evidence of one sort or another in order to reconstruct the ancient contexts. Some essays supplement textual evidence with cross-cultural comparisons (Grabbe and Hamori) or approaches based in literary theory (Boer).

Presenters were instructed to consider gender broadly. They were invited to address not just female gender, but masculinity and sexual ambiguity. The result is a collection of essays that demonstrate how attention to gender dynamics in a variety of ancient contexts reveals other social and ideological dynamics at play in the ancient evidence. Attention to gender is not an optional category for understanding all the variety of texts in their ancient context—it is an essential element in these artifacts.

The volume is divided into two parts: prophecy in the ancient Near East and Greece, followed by prophecy in biblical texts. The essays in each set differ from those in the other in noticeable ways, with the Near Eastern essays more focused on historical reconstruction and the biblical essays providing literary analyses of the texts. This is due, in part, to the nature of the evidence available to each set of scholars but is also a result of the differences in the scholarly debates in the various academic disciplines.

Evidence for Israelite/Judean prophecy comes almost entirely from the biblical record, via long, complex texts that have undergone heavy editorial control. The explicit ideology of each text, which can only be partially corrected by epigraphic, annalistic, inscriptional evidence, must be explicitly engaged in one manner or another. The texts themselves are either long narratives within which prophetic activity is described or prophetic books that, while ostensibly containing collections of prophetic oracles, do so within a larger rhetorical framework. The biblical essays, then, more often utilize literary methods of analysis given the rhetorical elements in this ancient evidence.

The essays in the first part of the book, with the exception of Grabbe's, cover a very broad swath of evidence, both geographically and chronologically. While essays dealing with late antiquity do engage complex narrative texts, much of the other evidence comes from nonnarrative texts. While nonnarrative texts also employ rhetoric and reflect ideology, literary methods are not always the best means for revealing those forces. Thus the question raised by Mesopotamian references to the *assinu*s is whether they functioned as prophets or whether their function was something altogether different and their prophetic activity incidental to their other religious role. Even with this wide variety of material, however, questions of status, authority, and agency appear repeatedly in these essays, and we cannot fully understand these questions without engaging how status always engaged gendered status as well.

The volume starts with the essay by Lester Grabbe because of the way that it sets out broader anthropological categories for thinking about this intersection. Grabbe notes that, in the wide variety of settings he surveyed, female prophets were in fact prophets who happened to be female. That is, female prophets performed the same prophetic roles as male prophets. But he goes on to note that female prophetic behavior could be circumscribed by other gendered expectations within their respective societies.

These observations about female prophets raise questions about how masculinity or transgendered identity might also circumscribe prophetic performance. In patriarchal cultures, the performance of gender raises questions about status, power, and agency, which are explicitly addressed by Martti Nissinen, Anselm Hagedorn, Antti Marjanen, Dale Launderville, and Roland Boer. While prophetic activity deemed as authentic conveyed elements of status and power, these scholars query whether the matrix of prophetic status mapped differently onto nonmale prophets than it did onto high-status males. Whereas Grabbe sees female prophets as prophets who happen to be female, Esther Hamori's essay presents literary evidence that the prophetic office may have had different consequences for female and male prophets. Hanna Tervanotko takes the depiction of Miriam as a starting point to inquire whether there may have been forms of communication between the divine and human spheres that were more often practiced by women. Jonathan Stökl and Ilona Zsolnay test the evidence for gender ambiguity in ancient Near Eastern prophecy. The essays by Nissinen, Launderville, and Corrine Carvalho address how prophetic performance of gender also addressed issues of divine status.

Gendered Prophecy in the Ancient Near East and Greece

It is difficult to synthesize the results of these essays, since they cover such disparate locations and historical settings. Three of the essays focus on female prophets in the anthropological evidence (Grabbe), Greek literature (Hagedorn), and Montanist (Marjanen) settings. Two look at the gendered performances of the *assinu* (Stökl and Zsolnay). One provides a broader survey of gender and agency in both the ancient Near East and Greece (Nissinen). None of these essays focuses on masculinity per se, but Zsolnay and Stökl discuss (modern and ancient) expectations of gendered behavior. In spite of the disparate evidence, it is still possible to identify certain patterns related to female prophets.

Not all essays operate with the same terminology. Among the essays on ancient Near Eastern and Greek prophecy, the term *divination* is used to describe all forms of humans accessing divine information, be it through reading the gods' will in the stars, in a sheep's liver, in the flight of birds (all forms of technical divination), or through dreams and prophecy in which the divine will does not have to be interpreted into human speech (intuitive divination). The essays that focus on the biblical texts tend to use the word *divination* to refer to the use of technical manipulation as a means for prophetic interaction with the divine world.

First, unlike more technical forms of divination, ecstatic or charismatic forms of prophecy seems to have been open to women in most societies. To be sure, some cultures were more tolerant of female prophecy, and perhaps prophecy by people who did not fit into contemporary gender dichotomies. Ancient Greece had multiple cultic sites that featured female prophets (Hagedorn). In the ancient Near East, Mari was more tolerant of female prophets than West Semitic cultures such as Israel (Nissinen), but even the less-tolerant communities give evidence of some women who were deemed authentic prophets.

Second, if our evidence is to be trusted, the vast majority of Neo-Assyrian prophets were female. In Mari the numbers show a preference for male prophets, while the data in the Hebrew Bible mentions only five female prophets. Some ancient cultures appear to have required female prophets to be celibate (e.g., the Pythia at Delphi, the Montanists, and possibly some in the Hebrew Bible).

Third, in general, female prophets did not enjoy the same ease of prestige that their male counterparts did. Especially noteworthy is the degree to which the professionalization of prophetic activity seemed to have progressively excluded women. Grabbe speaks about the kinds of restrictions that female prophets would have experienced. The restriction that they not have control over men seems especially at play in this arena.

Fourth, on a related note, the nonbiblical evidence of prophecy gives a fuller picture of various types of prophetic activity: seers, diviners, those possessed by spirits, and so on. As a result of this fuller picture, another limitation sometimes seen for women is their exclusion from prophetic activities requiring training or education, such as the arts of technical divination.

This last observation raises the issue of the relationship between the divine and human realms that is at the heart of (divinatory and) prophetic activities. As implied by Nissinen's article, the ability to read the gods' writing in the stars or a sheep's liver conferred a higher status to a technical diviner, who could reliably inquire of the gods. In contrast, prophecy and other forms of intuitive divination place the agency more on the divine. As a rule, communities do not object to a deity speaking through a woman or someone else of lower status. The question whether the oracles of Montanist female prophets came true suggests that for early Christians it was not enough to deny that these women were prophets because of their gender; instead, the authenticity of their call depended on divine agency revealed through the fulfillment of these oracles.

The question remains whether these general patterns also apply to other nonmale prophets. Stökl's essay raises important questions of terminology and classification for nonmale persons in ancient Mesopotamia. Were they simply acting out nonmale gender roles in the context of a cult, or is there evidence for a standard social role for such persons within their religious system? Stökl shows that there is not enough evidence to assert an official class of nonmale prophets. Zsolnay questions the consensus that *assinnu*s are always nonmale performers suggesting instead that until the middle of the first millennium B.C.E. the *assinnu*s should be understood as specialists who performed a martial role in the cult of warlike forms of Ištar. Only in late texts is the reference to ambiguous gender clear; there is no reason to read that evidence back into earlier texts.

In general, these essays demonstrate that the significance of the gender of a given prophet depends in large part how that gender functions within its native culture. Prophecy, as a religious phenomenon, was one vehicle through which women could have some public expression of their religious identity. This path was safeguarded by the fact that it was a deity who paved it.

The Biblical World

Unlike the essays in the first part of this volume, the essays related to biblical prophecy deal with a far more focused collection of texts, mainly stemming from ancient Israel. Nissinen identifies Israel as less open to female prophets than many other ancient cultures, noting that only about 10 percent of the named prophets found in the biblical evidence were women. The biblical record asserts the nonparticipation of women as leaders in the official cult of Israel; for these texts there were no women priests of Yahweh in the national shrines. Although conclusions about women and the cult need to be cautious since Israelite literature was even more ideologically controlled than the evidence from Mesopotamia, there is no evidence to the contrary about the official cult.

Given the androcentric nature of the biblical literary record, it is noteworthy that positive portrayals of some female prophets remain. These records are the subject of essays by Tervanotko and Hamori. Both essays point to the fact that, although these biblical texts provide more detailed descriptions of individual female prophets in comparison to Mesopotamian texts, they nevertheless suggest that there were fuller traditions about female prophets that lie behind the textual record. Certainly the challenge raised about Moses' prophecy in Num 12 assumed that Miriam was known as a prophet, even though the title was not used in this text (Tervanotko). This evidence suggests that one factor contributing to the unequal representation of female prophets in the written record is the social factors related to writing itself, a topic explicitly addressed by Boer.

Hamori's essay is the only one in the volume to consider nonnormative female behavior as a mark of female prophets. Using broader anthropological parallels, as Grabbe does, her essay notes the prominence of separating female reproductive roles from prophetic ones. In some cases women's sexuality raised questions of purity; in others the role of mother was simply incompatible with the role of prophet. Hamori's cross-cultural survey asks readers to reconsider the reality that no woman in the Bible who functioned as a prophet was, at the same time, said to have children. Biblical texts do not mention an explicit prohibition, but Hamori's essay suggests that the texts could simply presume that female prophets were either virgins, celibate, or postmenopausal.

In addition to these essays on female prophets, this volume also contains three essays that explore the intersection of masculinity and prophecy in the books of Ezekiel and Jeremiah. Launderville's essay analyzes the rhetorical purpose of likening the male elite with menstruating women in Ezek 36:17. Boer examines how the images of Ezekiel promote a phallic power embodied in a male scribal prophet. Carvalho uses categories of gender and queer theory to explore how the notations of Ezekiel and Jeremiah's singleness function within their books.

These essays on the exilic prophets show that masculinity was an essential element in understanding the gender dynamics of the prophetic phenomena. Given the high status of the male elite within Israelite society, an effective way to unsettle that status in relationship to Yahweh was to liken those men to women. Launderville's essay shows that the rhetorical details of Ezek 36:17 expected the reaction of disgust as a tool to change the behavior and attitudes of the male elite toward Yahweh. Boer and Carvalho note that, on the divine side of the coin, hypersexualizing male metaphors attached to the divine realm (from the messengers in Ezek 9 to the hypermale Yahweh in Ezek 16, 23, and Jer 20) undercut the ideology of male control that was the foundation of the patriarchal system.

Boer's essay reads Ezek 9 as a site of ideological struggle over the hegemony of a masculine scribal class. Uncovering assertions of male sexual power undergirding texts like Ezek 2, 9, and Jer 36, Boer concludes that assertions about the phallic power of writing simultaneously revealed the ruling elite's inability to control or contain such power. The result was a set of texts that were merely self-serving, a kind of rhetorical masturbatory practice.

By examining the singleness of Ezekiel and Jeremiah, Carvalho also seeks to uncover the ways in which these texts reveal how the exile ripped out the foundation of male privilege on which preexilic Israel was built. The book of Ezekiel used standard gender categories to depict Yahweh as actively involved in shaming the male elite. Jeremiah's singleness, on the other hand, undercuts Jeremiah's performance of masculinity, an image in continuity with a broader attempt found throughout other sections of the book to complicate gender norms.

In all of these essays on exilic prophets, masculinity was played out not only against the backdrop of Israelite social structures, but against its religious backdrop as well. These essays point out the way that gender was used as a rhetorical feature in these texts to advance certain ideologies and undercut others. All three essays show that in these texts gender was performed in a way that raised the status of the divine realm while simultaneously lowering the status of males who were experiencing exile.

Outcomes

The gendered performances of ancient prophets functioned with a variety of other performances of social roles. In order to explore the significance of gender in each case, then, awareness of this larger social matrix must be kept in mind. Grabbe concludes that female prophets are prophets who happened to be female, but the question remains in what ways gender was always a factor in the way the prophets acted, spoke, and were received by the societies in which they operate. The essays in this volume suggest three areas for further inquiry.

First, the texts about female prophets raise questions about the agency and authority of these women, questions inextricably linked to issues of social status within the gendered matrix of status of each culture. Female prophets seem to have been common both in Greece and in the Neo-Assyrian Empire for reasons that are still not entirely understood. While the texts suggest that in all ancient societies female prophetic activity was probably more widespread than the written evidence records, in most situations female and nonmale prophets were less common than male ones; the one obvious exception to this rule is the Neo-Assyrian Empire, which, according to the available evidence, seems to have preferred its prophets to be female. When the written record includes objections to female prophets, it was usually an issue of status and power relative to men. There are hints in some texts from Greece, however, that there was a tendency for some female prophets to be celibate (although purity language is rarely used in these cases), an issue that may have elevated their status by denying those activities that were most often associated with female gender performance.

Second, the performance of masculinity by prophets and other cult functionaries could be undermined in order to preserve the status of the divine realm vis-à-vis human power. Although in the cult of Ištar cult functionaries (*assinnu*s) performed her martial attributes, for a long time without reference to cross-dressing or nonmale gender performance by male cult functionaries, at a later date reference to such behavior is found in the textual evidence. In Israelite literature, male elites had their status rhetorically deflated, by confrontations with phallic angels, comparisons to menstruating women, and loss of personal agency by becoming Yahweh's mouthpiece, in order to maintain the status of their God. In this way, the feminization of males in the Israelite literature expressed the ancient male audience's awe of their god.

Third, gendered identities that do not match modernist dichotomies of male/female were certainly known in the ancient world outside prophecy. Such identities did not preclude someone from being viewed as an authentic prophet. In Israel and Judah gender-bending and sexual language are apparent in prophetic texts; in Mesopotamia nonstandard gender roles can be found in the textual record, but the evidence is ambiguous as to whether it also occurs in connection to prophecy (Stökl). The question remains whether these were persons already viewed as third (or fourth) gendered by their societies, or whether these were simply cult functionaries playing out set roles.

Lastly, the essays in this volume demonstrate that gender was an essential component of all life in ancient and modern societies and can therefore also be found in most prophetic activity. While female prophets did not prophesy differently than their male counterparts, the ways in which they were accepted, the roles they played in the cult, and their relationship to the divine agent all reveal hidden social structures that impinged on ancient religious expressions. Although more attention has been paid to female identity, the essays as a whole point out that every prophetic expression was a gendered expression, and that attention to those gender dynamics will continue to open up the ancient contexts of prophetic texts.

Part 1
Prophecy in the Ancient Near East and Greece

"Her Outdoors":
An Anthropological Perspective
on Female Prophets and Prophecy*

Lester L. Grabbe

In traditional societies certain roles are often gender specific. This frequently applies to prophet-like figures, such as prophets, shamans, and those possessed by a spirit. In the Jewish and Christian Bibles we find most references to prophets as having male figures in mind, but a number of female prophets are clearly designated as such (Judg 4:14; Exod 15:20; 2 Kgs 22:14; Isa 8:3; Neh 6:14; 2 Chr 34:22).[1] My task in this paper is to consider examples of female prophet-like figures in various cultures with the aim of better understanding the prophetesses of the Bible.

The reason for making this study is the firm belief in the value of drawing on examples of prophetlike figures in other cultures for comparative purposes. To some, any deviation from the figure of an Israelite prophet—

---

* In the traditional argot of (some) Londoners, "indoors" means "at home." Thus a man who says he is going to "eat his dinner indoors" has in mind that he will go home for lunch. Likewise, "her indoors" is a common way for a man to refer to his wife. Anthropologists are noted for their penchant of reasoning from analogies and models. I am not aware that "outdoors" means in public, but logic says it should. Hence, although prophets—whether male or female—are somewhat thin on the ground in today's London, it seems to me logical that a prophetess would be "her outdoors." This remains to be confirmed by anthropologists—or dyed-in-the-wool Londoners.

1. For information on female prophets in the Bible, see Esther J. Hamori's paper in this volume; also Hugh G. M. Williamson, "Prophetesses in the Hebrew Bible," in *Prophets and Prophecy: Proceedings of the Oxford Old Testament Seminar* (ed. John Day; LHBOTS 531; London: T&T Clark, 2010), 65–80. One book that also relates to the matter is Esther J. Hamori, *Women's Divination in Biblical Literature: Prophecy, Necromancy and Other Arts of Knowledge* (AYBRL; New Haven: Yale University Press, forthcoming).

or their concept of an Israelite prophet—invalidates the comparative example. This misses the aim of cross-cultural comparisons, which is not to provide exact counterparts but to open up the study of Israelite prophecy to new ideas and possibilities. Ultimately, any such comparisons must be tested against the data from the Hebrew Bible.

Cross-Cultural Examples

In the examples that follow, I describe the revelations as they are presented in the sources. I make no judgment on the revelations as to whether they are authentic (whatever "authentic" might mean). In cultures with prophetlike figures there may be considerable skepticism toward individual practitioners, even though society believes in the institution as such. Although there are documented examples of deception, it appears that most "possessed" individuals are convinced of being under the control of a higher power of some sort.[2]

Alice Lakwena

In the period after the fall of Idi Amin, a civil war developed between the army that liberated Uganda from his grip and another group called the National Resistance Army.[3] The National Resistance Army won out but sent soldiers to occupy the region of Acholi. Internal resistance to this occupation began to develop in the form of the Uganda People's Democratic Army. A young woman named Alice Auma was seized by the spirit of a deceased Italian army officer in 1985. Her father had himself been a spirit medium, and Alice claimed to be the one chosen to inherit the spirits. Alice's spirit was named Lakwena, and for a time she practiced as

---

2. This judgment arises from reading many anthropological accounts of prophetlike figures. This is especially clear from call accounts, where the figure involved quite frequently attempts to evade the call. Examples can be found in the literature cited later in this article and in Grabbe, *Priests, Prophets, Diviners, Sages: A Socio-historical Study of Religious Specialists in Ancient Israel* (Valley Forge, Pa.: Trinity Press International, 1995), ch. 4.

3. The information in this section is derived from Heike Behrend, *Alice Lakwena and the Holy Spirits: War in Northern Uganda 1985–97* (Eastern Africa Studies; Oxford: James Currey, 1999); idem, "Power to Heal, Power to Kill: Spirit Possession and War in Northern Uganda (1986–1994)," in *Spirit Possession: Modernity and Power in Africa* (ed. Heike Behrend and Ute Luig; Oxford: James Currey, 1999), 20–33.

a healer, on behalf of infertile women and soldiers wounded in battle. But after about a year Lakwena told her to give up healing and lead the fight against evil in Uganda.

She convinced some soldiers to support her and eventually negotiated to lead a section of the Uganda People's Democratic Army, from which she began to organize the Holy Spirit Mobile Army. It should be noted, however, that she did not claim military leadership skills. She stated that she was only a woman and sometimes prepared food and distributed it along with the other women. Indeed, there was initially reluctance on the part of some soldiers to follow her because she was not a military leader. But the spirits who possessed her included a variety of military leaders, and they provided the military leadership. This hierarchy included, in addition to the leader Lakwena, several Islamic spirits who were fighters, a female spirit who was a nurse and healer (the only indigenous spirit), a Korean or Chinese spirit, and an American spirit named Wrong Element. This last was a trickster figure who would sometimes test the soldiers by making misleading statements. He would sometimes even change sides and fight against his own troops when they did not obey the regulations.

Alice developed a code of ethics that all soldiers had to follow, called "the Holy Spirit Precepts." Some of these were clearly Christian borrowings ("you shall not commit adultery," "you shall not kill," "you shall love one another as you love yourselves"), but others were traditional regulations for elders in times of crisis in precolonial times (forbidding witchcraft, quarreling, and sexual intercourse). As with many prophets in traditional societies, morality was an important part of Alice's message. Furthermore, the Holy Spirit Army had a "Moral Education Section" charged with the duty of educating the public in the Holy Spirit Precepts.

The spirits would take possession of Alice twice a day, and at other times when required, and give messages and instructions about the conduct of the military campaign. A "chief clerk of the spirit" would translate and record her words. During this time of possession, Alice would be unconscious and would later have no memory of what her mouth had uttered. The power to translate was apparently granted by Alice's main spirit Lakwena directly to the chief clerk (there were three during the brief period of her ministry). He would also translate when she spoke in foreign languages (except that Alice would herself translate the statements of the Korean/Chinese spirit). The person to be chief clerk was chosen by Lakwena, and he would not only report what the spirits said but would also ask questions of the spirits and would make reports to the spirits of what was happening externally. This description makes it obvious that the chief clerk had a position of great power, yet oddly no one within the movement seemed to realize this. He was seen simply as Alice's secretary.

She freed the soldiers from the threat of witchcraft and evil spirits and promised protection again enemy bullets. After some remarkable successes, she marched on Kampala. Some of those around her noticed, however, that she began to ignore the instructions of the spirits and make decisions without them. This sudden shift to a dictatorial approach became quite significant in the aftermath of the decisive defeat before Kampala. She lost the confidence of her soldiers and fled to Kenya. Her spirits abandoned her, and she eventually died in January 2007. This did not end the resistance, however. Her father, who had remained aloof from his daughter's movement, now inherited her spirits and took leadership of a remnant of Alice's followers. There was also a rival movement led by Joseph Kony, who was possessed by a set of spirits that looked remarkably like Alice's in function, though they went by entirely different names. Thus Kony formed a third Holy Spirit Army (called the Lord's Resistance Army), but in fact there were as many as five such groups at one time. The movement of Alice's father was apparently short-lived, but Kony's was more successful. He formed alliances with other military groups and continues to exist until the present time, becoming notorious for his child soldiers and indicted by the International Criminal Court in 2005 for crimes against humanity.

Tromba Spirits of Northwest Madagascar

In northern Madagascar the Sakalava people were organized into a kingdom before the coming of the French.[4] The site of the royal tombs was an island called Nosy Faly. The spirits of dead royal ancestors were called *tromba*. The greatest and oldest of the spirits would occasionally possess a woman, who would then journey in a trance to the island of Nosy Faly. She would be subjected to stringent tests; but if she passed them, she would be allowed to join the *saha*, the small group of mediums possessed by these spirits (there were four such mediums in 1987). For the rest of her life she

---

4. This section depends on Lesley A. Sharp, *The Possessed and the Dispossessed: Spirits, Identity and Power in a Madagascar Migrant Town* (Comparative Studies of Health Systems and Medical Care; Berkeley: University of California Press, 1993); idem, "The Power of Possession in Northwest Madagascar: Contesting Colonial and National Hegemonies," in Behrend and Luig, *Spirit Possession*, 3–21.

would usually remain in the royal village, where royalty would consult her spirit about policy and the future.

The French were not very sympathetic to spirit possession and eventually outlawed it. They also treated the Sakalava badly, taking some of their best land and favoring another ethnic group in the center of Madagascar called the Merino. The colonial policies were largely continued after independence in 1960, but the "Socialist Revolution" of the 1970s led to a movement to restore many traditional practices and also some recognition of precolonial landownership. The result has been an elevation of the importance of the *tromba saha* mediums. Their value became apparent in an outbreak of possession of young people by evil spirits. The traditional healers could not deal with them, and the more powerful *tromba* mediums had to be called in. Their aid was further enlisted in a dispute over profitable fishing rights around the island of Nosy Faly. In another example, they were consulted on and approved the opening of a new school that might have been opposed by the Sakalava.

Possession has increased greatly among ordinary people in recent years. This includes both men and women; however, the *saha* are always women. Here we see a possession cult that has considerable power and is able to pronounce on national matters and to be heeded by the powers that be.

Swahili Possession Cults

In the 1980s Linda Giles studied possession cults in a number of coastal sites in Kenya and Tanzania in which Islam was the dominant religious culture.[5] In spite of qur'anic teachings, spirit possession is not uncommon even among "good Muslims," affecting both men and women. The spirit may be Muslim or pagan. When spirit possession is suspected (because of illness, misfortune, or perhaps more direct manifestations), one can go to a diviner, who is able to provide a diagnosis as to whether the person is possessed. If he or she is, the diviner will refer the person to a *mganga*, who is able to treat such problems. Sometimes the spirit is exorcised, but more often the spirit is appeased and the person comes to terms with living with

---

5. The information here is taken from Linda L. Giles, "Possession Cults on the Swahili Coast: A Re-examination of Theories of Marginality," *Africa* 57 (1987): 234–58.

it. Because many people are possessed by the same spirit or spirits, the possessed individual will usually be initiated into a possession cult.

What Giles discovered is that such cults do not occupy the peripheral position often assumed. Possession cults are much more widespread than might be at first realized, even among Muslims. Giles "found all societal categories in the cult, including those from highly respected, well-educated or economically well-off families. I also found representatives from various racial and ethnic backgrounds, running the full continuum from 'Arab' to 'African,' as well as from various age groups."[6]

She goes on to argue that "spirit possession should be seen as an integrated part of coastal Islamic belief and practice."[7] Rather than being an opportunity for the marginal or powerless to protest, the cults provided a much more tangible set of benefits:

> Scholars have noted that such cults provide an explanation of illness and misfortune and, moreover, a means to combat it. They also argue that the cult provides psychological catharsis, as well as attention and support for the patient, whereas on the social level the cult provides an arena for conspicuous consumption as well as entertainment. I would suggest that the cult also provides ... a legitimate avenue to higher status and authority, not just within the context of the cult itself but also within the wider society.[8]

It does demonstrate that possession cults are not made up only of the marginalized and the powerless. This seems to counter I. M. Lewis's interpretation, though I expect that his thesis could be partially accommodated to it.[9] According to Lewis, women and others of low status in possession cults or related groups use this as a way of achieving status or of obtaining certain objectives in a society in which they are repressed or have a low status. Also, Lewis labeled them as "peripheral cults," as opposed to official "central cults."

---

6. Ibid., 242.
7. Ibid., 245.
8. Ibid., 247.
9. Lewis, *Ecstatic Religion: A Study of Shamanism and Spirit Possession* (3rd ed.; London: Routledge, 2003).

Mhondoro Mediums in Zimbabwe

Among the Shona of Zimbabwe both chiefs and mediums traditionally derived their power and authority from the royal ancestral spirits known as *mhondoro*.[10] The colonial powers had disrupted the traditional chieftainship, by giving the office to those who showed loyalty and dismissing those regarded as untrustworthy. The result was that the people tended to look on *mhondoro* mediums for leadership. When guerrilla movements arose, they found it important to obtain the approval of *mhondoro* mediums. Such figures were central in the rebellion of 1896–1897 and also in the war of independence in 1966–1980.

The duties of the *mhondoro* mediums were various. They were involved in ceremonies to bring rain, and in general looked after their people by protecting the crops and animals and providing fertility. They could convey any message that the ancestors wanted to pass on to the people, including foretelling the future. Because the ancestors were past chiefs of experience, they were especially important in leading and advising during times of war.

Most of the *mhondoro* were male, and the office of *mhondoro* medium was usually held by men. A couple of the *mhondoro* were female, however, including Nehanda, a female deity who ruled over two regions, Mazoe and Dande. Her mediums in each place were female. According to the traditional worldview of the Shona, maturing and aging was a process of "drying out." All were born "wet," and because of fertility, menstruation, and childbirth women periodically reverted to the wet state. After menopause, however, women really begin to "dry out" and could take on certain tasks that required them to be "dry" (e.g., the making of ceremonial beer).

In 1896–1897 Charwe, a medium of Nehanda from Mazoe, was a major leader. She was captured at the end of the rebellion and hanged, but traditions grew up around her persona, making her a symbol of opposition to white rule. In the war of independence in 1964–1980, one of the mediums supporting the guerrillas was Kunzaruwa, a medium of Nehanda in the

---

10. The information in this section comes from David Lan, *Guns and Rain: Guerrillas and Spirit Mediums in Zimbabwe* (Perspectives on South Africa 38; Berkeley: University of California Press, 1985); and Terence O. Ranger, *Revolt in Southern Rhodesia, 1896–97: A Study in African Resistance* (1967; repr., London: Heinemann, 1979); supplemented by Mary Keller, *The Hammer and the Flute: Women, Power and Spirit Possession* (Baltimore: Johns Hopkins University Press, 2002), 125–61.

Zambezi Valley. She was very old but gave advice to the warriors coming from outside the region. When the area was discovered by government troops, the rebels decided to take her out of the country. She died and was buried there, a female medium in the tradition of Charwe and still recognized as a symbol of the independence fighters in present-day Zimbabwe.

Beata the Delaware Indian Prophetess

We first hear of Beata about 1805 along the White River in Indiana (near the present-day site of Muncie).[11] She was only one of a number of Delaware and Shawnee Indian prophets from the mid-eighteenth century, the best known of whom was Tenskwatawa, the brother of the famous Shawnee chief Tecumseh. A prophetic tradition had developed in this time and place, and the brief descriptions of the various prophets make them sound quite similar. They preached a message of morality and reform, blaming the sins of the Indians for the troubles they were experiencing in losing their lands and being driven further and further westward by the encroaching white settlements.

Beata was from a family that had been converted by the Moravians. She began to have visions and to preach a message of return to the old ways. In her first vision in February 1805, two angels appeared to her and spoke as follows:

> We came to tell you that God is not satisfied with you Indians, because at your sacrifices you do so many strange things with wampum [beaded leather objects that were used as a sort of money] and all sorts of juggling, and also do not keep separate spoons with which to stir the sacrificial meat and to dip it out. You Indians will have to live again as in olden times, and love one another sincerely. If you do not do this, a terrible storm will arise and break down all the trees in the woods, and all Indians shall lose their lives in it.[12]

---

11. The main source for this section is Jay Miller, "The 1806 Purge among the Indiana Delaware: Sorcery, Gender, Boundaries, and Legitimacy," *Ethnohistory* 41 (1994): 245–66. A brief account is also given by John Sugden (*Tecumseh: A Life of America's Greatest Indian Leader* [New York: Random House, 1997], 113–26) and James Mooney (*The Ghost-Dance Religion and the Sioux Outbreak of 1890* [Fourteenth Annual Report of the Bureau of Ethnology, 1892–93, part 2; 1896; repr., Lincoln: University of Nebraska Press, 1991]).

12. Miller, "1806 Purge," 252.

She preached to large crowds in a large hall that was loaned to her, making the focus of her teaching the renewal of the Big House (Gamwing) ceremony, an annual thanksgiving rite.

Beata's essential message was a return to the "old ways." She got various chiefs to pledge to renounce drinking, fornication, stealing, murder, and the like. She also denounced witchcraft and identified certain members of the community as witches. Belief in and fear of witchcraft was traditional in this tribal society, and prophetic-type individuals would be consulted on who might be causing the misfortunes ascribed to witchcraft. Her role as a witch-finder did not last long, however, because she gave it up with the excuse that she was only a woman. At this time, the soon-to-be-acclaimed prophet Tenskwatawa was asked to pronounce on the witches that she had identified, and Beata fades from the sources.

NUER PROPHETS

A female prophet Nyapuka Dan, from the Jagei, lived in the late nineteenth century.[13] She joined up with another prophet (named Wol Athiang) to direct raids by the Nuer onto the Dinka, in retaliation for Dinka raids on themselves. Nyapuka was killed on one of these raids in the 1890s.

A second female Nuer prophet, Nyakong Bar, is known to us because of her encounter with the famous prophet Ngundeng, who lived from about the 1830s to 1906. She challenged Ngundeng on his own turf. Ngundeng enlisted certain prophets, diviners, and magicians among his spiritual assistants (though he condemned and tried to suppress magic outside his circle). He accepted the existence of some distant prophets but generally opposed those nearby. His favorite method was to ridicule them in verse and song. Another way was to make personal predictions about them, which would show his superiority when such a prediction was fulfilled. Ngundeng had had the local people build up a huge mound of earth, an artificial hill about fifty feet high with steep sides, as a symbol of his "headquarters" and prestige. When prophets visited him, he sometimes challenged them to run up the side of his mound, a strenuous physical feat that Ngundeng was able to do. Nyakong Bar accepted the challenge;

---

13. The information in this section comes from Douglas H. Johnson, *Nuer Prophets: A History of Prophecy from the Upper Nile in the Nineteenth and Twentieth Centuries* (Oxford Studies in Social and Cultural Anthropology; Oxford: Clarendon, 1994). On Nyapuku Dan, see pp. 249, 279, 282.

unfortunately, she faltered halfway up, and her divinity disappeared into the mound. Ngundeng gave her to one of his assistants to grind grain and sleep with.

Another female prophet among the Nuer was Nyacan Ruea, who was a disciple of the prophet Deng Laka.[14] She was seized by the divinity Mandiu ("mother of Diu"; Diu was Deng Laka's divinity). She performed ceremonies in support of the Nuer tribe Gaawar, which made raids on the Dinka (a traditional activity of prophets). Along with Deng Laka she helped to organize and lead a raid against the Twic and the Cuor about 1900. The battle was bloody, and Nyacan Ruea was captured by the Twic. Since they believed that spears could not kill her, they dispatched her by driving a cattle peg into her vagina. Deng Laka managed to rally the Gaawar and drive the Twic back, but it was too late for her.

The female Jagei prophet Nyaruac Kolang was the daughter of the famous prophet Kolang Ket, who lived from about 1840 to 1925. Although he had several sons, his daughter inherited his spirit at his death.[15] She seems to have been highly successful. She served her people without drawing attention to herself from the British administration, to the point that she was overlooked for the most part for the first decade of her career. One of the reasons is that she did not act as a war prophet (though other Nuer prophets did, as noted above); she did not even spear the sacrificial animals herself but let her followers do it. Yet she performed the traditional activities of a prophet, such as sacrificing against diseases, both of cattle and humans, and providing blessings on herds and crops. She also reputedly used her influence to prevent fighting, unlike some of her spiritual sisters.

ELLEN G. WHITE, THE SEVENTH-DAY ADVENTIST PROPHET

The Seventh-Day Adventist prophet Ellen White is a valuable example because we know so much about her,[16] unlike a number of the figures

---

14. See esp. ibid., 155 and 159.
15. Ibid., 279–81.
16. Most of the unattributed statements in this section are documented in Gary Land, ed., *Adventism in America: A History* (Studies in Adventist History; Grand Rapids: Eerdmans, 1986). Some additional details (of major importance) are provided by Ronald L. Numbers, *Prophetess of Health: A Study of Ellen G. White* (2nd ed.; Knoxville: University of Tennessee Press, 1992).

discussed above. A self-taught Bible reader named William Miller had calculated that the world would end in 1843. His teachings eventually gained a wide following. After disappointments in 1843 and early 1844, he was convinced that Christ would return in the autumn of 1844, and many continued to look on his predictions as certain. When the appointed date came and went, many followers left in the subsequent "great disappointment." A number remained loyal to this "adventist" movement, though there were different conceptions of how the movement should go forward. The group that ended up being the most successful was that which became the Seventh-Day Adventists. A young woman of 17 named Ellen G. Harman (1827–1915) had a vision of reassurance in December 1844. This was only the first of many visions. She came to be recognized as a prophet and later married James White (1821–1881), who was a key individual in the development and success of the movement.

Ellen White's most important revelation was with regard to Miller's date of 1844 for the advent of Christ. An important event had taken place as predicted by the calculations based on biblical data, but it was Christ's entry into the heavenly sanctuary to begin the "investigative judgment" for the purification of sins (Dan 8:14; Rev 11:19), not an earthly event. Many of the visions that followed related to eschatology, but others were about doctrinal issues, for example, the doctrine of tithing in 1876. Many of her revelations related to diet, health, and healing. A vision in 1863 led to teachings against meat and drug-oriented medicine. The Seventh-Day Adventists began to publish the *Health Reformer* (*Good Health*) and founded the Western Health Reform Institute (1866). Later, a sanatorium headed by J. H. Kellogg was set up in 1878.

Interspersed with these weighty points were others that seem trivial to modern sensibilities. For example, Mrs. White pronounced on women's dress. Although opposing hoop skirts in the 1850s, she recommended a skirt several inches shorter than current fashion dictated (about nine inches above the floor, to avoid dragging in the dirt of the street). On the other hand, she described the "American costume" of Harriet Austin as immodest, falling "about half-way from the hip to the knee" or "six inches" above the knee.[17] This was declared to be inaccurate by Dr. Austin, who asserted that her skirt covered her knees when walking. In 1863 Ellen White stated that God would not have Adventist women adopt the "reform

---

17. Numbers, *Prophetess of Health*, 140.

dress," but in 1867 she was urging adoption of it, though according to her own specifications. She even took the pattern around to various churches and made it available by mail order (for a price, except to those unable to pay). She also issued a tract on appropriate dress, which was approved by the Seventh-Day Adventist General Conference in 1869. But many women did not like the costume. Finally, in 1875 she had a vision that dress was becoming a stumbling block, and she withdrew the previous regulations. But she continued to speak out against "pride in dress," and advocated plain styles and subdued colors.

The death of her husband in 1881 led to a focus on Ellen White as the main spiritual leader. She always shunned an official position and was often abroad in her later years, but she nevertheless had a great deal of influence. Her revelations often supported the position she took on controversial issues, such as in her dispute with Kellogg, who challenged her authority.[18] Her letters replying to questions and discussing issues of concern were widely used as a guide and source of truth and were subsequently published as a collection of *Testimonies*. A result of her dispute with Kellogg was that her teachings were affirmed by the church, though their status in relation to the Bible remained ambiguous; however, after her death it was officially agreed in 1919 that her teachings were not infallible or verbally inspired. More recently, a debate over her teachings took place in the 1970s.[19]

Main Points Arising from the Cross-Cultural Data

These cross-cultural examples suggest certain themes about female prophets and related persons. That is, they provide examples or conclusions that may have wider implications for prophetesses and related female figures in other cultures. Here are some of the points that emerge from the cross-cultural examples examined here:

1. The first thing one notices about female prophets is that they are prophets who happen to be female. Their revelations and activities do not,

---

[18]. This was a major challenge to Ellen White's authority and leadership in the period 1900–1910. Kellogg emphasized health and the social mission of the church (too much according to some). He and some other prominent individuals were perceived as attacking her "prophetic gift." Kellogg and an associate were forced out in 1907.

[19]. Numbers's first edition of *Prophetess of Health* (1976; 2nd ed. 1992) was part of this debate.

on the whole, differ from those of male prophets. There are often differences between male and female prophetic figures, but these usually concern issues that are not central to prophecy as such but are more peripheral. For example, Nyaruac Kolang did not lead the Nuer on the traditional raids against the Dinka. One might infer that this was because she was a woman. Yet other female Nuer prophets led such raids and, conversely, Nyaruac's father, Kolang Ket, had maintained peace in his later years.[20]

2. The activities of female prophetic-type figures will usually be canalized by the expectations and restrictions on female behavior in their traditional society. Thus, among the Shona, where "dryness" is a major factor in leadership, women take on leadership roles (including spirit mediumship) only when they have passed menopause. Alice Lakwena took on traditional female roles in the Holy Spirit Mobile Army camp.

3. Gender transformation is also widely known in different cultures, with male prophets taking on some female features and vice versa. This is especially the case when the prophet is the opposite gender of the deity who seizes him or her. A good example concerns the female Nuer prophets who became war leaders, even though this was normally a male prerogative. Another example is Alice Lakwena, who led an army; her situation is complicated, however, in that it was her spirits—all male military types—who assumed leadership, using her as a vessel for their military commands. Indeed, her followers claim that just before her major defeat, she had begun to ignore her spirits and to give orders on her own authority. It is interesting that her successors and rivals were all men.

4. In some cases an all-female prophetic leadership has a major role to play in local, regional, or national society. (Usually prophets are of both genders, even when a preponderance of them are of one gender.) A good example is the *tromba* mediums (entirely female) in Madagascar, who continue to play a role even in the modern state.

5. The argument of I. M. Lewis that women in possession cults or related groups use this as a way of achieving status or of obtaining certain objectives in a society in which women are repressed or have a low status is only partially borne out. In some cases, other anthropologists argue that certain possession cults are actually "central," even though Lewis labeled them as "peripheral." In any case it is clear that the possession cult is not simply a way of achieving status but plays an important role in the

---

20. Johnson, *Nuer Prophets*, 248–53, 256–63.

particular society in question (e.g., the Swahili possession cults of Tanzania and Kenya). Also, being a prophet might be a way of achieving power without holding a formal office (as with Ellen White).

Implications for Better Understanding Biblical Prophets

The main points noted in the previous section suggest, above all, the sorts of questions that we need to put to the biblical tradition with the hope of gaining a greater insight into female prophets in ancient Israel. We can do some of that in this final section of the paper.

The number of female prophets in the Bible is not large. The first prophets mentioned in the text are Miriam (Aaron's sister) and the judge Deborah (Exod 15:20; Judg 4:4). The problem is that we are not told in what way they functioned as prophets. The next one was the woman with whom Isaiah had relations to produce the son Mahershalalhashbaz (Isa 8). This was not Mrs. Isaiah, as so many commentators have asserted on no basis whatsoever. The Hebrew language is perfectly capable of saying, "Isaiah had relations with his wife and she bore a son." It is clear in the context that Isaiah is being commanded to do something unusual as a sign, and this sign is to have relations with "the prophetess," who would bear a son.[21] Unfortunately, we know nothing further about this female prophet. In the time of Josiah, Huldah plays an important role in confirming the authenticity of the law book found in the temple. Finally, one of the prophets opposing Nehemiah was the woman Noadiah (Neh 6:14). We know nothing further about her, except her name, which is more than we know of the other prophets, whom Nehemiah does not even name.

It may be that Miriam and Deborah are נביאות mainly because of their association with a song, the Song of the Sea and the Song of Deborah, respectively. Otherwise, we have little indication that the prophetesses acted any differently from their male counterparts. For example, that Huldah was a female seems to have nothing to do with her duty of confirming the authenticity of the book found in the temple. That is, she appears to do this not because she is a woman but because she is a prophet, with the particular gender being irrelevant. The same seems to be the case with Noadiah. As far as we know, she did nothing differently

---

21. Jonathan Stökl has kindly drawn my attention to an article of Alfred Jepsen ("Die Nebiah in Jes 8, 3," ZAW 72 [1960]: 267–68) in which he argues that the "prophetess" in this passage took her title from her profession, not because of being Isaiah's wife.

from the other prophets who opposed Nehemiah. Why then is she named, whereas the male prophets are not? There are several possible reasons for singling her out: she was the only female prophet; it might have galled him to be criticized by a female; or she might have been a particular thorn in his side.

Female prophets may well have been restricted in certain areas of activity because of customary constraints on women in Israelite society. We have examples of this elsewhere, but we also find that certain sorts of female behavior might be tolerated in prophets but not in other women. On the other hand, such societal attitudes might also have made criticism of female prophets more stringent because they were women doing an activity that required a more active role in society than might have been the norm. This is an area that could bear further investigation, even though the amount of material to work with in the Bible is rather small.

Finally, the cross-cultural examples suggest that there might be other female prophetic figures in the biblical text, even though they are not labeled "prophet" as such. Here we get into the thorny question of how to define the term *prophet*, which cannot be taken up here. Yet some have already suggested that the women in Ezek 13 are prophets, even though they are not so designated. One might also consider the woman of Endor in 1 Sam 28; she is definitely a medium. If Miriam and Deborah can be called "prophets," why not some of the other female figures in the text? We should at least be encouraged to look and ask.

Cross-cultural comparisons from the field of anthropology are an important way of opening up study of prophets—male and female—in the biblical text. Although we may in the end decide that a particular figure in another culture should not bear the title "prophet," considering such individuals makes us see Israelite prophets in broader perspective and suggests that some of us are defining the term too narrowly. In any case, these examples should shake us out of our academic rut and make us ask more searching questions and consider different—even more radical—solutions to questions that have long been around in biblical scholarship. When we see the bizarre behavior of some prophetic figures in other cultures, we are less likely to be scandalized by Isaiah's having a child with the "prophetess" who was not his wife. And Ezekiel's long lie-in and unusual cooking techniques appear positively tame in comparison with some prophetic activity elsewhere. The area of female prophets is one ripe for asking sharp questions and considering new models. Anthropology may well provide us the knowledge and tools to do this.

Gender and Prophetic Agency in the Ancient Near East and in Greece*

Martti Nissinen

The Prophetic Texts and Their Ancient Contexts Group has devoted two consecutive sessions (2008-2009) to the topic of "Prophecy and Gender." This indicates an ongoing attention to gender issues, whether we discuss prophets as historical or literary characters, the language of the prophetic texts, or the representations of the Divine in the texts and their ideology. The interest in gender has hitherto resulted in a profusion of literature on prophecy and gender in the Hebrew Bible. Not too many studies have been written on this topic from a comparative perspective, however; hence in the present essay I attempt to provide an ancient Near Eastern view on prophecy and gender, supplemented by observations regarding Greek prophecy, which I presume to be culturally connected with the Near Eastern prophetic phenomenon, despite many differences.

I first present a taxonomy of gender of the prophets and deities in the ancient Near East. In the second part I discuss the agency[1] of the prophets from the gender point of view, and in the third part I analyze the gendered representations of deities —the female deity Ištar in particular—and their agency in the prophetic phenomenon.

---

* I am indebted to the Institute for Advanced Study (Princeton) for the opportunity of writing this article during a research visit in May–June 2011. I would also like to thank Esther Hamori, Saana Svärd, and Caroline Walker Bynum for their helpful comments, as well as Corrine Carvalho and Jonathan Stökl for their careful editing and help in improving the article.

1. The explanation of what I mean by "agency" is given below, pp. 36–37.

Taxonomy

My statistical survey of the gender of prophets and deities is based on the corpus of texts included in the SBLWAW volume *Prophets and Prophecy in the Ancient Near East*.[2] The references to the texts in this paper follow the numbering of that volume, which consists of 142 texts mostly written in Akkadian and coming from Mari (65 texts), Assyria (51 texts), and other places in Mesopotamia, but also a few West Semitic sources and one Egyptian story on events that are told to have happened in the Phoenician city of Byblos. In these texts, prophets are referred to in a variety of ways. In the letters and administrative documents from Mari, as well as in Assyrian prophetic oracles, prophets are often mentioned by name, but as often we encounter references to anonymous individuals or to a collective of prophets.

The gender of the prophets known by name is always indicated, but this is not always the case with anonymous prophets, especially if the prophecy is quoted without an explicit reference to the person of the prophet. Prophets whose names are mentioned are referred to in fifty-four texts, including twenty-seven references to twenty-one male individuals[3] and eighteen references to sixteen female individuals.[4] In addition, eight texts refer to five individual prophets whose gender is not clear, either because the prophet

---

2. Martti Nissinen, with contributions by Choon-Leong Seow and Robert K. Ritner, *Prophets and Prophecy in the Ancient Near East* (SBLWAW 12; Atlanta: Society of Biblical Literature, 2003). Meanwhile, a few texts have come to my notice that would deserve to be included in this collection. They have not been taken into account in the statistics because the information obtainable from them does not drastically change the picture.

3. Mari: Abiya (no. 2), Iṣi-aḫu (no. 5), Lupaḫum (nos. 9, 53, 62), Qišti-diritum (no. 18), Irra-gamil (nos. 33, 55/59, 65), Ḫadnu-El (no. 35), Iddin-kubi (no. 35), Iddin-ili (no. 43), Timlû (no. 45), Atamrum (no. 48), Ili-andulli (no. 54), Ea-maṣi (no. 55/59), Ea-mudammiq (no. 56/57), Qišatum (no. 60), Išḫi-Dagan (no. 63); Assyria: Lā-dāgil-ili (nos. 77, 80, 88), Nabû-ḫussanni (no. 78), Tašmētu-ēreš (no. 91), Quqî (no. 104); other texts from Mesopotamia: "Boatman" (no. 134); West Semitic texts: Balaam (no. 138). The numbers correspond to text numbers in Nissinen, *Prophets and Prophecy*.

4. Mari: Ḫubatum (no. 10), Innibana (no. 14), Aḫatum (no. 24), Ayala (no. 36), Zunana (no. 37), Kakka-lidi (no. 41), Šimatum (no. 44), Annu-tabni (no. 58); Assyria: Sinqîša-āmur (nos. 69, 82), Rēmūt-Allati (no. 70), Issār-bēlī-da"ini (no. 74), Aḫāt-abīša (no. 75), Urkittu-šarrat (no. 81), Mullissu-kabtat (no. 92), Dunnaša-āmur (nos. 94, 95), Mullissu-abu-uṣrī (no. 111).

bears the title *assinnu*, indicating a genderless or "third gender" role,[5] or because the reference to the prophet's gender is otherwise ambiguous; this is the case three times in the colophons of Assyrian prophecies,[6] to which I will return later. Altogether, forty-two individual prophets are known by their names.

Anonymous prophets whose gender is indicated are mentioned thirty-eight times; of these, twenty-seven are male[7] and thirteen female.[8] There is no way of knowing whether the same individuals are mentioned several times in these texts. When prophets are mentioned as a group, the prophets are sometimes referred to as "prophets" without gender specification (9 times);[9] as "male and female prophets" (5 times, one of which also mentions the *assinnu*s);[10] or as "female prophets" (twice: a ritual text from Mari and an administrative list from Assyria).[11]

When one compares the sources from Mari to those from Assyria, there is a perceptible difference between the gender profiles of prophets: at Mari, about two-thirds of the prophets mentioned in the texts surveyed here are male, whereas in Assyria two-thirds are female.

When it comes to the very meager documentation of West Semitic prophecy, we can observe that two prophets—not only Balaam in the Deir 'Allā inscription[12] but also a person called *Qn* in a seal amulet from Deir Rifa[13]—have male names, and the three others, appearing in the Lachish letters[14] and in the Egyptian Wenamon narrative,[15] are likewise of male

---

5. Šēlebum (nos. 7, 8, 23), Ili-ḫaznaya (no. 22).
6. Issār-lā-tašīaṭ (no. 68), Bāia (nos. 71, 79), Ilūssa-āmur (no. 72).
7. Nos. 1 (2x), 3, 4, 5, 16, 19 (2x), 25, 29, 30, 31, 32, 34, 38, 39, 40, 47, 51, 61, 64, 108, 119, 130, 139, 141, 142.
8. Nos. 7, 9, 11, 12, 13, 14, 20, 27, 42, 109, 113, 114, 115.
9. Nos. 26, 46, 49, 50, 97, 98, 99, 122, 137.
10. Nos. 1, 17, 105, 118, 123.
11. Nos. 52, 110.
12. No. 138.
13. A seal from Deir Rifa, Egypt (ca. 1700 b.c.e.?) includes the West Semitic name "*Qn* the seer" (UC 51354); see Gordon J. Hamilton, "A Proposal to Read the Legend of a Seal-Amulet from Deir Rifa, Egypt as an Early West Semitic Alphabetic Inscription," *JSS* 54 (2009): 51–79.
14. Nos. 139, 141.
15. No. 142. This literary text hardly reports a historical prophetic performance, but it demonstrates how an Egyptian contemporary would have viewed such a performance in Byblos; see Bernd U. Schipper, *Die Erzählung des Wenamun: Ein Litera-*

gender. Whether this refers to the preference of male prophets in West Semitic cultures is difficult to judge on the basis of five attestations only. However, the Hebrew Bible, with its five or so female prophets[16] over against the fifty or so male prophets, seems to point in the same direction.

The gender difference also plays a role when it comes to deities whose words the prophets are said to transmit or whose temples they are affiliated with. Again, there are divergences between the sources. In texts from Mari, a male deity is mentioned almost twice as many times (34)[17] as a female deity (18),[18] while in the case of Assyria, the thirty occurrences of a female deity[19] (always one of the manifestations of Ištar) drastically outnumber the eight cases of male deities mentioned in the texts.[20] In the four West Semitic sources in which the divine gender is revealed, the deity is always a male one: Baalšamayin in the Zakkur inscription, Amon in the Report of Wenamon, and, presumably, Yahweh in the Lachish letters;[21] note also the male god Tarhunza in the prophecy quoted in the Luwian stela of Hamiyata.[22]

---

turwerk im Spannungsfeld von Politik, Geschichte und Religion (OBO 209; Fribourg: Academic Press, 2005).

16. The following women carry the title נביאה in the Hebrew Bible: Miriam (Exod 15:20), Deborah (Judg 4:4), Huldah (2 Kgs 22:14–20 // 2 Chr 34:22–28), Noadiah (Neh 6:14), and the anonymous woman in Isa 8:3. For most recent treatments of these women, see Hugh G. M. Williamson, "Prophetesses in the Hebrew Bible," in *Prophecy and Prophets in Ancient Israel: Proceedings of the Oxford Old Testament Seminar* (ed. John Day; LHBOTS 531; London: T&T Clark, 2010), 65–80; see also Irmtraud Fischer, *Gotteskünderinnen: Zu einer geschlechtsfairen Deutung des Phänomens der Prophetie und der Prophetinnen in der Hebräischen Bibel* (Stuttgart: Kohlhammer, 2002); Susan Ackerman, "Why Is Miriam Also among the Prophets (And Is Zipporah among the Priests?)," *JBL* 121 (2002): 47–80; Wilda C. Gafney, *Daughters of Miriam: Women Prophets in Ancient Israel* (Minneapolis: Fortress, 2008); Esther J. Hamori, *Women's Divination in Biblical Literature: Prophecy, Necromancy, and Other Arts of Knowledge* (AYBRL; New Haven: Yale University Press, forthcoming).

17. Nos. 1 (3x), 2, 3, 4, 7, 9 (2x), 12, 15, 16, 19, 20, 25, 30, 31, 34, 37, 38, 39, 41, 46, 47, 48, 49, 50, 53, 55/59 (2x), 60, 61, 62, 63.

18. Nos. 5, 7, 8, 10, 18, 19, 21, 22, 23, 24, 29, 42, 43, 45, 51, 52, 56/57, 58.

19. Nos. 68, 69, 70, 72, 73, 74, 75, 76, 77, 78, 79, 80, 81, 82, 83, 87, 88, 90, 91, 92, 94, 95, 97, 99, 100, 101, 107, 113, 114, 118.

20. Nos. 71 (2x), 84, 85, 86, 106, 112, 115.

21. Nos. 137, 139, 141, 142.

22. Tell Ahmar 6 §§21–23; editio princeps: J. David Hawkins, "Inscription," in Guy Bunnens, *A New Luwian Stele and the Cult of the Storm-God at Til Barsib–Masu-*

Is there a correspondence, then, between the gender of the prophets and that of the deities?[23] According to my statistics, in the cases where the gender of both the prophet and the deity can be detected, male prophets are associated twenty-six times with male deities and fourteen times with female deities.[24] Female prophets are affiliated fifteen times with a female deity and seven times with a male one,[25] and the people with ambiguous or undetermined gender exclusively appear as prophets of a female deity, except for one Assyrian text (no. 71), where Bāia speaks in the voice of three different gods.

Leaving the statistics based on the text corpus published in *Prophets and Prophecy*, it is worth noting that the pivotal role of women in prophecy is not restricted to the ancient Near East, but can also be observed in Greek literature.[26] Greek seers (μάντεις) who practice divination involving observation of the livers of sacrificial animals and the flight of birds were, as a rule, male. However, there are a few hints at women involved in it in Greek sources,[27] such as the epitaph with the inscription "Satyra the seer" (ΣΑΤΥΡΑ Α ΜΑΝΤΙΣ);[28] the epigram attributable to Posidippus of Pella, mentioning "Asterie the seer" who interprets bird signs;[29] and a grave stela from Mantinea depicting a woman holding a liver in her left hand.[30]

---

wari (Tell Ahmar 2; Publications de la Mission archéologique de l'Université de Liège en Syrie; Leuven: Peeters, 2006), 11–31, esp. 15, 27–28, no. 143h.

23. So, on the basis of Assyrian and biblical texts, Jonathan Stökl, "Ištar's Women, YHWH's Men? A Curious Gender-Bias in Neo-Assyrian and Biblical Prophecy," *ZAW* 121 (2009): 87–100.

24. Male prophet, male deity: nos. 1 (2x), 2, 3, 4, 9, 16, 19, 25, 30, 31, 34, 38, 39, 47, 48, 53, 55/59 (2x), 60, 61, 62, 63, 139, 141, 142; male prophet, female deity: nos. 5, 18, 19, 29, 43, 45, 56/57, 77, 78, 80, 88, 91, 119, 134.

25. Female prophet, female deity: nos. 10, 24, 42, 58, 69, 70, 74, 75, 81, 82, 92, 94, 95, 113, 114; female prophet, male deity: nos. 7, 9, 12, 20, 37, 41, 115.

26. See Anselm Hagedorn's article in this volume.

27. See Michael Attyah Flower, *The Seer in Ancient Greece* (Joan Palevsky Imprint in Classical Literature; Berkeley: University of California Press, 2008), 212–15.

28. SEG 35.626. This epitaph, found in Larissa in Thessaly, dates to the third century B.C.E.

29. Poem 6 in *Labored in Papyrus Leaves: Perspectives on an Epigram Collection Attributed to Posidippus (P.Mil.Vogl. VIII 309)* (ed. Benjamin Acosta-Hughes, Elizabeth Kosmetatou, and Manuel Baumbach; HellSt 2; Washington, D.C.: Center for Hellenic Studies, 2004), also dated to the third century B.C.E.

30. For this late-fifth-century B.C.E. stela, see Hans Möbius, "Diotima," in *Studia*

While the female seers remain the exception to the general rule, the picture changes when it comes to the delivery of divine messages by nontechnical means. The historically attested Greek prophets who are likely to have acted in an altered state of consciousness[31] are almost exclusively female. The Pythias of Delphi, who constituted one of the most highly appreciated and long-lived divinatory institutions in the Eastern Mediterranean, could only be women.[32] A likewise strictly gender-specific role was assumed by the female prophet of the temple of Apollo at Didyma, at least after the reestablishment of the temple in the 330s B.C.E.,[33] as well as "the female priests, who were also the female prophets"[34] of the temple of Zeus at Dodona.[35]

---

varia: Aufsätze zur Kunst und Kultur der Antike mit Nachträgen (ed. Wolfgang Schiering; Wiesbaden: Steiner, 1967), 33–46; see also the image in Flower, *Seer in Ancient Greece*, 213 (fig. 18).

31. See Martti Nissinen, "Prophetic Madness: Prophecy and Ecstasy in the Ancient Near East and in Greece," in *Raising Up a Faithful Exegete: Essays in Honor of Richard D. Nelson* (ed. K. L. Noll and Brooks Schramm; Winona Lake, Ind.: Eisenbrauns, 2010), 3–29, esp. 17–27.

32. For the Delphic oracle and the Pythia, see, e.g., Joseph Fontenrose, *The Delphic Oracle: Its Responses and Operations, with a Catalogue of Responses* (Berkeley: University of California Press, 1978); Catherine Morgan, "Divination and Society at Delphi and Didyma," *Hermathena* 147 (1989): 17–42; Lisa Maurizio, "Delphic Oracles as Oral Performances: Authenticity and Historical Evidence," *Classical Antiquity* 16 (1997): 308–34; Hugh Bowden, *Classical Athens and the Delphic Oracle: Divination and Democracy* (Cambridge: Cambridge University Press, 2005); Sarah Iles Johnston, *Ancient Greek Divination* (Blackwell Ancient Religions; Chichester: Wiley-Blackwell, 2008), 82–90; Flower, *Seer in Ancient Greece*, 215–35.

33. See, e.g., Joseph Fontenrose, *Didyma: Apollo's Oracle, Cult, and Companions* (Berkeley: University of California Press, 1988); Morgan, "Divination and Society"; Christian Oesterheld, *Göttliche Botschaften für zweifelnde Menschen: Pragmatik und Orientierungsleistung der Apollon-Orakel von Klaros und Didyma in hellenistisch-römischer Zeit* (Hypomnemata 174; Göttingen: Vandenhoeck & Ruprecht, 2008).

34. Ephoros, *FGH* 70 F 119 = Strabo, *Geogr.* 9.2.4: τὰς ἱερείας· ταύτας δ'εἶναι τὰς προφήτιδας (cf. Proklos in Photius, *Bibliotheca* 239.321b–322a).

35. See, most recently, Esther Eidinow, *Oracles, Curses, and Risk among the Ancient Greeks* (Oxford: Oxford University Press, 2007); Barbara Kowalzig, *Singing for the Gods: Performances of Myth and Ritual in Archaic and Classical Greece* (Oxford Classical Monographs; Oxford: Oxford University Press, 2007), 331–52; Martina Dieterle, *Dodona: Religionsgeschichtliche und historische Untersuchungen zur Entstehung und Entwicklung des Zeus-Heiligtums* (Spudasmata 116; Hildesheim: Olms, 2007); Johnston, *Ancient Greek Divination*, 60–72.

The only major oracle site where the prophets seem to have been consistently of male gender was the temple of Apollo at Claros,[36] where, according to Iamblichus, a male προφήτης prophesied after having drunk water from the holy spring.[37] It is noteworthy, moreover, that in mythical sources the prophets at Dodona appear as male (the Σελλοί),[38] while the historical practice knows only female prophets. In an etiological story recorded by both Ephoros and Proklos, a parallel office of male and female prophets is taken for granted, as if at some point a change from male to female prophets took place at Dodona.[39] Also at Didyma, the speakers of the oracles may have been male members of the Branchidae family until the destruction of the temple in 494 B.C.E.[40] Generally speaking, only very few male persons can be found practicing the prophetic kind of divination in Greek sources; according to Armin Lange, "[p]rophetic *manteis* occur only in archaic legend. And even there, they are the exception to the rule."[41]

---

36. Tacitus (*Ann.* 2.54) calls specific attention to the fact that it is not a woman, as at Delphi, but a male person who delivers the oracular response at Claros, as if this were something unexpected.

37. Iamblichus, *De mysteriis* 3.11; cf. Pliny, *Nat.* 2.232 and Tacitus, *Ann.* 2.54; cf. Aude Busine, *Paroles d'Apollon: Pratiques et traditions oraculaires dans l'Antiquité tardive (IIe–VIe siècles)* (RGRW 156; Leiden: Brill, 2005), 48–52. Even though there are no direct references to ecstatic practices in the extant oracles from Claros from the first through fourth centuries C.E., one fragmentary strophe in the oracle for Kallipolis (no. 9 in Reinhold Merkelbach and Josef Stauber, "Die Orakel des Apollon von Klaros," *Epigraphica Anatolica* 27 [1996]: 1–53, esp. 21) has been interpreted in terms of prophetic ecstasy; see Oesterheld, *Göttliche Botschaften für zweifelnde Menschen*, 162, 165–66: "Wie mir in Eingeweiden ... des Mundes ... eine kleine ... Kampf ... bedrückt ist das Herz."

38. E.g., *Il.* 16.234.

39. Thus Kowalzig (*Singing for the Gods*, 347), who connects the arrival of the female prophets historically with the move of the sanctuary from Thessaly to Dodona; it is written that "most women, whose descendants are now the female prophets," accompanied the shrine, subsequently acting as female priests for it (Suidas in Strabo, *Geogr.* 7.7.12). It should be noted that while Sophocles knows both male (*Trach.* 1164–72: Σελλοί) and female (*Odysseus Akanthlopes* 456: "the prophesying priestesses of Dodona") prophets, Herodotus (*Hist.* 2.55) is completely silent about the Σελλοί.

40. They are always referred to as "the Branchidae of the Milesians" by Herodotus (*Hist.* 1.46, 92, 141, 157; 2.159; 5.36; 6.19) which, admittedly, does not indicate the gender of the speakers of oracles with certainty; cf. Morgan, "Divination and Society," 27.

41. Armin Lange, "Greek Seers and Israelite-Jewish Prophets," *VT* 57 (2007): 461–82, esp. 480. Lange's examples include Helenus (Homer, *Il.* 7.44–53), Theocly-

Such an exception may appear in a third-century c.e. inscription from Didyma, in which a person called Titus Flavius Ulpianus seems to report a vision of his own.[42]

Female gender is typical of even nonhistorical prophetic figures in Greek literature (discussed by Anselm Hagedorn in the present volume), such as the women prophesying the oracles of Loxias (Apollo) in the temple of Phoibos;[43] Cassandra in Aeschylus's *Agamemnon* and in other sources;[44] Manto (also called Daphne), daughter of the seer Teiresias and mother of the seer Mopsus, who not only spoke but also wrote oracles;[45] or the Sibyls, whose oracles were considered significant enough to be adopted by even the Jews and Christians.[46]

Outside the realm of cuneiform literature, female deities seem to disappear as oracular deities. The few West Semitic prophets we know are all male, associated with male deities. In Greek literature, again, female prophets are presented as mouthpieces of male deities, Zeus or Apollo (in fact, Apollo can be called μάντις[47] or the προφήτης of Zeus[48]), while female deities only exceptionally appear as sources of prophetic oracles. The Hebrew Bible endorses only one god, Yahweh, whose image is predominantly male and whose prophets likewise tend to be men rather than women, despite the few well-known cases demonstrating that the biblical writers did not consider the idea of a female prophet of Yahweh impossible.

---

menus (Homer, *Od.* 17.160–161; 20.350–357), Amphilytus (Herodotus, *Hist.* 1.62–63), and Teiresias (Homer, *Od.* 10.494–495; 11.150–151; Sophocles, *Ant.* 998–1014; *Oed. tyr.* 297–299, 300–304).

42. Albert Rehm and Richard Harder, *Didyma II : Die Inschriften* (Berlin : Mann, 1958), 277.13-20; see Fontenrose, *Didyma*, 203-4.

43. Euripides, *Melanippe Desmotis*, fr. 494.

44. Aeschylus, *Ag.* 1072-1340; cf. Pindar, *Pyth.* 11.33, where she is called μάντις, and the narrative of the Hellenistic historian Anticlides, who tells about how she received the gift of prophecy while being left in a sanctuary as a child together with her brother (Anticlides, *FGH* 140, fr. 17). For Cassandra see Seth L. Schein, "The Cassandra Scene in Aeschylus' Agamemnon," *Greece and Rome* 29 (1982): 11-16.

45. Diodorus Siculus 4.66.6. Her name literally means "(female) diviner."

46. See, e.g., Herbert W. Parke, *Sibyls and Sibylline Prophecy in Classical Antiquity* (ed. Brian C. McGing; Croon Helm Classical Studies; London: Routledge, 1988); Rieuwerd Buitenwerf, *Book III of the Sibylline Oracles and Its Social Setting with an Introduction, Translation, and Commentary* (SVTP 17; Leiden: Brill, 2003).

47. Aeschylus, *Ag.* 1203.

48. Aeschylus, *Eum.* 614-619.

The statistics show that there was no universal gender correspondence between prophets and deities in the ancient Eastern Mediterranean. Nonetheless, some patterns can be tentatively outlined according to the provenance of the texts. The biblical and West Semitic sources seem to favor the male god/male prophet pattern, while in Greece the male god/female prophet model prevails. In the texts from Mari, the prophets, regardless of their gender, more often appear as prophets of male than of female deities, and there is a majority of male prophets among them. In Assyrian sources, again irrespective of the gender of the prophet, the deity speaking in prophetic oracles is virtually always female, and female prophets clearly outnumber the male ones.

This variation may well go back to differences in socioreligious contexts and traditions, but we should always bear in mind that our dependence on written sources impedes a direct access to historical circumstances, and that our image of ancient prophecy is decisively informed by the nature of source materials. Biblical prophecy, for example, cannot be straightforwardly equated with the prophetic phenomenon in the ancient kingdoms of Israel and Judah, even when it comes to the gender ratio of biblical prophets, because biblical prophecy is ultimately the construct of biblical writers, reflecting their ideologies. In a similar vein, the Assyrian construct of prophecy clearly favors the state ideology as propagated in temples of Ištar.[49] Hence both the biblical paucity of women prophets and the Assyrian prevalence of Ištar may at least partly go back to an intended construct.

Gender and Human Agency

It is well known from anthropology and the history of religion that, virtually regardless of time and place, women and other nonmale individuals occupy important positions usually related to their alleged receptiveness to divine inspiration and the ability to mediate between the divine and human worlds.[50] The prophetic action as such is not gender-specific. Anyone can achieve an altered state of consciousness required for prophe-

---

49. See my "Prophecy as Construct, Ancient and Modern," in *"Thus Speaks Ishtar of Arbela": Prophecy in Israel, Assyria and Egypt in the Neo-Assyrian Period* (ed. Robert P. Gordon and Hans M. Barstad; Winona Lake, Ind.: Eisenbrauns, forthcoming).

50. See the article of Lester Grabbe in this volume.

sying, and there is no difference between men and women in this respect.[51] The above statistics point in the same direction: in the ancient Near East, prophecy was open to both, or should we say, *all* genders.

Whatever local variations there might have been in the relative status of prophets representing different genders, it appears as a continuing pattern that in the ancient Eastern Mediterranean, the prophetic role could be assumed by male and nonmale persons alike. This cannot be said of most professions; at least in Mesopotamia, femininity and masculinity "were considered two of the divinely-ordained organizing principles by which society was thought to be governed,"[52] and this was reflected in gendered professional roles. Technical divination in particular (astrology, extispicy, augury, etc.) was a male domain in which women seem not to have been involved in Mesopotamia.[53] A few female seers (μάντεις) are known from Greek sources (see above), and some branches of divination are said to have been practiced by women in the Hebrew Bible; it mentions the necromancer of Endor (1 Sam 28) and the women who "prophesy" in some rather technical way in Ezek 13.[54] In general, however, the prophetic role appears to be clearly less dependent on gender than other methods of divination. There must be features in the prophetic and/or magical *agency* that explain the gender flexibility that makes prophecy different from the divinatory agency in general, enabling a socioreligious role that was not gender-specific.

At this juncture, it is necessary to explain the meaning of the concept of agency in this essay. As prophecy, by any definition, is religious activity

---

51. See the textual evidence in Nissinen, "Prophetic Madness."
52. Ilona Zsolnay, "Do Divine Structures of Gender Mirror Mortal Structures of Gender?" in *In the Wake of Tikva Frymer-Kensky* (ed. Steven Holloway, JoAnn Scurlock, and Richard Beal; Gorgias Précis Portfolios 4; Piscataway, N.J.; Gorgias, 2009), 103–20, esp. 107. See also Julia Asher-Greve, "Decisive Sex, Essential Gender," in *Sex and Gender in the Ancient Near East: Proceedings of the 47th Rencontre Assyriologique Internationale, Helsinki, July 2–6, 2001* (ed. Simo Parpola and Robert M. Whiting; CRRAI 47; Helsinki: Neo-Assyrian Text Corpus Project, 2002), 11–26.
53. Note, however, the two Neo-Assyrian oracular queries (SAA 4 321 and 322) in which the inquirer appears to be an unidentified female writer. The last lines of both queries present a unique formula: "disregard that a woman has written it and placed it before you." I am indebted to Saana Svärd for this reference.
54. See Esther Hamori's article in this volume; cf. Nancy R. Bowen, "The Daughters of Your People: Female Prophets in Ezekiel 13:17–23," *JBL* 118 (1999): 417–33; Jonathan Stökl, "The מתנבאות of Ezekiel 13 Reconsidered," *JBL* 132 (2013): 61–76.

and is practiced within a religious framework, *prophetic agency* should be understood as a subspecies of *religious agency*, which the sociologist Laura M. Leming understands "as a personal and collective claiming and enacting of dynamic religious identity. As *religious* identity, it may include, but is not limited to, a received or an acquired identity, whether passed on by family, religious group, or other social entity such as an educational community, or actively sought. To constitute religious *agency*, this identity is claimed and lived as one's own, with an insistence on active ownership."[55]

Although Leming's definition arises from the modern world (her case study is about woman-conscious Catholic women in America), she underlines that agency "is not practiced in a vacuum but is enacted within specific social contexts," which, in my view, makes her idea of religious agency equally applicable to other contexts, including ancient sources. Importantly, this definition encompasses both the received tradition and an "active ownership," thus making it possible to understand religious agency in terms of both transmission and transformation.[56]

Prophetic agency, therefore, can be understood as *instrumental* (silenced subjectivity: prophets as passive intermediaries) as well as *independent* (endorsed subjectivity: prophets as active agents).[57] These types of agency are neither gender-specific nor mutually exclusive, because the prophetic agency is ultimately defined by the audience. The agency of one and the same prophet can be interpreted simultaneously as instrumental from the point of view of contemporary religious authorities, and independent from that of contemporary critics or modern scholars. When interpreted as passive intermediaries, the actual agency is ascribed to the divinity, whose authority the transmissive action of the human prophet does not threaten. When seen as active agents, the prophets, both male and nonmale, are not merely regarded as instruments of the divine agent but also as acting on their own.

---

55. Laura M. Leming, "Sociological Explorations: What Is Religious Agency?" *Sociological Quarterly* 48 (2007): 73–92, esp. 74.

56. Cf. ibid., 88.

57. I owe these two aspects of agency to Tuija Hovi, "Sukupuoli, toimijuus ja muutos: Uuskarismaattisen liikkeen 'uutuus'" [Gender, Actorship and Change: "Novelty" in the Neo-Charismatic Movement], *Teologinen Aikakauskirja* 116 (2011): 195–207, esp. 199: "(1) Agency as transmission, effectuation, representation: rhetorically silenced subjectivity, 'working as God's instrument'; (2) agency as subjectivity, independent action, decision making: implicit accent on subjectivity, 'the authority of a Christian as an independent individual'" (my trans.).

Prophecy aims at influencing the audience by way of referring to the divine authorization behind the word spoken by the human prophet. Therefore, it has *both* the transmissive function as reflecting the religious framework known to the audience, *and* the transformative function, urging the addressees to accept potentially unexpected divine ordinances. These two functions are characteristic of ancient divination in general; Walter Burkert speaks of a paradox of divination "between establishment and crisis or even revolt, between the integration of divination's proceedings and representatives into the social-political system and divination as a disruptive, revolutionary, sometimes uncontrollable power."[58]

The gender aspect of religious, or prophetic, agency is fundamentally dependent on the prevailing gender matrix in the given social context of prophetic activity; in other words, gender matrix precedes prophetic agency, not vice versa. Therefore, whatever observations are made concerning the significance of gender in prophetic goings-on, they must always be measured against the gendered structure of the given (usually patriarchal) society, paying attention to features in prophetic agency that deviate from the standard expectations of gender roles and their enacting.

One conspicuous and potentially significant contextual factor that sets prophets apart from technical diviners is their education or—as our sources suggest—the lack thereof. While female scribes existed in Mesopotamia,[59] only male persons are known as practitioners of scholarly divination.[60] There is no indication that any such skills were required of prophets regardless of their gender, whether we look at Mari, Assyria, or Greece.

Particular techniques were probably needed in prophecy as well, but these could have been learned in temple communities. However, prophecy was not always a permanent role confined to temples and based on a

---

58. Walter Burkert, "Signs, Commands, and Knowledge: Ancient Divination between Enigma and Epiphany," in *Mantikê: Studies in Ancient Divination* (ed. Sarah Iles Johnston and Peter T. Struck; RGRW 155; Leiden: Brill, 2005), 29–49, esp. 43.

59. See, e.g., Samuel A. Meier, "Women and Communication in the Ancient Near East," *JAOS* 111 (1991): 540–47; Brigitte Lion, "Dame Inanna-ama-mu, scribe à Sippar," *RA* 95 (2001): 7–32; for Neo-Assyrian evidence see, e.g., SAA 7 24: r.2, mentioning six female Aramean (?) scribes.

60. For Mesopotamian education, see, e.g., Petra D. Gesche, *Schulunterricht in Babylonien im ersten Jahrtausend v.Chr.* (AOAT 275; Münster: Ugarit-Verlag, 2001); and, concisely, Karel van der Toorn, *Scribal Culture and the Making of the Hebrew Bible* (Cambridge: Harvard University Press, 2007), 54–67.

systematic education but could be assumed by anyone whose divine possession, however transient, was acknowledged by the audience. This may partly explain the gender flexibility of prophecy. The image of prophecy obtainable from Mesopotamian, biblical, and Greek texts alike tolerates individuals who occasionally speak divine words without carrying a prophetic title or otherwise acknowledged prophetic role. Wives, servants, and "slave girls" act as mediators of divine words in texts from both Mari and Assyria.[61]

In these cases, the idea of the divine possession as a way for women to act out despite their otherwise underprivileged agency may suggest itself. The prophetic role enabled women to open their mouth in public because they were expected to talk divine words—not as themselves but as mere instruments of gods speaking through them.[62] I will return later in this paper to the question whether this deprived them of their own agency altogether.

In the majority of cases recorded in our sources, the appreciation of male and female prophets and their sayings is due to their affiliation with temples that provide them with an accredited background. It indeed seems to have mattered where the oracles were spoken: the temples of Apollo at Delphi and Didyma, the temples of Annunītum at Mari and Dagan in Terqa, as well as the temple of Ištar in Arbela were acknowledged as sources of reliable prophecy.[63] This is not to say that prophetic agency would never have been acknowledged without such a background, but it deserves attention that temples, alongside the royal palace, were institutions where women actually had an acknowledged agency as priests, prophets, and in other roles, as members of communities that communicated with other parts of the society.[64]

---

61. E.g., the "spouse of a free man" in no. 20; Aḫatum, the servant girl of Dagan-malik in no. 24; the slave girl of Bēl-aḫu-uṣur in no. 115.

62. For the possessed women's instrumental agency, see esp. Mary Keller, *The Hammer and the Flute: Women, Power, and Spirit Possession* (Baltimore: Johns Hopkins University Press, 2002); for a critical review of her theory see Jonathan Stökl, "The Role of Women in the Prophetical Process in Mari: A Critique of Mary Keller's Theory of Agency," in *Thinking towards New Horizons: Collected Communications to the XIXth Congress of the International Organization for the Study of the Old Testament, Ljubljana 2007* (ed. Matthias Augustin and Hermann Michael Niemann; BEATAJ 55; Frankfurt am Main: Lang, 2008), 173–88.

63. Cf. Nissinen, "Prophetic Madness," 26–27.

64. For the royal women's position and agency, see Saana Teppo, "Agency and

Especially in Mesopotamian sources, there are several implications of communication between palace women and women affiliated with temples, and it would be worth investigating to what extent the personal ties between the women in palaces and temples actually contributed to the public role of the prophets, female prophets in particular, in the society at large. Palace women, such as Queen Šibtu and the royal ladies Addu-duri and Inib-šina at Mari,[65] and Queen Mother Naqī'a of Assyria,[66] seem to have maintained a close contact with temples where prophecies were uttered, and they turn out to have been decisive vehicles of not only the reception of prophecy in their own times but also the political use of prophecy and preservation of prophetic oracles for posterity.[67]

The prophetic role could be assumed continuously. This was most likely the case in the temple of Apollo at Delphi, where the Pythias held a permanent post involving sexual abstinence as a guarantee of their ritual purity.[68] Whether lifelong commitments or chastity were required of Mes-

---

the Neo-Assyrian Women of the Palace," StudOr 101 (2007): 381–420; idem, "The Role and the Duties of the Neo-Assyrian *šakintu* in the Light of Archival Evidence," SAAB 16 (2007): 257–72; Saana (Teppo) Svärd, *Women's Roles in the Neo-Assyrian Era: Female Agency in the Empire* (Saarbrücken: VDM, 2008); idem, "Power and Women in the Neo-Assyrian Palaces" (diss., University of Helsinki, 2012; http://hdl.handlenet/10138/29538); Sarah C. Melville, "Neo-Assyrian Royal Women and Male Identity: Status as a Social Tool," *JAOS* 124 (2004): 37–57.

65. See, e.g., Bernard F. Batto, *Studies on Women at Mari* (JHNES 5; Baltimore: Johns Hopkins University Press, 1974), 8–21; Abraham Malamat, *Mari and the Bible* (SHCANE 12; Leiden: Brill, 1998), 175–91; Stephanie Dalley, *Mari and Karana: Two Old Babylonian Cities* (London: Longman, 1984), 97–111.

66. See Sarah C. Melville, *The Role of Naqia/Zakutu in Sargonid Politics* (SAAS 9; Helsinki: Neo-Assyrian Text Corpus Project, 1999); Svärd, *Women's Roles*, 31–33; Kateřina Šašková, "Esarhaddon's Accession to the Assyrian Throne," in *Shepherds of the Black-Headed People: The Royal Office vis-à-vis Godhead in Ancient Mesopotamia* (ed. Kateřina Šašková, Lukáš Pecha, and Petra Charvát; Plzeň: Západočeská univerzita, 2010), 147–79, esp. 153–54, 170–71.

67. For Naqī'a and the prophets, see also Martti Nissinen, *References to Prophecy in Neo-Assyrian Sources* (SAAS 7; Helsinki: Neo-Assyrian Text Corpus Project, 1998), 22–24, 92.

68. Rather than implying an imagined sexual relationship with the god Apollo (thus Giulia Sissa, *Greek Virginity* [Revealing Antiquity 3; Cambridge: Harvard University Press, 1990]), the "virginity" of the Pythia has to do with her need to be free of bodily pollution. "The best way to accomplish this would have been to forbid the Pythia from engaging in sex at all during her term of office" (Johnston, *Ancient Greek Divination*, 42; cf. Flower, *Seer in Ancient Greece*, 224–25).

opotamian prophets escapes our knowledge, but several administrative documents from different periods use "prophets" (male and nonmale) as classifications that define their place within the temple community in a way that suggests a fixed role and position.[69]

At Mari, however, some palace women seem to have assumed the prophetic role themselves.[70] This, among other things, suggests that the prophetic role was not always understood as a permanent function or profession; rather, it was a role that could be assumed according to personal qualifications. This may also have been the case with the woman with the title *qammatum* at Mari,[71] or the votaresses (*šēlūtu*), that is, women dedicated to a temple, who are attested as prophets in two Assyrian texts.[72] Acting as a prophet was probably not a fixed part of their job description, but some votaresses transmitted divine words because of their acknowledged personal ability to achieve the required state of consciousness.

The same could apply to the sexually ambivalent or intersex people; indeed, the representation of nonmale persons other than women deserves full attention. The Greek sources include, to my knowledge, only one reference to the androgynous Scythian prophets, Ἐνάρεες οἱ ἀνδρόγυνοι (Herodotus, *Hist.* 4.67), who received their divinatory power from Aphrodite;[73] but we should not forget Teiresias, the mythical blind diviner who mastered both intuitive and technical types of divination and appeared mostly as male but sometimes as female.[74]

In Mesopotamia, devotees of Ištar called *assinnu, kurgarrû, sinnišānu*, sometimes also *kalû* and *kulu'u* are mentioned in several texts from dif-

---

69. E.g., nos. 110 (Neo-Assyrian), 119 (Ur III), 123 (Middle Assyrian), 130 (Neo-Babylonian).

70. Thus Addu-duri, King Zimri-Lim's mother (no. 42); Zunana, an otherwise unknown servant of the king (no. 37); and Šimatum, Zimri-Lim's daughter (no. 44).

71. Nos. 7, 9, 13.

72. Nos. 74, 114. For the *šēlūtu* see Svärd, *Women's Roles*, 70–80.

73. Unfortunately, the Ph.D. dissertation of Donat Margreth, *Skythische Schamanen? Die Nachrichten über Enarees-Anarieis bei Herodot und Hippokrates* (Schaffhausen: Meier, 1993), was not available to me.

74. For Teiresias, see Luc Brisson, *Le mythe de Tirésias: Essai d'analyse structurale* (Études préliminaires aux religions orientales dans l'Empire romain 55; Leiden: Brill, 1976); idem, *Sexual Ambivalence: Androgyny and Hermaphroditism in Graeco-Roman Antiquity* (trans. Janet Lloyd; Berkeley: University of California Press, 2002), 116–30; Gherhardo Ugolini, *Untersuchungen zur Figur des Sehers Teiresias* (Classica Monacensia 12; Tübingen: Narr, 1995); Lange, "Greek Seers," 473–75, 477–80.

ferent periods as representatives of an ambivalent gender.[75] These people feature in different roles including cross-dressing, ritual dance, healing, prophecy, lament—and prophecy, as evidenced by texts from Mari and probably also from Assyria. Two *assinnu*s, Šēlebum and Ili-ḫaznaya, are known to have prophesied at Mari, while in Assyrian sources the gender ambiguity is suggested by unclear gender specifications in three out of ten colophons of the tablet SAA 9 1: "Issār-lā-tašīaṭ, a man from Arbela,"[76] "the woman Bāia, a man from Arbela,"[77] and "the woman Ilussa-am[ur], a m[ale citizen] of Assur."[78] Some scholars have expressed their doubts about these colophons as reflecting a real gender ambivalence, suggesting scribal errors as the reason for the ambiguity,[79] but I find it improbable that the otherwise very competent and meticulous scribe had managed to create no less than three mistakes on one and the same tablet, hence I follow Simo Parpola's readings, which to me make perfect sense.[80]

---

75. For them see, e.g., Martti Nissinen, *Homoeroticism in the Biblical World: A Historical Perspective* (Minneapolis: Fortress, 1998), 28–34; Uri Gabbay, "The Akkadian Word for 'Third Gender': The *kalû* (gala) Once Again," in *Proceedings of the 51st Rencontre Assyriologique Internationale Held at the Oriental Institute of Chicago, July 18–22, 2005* (ed. Robert D. Biggs, Jennie Myers, and Martha T. Roth; SAOC 62; Chicago: Oriental Institute of the University of Chicago, 2008), 49–56; Saana Teppo, "Sacred Marriage and the Devotees of Ištar," in *Sacred Marriages: The Divine-Human Sexual Metaphor from Sumer to Early Christianity* (ed. Martti Nissinen and Risto Uro; Winona Lake, Ind.: Eisenbrauns, 2008), 75–92; Julia Assante, "Bad Girls and Kinky Boys? The Modern Prostituting of Ishtar, Her Clergy and Her Cults," in *Tempelprostitution im Altertum: Fakten und Fiktionen* (ed. Tanja Scheer; Oikumene 6; Osnabrück: Antike, 2009), 23–54, esp. 34–49; Ilan Peled, "On the Meaning of the 'Changing *pilpilû*,' " *NABU* 1/2013: 3–6 (no. 3).

76. No. 68 i 28–29 (ᵐⁱᵈ15—*la—ta-ši-ia-aṭ* DUMU URU.*arba-il*); the masculine determinative preceding the name is written over an erased feminine determinative.

77. No. 71 ii 40 (MÍ.*ba-ia-a* DUMU URU.*arba-il*); the discrepancy here is between the feminine determinative MÍ and the attribute DUMU, "son/man."

78. No. 72 iii 5–6 (MÍ.DINGIR-*ša—a-m*[*ur*] URU.ŠÀ— URU-*a*-[*a*]); here the *nisbe* form indicating the domicile of the prophet can only be reconstructed as masculine, hence it contradicts the feminine determinative.

79. See Jonathan Stökl's contribution to this volume, and cf. Manfred Weippert, "'König, fürchte dich nicht!': Assyrische Prophetie im 7. Jahrhundert v. Chr.," *Or* 71 (2002): 1–54, esp. 33–34; Jonathan Stökl, "Female Prophets in the Ancient Near East," in Day, *Prophecy and Prophets*, 47–61, esp. 55–56; idem, "Ištar's Women, YHWH's Men?" 96–98.

80. Simo Parpola, *Assyrian Prophecies* (SAA 9; Helsinki: Helsinki University Press, 1997), 5, 6, 7; cf. il [xlix] –l.

The *assinnu*s and their colleagues are impossible to classify in modern gender categories, because the sources do not inform us about their sexual orientation or bodily appearance. They have sometimes been called "transvestites," "bisexuals," even "cult homosexuals," but these designations are all misleading since they all derive from the modern understanding of "sexuality." Perhaps the best word to describe them is "queer," because that is what they seem to have been even in the eyes of their contemporaries.[81] Their third-gender role was probably not considered "normal"; nevertheless, their permanent difference from other people was divinely sanctioned. They were what they were by divine ordinance, and their very appearance conveyed a message to the people. Their existence had a mythological explanation, and their role was institutionalized because they "existed between myth and reality and embodied the divine Otherness."[82] This was also the justification of their manifest transgression of conventional sexual roles: being neither men nor women, they were not expected to engage in ordinary family life or to conform either to the dominant and reproductive sexual role of a male citizen or to the motherly role of a woman. Rather, they reflected Ištar's alterity,[83] emulating her power to transgress sexual boundaries, thus highlighting acceptable gender roles by way of manifestly violating them.

Even though the documented evidence of gender-ambiguous prophets is relatively rare, it nevertheless demonstrates the gender flexibility of prophecy. It also tells about their affiliation with temples of Ištar and their intimacy with the worship of the female deity. They were appreciated as flesh-and-blood manifestations of the alterity of Ištar, who was believed to have created them; hence their social status was due to their otherness. The prophetic role (probably unlike their transgender role) is not likely to

---

81. For the concept of "queer," see Annamarie Jagose, *Queer Theory: An Introduction* (New York: New York University Press, 1996); Ken Stone, "Queer Commentary and Biblical Interpretation: An Introduction," in *Queer Commentary and the Hebrew Bible* (ed. Ken Stone; JSOTSup 334; Sheffield: Sheffield Academic Press, 2001), 11–34; for recent applications of queer theory, see, e.g., Anthony Heacock, *Jonathan Loved David: Manly Love in the Bible and the Hermeneutics of Sex* (BMW 22; Sheffield: Sheffield Phoenix, 2011); Teresa J. Hornsby and Ken Stone, eds., *Bible Trouble: Queer Reading and the Boundaries of Biblical Scholarship* (SemeiaSt 67; Atlanta: Society of Biblical Literature, 2011).

82. Teppo, "Sacred Marriage," 87.

83. See esp. Zainab Bahrani, *Women of Babylon: Gender and Representation in Mesopotamia* (London: Routledge, 2001), 141–60.

have been their permanent occupation, but as members of temple communities they could assume this role if they, like the female members of the same communities, fulfilled its requirements.

However fixed and permanent, the prophetic role constituted a specific agency through which the people acknowledged as prophets enjoyed whatever appreciation belonged to that role in their societies. An essential constituent of this role was the idea of the prophets as intermediaries of divine words; from the point of view of agency, this idea raises the question of whose agency, in fact, is at issue. The cultural theory of divine possession makes the prophets mouthpieces of deities who do not express their own opinions or even use words of their own, but through whom the deities speak.[84] According to this theory, the authority behind them was that of the temple and the deity, which, at least theoretically, deprived the prophets of their personal agency altogether. If the prophets were not thought of as representing themselves (or their gender, for that matter), does it make any sense at all to talk about agency in their case, and is there a difference between male and nonmale prophets in this respect?

We have seen that female prophecy was, by and large, well established in the ancient Near East. Even the Hebrew Bible acknowledges female prophets, some of them assuming important roles, such as Huldah in the initial phase of the Josianic reform (2 Kgs 22:14–20), or Noadiah as the primary opponent of Nehemiah (Neh 6:14). That their number is considerably smaller than that of male prophets, however, makes women prophets look like an exception rather than the rule. To whatever extent the paucity of women prophets conforms to the historical reality, or reflects a patriarchal bias of the editors of the biblical texts, remains a matter of dispute.[85] At any rate, it is evident that in the Hebrew Bible, the agency of the female prophets is consistent with the ideology of the literary construction within which they appear. This can be seen, for instance, in the profoundly Deuteronomistic presentation of Huldah in 2 Kgs 22.[86]

---

84. E.g., Keller, *Hammer and Flute*.

85. E.g., Fischer (*Gotteskünderinnen*) believes that the impact of women prophets in ancient Israel was much more significant that the editors of the biblical texts want to admit. Stökl ("Ištar's Women, YHWH's Men?"), on the other hand, thinks that the prevalence of male prophets in the Hebrew Bible corresponds to the male gender of Yahweh and is, therefore, not primarily the construction of the editors.

86. See, e.g., Tal Ilan, "Huldah, the Deuteronomic Prophetess of the Book of Kings," *lectio difficilior* 1/2010. Online: http://www.lectio.unibe.ch.

More tangible information of women's divinatory role as potentially inferior to that of male persons may be drawn from the Mari letters. Esther Hamori has recently paid attention to the references to the enclosure of the prophet's "hair and fringe" (*šārtum u sissiktum*) in a letter reporting the prophet's performance, which are twice as common if the prophet is a woman or an *assinnu* than if the prophet is a man. Since the hair and fringe were used for a ritual verification of the prophecy, this evidence suggests that prophecies uttered by women and the *assinnus* were thought of as less reliable, hence implying a lower status of nonmale prophets.[87] Both at Mari and in Assyria, the social standing of women prophets was probably related to their association with influential palace women on the one hand, and to the prestige of their home temples on the other hand.

Sometimes, as in the case of the Delphic Pythia, influential positions of women as mediators were well established and based on a long-term tradition (which did not necessarily spare them from male criticism[88]). Whose agency is it, then, that these women are executing? One can certainly say, from the emic point of view, that since prophets were regarded as mouthpieces of a deity, their own personality was indifferent. The speaker, after all, was the deity, hence the person of the prophet did not matter. The instrumental understanding of prophetic agency, however, does not sufficiently explain the recurrent appreciation of individual women whose impact was quite evidently bound to their institutional background and personal qualifications, which sometimes provided them with considerable authority. Prophets, whether male or female, did not just passively repeat divine words, barely aware of what they said, but really did *act* as independent individuals. Speaking with a divine voice enabled not only male but also nonmale individuals to raise their own voices as well.

We should not, however, forget the gendered social context within which the prophetic agency was enacted. The instrumental aspect is emphasized in a male-dominated environment where the nonmale prophetic voice is acknowledged and authorized as an echo of the divine speech. Even the independent agency, while occasionally intruding into

---

87. Esther Hamori, "Gender and the Verification of Prophecy at Mari," *WO* 42 (2012): 1–22. The texts in question are nos. 10, 11, 13, 14, 24, 27, 36, 42 (woman); 8, 23 (*assinnu*); 2, 25, 29, 39, and ARM 26 226 (man).

88. Cf. the rather slanderous downplaying of the Delphic Pythia in the second century C.E. by Aelius Aristides, who claims the Pyhtian προμάντεις cannot even remember what they prophesied (*In Defence of Oratory* 34–35).

the hierarchical structures of the society, is ultimately dependent on the same structures that in due course harness the prophetic agency to serve its purposes. This can be seen, for instance, in the Assyrian oracles, which as a whole preach the Assyrian state ideology, hiding the personal input of the prophets, whether male or nonmale.

As the prophetic action is not gender-specific, it is not primarily *women's* agency the female prophets execute but, rather, *prophetic* agency insofar as the action is presented as part of the prophetic activity. This notwithstanding, gender does matter because prophecy appears as one of the few public, socially appreciated roles that were not inextricably linked with male gender and therefore could be assumed by nonmales even in a patriarchal society. The female contribution to different kinds of divine-human communication exhibits specific domains where nonmales are allowed to transgress the socially sanctioned gender-based boundaries.

Gender and Divine Agency

As much as the human agency, more or less gendered, can be seen by today's scholars as the driving force behind the prophetic phenomenon and institution, the ancient audiences of prophecy perceived of it as based entirely on a superhuman, divine agency. As one of the branches of the art of divination,[89] prophecy was one of the channels of divine-human communication, in which the human prophet's action, whether male or nonmale, was indeed understood in an instrumental manner. Divine agency, of course, is something that can only be believed; however, if divine agency is taken for granted, as was and is done wherever the concept of divination has any meaning, agency can be attributed to divine beings on the basis of each person's own experience of agency.[90]

---

89. For prophecy as divination see, e.g., Martti Nissinen, "Prophecy and Omen Divination: Two Sides of the Same Coin," in *Divination and Interpretation of Signs in the Ancient World* (ed. Amar Annus; OIS 6; Chicago: Oriental Institute of the University of Chicago, 2010), 341–51.

90. Ilkka Pyysiäinen, *Supernatural Agents: Why We Believe in Souls, Gods, and Buddhas* (New York: Oxford University Press, 2009), 41–42: "Humans have immediate experience of their own agency and also attribute agency to others whose behavior shows regular patterns.… Agency can also be (counterintuitively) transferred to natural objects and artifacts"—and, of course, to divine beings. For God as supernatural agent, mainly from the Christian point of view, see ibid., 95–136.

The gendered theological model that prevailed everywhere in the ancient Eastern Mediterranean (which is not primarily a matter of "polytheism" but of a gendered image of the divine[91]) raises the question of the role of gender in the divine prophetic agency. As we have seen, both male and female deities can be found as divine speakers of prophetic oracles. Fourteen male deities[92] and six female deities[93] are mentioned by their names in the SBLWAW corpus as the source of prophecy.[94]

Among them, one male and one female god stand out as principal Near Eastern deities of prophecy: Dagan, who appears in almost a half of all the cases where a male deity is involved (22/47); and Ištar or one of her manifestations, who is the god of prophecy in no less than 47 out of 55 occurrences of female deities. At Mari Dagan is the deity in two-thirds of the cases involving a male god (22/33). In Assyria Ištar is the sole female deity of prophecy, appearing in her different local manifestations, such as Mullissu (Ištar of Nineveh), Bēlet Kidmuri (Ištar of Calaḫ), and Urkittu (Ištar of Uruk). She is by far the most important female oracular deity

---

91. Cf. Stökl, "Ištar's Women, YHWH's Men?" 99. Even in Simo Parpola's "monotheistic" model of the Assyrian religion ("Monotheism in Ancient Assyria," in *One God or Many? Concepts of Divinity in the Ancient World* [ed. Barbara Nevling Porter; Transactions of the Casco Bay Assyriological Institute 1; Chebeague, Me.: Casco Bay Assyriological Institute, 2000], 165–209), the image of the divine is gendered, since different manifestations of the one god Aššur are both male and female, Ištar among the foremost of them.

92. Adad no. 50, 61; Adad of Kallassu no. 1 (3x); Adad of Aleppo no. 2; Amu of Hubšalum no. 49; Amon no. 142; Aššur nos. 84, 85, 86; Baalšamayin no. 137; Dagan (as Dagan nos. 3, 9, 12, 15, 16, 20, 25, 30, 31, 34, 37, 46, 53, 60, 62; as Dagan of Ṣubatum no. 63; as Dagan of Terqa nos. 7, 9, 38, 39; as Dagan of Tuttul no. 19); Itur-Mer nos. 41, 55/59; Marduk (as Marduk no. 47, as Bēl nos. 71, 106, 112); Milcom no. 136; Nabû no. 71; Nergal no. 55/59; Nusku no. 115; Šamaš no. 4, 48; Yahweh nos. 139, 141.

93. Bēlet-biri no. 43; Bēlet-ekallim nos. 19, 21, 45; Diritum no. 18; Hišamitum no. 5; Ištar (as Ištar nos. 51, 52, 97, 118, 123; as Ištar of Arbela nos. 68, 69, 70, 71, 73, 75, 76, 77, 80, 81, 87, 88, 90, 91, 94, 100, 101, 107, 113, 114; as Ištar of Nineveh no. 107; as Annunītum nos. 7, 8, 10, 22, 23, 24, 42, 58; as Banitu no. 78; as Inana of Girsu no. 119; as Kititum nos. 66, 67; as Lady of Kidmuri no. 99; as Mullissu nos. 72, 81, 92, 94; as Nanaya no. 134; as Šauška of Nineveh no. 121; as Urkittu no. 83); Ninhursag nos. 29, 56/57.

94. Different manifestations of one single deity are grouped together in the previous footnotes; the list includes also the cases where the name of the deity is not mentioned but the deity is otherwise recognizable to a high degree of probability.

also at Mari (Annunītum), Ešnunna (Kititum), and Babylonia (Inana, Nanaya).

The two main corpora of prophetic texts hence give the impression that prophetic activity was centered in the temples of Dagan and Ištar without, however, having been restricted to them. The evidence coming from other sources is too meager to warrant similar conclusions regarding other Near Eastern societies. It deserves attention, however, that in the few West Semitic cases from Ammon, Hamath, and Judah, the oracular god is always the state god, which corresponds to the "henotheistic" or "monolatric" pattern of worship in these societies.

In Greece, as noted above, the principal oracular gods are Apollo and Zeus. Locally, a few other gods and ancient heroes are mentioned as giving oracles,[95] but it is quite exceptional to find female deities in this function. The Greek sources only know of an oracle of Hera Akraia in Perachora,[96] another of Gaia in Aegira,[97] and yet another of Nyx in Megara.[98] None of these counted among major oracle sites. Only Perachora is archaeologically attested, and only Aegira involves a female prophet, but the reference seems to be inspired by the analogy to the Delphic Pythia rather than historical circumstances. The prevalence of male gods as Greek oracular deities hence appears as an established and gendered cultural pattern.

We have seen that, even though there is no universal gender correspondence between prophets and deities, the female deity/nonmale prophet pattern clearly prevails in Assyria, and male deity/male prophet pattern seems to be the standard pattern in the West Semitic world, as far as the small number of sources yields a realistic picture of the historical

---

95. These include, e.g., Amphilochus in Mallos (Pausanias, *Descr.* 1.34); Dionysos (Pausanias, *Descr.* 10.33), Heracles in Bura and in Hyettos (SEG 26.524), and Teiresias, whose oracle site, according to Plutarch, was abandoned (Plutarch, *Mor.* 434c).

96. Strabo, *Geogr.* 8.6.22; see T. J. Dunbabin, "The Oracle of Hera Akraia at Perachora," *Annual of the British School at Athens* 46 (1951): 61–71; Blanche Menadier, "The Sanctuary of Hera Akraia and Its Religious Connections with Corinth," in *Peloponnesian Sanctuaries and Cults: Proceedings of the Ninth International Symposium at the Swedish Institute at Athens, 11–13 June 1994* (Skrifter utgivna av Svenska institutet i Athen 4o, 48; ed. Robin Hägg; Stockholm: Swedish Institute at Athens, 2002), 85–91.

97. Pliny (*Nat.* 28.147) mentions the oracle of Gaia at Aegira, located in a cave where a female priest, having drunk bull's blood, descended to utter prophecy; see Yulia Ustinova, *Caves and the Ancient Greek Mind: Descending Underground in the Search for Ultimate Truth* (Oxford: Oxford University Press, 2009), 88.

98. The only reference to this is Pausanias, *Descr.* 1.40.6.

phenomenon they reflect. What difference does it make, then, whether the speaking deity is male or female, and is the gender of the prophet significant in any way with regard to what the gods say?

Only the prophetic corpora of Mari and Assyria allow comparisons between the utterances of male and female oracular deities. The foremost topic of prophetic oracles in both corpora is the reign of the ruling king. The divine support for the king is affirmed by male and female gods alike and conveyed by both male and nonmale prophets, at Mari as well as in Assyria. The male god Adad of Aleppo claims to have restored Zimri-Lim to his father's throne,[99] while the female deity Diritum declares that the Upper Country is given to him.[100] The establishment of the rule of Esarhaddon is incessantly asserted by Ištar[101] and, on the occasion of his enthronement, also by Aššur;[102] the proclamation of Ashurbanipal's kingship has been preserved only as words of Ištar.[103] Another principal theme of prophecies, the destruction of enemies, is similarly non-gender-specific, abundantly proclaimed by male and female prophets.[104] Cultic instructions and criticism, too, can be found in different gender configurations,[105] and the same is true for political advice.[106] So far, thus, the divine prophetic agency does not show any clear traces of gender specificity of any kind.

This, however, is not the whole truth about gender and divine agency in ancient Near Eastern prophecy. What really makes a difference in this

---

99. No. 1 (male and female prophets), no. 2 (male prophet).

100. No. 18 (male prophet); cf. no. 21 (Bēlet-ekallim, unknown prophet).

101. E.g., no. 71 (genderwise ambiguous prophet), no. 73 (unknown prophet), no. 75 (female prophet), no. 77 (male prophet), no. 80 (male prophet).

102. Nos. 85, 86 (male prophet); cf. Bēl, no. 106 (unknown prophet).

103. Nos. 92, 94 (Mullissu and Ištar of Arbela; female prophets).

104. Cf. Mari: nos. 19, 38, 47 (male god, male prophet); nos. 5, 18 (female god, male prophet); no. 22 (female god, *assinnu*); Assyria: nos. 85, 86 (male god, male prophet), nos. 88, 101 (female god, male prophet); nos. 69, 74, 81, 82, 94 (female god, female prophet); nos. 68, 79 (female god, gender-ambiguous prophet); no. 100 (female god, unknown prophet).

105. Mari: nos. 4, 25, 30, 31 (male god, male prophet); no. 29 (female god, male prophet); Assyria: no. 80, 88 (female god, male prophet); no. 99 (female god, unknown prophet); nos. 111, 113 (unknown god, female prophet).

106. Mari: no. 4 (male god, male prophet); nos. 7, 9 (female god, female prophet); Assyria: no. 107 (female god; unknown prophet); no. 115 (male informant on the alleged word of a male god by a female prophet).

respect is the gender-specific language attached to the female deity Ištar in Assyrian sources. Belligerent language and warlike appearance, usually perceived of as markers of masculinity, may seem ill fitting for a female deity, but in the case of Ištar, "the most warlike among the gods,"[107] they form an indispensable part of her image. As a liminal figure, Ištar—who without doubt was identified as female and not as a hermaphrodite[108]— was "the place of all extremes,"[109] with formidable destructive powers but also with a great sexual allure and excessive femininity.

The Assyrian Ištar is not particularly well known as executing motherly care or other parental functions; this, however, is the role she is given often enough in the Neo-Assyrian prophetic oracles to make it one of the central metaphors used of her in this material.[110] In Neo-Assyrian oracles, the Ištars of Arbela and Nineveh present the Assyrian king as the "creation of their hands" (*binūt qātīšina*).[111] Esarhaddon, as the legitimate heir of the Assyrian throne, is called "son of Mullissu" (Mullissu is another name of Ištar of Nineveh),[112] and Ashurbanipal receives the message: "You whose mother is Mullissu, fear not! You whose nurse is the Lady of Arbela, fear not!"[113] Ištar declares herself as the father and mother of Esarhaddon, whom she raised between her wings;[114] while Ashurbanipal, in another context, claims he knew no father and mother but grew up in the lap of the female deities. He even calls Mullissu his mother who gave birth to him.[115] Sometimes the deity's motherly function is mixed with that of a midwife or wet nurse who carries the king on her hip, breastfeeds him, and hushes him like a baby.[116] This imagery reflects the Assyrian

---

107. No. 101 v 44.

108. See Brigitte Groneberg, "Die sumerisch-akkadische Inanna/Ištar: Hermaphroditos?" *WO* 17 (1986): 25–46.

109. Bahrani, *Women of Babylon*, 159; for the paradoxical character of Ištar, see ibid., 141–60.

110. See Parpola, *Assyrian Prophecies*, xxxvi–xli.

111. No. 94 5, r. 2.

112. No. 73 iv 2, 21.

113. No. 92 r. 6.

114. No. 82 iii 26–27.

115. SAA 3 3:13, r. 14.

116. "I am your great midwife, I am your excellent wet nurse" (no. 72 iii 15–18); "Like a nurse I will carry you on my hip. I will put you, a pomegranate, between my breasts. At night I will be awake and guard you; throughout the day I will give you milk, at dawn I will hush you" (no. 92 r. 7–10).

royal theology especially in Neo-Assyrian times and is not restricted to prophetic texts;[117] however, the motherly imagery is especially common in prophecy, probably because it gives the best possible expression for the prophetic agency of Ištar combined with the extraordinary relationship between the deity and the king.

Of the various manifestations of the deity, Ištar of Arbela appears as the god of prophecy par excellence.[118] "The Lady of Arbela"— often together with her alter ego, Ištar of Nineveh—is one of the most frequently mentioned deities in letters, inscriptions, and prophecies. Seven out of fifteen Neo-Assyrian prophets known by their names come from Arbela,[119] and two prophets who come from outside of Arbela speak the words of Ištar of Arbela.[120] Her words are paraphrased also in the inscriptions of Ashurbanipal.[121] All this indicates that Ištar of Arbela at this time was a national deity, not just another local manifestation of the deity.

Esarhaddon and Ashurbanipal had without any doubt a distinctive relationship with Ištar of Arbela and her worship. Her temple Egašankalamma was one of the major temples in Assyria[122] and the object of both kings' special devotion.[123] The prophetic scene described by Ashurbanipal

---

117. Cf. the references in Parpola, *Assyrian Prophecies*, c nn. 177–86.

118. See Martti Nissinen, "City Lofty as Heaven: Arbela and Other Cities in Neo-Assyrian Prophecy," in *"Every City Shall Be Forsaken": Urbanism and Prophecy in Ancient Israel and the Near East* (ed. Lester L. Grabbe and Robert D. Haak; JSOTSup 330; Sheffield: Sheffield Academic Press, 2001), 172–209.

119. Aḫat-abiša (no. 75), Bāia (nos. 71, [79]), Dunnaša-āmur (no. 94), Issār-lā-tašīaṭ (no. 68), Lā-dāgil-ili (nos. 77, 83, 88), Sinqīša-āmur (no. 69), Tašmētu-ēreš (no. 91); note that Dunnaša-āmur and Sinqīša-āmur may be one and the same person. In addition, letter no. 113 reports a prophecy delivered by a woman in a temple probably located in Arbela.

120. Urkittu-šarrat from Calah (no. 81) and Rēmūt-Allati from Dara-aḫuya (no. 70).

121. I.e., in his accounts of the campaigns against Mannea (no. 100) and Elam (no. 101).

122. See Brigitte Menzel, *Untersuchungen zu Kult, Administration und Personal* (vol. 1 of *Assyrische Tempel*; StP Series Maior 10.1; Rome: Biblical Institute Press, 1981), 6–33; Andrew R. George, *House Most High: The Temples of Ancient Mesopotamia* (MC 5; Winona Lake, Ind.: Eisenbrauns, 1993), 90, no. 351.

123. Esarhaddon: Erle Leichty, *The Royal Inscriptions of Esarhaddon, King of Assyria (680–669 BC)* (RINAP 4; Winona Lake, Ind.: Eisenbrauns, 2011), 155 (no. 77), lines 8–11; Ashurbanipal: Rykle Borger, *Beiträge zum Inschriftenwerk Assurbanipals: Die Prismenklassen A, B, C = K, D, E, F, G, H, J und T sowie andere Inschriften* (Wies-

in his inscription on the war against Elam (no. 101) serves as a good illustration of the ideology of prophecy and the theology of Ištar, presenting her as the creator and mother of the king in a language reminiscent of the above-quoted prophecies.

According to Simo Parpola, the prophecies presenting Ištar as the wet nurse or the mother of the king[124] should be understood not merely as metaphors but as referring to their upbringing as royal infants in the temples of Ištar in Nineveh and Arbela.[125] This practice may have begun only with Esarhaddon, whose mother Naqi'a seems to have maintained close contact with the prophets of Arbela.[126] If this theory is correct, it explains much of the special significance of Ištar, of the outstanding religious position of the city of Arbela, and of the special appreciation of prophecy during the rule of these two kings. In the case of Arbela, the prophetic agency of the deity was successfully administered by women of the palace and temple: queens, nonmale prophets, and other devotees of Ištar. Measured against the observation of Sarah Melville that "[n]ot only do the Assyrians refer officially to the king's women with intentionally impersonal language, but they also tend to ignore the relationship between royal mothers and their children,"[127] one is tempted to ask how much the backstage agency of these women actually influenced the structures of Assyrian religion and royal ideology.

The exclusive relationship between Ištar and the Assyrian king (or crown prince) has its roots in the ancient Mesopotamian tradition of alliances between female deities and kings. Beate Pongratz-Leisten has demonstrated that Ištar may assume the role of the beloved of the king in the sacred marriage, as well as the roles of divine mother, wet nurse, and midwife.[128] All these roles are emphatically and inevitably gendered and can be assumed by female deities only; however, they imply more than just the

---

baden: Harrassowitz, 1996), 140 ii 7–8. Esarhaddon visualized his enduring presence in this temple by letting his doubled image be placed on the right and left sides of Ištar; see SAA 13 140 and 141.

124. Cf. nos. 73, 82, 92; SAA 3 13: r.6–8, etc. In his hymn to the Ištars of Arbela and Nineveh, Ashurbanipal calls himself "product of Emašmaš and Egašankalamma" (SAA 3 3:10).

125. Parpola, *Assyrian Prophecies*, xxxix–xl.

126. She is addressed several times in the prophetic oracles (nos. 74, 75, 78, [83], 90); cf. Nissinen, *References to Prophecy*, 22–24; Melville, *Role of Naqia/Zakutu*, 27–29.

127. Melville, "Neo-Assyrian Royal Women," 54.

128. Beate Pongratz-Leisten, "When Gods Are Speaking: Toward Defining the Interface between Polytheism and Monotheism," in *Prophetie in Mari, Assyrien und*

aspect of motherliness and fertility. While in the sacred marriage the love between the female deity and the king (or even between a divine couple) bestows the king with the divine love and an intimate relationship with the divine world,[129] the role of the female deity as the (adoptive) mother of the king creates a familial tie between the king and the gods, and that of the midwife presents her as supervising the birth of the king and being its first witness.[130] In all these functions, the female deity is the mediator between the divine and human worlds, the one who transfers divine knowledge and favors to the people through the person of the king. This is the gendered divine agency of Ištar even in the case of prophecy.

The function of the female deity as mediator of the divine knowledge also belongs firmly to the concept of the divine council (Akk. *puḫur ilāni*) known all over the ancient Near East. Within this concept, the female deity often appears as the "diviner of the gods," that is, the divine figure who mediates the decisions of the council of gods to humans, and this makes the concept of the divine council significant also with regard to the gendered divine agency in prophecy.[131] The following quotation is not from Neo-Assyrian prophecies but from the oracles of Kititum (Ištar) to Ibal-pî-El II, king of Ešnunna: "O king Ibal-pî-El, thus says Kititum: The secrets of the gods are placed before me. Because you constantly pronounce my name with your mouth, I keep disclosing the secrets of the gods to you."[132]

Israel (ed. Matthias Köckert and Martti Nissinen; FRLANT 201; Göttingen: Vandenhoeck & Ruprecht, 2003), 132–68.

129. See Beate Pongratz-Leisten, "Sacred Marriage and the Transfer of Divine Knowledge: Alliances between the Gods and the King in Ancient Mesopotamia," in Nissinen and Uro, *Sacred Marriages*, 43–73; Pirjo Lapinkivi, "The Sumerian Sacred Marriage and Its Aftermath in Later Sources," in Nissinen and Uro, *Sacred Marriages*, 7–41; Martti Nissinen, "Akkadian Rituals and Poetry of Divine Love," in *Mythology and Mythologies: Methodological Approaches to Intercultural Influences* (ed. Robert M. Whiting; Melammu Symposia 2; Helsinki: Neo-Assyrian Text Corpus Project, 2001), 93–136.

130. Cf. Pongratz-Leisten, "When Gods Are Speaking," 150–55.

131. See, with more evidence, Martti Nissinen, "Prophets and the Divine Council," in *Kein Land für sich allein: Studien zum Kulturkontakt in Kanaan, Israel/Palästina und Ebirnâri für Manfred Weippert zum 65. Geburtstag* (ed. Ulrich Hübner and Ernst Axel Knauf; OBO 186; Fribourg: Universitätsverlag, 2002), 4–19. For prophecy and the divine council in the Hebrew Bible, see also Alan Lenzi, *Secrecy and the Gods: Secret Knowledge in Ancient Mesopotamia and Biblical Israel* (SAAS 19; Helsinki: Neo-Assyrian Text Corpus Project, 2008), 233–71.

132. No. 66 1–8.

The message of this oracle, probably pronounced on the occasion of Ibal-pî-El's accession to the throne,[133] is that the divine council has decided that the throne of Ešnunna belongs to Ibal-pî-El. Kititum, knowing the "secrets (*niṣirtu*) of the gods,"[134] functions as the divine intermediary, who constantly communicates the arbitrations of the council of gods to the king. The same pattern is attested a full millennium later in Neo-Assyrian prophecy, where Ištar in her two manifestations as Ištar of Arbela and Mullissu makes the following statement to Ashurbanipal by the mouth of the female prophet Dunnaša-āmur:

> In the assembly of all the gods (*ina puḫur ilāni kalāmi*) I have spoken for your life. My arms are strong and will not cast you off before the gods. My shoulders are always ready to carry you, you in particular. I keep desiring your life with my l[ip]s […] your life, you increase life.… [In the assembly] of all [the gods I incessantly spe]ak for your good.[135]

In this text the role of the deity as mediator is combined with her maternal aspect: Ashurbanipal is described as the "creation of their [scil. both Ištars'] hands" (*binût qātīšina*), and the oracle is replete with the deity's compassion toward Ashurbanipal.[136] Again, it is the intimate relationship between the king and the female deity that ultimately counts before the divine council.

The idea of the female deity's intimacy with the world of the humans, as well as her prophetic agency within the divine council, is not restricted to Mesopotamian sources but, interestingly and importantly, finds a clearly

---

133. For this text see Maria deJong Ellis, "The Goddess Kititum Speaks to King Ibalpiel: Oracle Texts from Ishchali," *MARI* 5 (1987): 235–66.

134. For the "secrets of the gods" in this text, and in divination in general, see Lenzi, *Secrecy and the Gods*, 55–62.

135. No. 94 16–24.

136. Cf. Dialogue of Ashurbanipal and Nabû (SAA 3 13), a text written by the same scribe and deriving from the same historical situation (Ashurbanipal's war against his brother Šamaš-šumu-ukin) as no. 94. In this text, Ashurbanipal pleads with Nabû not to leave him "in the assembly of those who wish him ill" (*ina puḫur ḫaddānūtīšu*, line r. 3; cf. lines 6, 22, r. 4), and Nabû asserts: "My pleasant mouth shall ever bless you in the assembly of great gods" (*ina puḫur ilāni rabūti*, line 26; cf. line r. 11). The reason for Nabû's intercession is that Ashurbanipal, who in his childhood "sat in the lap of the Queen of Nineveh" (line r. 7), "grasps the feet of the Queen of Nineveh" and "sits next to Urkittu" (lines r. 2–3).

recognizable echo in the figure of Lady Wisdom in early Judaism.¹³⁷ Lady Wisdom's lovers, like those of Inana/Ištar, are both divine and human.¹³⁸ The language used of her in Prov 8:22–31 subtly suggests an intimate relationship with God, something that Philo of Alexandria develops further in his description of the cosmogonic union between Wisdom and the creator, as the result of which Wisdom receives the seed of God and becomes the mother and the wet nurse of the universe.¹³⁹ In Wisdom of Solomon, too, Wisdom and God are presented in terms of a divine marriage: Wisdom is called God's πάρεδρος (Wis 9:4), who lives in a συμβίωσις with him, her function being the μύστις of God's knowledge (8:3–4).¹⁴⁰ But she is also the companion of her student, King Solomon, who is engaged in a love relationship with her (6:12–25; 7:7–14; 8:2–21); this compares well to the virtual equation of Wisdom with a wife in Prov 8:35 and 18:22.¹⁴¹

Ben Sira (Sir 51:13–30 = 11QPsᵃ XXI 11–17) also describes the young man's burning desire for Lady Wisdom; especially the original Hebrew text uses euphemisms that do not even try to veil the sexual connotations of the relationship between the two. Even God is involved in this love affair, because "Those who serve her serve the Holy One; God loves those who love her" (Sir 4:14). By virtue of this love, the divine knowledge will be revealed to the lover by Wisdom herself: "When his heart is fully with me, I will set him again upon the straight path and will reveal to him my secrets (מסתרי)" (Sir 4:17–18 Heb.). Lady Wisdom's key position in revealing divine secrets¹⁴² is so closely reminiscent to Ištar-Kititum's role in the oracles to kings Ibal-pî-El of Ešnunna and Ashurbanipal of Assyria

---

137. For the figure and functions of Lady Wisdom, see, e.g., Silvia Schroer, *Wisdom Has Built Her House: Studies on the Figure of Sophia in the Bible* (Collegeville, Minn.: Liturgical Press, 2000).

138. For the following, see Ruben Zimmermann, "The Love Triangle of Lady Wisdom: Sacred Marriage in Jewish Wisdom Literature?" in Nissinen and Uro, *Sacred Marriages*, 243–58.

139. Philo of Alexandria, *Ebr.* 30–36: μητρὸς καὶ τιθήνης τῶν ὅλων (31).

140. Wis 8:4: μύστις γάρ ἐστιν τῆς τοῦ θεοῦ ἐπιστήμης.

141. Cf. also Prov 4:5–8 and 4Q185 2:8–15. For Lady Wisdom in the Dead Sea Scrolls, see Sidnie White Crawford, "Lady Wisdom and Dame Folly at Qumran," *DSD* 5 (1998): 355–66.

142. See Pancratius C. Beentjes, "What about Apocalypticism in the Book of Ben Sira?" in *Congress Volume Helsinki 2010* (ed. Martti Nissinen; VTSup 148; Leiden: Brill, 2012), 207–27, esp. 214–16; Benjamin G. Wright, "Conflicted Boundaries: Ben Sira, Sage and Seer," in Nissinen, *Congress Volume Helsinki 2010*, 229–53, esp. 236–37.

that it cannot be coincidental but must belong to the same ancient Near Eastern tradition.

What, then, has all this divine-human intimacy to do with divine *prophetic* agency? In Mesopotamia, both prophecy and the sacred marriage were vehicles for conferring divine knowledge and creating a close relationship between gods and the king, and through him, the people.[143] Even in Jewish sources, the ultimate purpose of the intimate liaison between God and the wise man is to become acquainted with divine knowledge (often read: Torah); the love affair with Wisdom symbolizes the closest possible proximity to God himself. According to Alan Lenzi, Wisdom in Prov 8:22–31 "is implicitly a messenger sent by Yahweh to humanity and therefore can communicate to mortals her unique cosmological knowledge"; dwelling among humanity she is a "uniquely qualified prophetic-like messenger from Yahweh bearing his wisdom to them."[144]

The prophetic aspect comes into play with the position of Lady Wisdom in the heavens, blatantly similar to that of Ištar in the Assyrian divine council. That Lady Wisdom's dwelling was with (other) divine beings is well known from various sources, such as the Aramaic book of *Ahiqar*, where she is said to be set in heaven and exalted by the Lord of the holy ones (i.e., of the divine council);[145] and possibly in one of the Dead Sea Scrolls, 4Q491, where an anonymous speaker claims to be "in the assembly of gods" (בעדת אלים), "with gods" (עם אלים), and "in the congregation of the holy ones" (בעדת קדוש).

The clearest evidence, however, is provided by the book of Ben Sira,[146] where the self-praise of Lady Wisdom is introduced as follows: "In the assembly of the Most High [ἐν ἐκκλησίᾳ ὑψίστου] she opens her mouth, in

---

143. Cf. Pongratz-Leisten, "Sacred Marriage," 68–69.

144. Lenzi, *Secrecy and the Gods*, 361.

145. "To gods, moreover, she is pre[c]ious; wi[th her ...] kingdoms. In heav[e]n she is set, for the Lord of the holy ones exalted [her]" אף לאלהן יק[י]ר[י הי / ענ]ל[...] / מלכותא בשמ[י]ן שימה הי כי בעל קדשן נשא[ה] [...]). For the text, see Bezalel Porten and Ada Yardeni, *Textbook of Aramaic Documents from Ancient Egypt: Newly Copied, Edited, and Translated into Hebrew and English* (Jerusalem: Hebrew University Department of the History of the Jewish People, 1993), 3:36–37 (C 1.1:79).

146. For the following, see Martti Nissinen, "Wisdom as Mediatrix in Sirach 24: Ben Sira, Love Lyrics, and Prophecy," in *Of God(s), Trees, Kings, and Scholars: Neo-Assyrian and Related Studies in Honour of Simo Parpola* (ed. Mikko Luukko, Saana Svärd, and Raija Mattila; StudOr 106; Helsinki: Finnish Oriental Society, 2009), 377–90.

the presence of his host she declares her worth" (Sir 24:2). The source of this idea can hardly be anything else than the common Near Eastern concept of the divine council, and it is easy to see how similar the position of Wisdom is to that of Ištar in the Mesopotamian divine council—especially because it is the divine knowledge, that is, Torah, that Wisdom transfers to the people: "All this is the book of the covenant of God Most High, the law which Moses imposed upon us as inheritance of the assemblies of Jacob" (Sir 24:23). In the scenario of Sir 24, prophetic agency is enacted in both forms, as divine agency in the activity of Lady Wisdom, and as human agency executed by Ben Sira himself, who identifies himself as "a rivulet from her stream," whose task it is to "pour out instruction like prophecy [διδασκαλίαν ὡς προφητείαν ἐκχεῶ], and leave it to all future generations" (24:33); in the words of Ben Wright, "although Ben Sira stops short of stating outright that his teaching is the product of revelatory activity, the comparison 'like prophecy' comes about as close as one can."[147] All this follows the pattern of the prophetic transmission of divine knowledge as we know it from the Near East, involving the divine council, the divine mediator, the prophet, and the audience. Even the aspect of erotic intimacy (sacred marriage, if we prefer) is not absent from Sir 24, where Lady Wisdom describes herself with imagery inspired by love lyrics, most probably by the Song of Songs (24:13–22).[148]

These texts demonstrate that there was a place for the female divine agency—prophetic agency in particular—even in the monotheistic theological model of early Judaism. The significant points of comparison with Mesopotamian patterns of divine-human communication suggest that the position of Lady Wisdom in early Judaism is rooted in a strong cultural pattern involving the concept of the divine council and the role of the female deity as the mediator.

Conclusion

The concept of "divine agency" presupposes the idea of divine beings as meaningful actors influencing everything that happens on the earth. Whether or not one thinks of divine beings as "really" existing, the idea

---

147. Wright, "Conflicted Boundaries," 236.
148. I have argued that Ben Sira knew the Song of Songs and utilized its imagery as a part of his construct of Lady Wisdom; the links between the texts are too many and detailed to be purely coincidental (Nissinen, "Wisdom as Mediatrix").

of divine agency indeed exists in the texts discussed above. They were written in a world where nothing was perceived as coincidence, and the acquisition of superhuman knowledge by means of divination was considered an indispensable tool in coping with risk and uncertainty. Within this conceptual framework, prophetic agency, among others, fulfilled an important function in mediating the divine knowledge indispensable for running any earthly business, a state or an empire in particular.

The divine world, like the human world, was conceived of as gendered, and so was the agency mediating between these two worlds—not in the form of an exact gender correspondence between the deities and their prophets, but structured in each case according to the prevailing cultural pattern (Greece: male god/female prophet; Assyria: female god/ nonmale prophet; Mari: mixed; West Semitic/biblical texts: male god/ male prophet). The remarkable feature of the prophetic agency is its nongender specificity, which, however, does not mean it was not gendered. Within the male-dominated, hierarchical society, the prophetic agency could be claimed and enacted by male and nonmale individuals alike, and the sources show no drastic differences between the prophetic agencies of male and nonmale persons. Nevertheless, gender difference does not fade away completely. At Mari, for example, the words pronounced by a female prophet seem to have been confirmed by technical divination more often than those spoken by male prophets. In Assyria, again, the religio-political power of the temples of Ištar probably bolstered the position of nonmale prophets and other devotees.

From the emic point of view, prophetic agency was socially sanctioned as an instrumental and transmissive agency in which the person and, consequently, the gender of the prophet were a matter of indifference. This, however, enabled the prophets, the nonmale ones in particular, to raise their voices even in a way that was not purely instrumental. Under the aegis of the deity believed to act as the actual agent (and under the control of religious authorities, the earthly administrators of the divine agency), both male and nonmale prophets could also execute an independent and transforming actorship in their societies.

Gender "Ambiguity" in Ancient Near Eastern Prophecy? A Reassessment of the Data behind a Popular Theory*

Jonathan Stökl

Introduction

"There is a clear connection between ambiguous gender and prophecy."[1] In this sentence Saana Teppo sums up the general consensus among theologians and Assyriologists on the nexus between "gender ambiguity" and ancient Near Eastern prophecy. Lester Grabbe has challenged the ease with which a consensus can be upheld simply because it is easier not to challenge it.[2] Following Grabbe's call to challenge consensuses, I will argue

---

* I would like to thank Martti Nissinen for inviting me to speak at the session on Female Prophets and Gender of the Prophetic Texts and Ancient Contexts group at the SBL annual conference in New Orleans in 2010. I would also like to thank the other panel members and the discussants at that meeting, in particular Ann Guinan and Kathleen McCaffrey. Further thanks are due to Carly Crouch and Kathleen McCaffrey for reading drafts of this paper and making valuable suggestions. This essay is meant to challenge and to open the door for a renewed and more informed discussion. This essay was first written between 2009 and 2011, during my time as Naden Research Assistant at St. John's College, Cambridge. It was revised while I was a research assistant at the ERC project BABYLON at University College London. I would like to thank Makenzi Crouch for improving my English.

1. Saana Teppo, "Sacred Marriage and the Devotees of Ištar," in *Sacred Marriages: The Divine-Human Sexual Metaphor from Sumer to Early Christianity* (ed. Martti Nissinen and Risto Uro; Winona Lake, Ind.: Eisenbrauns, 2008), 82. To make this study easier on the eye, I will use anglicized rather than Akkadian or Latin plurals, e.g., *assinnu*s instead of *assinnū*.

2. Lester L. Grabbe, "The Case of the Corrupting Consensus," in *Between Evidence and Ideology: Essays on the History of Ancient Israel Read at the Joint Meeting of the*

that the connection between "gender ambiguity" and ancient Near Eastern prophecy has been exaggerated; indeed, "ambiguous" gender does not play a stronger role in ancient Near Eastern prophecy than in most other parts of ancient Near Eastern society. Whether or not a certain view is a consensus view is immaterial to the question whether it is correct or not. However, once a consensus is established it is challenged less often, and the evidence starts to be read in its light so that this consensus then has a greater chance of not being overturned. Indeed, in this case the dynamics are exactly as Grabbe described them: a theory was put forward and remained unchallenged. It has subsequently been accepted as "writ" and is now repeated in many studies with few scholars scrutinizing the textual data behind the theory.[3] In this paper I intend to look at the available data for "gender ambiguity" in ancient Near Eastern prophecy and reassess the theory. I will start by defining the unfortunate expression "gender ambiguity"; the rest of the paper is concerned with a detailed scrutiny of the data. I am aware that at the same time it appears as if this paper were going along with another consensus according to which the ancient Near Eastern gender system is equivalent to that operating in the West in the nineteenth and much of the twentieth century. As will become obvious, I do not think that this is the case. And I do not think that the evidence supports the majority view on the connection between "gender ambiguity" and prophecy.

Scholarship that detects evidence for the existence of gender systems in the ancient Near East that does not directly correspond to gender constructions in traditional Western societies (i.e., there are two genders, which map directly to biological sex) is itself relatively recent and challenges a false consensus among Assyriologists. It is important to note here that I do agree with those scholars who see gender systems in the ancient

---

Society for Old Testament Study and the Oud Testamentisch Werkgezelschap, Lincoln, July 2009 (ed. Bob Becking and Lester L. Grabbe; OTS 59; Brill: Leiden, 2011), 83–92.

3. I would like to point out that Teppo ("Sacred Marriage") is innocent of this particular accusation; she closely examines all the evidence for the *assinnu*, the *kurgarrû*, and the *kulu'u*/*kalû*/GALA, particularly in the first millennium. The question that I raise in this paper is the connection between these and institutionalized prophecy in the ancient Near East. On the *kalû* as a cult performer see also Uri Gabbay, "The Akkadian Word for 'Third Gender': The *kalû* (*gala*) Once Again," in *Proceedings of the 51st Rencontre Assyriologique Internationale Held at the Oriental Institute of the University of Chicago July 18–22, 2005* (ed. Robert D. Biggs, Jennie Myers and Martha T. Roth; SAOC 62; Chicago: Oriental Institute of the University of Chicago, 2008), 49–56.

Near East that go beyond traditional Western models.[4] My argument here is not against the existence of what has often been called "ambiguously" gendered people. Instead, I maintain that the evidence for this phenomenon in the prophetic texts is not convincing, as it relies mostly on some features of SAA 9 1 and the misunderstanding of the involvement of the *assinnu* in prophecy.

The *assinnu* at Mari is often regarded as the best example for a connection between "gender ambiguity" and prophecy. While *assinnu*s are involved in prophecy at Mari, I will argue that they are not professional prophets, nor were they regarded as such in antiquity; instead they are cult officials of Ishtar, who—like other people who are not professional prophets—can at times prophesy.[5] The case of the three prophets of seemingly ambiguous gender from the Neo-Assyrian Empire will be discussed before I show that what we find in the anthropological record more often than not agrees with Teppo's understanding of the expression "sacred marriage" rather than "gender ambiguity."[6] In the Neo-Assyrian Empire the data itself is ambiguous and may or may not reflect that an individual does not fit into the traditional Western gender system. The Mari data do not support the current consensus at all. This leads me to the conclusion that the claim that "gender ambiguity" and prophecy are intrinsically linked in the ancient Near East should be discarded.

Finally, many terms are used in modern research to refer to women who are prophets. The traditional term is *prophetess*, but I do not use this term as the English feminine ending /-ess/ has changed its semantics considerably and is now often understood as belittling. In light of this some scholars, particularly those from North America, have started using the

---

4. See, e.g., Zainab Bahrani, *Women of Babylon: Gender and Representation in Mesopotamia* (London: Routledge, 2001). I am sympathetic to Bahrani's and McCaffrey's position that the ancient Near Eastern gender system is binary but not directly linked to biological sex, but I am open to see further possible gender constructions in the ancient Near East. Bahrani's and McCaffrey's models suggest that people who were biologically recognized as female could perform a male gender role and be treated as men—and vice versa. This construction explains well the position of the *ḫarimtu* as presented by McCaffrey to the 2011 International SBL Meeting in San Francisco.

5. See the contribution by Ilona Zsolnay in this volume for the *assinnu*. For the question of professional prophets and other cult officials and ordinary people involved in prophecy, see Jonathan Stökl, *Prophecy in the Ancient Near East: A Philological and Sociological Comparison* (CHANE 56; Leiden: Brill, 2012).

6. Teppo, "Sacred Marriage."

term *woman prophet*.⁷ While theoretically English allows for the use of nouns as adjectives, I prefer the expression *female prophet* when referring to a woman who is a prophet. Similarly, a *male prophet* is a man who is a prophet. When I use the term *prophet* without a marker to indicate either gender or biological sex, I use it as a neutral form referring to both male and female prophets.

Definition of "Ambiguous Gender" with Regard to the Ancient Near East

The expression "ambiguous gender" is based on and a result of the work of a number of philosophers and thinkers that has become very influential in the study of literature and society as well as in more historically oriented subjects.⁸ The very influential work by Judith Butler considers the role society demands us to perform, which depends on that society's perception of "gender." For much of the history of Western society there have been two distinctly defined roles, feminine and masculine, and most people have regarded these as indicative not only of gendered behavior but also of the biological sex of the person who performed them: men largely perform male gender roles and women largely perform female gender roles. These norms can be brutally enforced—with the possible exception of transvestite and transgender roles in the performing arts. The performing arts, in turn, reinforce the otherwise strict norms by breaking them in ways acceptable within society.⁹ Butler and others have questioned the determinative link between biological sex and performed gender roles and noted that in a number of cultures "masculine" and "feminine" are not the

---

7. See, e.g., Wilda C. Gafney, *Daughters of Miriam: Women Prophets in Ancient Israel* (Minneapolis: Fortress, 2008).

8. See particularly Judith Butler, *Bodies That Matter: On the Discursive Limits of "Sex"* (New York: Routledge, 1993); idem, *Gender Trouble: Feminism and the Subversion of Identity* (Thinking Gender; New York: Routledge, 1990); idem, *Undoing Gender* (New York: Routledge, 2004).

9. In Britain the obvious example is the performance of a female role by a male—often heavily built—during a panto (short form of pantomime), a form of theater performed during Advent and the Christmas season and usually based on a fairy tale. The fairy tale is then often adapted to express issues a local community encountered in the past year. More recently, there has been considerable play with traditional gender and transgender roles in pantos.

only two recognized genders and that gender and sex are not necessarily mapped in one way only.

Matters become even more complicated when one realizes that biological sex is also not as binomial as sometimes assumed and is itself dependent on the conceptualization of gender.[10] Instead of a simple, single factor that would indicate either "male" or "female," there are several such indicators, not all of which always agree. A recent example is the famous case of the South African middle-distance runner Caster Semenya, whose gold medal was taken away at the 2009 Athletics World Championships in Berlin because a test showed that, although her body looks female on the outside, her chromosomes are XY (i.e., "male") rather than XX ("female"). Is this runner biologically male or female? From a biological point of view the possibility of XXY chromosomes makes the situation yet more complex.[11] Some bodies also show outward signs of both male and female genitalia. These phenomena used to be called "intersex," but recently the expression "disorder of sex development" has been used in the medical discourse and also by the American intersex society.[12] Due to the con-

---

10. Rachel Alsop, Annette Fitzsimons, and Kathleen Lennon, *Theorizing Gender* (Cambridge: Polity, 2002); Suzanne J. Kessler, "From Sex to Sexuality: The Medical Construction of Gender," in *Theorizing Feminism: Parallel Trends in the Humanities and Social Sciences* (ed. Anne C. Hermann and Abigail J. Stewart; Boulder, Co.: Westview, 1994), 135–57. Sexual preference may be related to gender roles but it need not be. Like so many other issues, this is contingent on the culture in which a gender system is operating and self-enforced.

11. It is not clear how the sports courts will decide on this and related matters. Which factor counts for the decision whether an athlete should compete among women or men? Outer appearance is clearly not enough. On the legal issues of intersex not addressed in many Western legal systems, see, e.g., P.-L. Chau and Jonathan Herring, "Defining, Assigning and Designing Sex," *International Journal of Law, Policy and the Family* 16 (2002): 327–67.

12. See the statement of the Intersex Society of North America on the topic (http://www.isna.org/node/1066, accessed on 27/01/2011). Apparently, the intent of the change in terminology is to facilitate communication with medical professionals and parents who might find it easier to cope with. To me it seems counterintuitive, to say the least, as it describes intersex as a "disorder," i.e., as something that is medically wrong, not something that is merely unusual. Intersex can of course be caused by underlying disorders, but it is not clear whether this is always the case. In Europe the expression "differences of sex developments" seems to be more common; see, e.g., Claudia Wiesemann, Susanne Ude-Koeller, Gernot H. G. Sinnecker, and Ute Thyen, "Ethical Principles and Recommendations for the Medical Managements of Differ-

notations of the term *disorder* I will continue to use the term *intersex* in this essay. For the study of the ancient world, chromosomes are not an important factor, since they would not have been discernible. In contrast, outer appearance may have been more visible, so that it is more likely that hermaphrodites—people who have various combinations of male and female genitalia—would have been recognized.[13] While the phenomenon of intersex is considerably more common than often thought, most modern statistics do not include specific numbers of people who could be recognized as intersex without the use of DNA testing, a method to which ancient Near Eastern physicians, priests, and scholars did not have access. Estimates range from 0.18 percent to 1.7 percent of the general population today.[14]

---

ences of Sex Development (DSD)/Intersex in Children and Adolescents," *European Journal of Pediatrics* 169 (2010): 671–79.

13. But see Kathleen McCaffrey, *Changed by the Goddess: Lay and Cultic Gender Variance in the Ancient Near East* (forthcoming), who points out that most people without medical training do not recognize the majority of hermaphrodism; she cites Alice Domurat Dreger, *Hermaphrodites and the Medical Invention of Sex* (Cambridge: Harvard University Press, 1998), 55–56, 77, 111, 120; Suzanne J. Kessler, *Lessons from the Intersexed* (New Brunswick, N.J.: Rutgers University Press, 1998), 100. McCaffrey also quotes Kessler, "From Sex to Sexuality," 152–53, when pointing out the difficulties of attaining statistics of "obvious" cases of intersex in general.

14. The high estimate can be found in Anne Fausto-Sterling, *Sexing the Body: Gender Politics and the Construction of Sexuality* (New York: Basic Books, 2000), 53; while the low estimate was suggested by Leonard Sax, "How Common Is Intersex? A Response to Anne Fausto-Sterling," *Journal of Sex Research* 39 (2002): 174–78. Kenneth Kipnis and Milton Diamond ("Pediatric Ethics and the Surgical Assignment of Sex," *Journal of Clinical Ethics* 9 [1998]: 398–410) suggest a middle ground, with one intersex person per about two thousand people (= 0.5 percent). There are no such statistics for the premodern era so that it is impossible to be certain that intersex was as common in the first millennium B.C.E. as it is in the twentieth–twenty-first centuries C.E. As McCaffrey (*Changed by the Goddess*), argues, numbers for genuine hermaphrodism would have been significantly lower in antiquity since many forms of hermaphrodism are linked to life-threatening diseases so that many would have died at a very early age (I would like to thank McCaffrey for sending me a section of her manuscript before publication). She points to Arye Lev-Ran, "Sex Reversal as Related to Clinical Syndromes in Human Beings," in *Genetics, Hormones and Behavior* (vol. 2 of *Handbook of Sexology*; ed. John Money and Herman Musaph; New York: Elsevier, 1978), 157–71. I am not aware of medical studies on intersex that take ethnic origin into account as a distinguishing factor, which suggests that the teams conducting the research regard it as nonindicative. It is mentioned anecdotally in anthropological literature; see, e.g.,

The example of Caster Semenya is helpful, because it shows that biological sex and performed gender are not directly and unequivocally linked. The athlete has performed a role that in her (and our) society is recognized as feminine, so that people related to her as female. It has become clear that, as in so many other phenomena, different societies have different concepts of "gender." Most societies regard their particular concepts as "natural," as somehow inspired by biological differences. In other words, most societies regard the social performativity of gender as in some form of dialogue to a person's biological sex; but as we have just seen, this is not strictly speaking the case. Physical appearance and gender performance are not entirely unrelated, but physical appearance does not determine gender totally.[15]

Many Western scholars seem to work with gender roles that are more at home in nineteenth-century Europe, transferring these onto the ancient world. This is not surprising, since to some degree nineteenth-century scholarship still forms the basis for most scholarship on the ancient world. Kathleen McCaffrey has recently shown how this can lead scholars to assume that grave goods given to female skeletons in graves at Ur are "ritual" in nature while the same goods next to a male skeleton turn him

---

Gilbert Herdt, "Mistaken Sex: Culture, Biology and the Third Sex in New Guinea," in *Third Sex, Third Gender: Beyond Sexual Dimorphism in Culture and History* (ed. Gilbert Herdt; New York: Zone, 1994), 419–45. It is difficult to know whether the factors are cultural or biological, and in the absence of good evidence that could distinguish, I think it is better to withhold judgment. A factor not usually discussed outside the medical literature is GID, "Gender Identity Disorder," which is usually approached as part of an individual's psychosexual makeup; see, e.g., Alexander Korte et al., "Gender Identity Disorders in Childhood and Adolescence," *Deutsches Ärzteblatt International* 104 (2008): 834–41. It does not seem possible to disentangle cultural, biological, and psychological factors from one another in this question. In a city like Sennacherib's Nineveh, with a population of about 75,000, there would have been between 13 and 1,275 intersex people. For comparison, albinos are usually estimated to be around 0.05 percent (about 3-4 albinos for Neo-Assyrian Nineveh), more than a third fewer than even the most conservative estimates for intersex. The population estimate of Nineveh after Sennacherib's extensions is from Julian E. Reade, "Ninive (Nineveh)," *Reallexikon der Assyriologie* 9.5–6 (ed. Erich Ebeling, Bruno Meissner, Ernst Weidner, Wolfram von Soden, and Dietz Otto Edzard; Berlin: de Gruyter, 2001), 388–433.

15. Butler, *Undoing Gender*. Nor does sexual activity. Good evidence for this can be found in Peter Drucker, ed., *Different Rainbows* (London: Gay Men's Press, 2000); Gilbert Herdt, *Sambia Sexual Culture: Essays from the Field* (Worlds of Desire; Chicago: University of Chicago Press, 1999).

into a warrior.[16] The question therefore is: What are the implications of the labels "male" and "female" in any given society and, in our case, in Old Babylonian Mari and the Neo-Assyrian Empire; or, what makes a woman a woman, a man a man, and someone of third (or fourth, or …) gender into someone of third (or …) gender?[17] Theoretically, there is no limit to the number of gender roles that could be performed.

This discussion has focused on the terminology of gender and so far has left out the term *ambiguous*. Taking the term seriously, we have several distinct possibilities for "ambiguous" gender, all of which can be defined as: someone who performs a gender role that is not recognized by their society. Therefore, in many societies a (biologically) male individual who performs a feminine gender role may be said to perform an ambiguous gender role if, and only if, the society does regard this as unusual or "ambiguous." Not all societies consider someone with a male body who performs a female gender role to perform an ambiguous gender role. For example, some shamans among the Siberian Chukchi are biologically male, but they perform entirely female gender roles and are regarded by their society as female rather than male. Early Western anthropologists had difficulties with the category and understood them as homosexual shamans, and that is how these shamans entered the scholarly arena. However, there does not appear to be any evidence for this understanding. Their marriages to male masculine Chukchi are only logical, once it is understood that they are regarded as female by their fellow tribespeople. Indeed, McCaffrey has recently proposed that the *ḫarimtu* may be best understood in a similar way, only in the *ḫarimtu*'s case it is not males performing feminine gender roles but females performing masculine roles.[18]

I would therefore prefer to avoid using the expression "ambiguous gender" altogether when describing the genders performed by ancient Near Eastern prophets, whether they are male, female, masculine, feminine, or

---

16. Kathleen McCaffrey, "The Female Kings of Ur," in *Gender through Time in the Ancient Near East* (ed. Diane Bolger; GAS; Lanham, Md.: AltaMira, 2008), 173–215.

17. In "Reconsidering Gender Ambiguity in Mesopotamia: Is a Beard Just a Beard?" in *Sex and Gender in the Ancient Near East: Proceedings of the 47th Rencontre Assyriologique Internationale, Helsinki, July 2–6, 2001* (ed. Simo Parpola and Robert M. Whiting; CRRAI 47; Helsinki: Neo-Assyrian Text Corpus Project, 2002), 379–91, Kathleen McCaffrey convincingly works with three to four possible genders in the ancient Near East.

18. Presentation to the SBL Annual Meeting in San Francisco, 2011.

something altogether different.[19] Queer theory would suggest the term *queer* for biological women who perform a masculine gender role. However, ancient Near Eastern society would not have perceived people like the *ḫarimtu* or the *assinnu* as not fitting into their gender system—in their own context their gender is neither ambiguous nor "queer." Since my analysis is a historical one I will try to take seriously the models and systems operating within the society that created them, as far as we can discern them. For that reason I will also not use the term *queer*, even though to our Western society some of the individuals who will be mentioned here—and certainly the ancient Near Eastern gender system—would be "queer."[20] *Transgender* is also not necessarily helpful since it implies the changing from one gender to another. But it may be appropriate in the case of the first-millennium *assinnu* "whom the goddess has turned into one like a woman." *Nonbinary* may also be unhelpful as it suggests that more than two genders existed in the society.[21] I will, therefore, reluctantly retain the expression "ambiguous gender" in order to avoid lengthy circumlocutions and indicate my unease with the expression by using quotation marks.

The biological sex of the ancient individual is not necessarily discernible to the modern reader, since it is not clear whether cuneiform writing indicates gender or biological sex, or indeed, at least sometimes, social status.[22] On the surface, social status and gender appear to be interpreta-

---

19. A good example for the misunderstanding of ancient Near Eastern gender constructions can be seen in John Barclay Burns, "Devotee or Deviate: The 'Dog' (*keleb*) in Ancient Israel as a Symbol of Male Passivity and Perversion," *Journal of Religion and Society* 2 (2000). Online: http://moses.creighton.edu/JRS/2000/2000-2006.html].

20. Donald E. Hall, *Queer Theories* (Transitions; New York: Palgrave Macmillan, 2003); Jarrod Hayes, Margaret R. Higonnet, and William J. Spurlin, "Comparing Queerly, Queering Comparison: Theorizing Identities Between Cultures, Histories, and Disciplines," in *Comparatively Queer: Interrogating Identities Across Time and Cultures* (ed. Jarrod Hayes, Margaret R. Higonnet, and William J. Spurlin; New York: Palgrave Macmillan, 2010), 1–19. In other words, by not using the term *queer* I am effectively queering queer theory and its application to a culture that is by mere fact of being extinct subservient to theory in general. Thus my decision not to use the term is entirely within the spirit of queer theories as suggested by Hall, *Queer Theories*, 1–18, 86–108.

21. I am grateful to Kathleen McCaffrey for pointing this out to me in her extensive and helpful response to an earlier draft of this paper.

22. On the question in general see Julia M. Asher-Greve, "The Essential Body: Mesopotamian Conceptions of the Gendered Body," *Gender and History* 9 (1997):

tions that exclude each other. Since in most societies, however, gender and social status are intricately linked, it seems to me that a woman at Nuzi who is referred to as a son and with masculine pronouns at that time is understood to be performing masculine social status, which implies some form of a masculine gender. While it is often assumed that cuneiform differentiates clearly between male and female, with the use of signs in front of the name indicating the gender of that person—either a single vertical wedge (DIŠ) for a man or the more complicated sign (MUNUS) for a woman—the matter is not quite that clear-cut. These two signs are derived from drawings of male and female genitalia and generally stand for male and female. The sign LÚ stands for "person," and DIŠ is sometimes known as *Personenkeil* and regularly stands before female names. The only way we could trace the question whether cuneiform writing indicates gender or biological sex would be to find a theoretical treatise on gender. Otherwise, it remains impossible to establish definitively whether during a certain period and at a certain time a gender preformative (male, female) refers to biological sex or gender. Since it is extremely unlikely that theoretical treatises on gender will ever be found in ancient Mesopotamia's textual record, we are limited to inferring solutions to this question from other information provided in the relevant texts.

In the following I will discuss the evidence that has been adduced to support an understanding of a close link between prophecy and gender roles in which sex and gender are not aligned in ancient Mesopotamia. As will become clear, in my view "ambiguous" gender does not play a more significant role in (professional) prophecy than it does elsewhere in Mesopotamian societies, and it is therefore an exaggeration to claim that there is a particularly strong connection between transgender and prophecy. I do not claim that none of the attested prophets performed an "ambiguous" gender identity, but I do not believe there to be a strong connection

---

432–61. For the suggestion that social status may at times be denoted see John A. Brinkman, "Masculine or Feminine? The Case of Conflicting Gender Determinatives for Middle Babylonian Personal Names," in *Studies Presented to Robert D. Biggs* (ed. Martha T. Roth, Walter Farber, Matthew W. Stolper, and Paula von Bechtolsheim; From the Workshop of the Chicago Assyrian Dictionary 2; AS 27; Chicago: Oriental Institute of the University of Chicago, 2007), 1–10. Asher-Greve discusses the subject mainly on the basis of the interpretation of statues and their sex/gender. She continues the discussion in "Decisive Sex, Essential Gender," in Parpola and Whiting, *Sex and Gender*, 11–26; idem, "Images of Men, Gender Regimes, and Social Stratification in the Late Uruk Period," in Bolger, *Gender through Time*, 119–71.

between "ambiguous" gender and prophecy. The evidence is much stronger for the connection between "ambiguous" gender and ecstatic religion in the cult of a number of deities, with various forms of Ishtar featuring particularly strongly.

The *Assinnu* at Mari

The evidence for the connection between gender "ambiguity" and prophecy at Mari is limited to two *assinnu* in the texts, Šēlebum (ARM 26 197, 198, and 213) and Ili-ḫaznaya (ARM 26 212).[23] It is clear that both transmit divine messages from Annunītum, a martial manifestation of Ishtar, to Queen Šibtu, which the latter transmits to her husband, King Zimri-Lim.[24] My argument in this section is that there is no evidence that the two (incidentally) prophesying *assinnu*s at Mari in the second millennium were transgendered. At the same time, no evidence connects prophecy and *assinnu*s in the first millennium. Even if there may be evidence for a transgender identity of *assinnu*s in some first-millennium texts, they should not be connected to the Mari *assinnu*s with too much haste.

In texts from the first millennium we meet the *assinnu* as a cult official of manifestations of Ishtar. The *assinnu* is often attested together with the *kurgarrû*, and their cultic duties are represented as dancing and singing.[25] The *assinnu* is a cult performer who "responds with joy" to the singing of the *kurgarrû*.[26] In traditional scholarship both are portrayed as performing gender roles in flux or, indeed, at times as homosexual.[27] This is in

---

23. Martti Nissinen and I use different ways of counting those prophets for whom the texts do not indicate a gender. I only count those as of "ambiguous" gender for whom all information regarding grammatical gender is given in the text and it does not align. When such information is missing I do not regard their gender as not clearly indicated by the text, which is, in my view, a different category. This procedure reduces the number of prophets with "ambiguous" gender substantially.

24. On Annunītum and *assinnu*s more generally see the contribution by Ilona Zsolnay in this volume. For the absence of evidence for nonnormative gender roles of the *assinnu* in Old Babylonian texts see Richard A. Henshaw, *Female and Male: The Cultic Personnel: The Bible and the Rest of the Ancient Near East* (PrTMS 31; Allison Park, Pa.: Pickwick, 1994), 284.

25. *CAD* K s.v. *kurgarrû*; and *CAD* A/2 s.v. *assinnu*.

26. *CAD* K:558, citing K.3438a + 9912, line 8: *yarurūtu usaḫḫurū*.

27. As said above, gender and sexual orientation can be connected but in many societies are not.

large part based on texts from the first millennium: in the Epic of Erra both the *kurgarrû* and the *assinnu* are described as those "whom Ištar had changed from men into women to show the people piety."[28] In the lexical list ḪAR-gud B, line 133, the *assinnu* is explained as *sinnisānu* ("one who is like a female").[29] While there is some evidence for homosexual acts in connection to the *assinnu*, they are by no means pervasive.[30] It has been suggested that the *assinnu* was also involved in homosexual cultic prostitution, but in view of the discussion surrounding cultic prostitution and the accumulating evidence, this modern (male) construct can safely be abandoned.[31]

---

28. *Kurgarrî* $^{(m)}$*issinnī ša ana šupluḫ nišī Ištar zikrūssunu utēru ana sin*[*ništi*]; Erra col. iv, lines 55–56; Luigi Cagni, *Das Erra-Epos: Keilschrifttext* (StP 5; Rome: Päpstliches Bibelinstitut, 1970), 26; Luigi Cagni, *L'epopea di Erra* (Studi semitici 34; Rome: Istituto di Studi del Vicino Oriente dell'Università, 1969), 110. See also the Hellenistic "Fête d'Ištar" AO. 7439+, rev. line 25´, Sylvie Lackenbacher, "Un nouveau fragment de la 'Fête d'Ištar,'" *RA* 71 (1977): 39–50; Marc J. H. Linssen, *The Cults of Uruk and Babylon: The Temple Ritual Texts as Evidence for Hellenistic Cult Practises* (CM 25; Leiden: Brill Styx, 2004), 238–44. *Issinnu* is a variant of *assinnu*, CAD A/2:341.

29. MSL 12 6.22:133, Miguel Civil, *The Series lú = ša and Related Texts* (MSL 12; Rome: Pontifical Biblical Institute, 1969), 226.

30. *CT* 39 45, line 32. Further, the lexical list Malku = *šarru* col. I, line 135, attests the feminine form *assinnatu*, which in that text is equated to the *entum* ("female high priest"); see Anne Draffkorn Kilmer, "The First Tablet of *malku* = *šarru* together with Its Explicit Version," *JAOS* 83 (1963): 421–46.

31. In favor of this interpretation see, e.g., Stefan M. Maul, "*kurgarrû* und *assinnu* und ihr Stand in der babylonischen Gesellschaft," in *Aussenseiter und Randgruppen: Beiträge zu einer Sozialgeschichte des Alten Orients* (ed. Volkert Haas; Xenia 32; Konstanz: Universitätsverlag, 1992), 159–71. In contrast see Julia Assante, "Bad Girls and Kinky Boys? The Modern Prostituting of Ishtar, Her Clergy and Her Cults," in *Tempelprostitution im Altertum: Fakten und Fiktionen* (ed. Tanja S. Scheer; Oikumene 6; Berlin: Antike, 2009), 23–54; idem, "From Whores to Hierodules: The Historiographic Invention of Mesopotamian Female Sex Professionals," in *Ancient Art and Its Historiography* (ed. A. A. Donohue and Mark D. Fullerton; Cambridge: Cambridge University Press, 2003), 13–47; idem, "The kar.kid/ḫarimtu, Prostitute or Single Woman? A Reconsideration of the Evidence," *UF* 30 (1998): 5–96; idem, "What Makes a 'Prostitute' a Prostitute? Modern Definitions and Ancient Meanings," *Historiae* 4 (2007): 117–32; Phyllis A. Bird, "The End of the Male Cult Prostitute: A Literary-Historical and Sociological Analysis of Hebrew *Qādēš-Qĕdēšîm*," in *Congress Volume: Cambridge, 1995* (ed. John A. Emerton; VTSup 66; Leiden: Brill, 1997), 37–80; Stephanie Lynn Budin, *The Myth of Sacred Prostitution in Antiquity* (Cambridge: Cambridge University Press, 2008); Mayer I. Gruber, "Hebrew *qedeshah* and Her Canaanite and Akkadian Cognates," *UF* 18 (1986): 133–48.

In some more recent interpretations of the *assinnu* it has been suggested that they are the Mesopotamian form of a shaman, on the basis of their mythical ability to travel into the land of the dead. In *Ishtar's Descent into the Underworld* they are created for that purpose and Ea/Enki provides them with the water and herb of life.[32] The interpretation of the *assinnu*'s mythical journey into the underworld as an equivalent to shamanistic spirit journeys is interesting, but since in general shamans only rarely cooperate in large groups or with other religious specialists and since they are not usually integrated into the worship of a deity at a temple where they are only subservient, it is not necessarily helpful.

As the preceding makes clear, I am willing to accept the *assinnu*'s transgendered role as it appears in first-millennium texts. Ilona Zsolnay is skeptical about most of the evidence in favor of this as well and stresses that the vast majority of texts do not ascribe a transgendered identity to the *assinnu*, but she allows for some nonheteronormative behavior—whether alleged or real—in some later texts. What is most important in the current context, however, is that there is currently no evidence for the *assinnu* as transgendered in early-second-millennium B.C.E. Mari. And it is exclusively in the second millennium that we see the *assinnu* linked to prophecy. In addition, there are other cult officials at Mari, such as the *muḫḫûm* and *qammatum*, who are linked to ecstatic behavior but who only incidentally prophesy (as opposed to "professional" prophets like the *āpilum*). The distinction drawn here between ecstasy and prophecy is not yet very common in the scholarship on ancient Near Eastern and biblical prophecy, but it can be useful. Some ecstatics performed ecstatic dances; others used their voices in ecstatic vocal displays; others yet were linked to lamentation rites.[33] Indeed, many ecstatic cult officials, such as the *kurgarrû*, are attested in rituals without ever being linked to prophetic activity. This indicates that at Mari, cult officials who were linked to war dances (*assinnu*) or mourning (*muḫḫûm*) could occasionally prophesy.[34]

---

32. Maul, "*kurgarrû* und *assinnu*," 163–64; and Herbert B. Huffmon, "The *Assinnum* as Prophet: Shamans at Mari?" in *Amurru 3: Nomades et sédentaires dans le Proche-Orient ancien. Compte rendu de la XLVIe Rencontre Assyriologique Internationale (Paris, 10–13 juillet 2000)* (ed. Christophe Nicolle; Paris: ERC, 2004), 241–47.

33. Ilona Zsolnay's essay in this volume shows that the *assinnu* is an ecstatic but essentially nonprophetic cult official. On the distinction between ecstasy and prophecy see also my *Prophecy in the Ancient Near East*.

34. For a discussion of these specialists see Stökl, *Prophecy in the Ancient Near East*.

Initially, Huffmon had urged caution about conflating the *assinnus'* later first-millennium role with their role in the Old Babylonian Mari, but more recently he has expressed support for the view that they were transgendered already in the early second millennium.[35]

There is no evidence for transgendered *assinnu* in Mari in the second millennium and no evidence for the *assinnus'* involvement in prophetic behavior, professional or not, in the first millennium. Considering the relatively large amount of data we possess for the first millennium and the absence of references to prophecy there, it is likely that first-millennium *assinnu*s did not regularly prophesy; more importantly, they were not considered to be professional prophets. This suggests that the four Mari texts in which an *assinnu* prophesies (ARM 26 197, 198, 212, and 213) are the exception to the rule.

It is, in my view, important to realize that the two Mari *assinnu*s who prophesy present an extremely weak link between prophecy and "ambiguous" gender. Unless we redefine prophecy to automatically include all forms of ecstatic behavior, rather than more precisely to refer to the transmission of divine messages to human addressees, ecstasy is a related but distinct form of religious behavior from prophecy.[36] In sum, the two attestations of prophesying *assinnu*s at Mari simply show that *assinnu*s occasionally prophesied, while the first-millennium data shows that *assinnu*s could display transgendered identities. They most certainly should not be understood as an indicator that Mariotes would have assumed that their prophets routinely displayed "ambiguous" gender roles.

---

35. The cautionary view can be found in Herbert B. Huffmon, "Prophecy in the Mari Letters," *BA* 31 (1968): 101–24. For his later view see idem, "Ancient Near Eastern Prophecy," *ABD* 5:477–82; idem, "A Company of Prophets: Mari, Assyria, Israel," in *Prophecy in Its Ancient Near Eastern Context: Mesopotamian, Biblical, and Arabian Perspectives* (ed. Martti Nissinen; SBLSymS 13; Atlanta: Society of Biblical Literature, 2000), 47–70; idem, "The Origins of Prophecy," in *Magnalia Dei, the Mighty Acts of God: Essays on the Bible and Archaeology in Memory of G. Ernest Wright* (ed. Frank Moore Cross, Werner E. Lemke, and Patrick D. Miller; Garden City, N.Y.: Doubleday, 1976), 171–86; idem, "Prophecy in the Ancient Near East," *IDBSup*, 697–700.

36. See also Zsolnay in this volume. It is peculiar that Assante ("Bad Girls"), who is so careful elsewhere not to mix her categories, falls into this trap when she describes the *assinnu* as prophetic.

Ambiguous Ambiguity: Neo-Assyrian Prophets

The idea of a close link between prophecy and "ambiguous" gender roles originated in the study of Neo-Assyrian prophetic texts; it is to these that we now turn. I will quickly rehearse the evidence before offering an alternative suggestion, ultimately concluding that the link between "ambiguous" gender and Neo-Assyrian prophecy is somewhat stronger than the evidence for "ambiguous" gender at Mari, but by no means incontrovertible.[37] Three prophets are often understood to display "ambiguous" gender: Ilūssa-āmur, Bāia, and Issār-lā-tašīaṭ. All three cases are to be found on the same tablet, SAA 9 1. The tablet is one of the *Sammeltafeln*, archival copies combining several oracles. This indicates that either the prophets in question were known to be performing "ambiguous" gender roles, or the scribe who wrote the *Sammeltafel* copied information that was found on the tablet or in dictation.

Ilūssa-āmur, the first of the three, is spelled with a female determinative in two texts: SAA 9 1.5, line 5´ and KAV 121, line 5, suggesting that she is regarded as female by her contemporaries.[38] In his edition of the Neo-Assyrian prophetic texts, however, Simo Parpola reads the gentilic following her name in SAA 9 1.5, line 6´, as masculine: ^{uru}šÀ-URU-a!-[a], resulting in a reading: *libbālā[ya]* ("[male] Aššuri[te]").[39]

---

37. For the following see also Jonathan Stökl, "Ištar's Women, YHWH's Men? A Curious Gender-Bias in Neo-Assyrian and Biblical Prophecy," *ZAW* 121 (2009): 87–100. The spelling of Neo-Assyrian names follows *PNA*.

38. Simo Parpola, *Assyrian Prophecies* (SAA 9; Helsinki: Helsinki University Press, 1997), 7; Otto Schroeder, *Keilschrifttexte aus Assur verschiedenen Inhalts: Autographiert, mit Inhaltsübersicht und Namenliste versehen* (WVDOG 35; Ausgrabungen der Deutschen Orient-Gesellschaft in Assur. E, Inschriften 3; Leipzig: Hinrichs, 1920), 83. For Ilūssa-āmur see Martti Nissinen, "Ilūssa-āmur," in *PNA* 2/I:535.

39. Parpola, *Assyrian Prophecies*, 7. Manfred Weippert ("'König, fürchte dich nicht!' Assyrische Prophetie im 7. Jahrhundert v. Chr.," *Or* 71 [2002]: 1–54) had suggested restoring an UD (with the reading *tú*) instead of Parpola's A: ^{uru}šÀ-URU-a[-a-tú], resulting in the reading *libbāla[yyatu]* ("[female] Aššuri[te]"). In "Ištar's Women," 96, I recently suggested a slightly different restoration, ^{uru}šÀ-URU-a!-[i-tú], resulting in the reading *libbāla[yyītu]*—"[female] Aššuri[te]." While *libbālayyītu* is theoretically a correct form of the feminine gentilic (*GAG* §56p; John Huehnergard, *A Grammar of Akkadian* [2nd ed.; HSS 45; Winona Lake, Ind.: Eisenbrauns, 2005], 40–41), Neo-Assyrian so far exclusively attests to the ending /-ītu/ for the feminine gentilic. The feminine gentilic *aššurītu* ("female Aššurite") is attested at least seven times: Jaakko Hämeen-Anttila, *A Sketch of Neo-Assyrian Grammar* (SAAS 13; Helsinki: Neo-Assy-

In his grammar of Neo-Assyrian, Jaakko Hämeen-Anttila mentions one further example of an evidently feminine name spelled with a masculine determinative, pointing to Karlheinz Deller's unpublished Ph.D. thesis.[40] This suggests that this kind of spelling is part of a wider phenomenon. Recent research on the Nuzi texts confirms this: in his study on the phenomenon of spelling female names with both a male (*Personenkeil*) and a female gender determinative, a relatively common occurrence in that corpus, John A. Brinkman concludes that this spelling indicates that these women had a higher social and economic position.[41] He rejects out of hand that this spelling represents "ambiguous" roles, not taking into account that the higher social status of the women involved probably required their performing at least a partially masculine gender role with respect to their adoptive parents. While the *Personenkeil* normally only indicates personhood and not necessarily masculinity, Brinkman's results are interesting.

It is likely that Parpola's reconstruction of this line is correct and that Ilūssa-āmur is described as an Aššurite using a masculine form of the adjective. The question, then, turns from one of the interpretation of writing to the interpretation of grammar. It is a well-known phenomenon that Semitic—and Indo-European—languages have a tendency to use masculine forms for groups of men and women, and occasionally also for individual women, without necessarily indicating gender. However, since it is certainly possible that the writer of the text wanted to express that Ilūssa-āmur has the social status of a man (as in the Nuzi texts) or that she performed a masculine gender role, we have to withhold judgment on the question—in this case the evidence itself is ambiguous.

---

rian Text Corpus Project, 2000), 84. I would like to thank professors Simo Parpola and Martti Nissinen for making available to me the list of attested feminine gentilics in Neo-Assyrian, all of which have the ending /-ītu/. The following spellings are attested: *aš-šur-i-tú* (SAA 7 145, line 7; A 2484, line r. 7; SAA 19 17, line 8), *aš-š]ur-i-tu* (SAA 12 40, line 13'), *áš-šu-ri-te* (SAA 12 10, line 7'), *áš-š]u-ri-tú* (SAA 12 13, line 9') and *áš-šu-ri-tú* (SAA 19 49, line 74). It is often part of the name Ishtar of Aššur (Aššurītu). This renders my previous suggestion highly unlikely.

40. This work has not been available to me.

41. Brinkman, "Masculine or Feminine?" See also Philippe Abrahami, "Masculine and Feminine Personal Determinatives before Women's Names at Nuzi: A Gender Indicator of Social or Economic Independence?" *CDLI Bulletin* 1 (2011). Online: http://cdli.ucla.edu/pubs/cdlb/2011/cdlb2011_2001.html.

The second of the three is Bāia. It appears that name itself is not gendered, similar to the names Ashley, Carly, or Lindsay, bearers of which can be either male or female.[42] The particular Bāia with whom we are concerned is attested in SAA 9 1.4, line 40′; in *STT* 406, line rev10; and, according to Parpola's reconstruction, also in SAA 9 2.2.[43] *STT* 406 is not much help for our question, as Bāia is simply referred to as a "[servant of] Ishtar of Ḫuzirina."

In SAA 9 1.4, line 40′, we read: *ša pi-i* ᶠ*ba-ia-a* DUMU uruLÍMMU. DINGIR, which can be normalized as *ša pî Bāia mār Arba'ilī* ("from the mouth of Bāia, son of Arbela"). Bāia is spelled with a feminine determinative, indicating that the writer understands the name to refer to a woman, while the following gentilic (*mār Arba'ilī*) is masculine. As in the case of Ilūssa-āmur, the spelling may refer either to Bāia's social position or to an "ambiguous" gender role. Additionally, DUMU is occasionally used as an abbreviated spelling of DUMU.MUNUS (which would be read as *mārtu*, "daughter").[44] Indeed, under the lemma *mārtu*, CAD lists several cases of ᶠPN DUMU ᶠPN, which suggests that DUMU could describe daughters as well as sons.[45] It is also possible that a grammatically masculine adjective is used for a woman, or the scribe could have heard the name and started writing using the feminine determinative, as he thought that she was probably a woman—as I would when hearing the names Ashley, Carly, and Lindsay. Yet, just as I have met men with these names as well, so the scribe may have been too quick in turning this particular Bāia into a woman. As in the case of Ilūssa-āmur, it is possible that SAA 9 1.4 indicates an "ambiguous" role for Bāia, but a number of other explanations are also possible.

---

42. *PNA* lists eleven individuals of this name, six of whom are men and five women; see Martti Nissinen and Marie-Claire Perroudon, "Bāia," *PNA* 1/II: 253.

43. For *STT* 406 see O. R. Gurney, *The Assyrian Tablets from Sultantepe* (Proceedings of the British Academy 41; London: Oxford University Press, 1955); O. R. Gurney and J. J. Finkelstein, *The Sultantepe Tablets I* (2 vols.; Occasional Publications of the British Institute of Archaeology at Ankara 3, 7; London: British Institute of Archaeology at Ankara, 1957). For SAA 9 1.4 and 9 2.2 see Parpola, *Assyrian Prophecies*, 6–7, 14–15.

44. See also Asher-Greve, "Essential Body," 437–38. View with caution, however, Asher-Greve's comments on castration.

45. MDP 22 73, line 23; 23 227, line 27; 230, line 10; 24 353, line 30; 382, line 29; 28 414, line rev.2ff. Further, DUMU.SAG can stand for *martu reštītu*; see *SBH* 65, line 13. DUMU.É can stand for *marat bīti* ("[adult] daughter of the house").

In the case of SAA 9 2.2 we should be even more careful. Line 35´ reads: [...]*a*? ᵘʳᵘLÍMMU.DINGIR-⌜*a-a*⌝, *Arba'ilāya* ("[male] Arbelan"). Based on the content of the preceding message, which is similar to that of SAA 9 1.4, Parpola suggests restoring [TA *pi-i* ᶠ*ba-ia*]-⌜*a*⌝ URU.*arba-il-*⌜*a-a*⌝, [*issu pî Bāi*]*a mār Arbailāya* ("[from the mouth of Bāi]a, son of Arbela"). The first three signs of Parpola's reconstruction, TA *pi-i*, are part of a formulaic expression at the end of most of the oracles on the *Sammeltafeln* and thus fairly certain. As only parts of the final A of Bāia's name are visible, I am less convinced by the reconstruction of the name. We do not possess enough material to be certain that similar content means that the same prophet delivered the oracle. That two different forms of the gentilic are used in the two oracles argues against restoring Bāia's name in this lacuna.

The third and last person we will deal with here is Issār-lā-tašīaṭ, who appears in SAA 9 1.1.⁴⁶ There has been an ongoing debate on how to read the determinative before her name. According to Parpola, the scribe superimposed a DIŠ (masculine) and DINGIR (divine) on a MUNUS (feminine), while Weippert only sees MUNUS.DINGIR and implies modern damage to the tablet.⁴⁷ While collating the tablet myself, I saw a ligature or "optical sandhi" spelling in which the final horizontal of the MUNUS (𒊩) is at the same time the first of the DINGIR (𒀭). This is certainly unusual, but can be attributed to scribal idiosyncrasy.

Further supporting the interpretation of the peculiar spelling is that the name Issār-lā-tašīaṭ itself is masculine; as Dietz Otto Edzard has shown, the female form would have had to be *Issār-lā-tašiṭṭī.⁴⁸ Thus the name itself is obviously masculine and would have been so to ancient Mesopotamian ears. Further, the tablet SAA 9 1 is an archival copy, and thus most probably contains copies of individual reports. It follows that the scribe who wrote Issār-lā-tašīaṭ's name did not see the prophet, and could not be confused about the gender of the person about whom they were writing. In addition, Ishtar's name does occasionally get the feminine determinative—and naturally also the divine determinative—and so, as it stands, the signs could be regarded as referring to Ishtar's name as part of Issār-lā-tašīaṭ's. It is this latter reading that I regard as the most likely.

---

46. On her see Nissinen, "Issār-lā-tašīaṭ," *PNA* 2/I: 572–73.

47. Parpola, *Assyrian Prophecies*, 83; Weippert, "König, fürchte dich nicht!" 33–34. Nissinen ("Issār-lā-tašīaṭ") allows either for error or for "ambiguous" gender.

48. Dietz Otto Edzard, "ᵐNingal-gāmil, ᶠIštar-damqat: Die Genuskongruenz im akkadischen theophoren Personennamen," *ZA* 55 (1962): 113–30.

While an "ambiguous" gender role cannot be ruled out, the evidence is hardly sufficient to argue in favor of castration, as Parpola and Huffmon have suggested.[49]

Conclusions

In her recent essay on the cult personnel of Ishtar, Saana Teppo understands "sacred marriage" as the performance of an intermediary role between the divine and the profane—or human—spheres.[50] This definition helps to articulate the curious fact that in many societies the relationship between ecstatics/prophetic figures and the deity or spirit for whom they speak is described in terms of a human-divine relationship, often in explicitly sexual terms.[51] These relationships are often regarded as heterosexual, but they are by no means exclusively so. Among the aforementioned Chukchi in Siberia there are heterosexual shamans whose human partners have to arrange themselves within a triangle of spiritual love. The Chukchi also allow for transgendered persons, in which (biological) men perform female gender roles and (biological) women perform male gender roles and are regarded by society as feminine and masculine, respectively. In couples—irrespective of whether they are shamans—in which one partner is transgendered, a third partner may also be included in the relationship to allow for procreation. Thus three-way partnerships are possible not only when one partner is the spirit mate of a shaman, but also when a transgendered person's main partner and the transgendered person are unable to procreate, another may join for the express purpose of procreation. A transgendered male-to-female shaman will have a male human partner and a male spiritual partner. I am unaware of female-to-male shamans among the Chukchi, but the possibility cannot be excluded a priori.[52]

---

49. Parpola, *Assyrian Prophecies*, xxxiv. While Huffmon ("Prophecy in Mari Letters," 111) argues not to read the Neo-Assyrian cross-dressing behavior of the *assinnu* into the Old Babylonian *assinnu*, he later suggests the opposite, e.g. Huffmon, "*Assinnum* as Prophet," 246.

50. Teppo, "Sacred Marriage."

51. See, e.g., I. M. Lewis, *Ecstatic Religion: A Study of Shamanism and Spirit Possession* (3rd ed.; London: Routledge, 2003). Stephen O. Murray (*Homosexualities* [Worlds of Desire; Chicago: University of Chicago Press, 2000], 295–355) collects a number of cases of homosexual and transgendered religious practitioners, including the *assinnu*.

52. It is not entirely clear whether transgendered life and shamanism go hand in hand; see Murray, *Homosexualities*, 325.

Naturally, transgendered religious practitioners can also be found in other parts of the world, but listing further examples does not provide any additional benefit for the question at hand.[53]

In this paper, we have seen that the reality of transgender and intersex is much more widespread than usually assumed. It should therefore not surprise us to find such phenomena in the ancient Near East. We have to be careful not to import Western gender stereotypes when doing so. It is equally important not to overinterpret every bit of potential evidence as pointing toward certain functionaries being third gender.

In reviewing the Old Babylonian evidence for *prophecy* being linked to ecstatic behavior and thereby to "ambiguous" gender roles, we have seen that the only evidence lies in the four texts that refer to two *assinnu*s, Ili-ḫaznaya and Šēlebum, transmitting divine messages. However, both the exact function and gender roles of these Old Babylonian *assinnu*s escapes us due to a lack of evidence. While cultic ecstasy in the service of forms of the deity Ishtar and "ambiguous" gender may be linked, this ecstatic behavior is not usually linked to prophecy. It is only occasionally that ecstasy may be linked to prophetic behavior in the strict sense.[54]

With regard to Neo-Assyria, the evidence is equally ephemeral. In one case it relies on the reconstruction of a name (Bāia) and in a second on the reconstruction of a masculine rather than a feminine gentilic (Ilūssa-āmur). In a third case the evidence relies on the assumption that the writer of the text physically saw the prophet in action and from that drew conclusions as to their gender, ignoring that the tablet is a *Sammeltafel* and thus an archival copy, as well as that the name is itself masculine but contains the female deity Issār (Issār-lā-tašīaṭ). The first two cases rest on a modern reconstruction of gender ambiguity—and even then could be explained in different ways—while the third is best explained as a scribal error. Although there is a considerable amount of Neo-Assyrian evidence

---

53. Ibid., 328–54.

54. Regarding a definition of prophecy I follow Martti Nissinen, "What Is Prophecy? An Ancient Near Eastern Perspective," in *Inspired Speech: Prophecy in the Ancient Near East: Essays in Honour of Herbert B. Huffmon* (ed. John Kaltner and Louis Stulman; JSOTSup 378; London: T&T Clark, 2004), 17–37. Additionally, I would like to quote David Clines, who in a conversation about prophecy once told me that presumably prophets had breakfast—but this does not mean that having breakfast is necessarily prophetic.

for "ambiguous" gender roles among cult ecstatics of Ishtar, this does not amount to evidence for "ambiguous" gender roles among prophets.

It is, of course, impossible to prove a negative statement along the lines of "prophecy and gender ambiguity are not linked." Consequently, my aim has been to show that, according to our available sources, prophecy and "ambiguous" gender are not intrinsically linked. In the absence of compelling evidence in favor of such a link and in the presence of a compelling connection between gender ambiguity and ecstatic cult practitioners, it seems better to me to abandon the popular theory in favor of a more differentiated view.

The Misconstrued Role of the *Assinnu* in Ancient Near Eastern Prophecy*

Ilona Zsolnay

Introduction

Mesopotamian gods communicated with the mortal world through omens (behavioral and exta), phenomena (terrestrial and astronomical), dreams, and, occasionally, prophetic declarations. Typically, this thriving field of divination employed trained male scholars who would parse out the meaning of transmissions using various compendia. The examiner (*bārû*) would "read" the marks upon and arrangement of the exta of animals, while the omen specialist would consult tomes of accumulated knowledge to decipher various occurrences. Prophecy, on the other hand, seems not to have required formal training; rather, because the prophet acted as a sort of megaphone for a god/gods, prophecy was not so much an active art as a cognitively passive activity.[1] Unlike other methods of divination that required logic, rational conscious thought may have actually been a hindrance for the prophet.[2]

---

* I would like to thank Jonathan Stökl for inviting me to be a participant in the Prophetic Texts and Ancient Contexts session Prophecy and Gender, convened at the 2010 meeting of the SBL. Although this article is a revision of the paper presented at that conference, it is also a work in progress and is part of a much larger project on the various manifestations of Ištar and their relationship to lamentation.

1. See Martti Nissinen, "Prophecy and Omen Divination: Two Sides of the Same Coin," in *Divination and Interpretation of Signs in the Ancient World* (ed. Amar Annus; OIS 6; Chicago: University of Chicago Press, 2010), 341–51; Jonathan Stökl, *Prophecy in the Ancient Near East: A Philological and Sociological Comparison* (CHANE 56; Leiden: Brill, 2012).

2. Numerous books and articles are devoted to the topic of ancient Near Eastern prophecy. For biblical prophecy see particularly Joseph Blenkinsopp, *A History of*

Reports of prophecies that date to the reign of the Old Babylonian king of Mari Zimri-Lim (ca. 1775–1761 B.C.E.) typically cite an "answerer" (*āpilum* [m.]/*āpiltum* [f.]) or an "ecstatic" (*muḫḫû* [m.]/*muḫḫūtum* [f.]) as the source of their messages, while during the late Neo-Assyrian period people functioning in the same capacity are called ecstatic (*maḫḫû*) or, more often, "proclaimer" (*raggimu* [m.]/*raggintu* [f.]).³ As these designations imply, in order to prophesy it seems that the transmitters of these messages needed to be in a sort of delirium or frenzy; and, while these texts do suggest a professional class of prophets, those perhaps trained to go into such an ecstasy, reports from Mari (modern Tell Hariri) also record that deities occasionally "spoke" through nonspecialists.⁴ Average people, such as a simple servant girl of the god Dagan, who is said to have gone into a frenzy (*immaḫḫima*), or a seemingly unassuming upper-class woman (*awīltum*), who conveys a message of Dagan, could function as prophets.⁵

In records from Mari, prophets speak for several different manifestations of Adad (e.g., Adad of Aleppo and Adad of Kallassu), Dagan (e.g., Dagan of Tuttul and Dagan of Terqa), Išḫara (Bēlet-biri), Itur-Mer, Marduk,

---

Prophecy in Israel (rev. ed.; Louisville: Westminster John Knox, 1996), and the various commentary series; for ancient Near Eastern prophecy see A. Kirk Grayson and Wilfred G. Lambert, "Akkadian Prophecies," *JCS* 18 (1964): 7–30; Maria deJong Ellis, "Observations on Mesopotamian Oracles and Prophetic Texts: Literary and Historiographic Considerations," *JCS* 41 (1989): 127–86; Martti Nissinen, ed., *Prophecy in Its Ancient Near Eastern Context: Mesopotamian, Biblical, and Arabian Perspectives* (SBLSymS 13; Atlanta: Society of Biblical Literature, 2000); and Matthias Köckert and Martti Nissinen, eds., *Propheten in Mari, Assyrien und Israel* (FRLANT 201; Göttingen: Vandenhoeck & Ruprecht, 2003); for compilations of the source material for ancient Near Eastern prophecies, see Simo Parpola, *Assyrian Prophecies* (SAA 9; Helsinki: Helsinki University Press, 1997); Martti Nissinen, *Prophets and Prophecy in the Ancient Near East* (SBLWAW 12; Atlanta: Society of Biblical Literature, 2003); idem, *References to Prophecy in Neo-Assyrian Sources* (SAAS 7; Helsinki: Helsinki University Press, 1998).

3. For an excellent survey of the various titles for possible prophets, see Herbert B. Huffmon, "A Company of Prophets: Mari, Assyria, Israel," in Nissinen, *Prophecy in Context*, 47–70.

4. Cf. Stökl, *Prophecy in Ancient Near East*. Stökl argues that there are classes of professional prophets (the Old Babylonian *āpilum/āpiltum* and the Neo-Assyrian *raggimu/raggintu*), as well as some cult officials and "common" people who prophesy occasionally.

5. ARM 26 214 and ARM 26 210.

Nergal, Šamaš, and Annunītum, a hypostasis of the goddess Inana/Ištar. Outside the Mari texts, there is little evidence for prophecy in the ancient Near East, until the late Neo-Assyrian period when Ištar becomes the chief deity for whom there are prophetic records.[6] During the Old Babylonian period, *assinnū* were employees of the temple of Annunītum at Mari, and there are accounts that they prophesied for her. Because of these reports and because Ištar became *the* prophetic god during the late Neo-Assyrian period, *assinnū* are assumed to have been yet another category of frenetic prophet, rather than being one of the attested "nonspecialists" who occasionally prophesied.[7]

Modern scholars conceive of the Ištar-Annunītum who communicated through prophetic agency as a benevolent goddess who wished to promote and protect kings, their land, and their people out of love and compassion. This Ištar is also thought to have had a mantic and bawdy cult populated by a colorful cast of characters of varying sexualities who performed all manner of ecstatic, lamenting, and lascivious acts. One of the purposes of these acts was to commune with the goddess and ultimately to be able to convey the words of Ištar through trance. As employees of the Ištar temple at Mari who are recorded to have prophesied, the *assinnū*, it then follows, must have been active participants in this frenetic love cult.

Forced to rely on difficult and fragmentary materials such as ritual, esoteric, and lexical texts, modern scholars have concluded that the *assinnu*'s "forte is the interpretation of sexuality, but seemingly abnormal

---

6. One should also note that compared with other forms of divination the cuneiform prophecy corpus is quite small and exceedingly delineated. Approximately thirty-five letters discovered at Mari record one or two prophecies each (an additional 15–20 tablets recount dreams or visions). These tablets date to the Old Babylonian period and from the reigns of the Amorite rulers Yaḫdun-Lim (late nineteenth century), his son Zimri-Lim, and the interregnum of Šamši-Addu's son Yasmaḫ-Addu (ca. 1792–1775 B.C.E.). Also dating to the Old Babylonian period are two tablets discovered at Ešnunna that seem to contain prophecies. A further eleven tablets, containing thirty prophecies (four of which contain "collections" and seven of which contain "fresh reports"), were discovered at Nineveh (modern Mosul). Though these Ninevite prophecies record revelations from the reigns of both Esarhaddon (680–669 B.C.E.) and his son Ashurbanipal (668–631 B.C.E.), the tablets themselves date to the reign of Ashurbanipal.

7. *Assinnū* are never recorded as having prophesied during the Neo-Assyrian period.

sexuality";[8] that *assinnū* took part in a transvestite cult;[9] that they should be, along with the *kurgarrû* and the *pilpili*, equated with the Hijra, a third gender class in Indian society;[10] and/or, as Simo Parpola has contended, that the *assinnu*, and other members of the Ištar cult, "lacerated himself or herself and, at the point of exhaustion, went into paranormal states and experiences: agitation of the eye (weeping) and mouth (lamenting)," in order to "trigger" possession by Ištar.[11] Although it may be the case that *assinnū* ultimately did take part in such a cult, it is unlikely that they did so during the Old Babylonian period, the period during which *assinnū* are recorded to have prophesied. Sumerian literary evidence, along with the Akkadian records of prophecy at Mari, suggest that the presence of *assinnū* in prophecy was likely a result of their positions as functionaries in a martial, not prophetic and/or bawdy, cult of Ištar.[12]

---

8. Richard A. Henshaw, *Female and Male: The Cultic Personnel: The Bible and the Rest of the Ancient Near East* (PrTMS 31; Allison Park, Pa.: Pickwick, 1994). However, Henshaw is ultimately forced to conclude that many of these titles of Ištar's cultic retinue cannot be translated (284–311).

9. See Brigitte Groneberg, "Die sumerisch-akkadische Inanna/Ištar: Hermaphroditos?" *WO* 17 (1986): 25–46; idem, "Namûtu ša Ištar: Das Transvestieschauspiel der Ištar," *NABU* 2 (1997): 64–66; Barbara Böck, "Überlegungen zu einem Kultfest der altmesopotamischen Göttin Inanna," *Numen* 51 (2004): 20–46; and Stefan M. Maul, "*Kurgarrû* und *assinnu* und ihr Stand in der babylonischen Gesellschaft," in *Aussenseiter und Randgruppen: Beiträge zu einer Sozialgeschichte des Alten Orients* (ed. Volkert Haas; Xenia 32; Konstanz: Universitätsverlag, 1992), 159–71.

10. Gwendolyn Leick, *Sex and Eroticism in Mesopotamian Literature* (New York: Routledge, 1994), 159. In *Homoeroticism in the Biblical World: A Historical Perspective* (Minneapolis: Fortress, 1998), Martti Nissinen, using late and problematic evidence, concurs, contending that *assinnū* (and *kurgarrû*) wore women's clothing and makeup. He further states that they were members of Ištar's cult because they, like Ištar, could transform their gender and that, because of this transsexuality, they were attractive to the goddess. He concludes that it may be necessary to view the *assinnū* (and *kurgarrû*) as members of a third gender (31–36).

11. Parpola, *Assyrian Prophecies*, xxxiv and xlvi. Seeming to model his understanding on Hellenistic cults, Parpola suggests that the Ištar cult was an "esoteric mystery cult promising its devotees transcendental salvation and eternal life" (xv). He compares this practice to Shakta Tantrism, contending that the initiates would have to journey through a series of metaphors, which once understood would reveal secret knowledge. Using the cuneiform text the Descent of Ištar as a guide, devotees of the goddess, he argues, strove for eternal life by emulating Ištar.

12. Although brought to my attention after this paper was completed (and so I could not fully incorporate it), one should compare the similar conclusions of Julia

Definition

According to certain cuneiform lexical texts, the logographic equivalences for the Akkadian term *assinnu* are saĝ.ur.saĝ and ˡᵘ²ur.sal. Translated literally, saĝ.ur.saĝ means either "hero" or "lead hero";[13] thus Adam Falkenstein suggests "heldenhaften Mannen" (heroic men),[14] while Wilfred G. Lambert conjectures that the term could mean "companion of a warrior or batman."[15] These would seem to be definitive translations, except that the alternative logographic equivalent ˡᵘ²ur.sal could mean "bitch," "lioness," "woman-man," or "feminine man" among other possibilities.[16] The last equivalence, which is not attested until the Neo-Assyrian period, has led some scholars to conclude that the *assinnu* was a temple prostitute or homosexual.[17] Due to a dearth of evidence and perhaps seeking to quell notions of Mesopotamian homosexuality and temple prostitution, the *CAD* defines an *assinnu* as simply "a member of the cultic personnel of

---

Assante, "Bad Girls and Kinky Boys? The Modern Prostituting of Ishtar, Her Clergy and Her Cults," in *Tempelprostitution im Altertum: Fakten und Fiktionen* (ed. Tanja S. Scheer; Oikumene 6; Berlin: Antike, 2009), 23–54.

13. ur.saĝ = "hero"; nam.ur.saĝ = "heroism"; and, saĝ = "front," "head," or "first." saĝ in this instance could also be acting as a signifier (similar to lu₂), thus carrying the meaning "individual" and having no English correspondence.

14. Adam Falkenstein, "*Sumerische religiöse Texte*," ZA 52 (1957): 56–75. In "A Hymn to Inanna and Her Self-Praise," *JCS* 40 (1988): 165–86, Åke W. Sjöberg contends that these two lines indicate that the *assinnu* had duties other than "cultic assignments." (177). This conclusion was rejected by Samuel N. Kramer (review of Adam Falkenstein, *Sumerische und akkadische Hymnen und Gebete*, BiOr 11 [1954]: 170–76, esp. 175 n. 32), who argues the saĝ.ur.saĝ are merely temple personnel.

15. Wilfred G. Lambert, "Prostitution," in Haas, *Aussenseiter und Randgruppen*, 127–57.

16. lu₂ = the determinative for "person" or "being;" ur = "dog," "lion," "man," "servant," etc.; and SAL, if read sal, = "feminine" or "thin"; or, if read munus, = "woman," or "female." It is even possible that the meaning for ˡᵘ²ur.munus could be "servant of women." (The reading "female servant" for ˡᵘ²ur.sal is unlikely, as this is regularly rendered geme₂ [SAL.KUR].)

17. E.g., Maul, "*Kurgarrû und assinnu*," who argues that the presence of transsexuals and homosexuals in the cult of Ištar were meant to incite fear in the people who witnessed their actions in order to regiment behavior; and Gertrud Farber-Flügge, *Der Mythos "Inanna und Enki" unter besonderer Berücksichtigung der Liste der ME* (StP 10; Rome: Biblical Institute Press, 1973), who, even though accepting that an *assinnu* may merely have been a courtier, defines the saĝ.ur.saĝ as a temple prostitute or temple attendant (248).

Ištar," cryptically adding at the end of the entry that "The [*assinnu*] seems to have functioned mainly in the cult of Ištar, to have sung specific songs and dressed in distinctive garments. There is no specific evidence that he was a eunuch or a homosexual; the Era passage may mean simply that Ištar turned his interest from the masculine role to the feminine role."[18]

Although certain early lexical lists, such as the simple corollary lists, can be extraordinarily useful, they do not provide any definition other than to equate one Sumerian lexeme with one Akkadian lexeme.[19] Furthermore, depending on the period to which they are dated, the terms listed may not have been fully understood by the scribe who indeed copied the list. Thus, other than to provide simple logographic or syllabic equivalences, these types of lists are of little help in accurate translation/interpretation. This situation is exacerbated in the case of the synonym lists. Created during the first millennium, in these lists all conceivable and inconceivable Sumerian words are given for a Babylonian word.[20] *Assinnū* are catalogued with mantic professionals such as prophets (*āpilum/āpiltum, muḫḫû/muḫḫūtum*), professional mourners (*lallarû*), and frenzied people (*zabbû*). They are also listed with other cultic functionaries, such as singers, the chief lamentation priest (*kalamāḫu*), and the simple lamentation priest (*munambû*), in addition to various other female and male clergy.[21]

---

18. *CAD* A/2:341–42 s.v. *assinnu*.

19. For a discussion of the various lexical lists and their development see Jonathan Taylor, "Babylonian Lists of Words and Signs," in *The Babylonian World* (ed. Gwendolyn Leick; New York: Routledge, 2007), 432–46; Niek Veldhuis, "How Did They Learn Cuneiform? 'Tribute/Word List C' as an Elementary Exercise," in *Approaches to Sumerian Literature in Honour of Stip (H. L. J. Vanstiphout)* (ed. Piotr Michalowski and Niek Veldhuis; CM 35; Leiden: Brill, 2006), 181–200; idem, "Continuity and Change in the Mesopotamian Lexical Tradition," in *Aspects of Genre and Type in Pre-Modern Literary Cultures* (ed. Bert Roest and Herman L. J. Vanstiphout; COMERS Communications 1; Groningen: Styx, 1999), 101–18; Miguel Civil, "Ancient *Mesopotamian* Lexicography," *CANE* 4:181–200.

20. Veldhuis, "Continuity and Change," 111–12 §7.1. It may even be more accurate to say that it is not all Sumerian equivalencies, but rather all logographic equivalencies, for it is likely that Sumerian was not at all well understood during this period and that scribes could have become quite creative.

21. E.g., Erimḫuš III 172ff ^{lu_2}an.sal (var. adds .la) = *as-sin-nu* (var. *i-[sin-nu]*) with *muḫḫû, zabbû, kurgarrû*; but also Malku I 134–135 *ug-bab-tum* = *en-tum, as-sin-na-tum*(!).

Attestations in Early Literary Texts

One of the earliest attestations for an *assinnu* is in a Sumerian royal inscription that records the construction and dedication of the Ningirsu temple in Lagaš (modern Tell al-Hiba). In it, Gudea (twenty-second century B.C.E.) proudly announces that "^{lu_2}si-gi$_4$-a, NITA.UD and women [munus-e] doing work he banished from the city; a woman wouldn't carry its [Lagaš's] basket [dusu-bi] only the best warriors [saĝ-ur-saĝ-e] would work for him."[22] It is unclear who either the ^{lu_2}si-gi$_4$-a or NITA.UD is; however, because the women mentioned are performing corvée labor, it must be assumed that these servile workers were considered of a less desirable cast and were thought to tarnish the environment so much that they had to be banished. Temple construction work (even if obligatory), it seems, was not meant to be done by lesser workers, thus the elite (?) saĝ.ur.saĝ are brought in. Perhaps analogously, in an Ur-Namma hymn, Ur-Namma (ca. 2113–2096) recounts the freedoms he brought to southern Mesopotamia including that "Its [i.e., Sumer's] finest warriors (saĝ-ur-saĝ) lifted their yoke." This may suggest that the *assinnū* were in some way held captive and perhaps had been pressed into labors inappropriate to their status.[23]

The heroic and splendid quality of the *assinnu* (saĝ.ur.saĝ) is emphasized in the Debate between Ewe and Grain. In this playful Sumerian contest text, Ewe and Grain dispute over who is superior (Ewe or Grain). In one heated segment, Grain cries to her rival:

> Sister, I am your better; I take precedence over you. I am the glory of the lights of the Land. I grant my power to the saĝursaĝ [*assinnu*]—he fills the palace with awe and people spread his fame to the borders of the Land. I am the gift of the Anuna gods. I am central to all princes. After I have conferred my power on the warrior [ur-saĝ-ra], when he goes to war he knows no fear, he knows no faltering (?)—I make him leave … as if to the playing field. (ETCSL 5.3.2:71–82)

Later in the text, continuing to emphasize her point, Grain proclaims: "I stand up as an equal to Iškur. I am Grain, I am born for the warrior [ur-saĝ-ra]—I do not give up."[24]

---

22. RIME 3 1.1.7.StB: iv 1–6.
23. Ur-Namma C 84 (TCL 15 12) Esther Flückiger-Hawker, *Urnamma of Ur in Sumerian Literary Tradition* (OBO 166; Göttingen: Vandenhoeck & Ruprecht, 1999).
24. ETCSL 5.3.2:140.

Similar to the Debate between Ewe and Grain, in the Old Babylonian version of the Sumerian hymn *Uru-Amirabi*, the *assinnu* receives not merely the power vital for acts of valor, but the actual art of being a hero. In this hymn, the goddess Inana (Ištar) is said to bring back multiple elements from the steppe.[25] Among other items, she brings back heroism (nam-ur-saĝ) for the saĝursaĝ (called *assinnu* in the later bilingual version).[26] *Uru-Amirabi* is also pertinent to this discussion because of its mention of the *kurgarrû* (kurĝara) and the *kalû* (gala), two figures with whom *assinnū* become associated and, at times, conflated. The text relays that after bringing heroism to the *assinnu*, Inana brings two types of weapons, the *patru* (ĝiri$_2$) and the *pattaru* (ba-da-ra), for the *kurgarrû*, and the xx (broken) for the *kalû*. These deliveries are also recorded in the Sumerian tale Inana and Ebiḫ. After subjugating the mountain Ebiḫ for its arrogance, and claiming to have created a firm foundation for rule, Inana states: "I have given the kur-ĝar-ra (*kurgarrû*) a ĝiri$_2$ (*patru*) and ba-da-ra (*pattaru*); I have given the gala (*kalû*) ub and lilis drums."[27] Finally, in the infamous "sacred marriage" text Iddin-Dagan A, a hymn dedicated to Ninsi'ana (a deity who was, at this point, equated with Ištar's manifestation as Venus)[28] and nominally written for the Old Babylonian king Iddin-Dagan (ca. 1974–1954 B.C.E.), *assinnū* and *kurgarrû* are said to parade with a variety of individuals. Some of these people carry musical instruments, perform a playful competition, or are girded with weapons, while others seem to perform blood rituals. Mentioned in the third *kirugu* (rubric), the *assinnu* would seem to be at the beginning of the parade. Although he is said to have a specific hairstyle, he is attributed no definitive actions; conversely, the *kurgarrû*, mentioned later in the fifth *kirugu*, once again is said to hold

---

25. It is also perhaps telling that in the Debate between Ewe and Grain, Grain tells Ewe that she (Grain) is similar to Inana (ETCSL 5.3.2:144).

26. VAT 1339 = VAS 2 29 (it should be noted that, unlike the later versions of this hymn, VAT 1339 does not contain reference to the u$_3$-bu-bu-ul/za-bu-bu): line 10: [saĝ]-ur-saĝ-da mu-un-da-dur$_2$-ru-ne-eš nam-ur-sag-e mu-ni-ib$_2$-DU, "she stays with the saĝursaĝ, she brings heroism"; and line 13: [kur-ĝa]r-ra-da mu-un-da-dur$_2$-ru-ne-eš me-er [ES for ĝiri$_2$] ba-da-ra-e mu-ni-ib$_2$-DU, "she stays with the kurĝara, she brings the ĝiri and the ba-da-ra."

27. ETCSL 1.3.2:171–175.

28. Wolfgang Heimpel, "Catalogue of Near Eastern Venus Deities," *Syro-Mesopotamian Studies* 4 (1982): 59–72.

the *pattaru* (ba-da-ra) and, likely, the *patru* (ĝiri₂).²⁹ He walks in front of a person who pours blood on a sword and throne.³⁰

The *patru* (ĝiri₂) is attested in Sumerian texts that date from the Early Dynastic through Old Babylonian periods and Akkadian texts from Old Akkadian until Neo-Babylonian periods, while the *pattaru* (ba-da-ra) appears in Sumerian texts that mainly date to the Old Babylonian period, but can appear in Akkadian texts from the Old Akkadian and Old Babylonian periods. Both implements tend to be defined as daggers or sharp knives, although the sign ĝiri₂ can indicate a sword, as it does in Anatolian texts,³¹ and the ba-da-ra may have been a mace, since it can also be listed with the *ḫutpalû*.

In the mortal world, the *patru* primarily seems to have been used as a butcher's implement or a symbol of heroic pride. On occasion, the Ur III kings would refer to themselves as the "dagger [ĝiri₂] of Sumer,"³² and in the Sumerian text Gilgameš and the Bull of Heaven, the legendary king Gilgameš carries a dagger (ĝiri₂) that weighs seven talents.³³ In Assyria the *patru* came to be used as an item to swear upon in judicial settings (i.e., the *patru* of Aššur or Ištar). In the divine world, it was a weapon of the gods, frequently in the hand of the war deities Ninurta, Inana, and Nergal. In Gudea Cylinder B, Gudea presents Ningirsu with, among other weapons, a ĝiri₂ (*patru*).³⁴ In the tales Angim and Inana and Ebiḫ, the *patru* seems to have been an assassin's weapon of choice. In the bilingual Angim, Ninurta declares, "I bear that which strips away the 'mountains' [Akkadian: severs necks], the sword [Sum. ĝiri₂-gal; Akk. *patru*],³⁵ my heavenly

---

29. This is somewhat unclear. It may be that he is preceded by both weapons, and then he grabs only the ba-da-ra.

30. Daniel Reisman, "Iddin-Dagan's Sacred Marriage Hymn," *JCS* 25 (1973): 185–202. See also Willem H. Ph. Römer, *Sumerische 'Königshymnen' der Isin-Zeit* (DMOA 13; Leiden: Brill, 1965), 128–208. This parade may also be referred to in *Innin-šagurra*, although it is entirely unclear what action the *assinnu* and *kurgarrû* are doing; furthermore, mention of the *assinnu* (saĝursaĝ) is extant in only one text from Nippur.

31. See *CAD* P:280 9′.

32. E.g., the Death of Ur-Namma (ETCSL 2.4.1.1:39) and Šulgi P (ETCSL 2.4.2.16).

33. Rev. col. i 94; Antoine Cavigneaux and Farouk N. H. Al-Rawi, "Gilgameš et Taureau de Ciel (šul-mè-kam) (Textes de Tell Haddad IV)," *RA* 87 (1993): 97–129.

34. ETCSL 2.1.7:1132.

35. Sum. ĝiri₂-gal, literally reads "big ĝiri₂."

dagger [Sum. ĝiri$_2$; Akk. *patru*]";[36] and, in a most graphic episode in Inana and Ebiḫ, Inana sharpens her dagger (ĝiri$_2$), grabs Ebiḫ by its tall grasses, and executes the mountain.[37] This latter scene is referenced in the Sumerian hymn in-nin ša$_3$-gur$_4$-ra. After recounting how Inana brought about the destruction and humbling of the mountain Ebiḫ, the text states, "the Mistress [Inana], the proud one, holds the hip-dagger [ĝiri$_2$] in her hand, [she is full of] radiance which covers the land."[38] Finally, in two late texts, Nergal, whose ferocity rivals only Ištar's, possesses the dagger. In the maledictory section of the succession treaty of Esarhaddon, he is invoked: "may Nergal bring your life to an end with his merciless dagger [ĝiri$_2$-šu$_2$]";[39] and, in a Neo-Babylonian hymn, Nergal is referred to as the one "who wields knife [*nāš patri*], who knows fighting."[40]

The Debate between Ewe and Grain, Inana and Ebiḫ, as well as *Uru-Amirabi* and Iddin-Dagan A, record differing traditions for each professional. In the Debate and *Uru-Amirabi*, the *assinnu* receives heroism, an art that seems fitting for a person whose Sumerian name may mean lead or best warrior. In Inana and Ebiḫ and *Uru-Amirabi*, it is the *kurgarrû* who receives two weapons: the *patru* and the *pattaru*, while the *kalû* receive instruments of lamentation. Finally, in Iddin-Dagan A, though not given the weapons, the *kurgarrû* does carry the *patru* and the *pattaru*. The function of *kalû* as a professional lamentation singer is well documented; thus the gift of lamentation instruments is appropriate. Unlike the activities of the *kalû*, the function of the *kurgarrû*, like the *assinnu*, is not as clear. Since *kurgarrû* are continually linked to the *kalû*, it is possible that they too function as lamenters; however, the *patru* is a weapon wielded by gods and one to which kings compare themselves. It is difficult to believe that this object served a mourning function. In any case, it is of note that in the Debate between Ewe and Grain the *assinnu*, as in the Ur III royal texts, is not mentioned with either the *kurgarrû* or the *kalû*. He is an independent

---

36. Angim III 32 = 140; see Jerrold S. Cooper, *The Return of Ninurta to Nippur: An-gim dím-ma* (AnOr 52; Rome: Pontifical Biblical Institute, 1978).

37. ETCSL 1.3.2:139–141.

38. Line 64; see Åke W. Sjöberg, "in-nin šà-gur$_4$-ra: A Hymn to the Goddess Inanna by the en-Priestess Enḫeduanna," *ZA* 65 (1975): 161–253.

39. SAA 2 6: 455; see Simo *Parpola* and Kazuko Watanabe, *Neo-Assyrian Treaties and Loyalty Oaths* (SAA 2; Helsinki: Helsinki University Press, 1988), 48.

40. F. M. Th. de Liagre Böhl, "Hymne an Nergal, den Gott der Unterwelt," *BiOr* 6 (1949): 165–70: 10b.

figure. Similarly, the *kurgarrû* and *kalû* are mentioned without the *assinnu* in Inana and Ebiḫ and are mentioned in separate *kirugu* in Iddin-Dagan A. It is only in *Uru-Amirabi* that the three are brought together, perhaps suggesting that they did not originally act together.

An additional aspect of the role of the *kurgarrû* may be suggested in Iddin-Dagan A. The Sumerian verb used to indicate the movement of the *kurgarrû* in the parade is ed (written with the ed$_3$ sign). Although it can be used to indicate other actions, the intrinsic meaning of this verb is to change levels, to ascend or to descend.[41] Although difficult to conceptualize in a parade, this action may refer to the same ability recorded in the Sumerian story the Descent of Inana.[42] In this dysfunctional family tale, Inana famously travels to the netherworld, perhaps to wrest power from the goddess Ereškigal. Possibly because of this hubris, once there she is perfunctorily turned into a slab of meat. Inana's vizier Ninšubar is then forced to convince the god Enki to save her mistress. This he does by creating the *kurgarrû* (kur-gar-ra) and the "little" *kalû* (gala-tur-a) and by giving a life-giving plant to the *kurgarrû* and life-giving waters to the *kalû*. They in turn sprinkle these items on Inana and revive her. The story also informs that, in order for this plan to have worked, the *kurgarrû* and *kalû* needed to gain Ereškigal's trust by empathizing with her great emotional and physical pain. As professional mourners who took on the pain of their charges, the actions the *kalû* perform in the Descent of Inana are expected;[43] however, the tale may suggest a new or different function for the *kurgarrû*. At no point in the story are either the *kurgarrû* or *kalû* given weapons or instruments. Instead, it would seem, they are endowed with the knowledge of being able to ascend from and descend to the netherworld.

In the Sumerian tale Inana and Enki, another story in which Inana characteristically transports aspects of society, the *kurgarrû* and *assinnu* are mentioned after a series of priests.[44] In the text, Ninšubar says to her mistress:

---

41. See also Reisman, "Iddin-Dagan's Sacred Marriage Hymn," 196 line 74.

42. William R. Sladek, "Inanna's Descent to the Nether World" (Ph.D. diss., Johns Hopkins University, 1974).

43. See Uri Gabbay, *The Ersema Prayers of the First Millennium BCE* (Heidelberger Emesal-Studien 2; Wiesbaden: Harrassowitz, forthcoming).

44. The egir-zid priestess, the nin-diĝir priestess, the išib priest, the office of lu-maḫ priest, and the office of gudug (priest?).

> You have brought with you constancy, you have brought with you…, you have brought with you…, you have brought with you going down to the underworld [ed$_3$-de$_3$], you have brought with you coming up from the underworld [ed$_3$-de$_3$], you have brought with you the kur-ĝar-ra (*kurgarrû*). You have brought with you ĝiri$_2$ (*patru*) and ba-da-ra (*pattaru*), you have brought with you the saĝ.ur.saĝ (*assinnu*), you have brought with you the black garment, you have brought with you the colourful garment, you have brought with you the … hair-style, you have brought with you the … hair-style. (ETCSL 1.3.1: segment I, 16–21, 22–27)

In Inana and Enki, the *patru* and the *pattaru* are brought with the *assinnu*, not the *kurgarrû*. The *kurgarrû* are instead brought with the skill of coming up from and going down to the netherworld, the skill with which they were endowed by Enki in the Descent of Inana. This blending of traditions is also evident in festival descriptions that mention the participation of *assinnū*, *kurgarrū*, and *kalû*.

In texts dating to the Ur III period, *assinnū* are mentioned in connection with the moon festival, the ešeš (eš$_3$-eš$_3$), "Holiday of Holidays" or "Great Holiday" (perhaps even the "Ever-Repeating Holiday"). So important was this occasion that Šulgi boasts that he ran the journey from Nippur to Ur and back in one day (approximately 150 km) in order to celebrate the ešeš in both cities. He further declares, "my saĝ-ur-saĝ-ĝu$_{10}$-ne (*assinnī*) looked at me with admiration," perhaps implying their involvement in the celebration or at the very least demonstrating their appreciation of his prowess.[45] What occurred during these festivals is open to debate, as we have little remaining evidence. By Šulgi's own account, they may have been times to celebrate fallen rulers, thus having had some connection to a cult of the deified kings:

> In the cult-places, let no one neglect the songs about me, whether they are *adab*, whether they are *tigi* or *malgatum*, *šir-gida* or praise of kingship, whether they are *šumunša*, *kunĝar* or *balbale*, whether they are *gi-gid* or *zamzam*—so that they shall never pass out of memory and never lapse from people's mouths. Let them never cease to be sung in the shining E-kur! Let them be played for Enlil in his Shrine of the New Moon! (ETCSL 2.4.2.05:53–62)

---

45. ETCSL 2.4.2.01:77.

When celebrating the ešeš, clear beer (i.e., the good stuff) is served "endlessly like water" before the gods Enlil and Ninlil.⁴⁶ Unfortunately, there is no further information detailing the involvement of *assinnū* in the festival. If it was a celebration glorifying deified kings, did *assinnū* participate as heroic warriors? That the first-person possessive is used with saĝursaĝ does, however, indicate that they were members of Šulgi's royal staff.

In the Debate Between Ewe and Grain, although a festival as such is not mentioned, Grain tells Ewe that her heroic warrior, the *assinnu*, will go to war, as if to the playing field (ki-a-ne-di).⁴⁷ In Sumerian literary texts, the playground, specifically Ištar's playground, is a frequent metaphor for battle, as in the legend Enmerkar and the Lord of Aratta, in which Ištar is said to make the warriors dance her dance (i.e., war). This is also true of the Akkadian *mēlultu*, "to play." The creation of a type of battle festival to Ištar is recorded in the Old Babylonian hymn *Agušaya*.⁴⁸ In order to praise and celebrate the martial aspect of the goddess, Enki creates a whirl dance (*gūštu*), which may have been a type of war dance.⁴⁹

As the sovereign of war, Ištar is not only the goddess of battle itself but also the goddess of warriors. On the battlefield she aids the king, and, as recorded in the Middle Assyrian Epic of Tukulti-Ninurta, in the midst of the carnage the warriors cry out to Ištar, "*aḫulap*!"⁵⁰ The connection between Ištar, war, and play continues into the Neo-Assyrian period as is evidenced by her title in the inscriptions of Šalmaneser III. In the invocation unit of these inscriptions, Ištar is referred to as "Sovereign of Battle and Combat, whose game is fighting" (*bēlet qabli u tāḫāzi ša mēlultaša tuqumtu*). In the festival setting, *kurgarrû* and *assinnū* seem to have reenacted the turmoil of war. A Neo-Assyrian ritual text records that *assinnū* may have sung a song titled "Battle Is My Game, Warfare Is My Game" (*mēlili qablu mē[lilī] tāḫāzu*), after which the *assinnu* "goes down to battle" and executes the whirl dance (*gūštu*).⁵¹ In a similar ritual *kurgarrû*

---

46. ETCSL 2.4.05:61–62.
47. ETCSL 5.3.2:82.
48. Brigitte Groneberg, *Lob der Ištar: Gebet und Ritual an die altbabylonische Venusgöttin Tanatti Ištar* (CM 8; Groningen: Styx, 1997), 73–93.
49. Ibid., *Agušaya*, col. v 16.
50. Col. iii 40–53; see Peter Machinist, "The Epic of Tukulti-Ninurta I: A Study in Middle Assyrian Literature" (Ph.D. diss., Yale University, 1978).
51. BM 41005 obv. col. iii 16–17: *ù me-li-li qablu me-[li-li] tāḫāzu* (MÈ) *iqabbi* (DUG₄-GA)-*ma* ˡᵘ*assinnu*(UR.SAL) *ana qab-lu ur-rad gu-uš-tum i-za-x* [....] "'Battle is my game, warfare is my game,' he/she will utter and the Assinnu-priest will go down

are said to sing the song titled "Battle Is My Game" (*melulī qablu*), and *assinnū* answer with a kind of shout (*yarrurtu*).[52] The *assinnū* are then said to *milḫu imalluḫū*, an opaque phrase that has been understood to mean the wildly differing concepts of "rip and tear themselves" or, more likely, "perform a dance or song."[53]

Attestations in the Mari Prophecy Corpus

Returning now to the prophetic corpus from Mari, we find further evidence for the association of *assinnū* and the Ištar who governs war. As stated in the introduction, Ištar is not the only god who spoke via prophetic agency; she is but one of a multitude of deities for whom prophecies are recorded. She is, however, the only deity who speaks through an *assinnu*. She does this in the form of Annunītum, a martial and by no means tender deity. Annunītum is first attested in the inscriptions of the Sargonic king Nārām-Sîn (ca. 2260–2223 b.c.e.). In these early inscriptions, she appears as either an independent deity Annunītum or as a manifestation of Ištar, Ištar-Annunītum.[54] It is likely that this hypostasis of Ištar is West Semitic and that her name derives from the verb *anānum*, "skirmish"; thus Annunītum should be understood as "the (deified) Battle/Skirmish."[55] In the Nārām-Sîn texts, Annunītum is frequently found in the company of Ilaba, another West Semitic martial deity, and is not only responsible for "leading the troops of the city of Ilaba," but also is

---

to battle, he will . . a jig [....]" (Wilfred G. Lambert, "The Problem of the Love Lyrics," in *Unity and Diversity: Essays in the History, Literature, and Religion of the Ancient Near East* [ed. Hans Goedicke and J. J. M Roberts; JHNES 7; Baltimore: Johns Hopkins University Press, 1975], 98–135).

52. Henshaw, *Female and Male*, 285 3.2.5. There is even an Ištar of the *ia-a-ru-ra-te* listed in An = Anum just prior to an Ištar of War (*tanūnqāte*) (*CT* 24 41:84).

53. *CAD* M/1:152–53 s.v. *malāḫu*. The verb is attested very infrequently.

54. Karin Gödecken, "Bemerkungen zur Göttin Annunītum," *UF* 5 (1973): 141–63.

55. Gerbhard J. Selz, "Five Divine Ladies: Fragments to Inana(k), Ištar, In(n)in(a), Annunītum, and Anat, and the Origin of the Title 'Queen of Heaven,'" *Nin* 1 (2000): 29–62. Cf. Ignace J. Gelb, "The Name of the Goddess Innin," *JNES* 19 (1960): 72–79; and Wilfred G. Lambert, "A Babylonian Prayer to Anuna," in *DUMU-E2-DUB-BA-A: Studies in Honor of Åke W. Sjöberg* (ed. Hermann Behrens, Darlene Loding, and Martha T. Roth; Occasional Publications of the Samuel Noah Kramer Fund 11; Philadelphia: University Museum, 1989), 321–36.

said to judge which leader is to be the victor in war.[56] Because of her connection to the Sargonic kings, it is likely that she is the deity intended by the designations *bēlet Akkade*, "the Sovereign of Akkade," and *bēlet tāḫāzi*, "the Sovereign of War."

In the entirety of the prophetic corpus, only three prophecies are said to have taken place in the temple of Annunītum at Mari and claim to convey the words of this goddess. Two of these prophecies, ARM 26 212 and 213, record the names of *assinnū* (Ili-ḫaznaya and Šēlebum) who prophesy. In a third prophecy, ARM 26 214, a servant girl is said to have prophesied.[57] Unfortunately, no content of the divine message of Ili-ḫaznaya can be discovered as there is a lacuna just as the *assinnu* is to give the message, which seems to have concerned Hammurabi, the king of Mari's rival, Babylon. The message from Šēlebum is slightly more helpful:

> *umma Annunītumma Zimrī-Lim ina bārtim ilattakūka pagarka uṣur wardē <l>ibbīka ša tarammu itâtīk[a] šukun šuzissunūtima liṣṣurūk[a] ana ramānīka[ma] lā tattana[lla]k u awīlū ša ila[ttakūk]a ana qātīka a[wīlī] šunūti umal[lam]*

> Thus says Annunītum: Zimri-Lim, you will be tested in a revolt! Protect yourself! Let your most favored servants whom you love surround you, and make them stay there to protect you! Do not go around on your own! As regards the people who would tes[t you]: those pe[ople] I deli[ver up] into your hands. (ARM 26 213:7–14)[58]

A similar message was given by the servant girl:

---

56. RIME 2 1.4 and 1 4.6.

57. In ARM 26 212, Šibtu, the wife of Zimri-Lim, says, *ittātim ašqi aštalm[a]*, "I gave him signs to drink." The *assinnu* Ili-ḫaznaya is given this special drink in order to prophesy. In ARM 26 213 the *assinnu* Šēlebum goes into a trance (*immaḫḫu*). Neither of these processes is particular to the *assinnu*. Šibtu also gives signs to drink to seemingly normal men and women in ARM 26 207. In ARM 26 214 the servant girl is also said to go into a trance (*immaḫḫima*), as does a male prophet in ARM 26 222 (*immaḫêm*). What is particular to the case of the *assinnu*, servant girl, and undesignated men and women is that it must be made explicit that they go into a state of frenzy before prophesying. It is not obvious that this happens.

58. See Nissinen, *Prophets and Prophecy*, 47.

ummāmi Zimrī-Lim u šumma atta mišâtanni anāku elīka aḫabbuṣ nakrīka ana qātīka umalla u awīlī šarrāqīya aṣabbatma ana karāš Bēlet-ekallim akammissunūti

Zimri-Lim: Even though you are neglectful about me, I will massacre on your behalf. Your enemy I will deliver up into your hand. The people that steal from me I will catch, and I will gather them into the camp of Bēlet-ekallim. (ARM 26 214:7–18)[59]

Annunītum's messages inform the king that he should safeguard himself from his enemies and that, even though he is not always properly pious, the goddess will destroy his enemies. In each of her messages she also states that she will deliver up his enemy.

Although the Mari texts merely record prophetic statements (i.e., the actions had not yet occurred, but were only declared), the action "to place enemies into the hands" is commonly invoked of martial Ištar and appears regularly in Babylonian and Assyrian inscriptions into the early Neo-Assyrian period.[60] Two of these attestations are particularly pertinent to this discussion. In a bilingual inscription from Kish, written for the son of Hammurabi, Samsu-iluna (ca. 1749–1712 B.C.E.), siblings Zabāba and Ištar, designated as the Heroes of the Igigi (*qārdūtim ina Igigi*), are commanded by Enlil:

lu nu-úr-šu na-aw-ru-um at-ta-nu-ma it-ta-ku-nu da-mi-iq-tum li-ib-ši-šum-ma a-a-bi-šu na-e-ra za-e-ri-šu a-na qá-ti-šu mu-l-li-a-ma

Be [Samsu-iluna's] illumination. May you bestow a good omen on him: kill his enemies (and) deliver into his hands his foes. (RIME 4 3.7.7:36b–42)

In the same inscription, Zabāba and Ištar respond to Samsu-iluna:

---

59. Ibid., 48.

60. See Ilona Zsolnay, "The Function of Ištar in the Assyrian Royal Inscriptions: A Contextual Analysis of the Actions Attributed to Ištar in the Inscriptions of Ititi through Šalmaneser III" (Ph.D. diss., Brandeis University, 2009).

in im-ni-ka ni-il-la-ak za-i-ri-ka ni-na-ar a-a-bi-ka a-na qá-ti-ka nu-ma-al-la

We will go at your right side, kill your enemies, (and) place your foes into your hands. (RIME 4 3.7.7:71–75)

The inscription then states that Samsu-iluna went out and killed his enemies. The inscription does not state the method by which the gods respond to Samsu-iluna, but the episode does seem to mirror that recorded in the Mari prophecies and demonstrates that the actions recorded in those prophecies were common to Mesopotamia proper.

Also of interest to this discussion is an inscription of Yarim-Lim (ca. 1781–1765 B.C.E.), ruler of the Northwest Semitic city Alalakh (modern Tell Atchana). The extremely problematic maledictory unit of the inscriptions reads:

Adad (^{d}IŠKUR) *i-na kakkī* (^{GIŠ}TUKUL) *ša qa-ti-šu li-iḫ-bu-us-su* ^{d}*ḫé-pát* ^{d}*eš₄-tar₂ šukurrūšu* (^{GIŠ}SUKUR-*šu*) *li-iš-bi-ir* ^{d}*eš₄-tar₂ a-na qa-ti mu-ka-aš-ši-di-šu li-ma-al-li-šu*

May Adad crush him with the weapon which is in his hand; may Ḫepat (and) Eštar shatter his spear; may the goddess deliver him into the hand of his pursuers. (RIME 4 34.1.1:16–18)

^{d}*eš₄-tar₂ assinnu* (SAG.UR.SAG) *pa-ra-ú-ra-am i-na bi-ir-ki-šu li-te-eb-bi*

and may Eštar (and) the *assinnu* cause potency to leave his groin. (RIME 4 34.1.1:19–20)[61]

As can be seen, Ištar is once again invoked to deliver up the enemy of the king. And, while it is indeed interesting that she is also invoked to break

---

61. Translation mine. For an extensive treatment of this curse see Ilona Zsolnay, "'Goddess of War, Pacifier of Kings': An Analysis of Ištar's Martial Role in the Maledictory Sections of the Assyrian Royal Inscriptions," in *Language in the Ancient Near East* (vol. 1 of *Proceedings of the 53e Rencontre Assyriologie Internationale*; ed. Leonid Kogan, N. Koslova, S. Loesov, and S. Tishchenko; Orientalia et Classica 30/1; Babel und Bibel 4/1; Winona Lake, Ind.: Eisenbrauns, 2010), 389–402.

the sword of this king, it is the final curse which is most intriguing. In this curse we find mention of sag.ur.sag. Unfortunately, it is entirely unclear how to read this. It is possible that, as in the first curse, a conjunctive *u* "and" is missing (cf. ^dḪepat ^dEštar). It is also possible that sag.ur.sag (= *assinnu*) is to be read in apposition with Ištar (i.e., Ištar, the *assinnu*) or even that *assinnu* is not meant at all and instead we should understand sag.ur.sag as a title, "Lead/Finest Warrior" (i.e., Ištar, the Lead/Finest Warrior).[62]

Conclusion

Although there are but a few early attestations for *assinnū*, when surveyed they indicate that, far from being gender-bending prophets who enter mantic states to bond with a loving form of the goddess Ištar, *assinnū* were more likely a special class of warriors. Occasionally found together, and later confused, *assinnū* and *kurgarrû* had different roles in southern Mesopotamian society and, until the Old Babylonian period, were differentiated in texts. The *assinnu* originally seems to have been an heroic strongman who worked for the palace during the Ur III period. During this time, he may have participated in a monthly ceremony called the "Repeating Festival," while during the early Old Babylonian period he took part in festivals devoted to Ištar. It is likely that because of his role as a hero and connection to a martial form of Ištar, he became associated and, at times, conflated with two additional cultic professionals: the weapon-wielding *kurgarrû* and the lament-singing *kalû*. All three figures were ultimately, if not originally, connected to this martial cult.

Rather than understanding multiple cults of Ištar, each dedicated to different (same or similar) hypostases of the goddess, studies of Mesopotamian prophecy have assumed (even stressed) a homogenous overarching cult for the goddess. As envisioned, this cult was filled with a list of flamboyant heterosexual, bisexual, and androgynous characters whose worship of the goddess led them to perform acts that would normally be deemed beyond societal bounds. In this conception, worship of the god-

---

62. Ištar *bēlet tāḫāzi u qabli*, "Sovereign of Combat and Battle," is also invoked to perform such an action in the epilogue of the Code of Hammurabi of Babylon and in several inscriptions from the reign of the Middle Assyrian king Tukulti-Ninurta I (ca. 1245–1208); further, she is also invoked in such a manner on a *kudurru* of the Babylonian king Meli-šipak (ca. 1186–1172).

dess involved extreme asceticism and mortification of the flesh with weeping and other ecstatic practices. In reality, very little is known about the practices of the cults, royal and otherwise, of any of the Mesopotamian deities. Furthermore, it is likely that, since there seem to have been a great variety of manifestations of Ištar, these different manifestations likely had differing attributes and therefore diverse cults. Certainly the cuneiform documentation suggests this.

With this said, we do know that at least some aspects of *a* cult of Ištar did have a cast of colorful characters, though the actual rituals involving these individuals can be very opaque indeed. Much of our information concerning possible ritual activities comes to us from literary texts created during the Old Babylonian period, from ritual texts dating to the Neo-Assyrian period, and from canonical lexical lists, which were consulted long after the collected terms were fully understood. Rather than participating in ecstatic rituals meant to channel Ištar for revelatory ends, *assinnū*, as members of her cultic retinue, took part in martial festivals meant to celebrate the goddess's love of and enthusiasm for battle. The Sumerian tales that record that *assinnū* were granted heroism complement this. The most typical activity for the *assinnu* in the cult of Ištar seems to be a kind of war game or dance; however, nothing about this dance suggests either a transcendental state or any type of ecstasy. Rather, it would seem to be a sort of martial celebration.

Similar to dreaming (not the actual art of divining the meaning of the dream), no intellectual training was necessary to be/become a prophet; thus, as the prophecies that come down to us demonstrate, anyone, male or female, feminine or masculine, could act as a prophet. That *assinnū* are connected to prophecy is a result of their connection to Ištar, specifically to the Ištar of war, Annunītum. This connection, however, relies on their martial natures and not on their sexualities nor on their occasional ability to prophesy.

The Role of the Female Seer/Prophet in Ancient Greece

Anselm C. Hagedorn

Introduction

In this essay I survey (some of) the evidence depicting female seers/prophets in ancient Greece using mostly literary sources. As such I offer some comparative evidence to the well-known biblical material as well as asserting the importance of female mantic personnel in antiquity.

Before we begin our investigation into the role of female seers or prophets in the ancient Greek world, we need to start with some definitions of what a prophet or a seer is.[1] Since they are often confused, I have to state at the outset that a prophet/seer has to be distinguished from a priest, though there might be some overlap as both the priest and the prophet/seer can be seen as mediators between humans and gods.[2] "In contrast to the priest,

---

1. See the discussion of the terminology in Michael Attyah Flower, *The Seer in Ancient Greece* (Joan Palevsky Imprint in Classical Literature; Berkeley: University of California Press, 2008), 22–30; and the observations in Jörg Rüpke, "Controllers and Professionals: Analyzing Religious Specialists," *Numen* 43 (1996): 241–62. The following presentation owes a lot to Flower's careful presentation of the material. For a first comparison with the biblical prophets see Armin Lange, "Greek Seers and Israelite-Jewish Prophets," *VT* 57 (2007): 461–82; Anselm C. Hagedorn, "Looking at Foreigners in Biblical and Greek Prophecy," *VT* 57 (2007): 432–48; and the comparative material amassed in Martti Nissinen, "Prophetic Madness: Prophecy and Ecstasy in the Ancient Near East and in Greece," in *Raising Up a Faithful Exegete: Essays in Honor of Richard D. Nelson* (ed. K. L. Noll and Brooks Schramm; Winona Lake, Ind.: Eisenbrauns, 2010), 3–29.

2. This function of the Greek priests has been observed by Christiane Sourvinou-Inwood, "What Is Polis Religion?" in *Oxford Readings in Greek Religion* (ed. Richard G. A. Buxton; Oxford: Oxford University Press, 2000), 38–42; contrast Rüpke, "Con-

whose prestige derived from the renown of the cult he administered, the seer owed his prestige to the success and reliability of his prophecies."[3] This stress on the reliability of the seer's prophecies reminds the biblical scholar of the Deuteronomistic criteria for distinguishing true from false prophecy,[4] a feature that seems to have influenced even the formation of the canon, as—for example—the placement of the book of Jonah in the Masoretic text indicates.[5]

Additionally we need to note that seers in the Greek world were neither appointed nor elected, and they generally did not inherit their position, though we will see in a moment that the gift of prophecy could run in a family. Generally speaking, anyone could become a seer but not everyone was good at the art of augury. The priests derived their prestige from the renown of the cult in which they served. In contrast, the source of the

---

trollers and Professionals," 245, who claims that "mediation is a central feature of the Christian concept of [a] priest"; we have to concede, however, that Greek mantic/prophetic activity appears to be a one-way street as the seer simply mediates the divine utterance to a human recipient.

3. Edward Monroe Harris, *Aeschines and Athenian Politics* (New York: Oxford University Press, 1995), 27.

4. On, e.g., Deut 18:9–20 and the role of the law in the formation of Deuteronomy, see Matthias Köckert, "Zum literargeschichtlichen Ort des Prophetengesetzes Dtn 18 zwischen dem Jeremiabuch und Dtn 13," in *Liebe und Gebot: Studien zum Deuteronomium: Festschrift zum 70. Geburtstag von Lothar Perlitt* (ed. Reinhard G. Kratz and Hermann Spieckermann; FRLANT 190; Göttingen: Vandenhoeck & Ruprecht, 2000), 80–100.

5. Jonah is generally thought to be one of the latest additions to the Book of the Twelve, and the manuscript evidence from 4Q76 (XII[a]) seems to support this, with Jonah coming at the end of the scroll. In the Masoretic text, however, Jonah is placed *before* Nahum. The reason for this placement is the final destruction of Nineveh announced in Nahum that was later seen as being fulfilled. Thus the existence of Nineveh at a later date—though only as a cipher for a metropolis—was not possible if one were to adhere to the criteria set out in Deut 18. The Targum explains the relationship between Nahum and Jonah as follows: "The oracle of the cup of malediction to be given to Nineveh to drink. Previously Jonah the son of Amittai, the prophet from Gath-hepher, prophesied against her and she repented of her sins; and when she sinned again there prophesied once more against her Nahum of Beth Koshi, as is recorded in this book" (ET: Kevin J. Cathcart and Robert P. Gordon, *The Targum of the Minor Prophets* [Aramaic Bible 14; Wilmington, Del.: Glazier, 1989], 131); for further discussion with additional bibliography see Anselm C. Hagedorn, *Die Anderen im Spiegel: Israels Auseinandersetzung mit den Völkern in den Büchern Nahum, Zefanja, Obdaja und Joel* (BZAW 414; Berlin: de Gruyter, 2011), 42–43.

seers' prestige was the accuracy of their predictions as well as the reliability of their prophecies.[6] Naturally the best seers were in high demand, and we know of several figures such as Sthorys,[7] Lampon, and Canon who were highly regarded.[8] It is further clear that the gift of prophecy could not be purchased, as—for example—priesthoods could.[9]

Greek tragedy defines the office of a prophet/seer (μάντις) as follows:

μάντις δ' ὁ δαίμων ὅδε· τὸ γὰρ βακχεύσιμον
καὶ τὸ μανιῶδες μαντικὴν πολλὴν ἔχει·
ὅταν γὰρ ὁ θεὸς ἐς τὸ σῶμ' ἔλθῃ πολύς,
λέγειν τὸ μέλλον τοὺς μεμηνότας ποιεῖ.

The god is also a prophet: for the ecstatic and the manic have mantic powers in large measure. When the god enters someone in force, he causes him in madness to predict the future.[10]

As we would expect in a polytheistic society with male and female gods, we find male and female religious personnel in the Greek world.[11]

---

6. Harris, *Aeschines and Athenian Politics*, 27.

7. See *IG* ii².17; on the problems regarding the figure of Sthorys in the inscription see Michael J. Osborne, "Honours for Sthorys (*IG* ii². 17): *IG* ii². 17+; Wilhelm, Attische Urkunden v 87-96; Meritt, Hesperia xxvi (1957) 51-2," *Annual of the British School at Athens* 65 (1970): 151-74.

8. See *IG* i² 76:47-48 (Eleusis ca. 423 B.C.E.) where we read: [Λ]άμπον εἶπε· τὰ μὲν ἄλλα καθάπερ αἱ χσυγγραφαὶ τε'ς ἀπαρχε'ς το' | καρπο' τοῖν θεοῖν. On Lampon see John Dillery, "Chresmologues and *Manteis*: Independent Diviners and the Problem of Authority," in *Mantikê: Studies in Ancient Divination* (ed. Sarah Iles Johnston and Peter T. Struck; RGRW 155; Leiden: Brill, 2005), 167-231; Lampon is mentioned in Aristophanes, *Birds* 521.988, and mocked for his augury; judging from a reference in Plutarch, *Pericles* 6.2, Lampon may have been associated with the circle around the Athenian politician.

9. See the examples and the discussion provided in Robert Parker and Dirk Obbink, "Aus der Arbeit der Inscriptiones Graecae VI: Sales of Priesthoods on Cos I," *Chiron* 30 (2000): 415-49; and Uta Kron, "Priesthoods, Dedications and Euergetism: What Part Did Religion Play in the Political and Social Status of Greek Women?" in *Religion and Power in the Ancient Greek World: Proceedings of the Uppsala Symposium 1993* (ed. Pontus Hellström and Brita Alroth; Acta Universitatis Upsaliensis: Boreas 24; Uppsala: Ubsaliensis S. Academiae, 1996), 140-55.

10. Euripides, *Bacchae* 298-301; ET: David Kovacs, *Euripides VI: Bacchae, Iphigenia at Aulis, Rhesus* (LCL; Cambridge: Harvard University Press, 2002), 37.

11. We will ignore questions of gender and gendering religious activity in this

As far as female priests are concerned, we have to note that they were not simply the female equivalent of male priests nor did they serve specifically the needs of the female population.[12] True, female priests tended to serve female deities, while male priests served male gods, but this does not allow for any conclusion regarding the gender of the worshippers. This distinction is also not always strictly maintained, since the two famous oracle shrines of male gods in the Greek world—Delphi and Dodona— had female priests.

It is precisely because of the role of the cultic personnel at the shrines of Apollo and Zeus that there emerges some confusion regarding the role of female seers/prophets. If we are guided by the evidence provided by the oracles, one is tempted to see all female seers as "passive agents of mediumistic possession."[13] To avoid such misconceptions and to stress the active role of female seers, we will look at other female figures who can be described as prophetesses and set aside the role of the Pythia at Delphi.[14]

First, we have to note that the role of female prophets is often regarded with deep suspicion by their male counterparts. In a fragmentary play by Euripides, the main character, Melanippe, deems it necessary to state the importance of women within the religion of Greece. Naturally she appeals to the special status of the women in Delphi and Dodona.

τὰ δ' ἐν θεοῖς αὖ· πρῶτα γὰρ κρινω
μέρος μέγιστον ἔχομεν. ἐν Φοίβου τε γὰρ
δόμοις προφητεύουσι Λοξίου φρένας

---

contribution and refer the reader to other articles addressing these issues in the current volume; see also the remarks in Joan Breton Connelly, *Portrait of a Priestess: Women and Ritual in Ancient Greece* (Princeton: Princeton University Press, 2007), 21–24; Janett Morgan, "Religion, Women, and the Home," in *A Companion to Greek Religion* (ed. Daniel Ogden; Blackwell Companions to the Ancient World: Literature and Culture; Oxford: Blackwell, 2007), 297–310; Froma I. Zeitlin, "Cultic Models of the Female: Rites of Dionysos and Demeter," *Arethusa* 15 (1982): 129–57.

12. On female priests see Matthew Dillon, *Girls and Women in Classical Greek Religion* (London: Routledge, 2002), 73–106; and Connelly, *Portrait of a Priestess*.

13. Flower, *Seer in Ancient Greece*, 211.

14. On the role and function of the Pythia see Flower, *Seer in Ancient Greece*, 215, 239; Robert Parker, "Greek States and Greek Oracles," in Buxton, *Oxford Readings in Greek Religion*, 76–108; Nissinen, "Prophetic Madness," 17–27, with comparative material from the ancient Near East. See also the contribution by Nissinen to this volume.

γυναῖκες, ἀμφὶ δ' ἁγνὰ Δωδώνης βάθρα
φηγῷ παρ' ἱερᾷ θῆλυ τὰς Διὸς φρένας
γένος πορεύει τοῖς θέλουσιν Ἑλλάδος.
ἃ δ' εἴς τε Μοίρας τάς τ' ἀνωνύμους θεὰς
ἱερὰ τελεῖται, ταῦτ' ἐν ἀνδράσιν μὲν οὐ
ὅσια καθέστηκ', ἐν γυναιξὶ δ' αὔξεται.

And in matters concerning the gods, for I consider these matters to be the most important, we women have the greatest share. For in the temple of Phoibos women prophesy the thoughts of Loxias, and around Dodona's holy foundation by the sacred oak it is the female sex which conveys the thoughts of Zeus to any Greek who seeks them. Also as to those rituals, which are performed for the Fates and the nameless goddesses, it is not holy for men to participate in them: all of them flourish in the hands of women. This is how the case for women stands in the dealings with the gods.[15]

In the verses just before, Melanippe also mentions the role of women in the running of a household, arguing that a household could neither prosper nor be clean without the hands of a woman.[16] What is stated here is that women can rightfully and honorably occupy both the private and the public sphere, and that prophetic or cultic involvement of women is an orderly and respectable process, not a frenzied affair as, for example, portrayed in the *Bacchae* of Euripides.[17]

The critical stance against female prophetic activity is a constant, however. Even in the second century C.E. Aelius Aristides is highly judgmental of female oracular utterances, and he accuses the Pythia in Delphi of not being able to know or to remember what she has prophesied.

ἃ δ' ἂν αἱ Πυθοῖ προμάντεις φῶσιν, ἐπειδὰν ἐκτῶσιν ἑαυτῶν, ταῦθ' ὡς ὁ Πύθιος εἶπε καὶ Πλάτων καὶ ἅπαντες λέγουσιν. καὶ τίνα ἐπίστανται δήπου τέχνην τότε, αἵ γε οὐχ οἷαί τέ εἰσι φυλάττειν οὐδὲ μεμνῆσθαι;

---

15. Euripides, *Melanippe Desmotis* fr. 494 (Nauck); ET: Dillon, *Girls and Women*, 1.
16. νέμουσι δ' οἴκους καὶ τὰ ναυστολούμενα | ἔσω δόμων σῴζουσιν, οὐδ' ἐρημίᾳ | γυναικὸς οἶκος εὐπινὴς οὐδ' ὄλβιος (Euripides, *Melanippe Desmotis* fr. 494.9–11 [Nauck]).
17. See Euripides, *Bacchae*, 32–36: τοιγάρ νιν αὐτὸς ἐκ δόμων ᾤστρησ' ἐγὼ | μανίαις, ὄρος δ' οἰκοῦσι παράκοποι φρενῶν· | σκευήν τ' ἔχειν ἠνάγκασ' ὀργίων ἐμῶν. | καὶ πᾶν τὸ θῆλυ σπέρμα Καδμείων, ὅσαι | γυναῖκες ἦσαν, ἐξέμηνα δωμάτων.

But as to the pronouncements of the priestesses at Pytho, when they are ecstatic, both Plato and all men declare that the Pythian has said these things. What art do these priestesses know, who are incapable of preserving and memorizing their predictions?[18]

Again, the criticism is leveled against official prophetic activity and not against accidental, or better, nonregulated, female prophecies, which—in general—seem to be regarded as more authentic as they cannot be influenced.[19] In the following we will look at precisely such activity and consider the role of three famous female seers from Greek literature: Cassandra, Manto, and the Sibyl.

1. Cassandra

In the *Iliad*, Cassandra is one of the three daughters of King Priam mentioned by name. Here her stunning beauty is noted even though the expression (εἶδος ἀρίστην) seems to be a set formula, since her sister Laodike is twice described in the same way:[20]

> πέφνε γὰρ Ὀθρυονῆα Καβησόθεν ἔνδον ἐόντα,
> ὅς ῥα νέον πολέμοιο μετὰ κλέος εἰληλούθει,
> ᾔτεε δὲ Πριάμοιο θυγατρῶν εἶδος ἀρίστην
> Κασσάνδρην ἀνάεδνον, ὑπέσχετο δὲ μέγα ἔργον,
> ἐκ Τροίης ἀέκοντας ἀπωσέμεν υἷας Ἀχαιῶν.

> For he [i.e., Idomeneus] slew Othryoneus of Cabesus, a sojourner in Troy, that was but newly come following the rumour of war; and he asked in marriage the comeliest of the daughters of Priam, even Cassandra; he brought no gifts of wooing, but promised a

---

18. Aristides, *In Defence of Oratory* 34–35; ET: Charles Allison Behr, *Panathenaic Oration and In Defence of Oratory* (vol. 1 of *Aristides in Four Volumes* [only vol. 1 published]; LCL; Cambridge: Harvard University Press, 1973), 301.

19. The problem of influencing oracular utterances has been discussed in connection to the role (and terminology) of the chresmologues and the *manteis* in ancient Athens; see, e.g., Hugh Bowden, "Oracles for Sale," in *Herodotus and His World: Essays from a Conference in Memory of George Forrest* (ed. Peter Derow and Robert Parker; Oxford: Oxford University Press, 2003), 256–74; and Dillery, "Chresmologues and *Manteis*."

20. Homer, *Il.* 3.124; 6.252.

mighty deed, that he would drive forth perforce out of Troy-land the sons of Achaeans. To him the old man Priam promised that he would give her, and bowed his head thereto, and Othryoneus fought, trusting in his promise.[21]

The superlative used to describe her beauty is intensified in *Il.* 24.699, when she is called a peer of Aphrodite (ἰκέλη χρυσέη Ἀφροδίτη):

οὐδέ τις ἄλλος ἔγνω πρόσθ' ἀνδρῶν καλλιζώνων τε γυναικῶν, ἀλλ' ἄρα Κασσάνδρη, ἰκέλη χρυσέη Ἀφροδίτη, Πέργαμον εἰσαναβᾶσα φίλον πατέρ' εἰσενόησεν ἑσταότ' ἐν δίφρῳ, κήρυκά τε ἀστυβοώτην·

Neither was any other ware of them, whether man or fair-girdled woman; but in truth Cassandra, peer of golden Aphrodite, having gone up upon Pergamus, marked her dear father as he stood in the car, and the herald, the city's crier; and she had sight of that other lying on the bier in the waggon drawn of the mules.[22]

We find the same expression once again in the *Iliad* (19.282) used in connection with Briseis, who has already suffered the fate Cassandra will suffer after the fall of Troy. The connection with Aphrodite stresses a certain erotic attractiveness, making her the quintessential adolescent beauty—a feature that will be used in later tradition.

Since Laodike and Medikaste, the other two daughters of Priam, are said to be married,[23] it is probably safe to argue that Cassandra was not married and thus still a virgin.[24] This finds support in the above quoted episode where Othryoneus asks for Cassandra in marriage without offering a (material) bride-price but instead promises to deliver Troy from the Achaeans. This plan fails, however, when Idomeneus kills him in battle. Cassandra remains unmarried.

---

21. *Il.* 13.363–368; ET: Augustus Taber Murray, *Homer: The Iliad* (2 vols.; LCL; London: Heinemann, 1925), 2:29, 31.

22. *Il.* 24.697–701; ET: Murray, 615.

23. *Il.* 3.121; 13.173.

24. See also Alcaeus, fr. 298.20 (Voigt) and Ibycus, fr. 303 (a), who transfers two attributes of virginal Athena to Cassandra: γλαυκώπιδα Κασσάνδραν | ἐρασιπλόκαμον Πριάμοιο κόραν | φᾶμις ἔχῃσι βροτῶν.

Nothing in the *Iliad* points to Cassandra's career as a seer, so well known from later tragedy. However, two indications enable us to see an *Anknüpfungspunkt* for the later literary development. First, Apollo notices her virginity and beauty. Second, in *Il.* 24.697–706 it is stated that she was the first person to "recognize" (εἰσενόησεν) her father Priam returning with the corpse of Hector and she subsequently announced this to the Trojans. It can be debated whether Homer wanted to allude to her as a seer, but the scenic setting as well as a remark of the scholiast to *Il.* 24.699 make this unlikely. Following the proposal by the scholiast, I would argue that the scene is created by Homer to emphasize the close relationship between Cassandra and her brother Hector and that Homer does not know of her as being a seer: διὰ τὴν συμπάθειαν ὡς Νέστωρ ‹οὐ› διὰ τὴν μαντείαν· οὐ γὰρ οἶδεν αὐτὴν μάντιν ὁ ποιητής.[25]

How Cassandra got transformed into a seer we do not know. Pindar, however, is the first one to call her explicitly so (μάντις): μάντιν τ' ὄλεσσε κόραν, "and he caused the destruction of the prophetic maiden."[26]

In a different place, he seems to report a prediction of Cassandra, when he describes her as δαιμόνιον κέαρ (i.e., a "divinely inspired heart") and states that Troy will suffer.[27] The use of the term σάμαινεν ("she alluded") for Cassandra's speech seems to refer to her later characteristic of speech and predictions that are difficult to understand.

Two traditions are known to us, explaining how Cassandra received her gift of prophecy. The more unusual one is reported by the Hellenistic historian Anticlides of Athens.[28] Here, after a festival, Cassandra and her twin brother Helenos are left in the sanctuary of Apollo. When they are discovered the next morning, two snakes are cleansing the ears of the chil-

---

25. Σ BT ad 24.699. Greek text according to Hartmut Erbse, *Scholia Graeca in Homeri Iliadem* (Berlin: de Gruyter, 1977), vol. 5.

26. Pindar, *Pyth.* 11.33. ET: John Sandys, *The Odes of Pindar including the Principal Fragments* (LCL; London: Heinemann, 1928), 275.

27. Pindar, *Paean* 8a (fr. 52i [A] M).

28. Anticlides, *FGH* 140, fr. 17: μυθεύεται τῶν ἐξ Ἑκάβης γεγνόντων Πριάμωι παίδων τὸν Ἕλενον καὶ τὴν Κασάνδραν διδύμους γεγενῆσθαι· τῶν δὲ γενεθλίων αὐτοῖς συντελουμένων ἐν τῶι τοῦ Θυμβραίου Ἀπόλλωνος ἱερῶι λέγεται τὸν Ἕλενον καὶ τὴν Κασάνδραν ἐν τῶι ναῶι παίζοντας κατακοιμηθῆναι, ὑπὸ δὲ μέθης ἐκείνων ἐκλαθομένων περὶ τῶν παίδων οἴκαδε χωρισθῆναι· τῆι δ' ὑστεραίαι ἐλόντας εἰς τὸ ἱερὸν θεάσασθαι τοὺς παῖδας ταῖς τῶν ὄφεων γλώτταις τοὺς πόρους τῶν αἰσθητηρίων καθαιρομένους. ὡς οὖν διὰ τὸ παράδοξον αἱ γυναῖκες ἀνέκραγον, συνέβη ἀπαλλαγῆναι τοὺς ὄφεις καὶ καταδῦναι ἐν ταῖς παρακειμέναις δάφναις τοὺς δὲ παῖδας ἀμφοτέρους τῆς μαντικῆς οὕτω μεταλαβεῖν.

dren with their tongues without hurting them. By this process the children receive the gift of prophecy. The same is reported about the seer Melampos receiving his prophetic gift; thus we might again have a literary topos here.[29]

How Anticlides learned of this story cannot be determined. We need to note, however, the connection to Apollo since this provides the link to the far better known story regarding Cassandra's prophetic gift.

Probably the most complex portrait of Cassandra can be found in Aeschylus's tragedy *Agamemnon*. Here she has become a full-fledged seer, and it is indeed her gift of prophecy that will guide her character. She is closely connected to Apollo, and her fate as a whole is determined by the actions of the god. This trait is most clearly expressed in the fact that the first intelligible word she utters is the name of the god.[30] How she received her gift of prophecy is described in a dialogue between the chorus (CH) and Cassandra (K):

K: μάντις μ' Ἀπόλλων τῷδ' ἐπέστησεν τέλει.
Ch: μῶν καὶ θεός περ ἱμέρῳ πεπληγμένος;
K: προτοῦ μὲν αἰδὼς ἦν ἐμοὶ λέγειν τάδε.
Ch: ἁβρύνεται γὰρ πᾶς τις εὖ πράσσων πλέον.
K: ἀλλ' ἦν παλαιστὴς κάρτ' ἐμοὶ πνέων χάριν.
Ch: ἦ καὶ τέκνων εἰς ἔργον ἤλθετον νόμῳ;
K: ξυναινέσασα Λοξίαν ἐψευσάμην.
Ch: ἤδη τέχναισιν ἐνθέοις ᾑρημένη;
K: ἤδη πολίταις πάντ' ἐθέσπιζον πάθη.
Ch: πῶς δῆτ' ἄνατος ἦσθα Λοξίου κότῳ;
K: ἔπειθον οὐδέν' οὐδέν, ὡς τάδ' ἤμπλακον.
Ch: ἡμῖν γε μὲν δὴ πιστὰ θεσπίζειν δοκεῖς.

K: The seer Apollo appointed me to this office.
Ch: Can it be that he, a god, was smitten with desire?
K: Before now I was ashamed to speak of this.
Ch: In prosperity all take on airs.
K: Oh, but he struggled to win me, breathing ardent love for me.

---

29. See Pliny, *Nat.* 10.137: "qui credat ista, et Melampodi profecto auguri aures lambendo dedisse intellectum avium sermones dracones non abnuat."

30. Aeschylus, *Ag.* 1073. Her importance is further stressed by the fact that she enters the stage with Agamemnon in 810 but is only acknowledged in 950ff. and starts to utter sounds in 1072.

Ch: Did you in due course come to the rite of marriage?
K: I consented to Loxias but broke my word.
Ch: Were you already possessed by the art inspired of the god?
K: Already I prophesied to my countrymen all their disasters.
Ch: How came it then that you were unharmed by Loxias' wrath?
K: Ever since that fault I could persuade no one of anything.
Ch: And yet to us at least the prophecies you utter seem true enough.[31]

Again, the gift of prophecy is connected with Apollo. Here in Aeschylus the god seemed to have struck a deal with Cassandra: he will give her the gift of prophecy in return for sexual favors. Apollo is said to be smitten with desire (περ ἱμέρῳ πεπληγμένος) and to breathe ardent love (ἦν παλαιστὴς κάρτ' ἐμοὶ πνέων χάριν). Cassandra, however, refused the god, after she had received the gift of prophecy. It seems that Apollo was unable to withdraw her ability to be a seer and thus he modifies it. From now on nobody will believe her prophecies (ἔπειθον οὐδέν' οὐδέν', ὡς τάδ' ἤμπλακον).[32] In this way it can be explained how Troy could have fallen, even though Cassandra announced its destruction. Being a seer is the central motif of Cassandra and this further emphasized by the plethora of words connected to the semantic field of prophecy used to describe her.[33] Additionally we learn from the Aeschylean figure that a female seer wore a special garment that allows others to recognize her, as well as setting her apart from ordinary people:[34]

τί δῆτ' ἐμαυτῆς καταγέλωτ' ἔχω τάδε
καὶ σκῆπτρα καὶ μαντεῖα περὶ δέρῃ στέφη;
σὲ μὲν πρὸ μοίρας τῆς ἐμῆς διαφθερῶ.
ἴτ' ἐς φθόρον· πεσόντα γ' ὧδ' ἀμείβομαι.
ἄλλην τιν' ἄτης ἀντ' ἐμοῦ πλουτίζετε.
ἰδοὺ δ', Ἀπόλλων αὐτὸς οὐκδύων ἐμὲ
χρηστηρίαν ἐσθῆτ', ἐποπτεύσας δέ με

---

31. Aeschylus, *Ag.* 1202-1214.
32. Aeschylus, *Ag.* 1212.
33. See the following list of terms used to characterize Cassandra in *Agamemnon*: τὸ θεῖον (1084), κλέος μαντικόν (1098), προφῆτις (1099), φρενομανής (1140), θεσπιῳδεῖν (1161), ψευδόμαντις (1195), τέχνησιν ἐνθέοις ᾑρημένη (1209), θεσπίζειν (1210, 1213), ὀρθομαντεία, (1215), ἀληθόμαντις (1241), μάντις (1275), πολλὰ σοφή (1295).
34. See Flower, *Seer in Ancient Greece*, 214.

κἀν τοῖσδε κόσμοις καταγελωμένην μέγα
φίλων ὑπ' ἐχθρῶν οὐ διχορρόπως, μάτην—
ἀλωμένη δὲ φοιτὰς ὡς ἀγύρτρια
πτωχὸς τάλαινα λιμοθνὴς ἠνεσχόμην—
καὶ νῦν ὁ μάντις μάντιν ἐκπράξας ἐμὲ
ἀπήγαγ' ἐς τοιάσδε θανασίμους τύχας.

Why, then, have I got this gear on to mock me, and this staff, and the prophetic bands about my neck? I'll destroy *you* before meeting my one fate! [*She breaks her staff and throws the pieces to the ground.*] Go to perdition [*throwing off her neck-bands*]—now you're on the ground this is how I get my own back on you [*trampling on them*]! Make some other woman rich with ruin, instead of me! [*As she tears off her robe*] Look, it is Apollo himself who is stripping me of my prophetic garb. He looked on when I, wearing all these accoutrements, was being roundly and unanimously mocked by friends who acted like enemies <while I prophesied the truth> in vain, <and he did nothing to help me>; I endured having to wander like an itinerant begging priestess, a wretched starving pauper. And now, the Seer, has collected his debt from me, the seer, by hauling me off to this deadly fate.[35]

The literary function of Cassandra in Aeschylus's tragedy can be described as being the link that connects past, present, and future enabling the poet to explore cause and effect.[36]

In Euripides' *Trojan Women* the picture of Cassandra changes slightly, though the main focus on Cassandra as the female seer par excellence remains.[37] Again, she is one of the main protagonists but with significant modifications. Her special role is already emphasized in the prologue when she alone from all children of Hecuba is given a detailed description.

φροῦδος δὲ Πρίαμος καὶ τέκν'· ἣν δὲ παρθένον

---

35. Aeschylus, *Agamemnon* 1264–1276. ET Alan H. Sommerstein, *Aeschylus: Oresteia* (LCL; Cambridge: Harvard University Press, 2008), 153, 155.

36. Dagmar Neblung, *Die Gestalt der Kassandra in der antiken Literatur* (Beiträge zur Altertumskunde 97; Leipzig: Teubner, 1997), 34.

37. See the statement in Euripides, *Hecuba* 676–677: οἴ 'γὼ τάλαινα· μῶν τὸ βακχεῖον κάρα | τῆς θεσπιῳδοῦ δεῦρο Κασσάνδρας φέρεις;

μεθῆκ' Ἀπόλλων δρομάδα Κασάνδραν ἄναξ,
τὸ τοῦ θεοῦ τε παραλιπὼν τό τ' εὐσεβὲς
γαμεῖ βιαίως σκότιον Ἀγαμέμνων λέχος.

Priam is gone, and her children too; Cassandra, whom the lord Apollo left to be a virgin, frenzied maid, has been forced by Agamemnon, in contempt of the god's ordinance and of piety, to a dishonoured wedlock.[38]

Euripides states that Apollo left her virginity untouched—an interesting variant to her refusal of the god in Aeschylus—and that she received the gift of prophecy from him.[39] Her relationship with Agamemnon, which does not seem to be a problem in Aeschylus, is here seen as an unholy act, defiling the property of a god (τὸ τοῦ θεοῦ τε παραλιπὼν τό τ' εὐσεβές). In similar terms her rape at the hands of Ajax is regarded as an act against Athena herself:[40]

Athena: οὐκ οἶσθ' ὑβρισθεῖσάν με καὶ ναοὺς ἐμούς;
Poseidon: οἶδ', ἡνίκ' Αἴας εἷλκε Κασσάνδραν βίᾳ.

Athena: Do you not know the insult done to me and to the shrine I love?
Poseidon: I do: when Ajax dragged away Cassandra by force.[41]

We can probably deduce from these statements that any form of violence against a seer is regarded as a sacrilege.

---

38. Euripides, *Trojan Women* 41–44; cf. ET of David Kovacs, *Euripides IV: Trojan Women; Iphigenia among the Taurians; Ion* (LCL; Cambridge: Harvard University Press, 1999), 17, 19.

39. In Euripides, *Trojan Women* 253, Hecuba states that Cassandra is the virgin of Apollo (τὰν τοῦ Φοίβου παρθένον) who belongs to him.

40. Apollodorus (*Epitome* 5.22) reports that because Ajax had raped Cassandra while she clung to the wooden statue of Athena, thus defiling the sacred law of asylum, the statue therefore looks up to heaven: διὰ ‹τοῦ›το τὸ ξόανον εἰς οὐρανὸν βλέπειν. Claude Calame (*Choruses of Young Women in Ancient Greece: Their Morphology, Religious Role, and Social Function* [Greek Studies; Lanham, Md.: Rowman & Littlefield, 1997], 145) sees in the rape of Cassandra the first stage of a female initiation rite; he argues that the place where the rape took place, i.e., the sanctuary of Athena, which is generally associated with (female) initiation, supports this conclusion.

41. Euripides, *Trojan Women* 69–70; cf. ET of Kovacs, *Euripides IV*, 21.

In the literary figure of Cassandra we are able to trace the transformation of the most beautiful daughter of King Priam of Troy who remains unmarried into a seer/prophetess. The exact reason for such a transformation is difficult to determine, but sexuality may have played a prominent role here. Her beauty led to the attempted rape by Ajax when she sought refuge in the sanctuary of Athena:[42]

Αἴας δὲ λ]ύσσαν ἦλθ᾽ ὀλόαν ἔχων
ἐς ναῦο]ν ἄγνας Πάλλαδος, ἂ θέων
θνάτοι]σι θεοσύλαισι πάντων
αἰνο]τάτα μακάρων πέφυκε·
χέρρεσ]σι δ᾽ ἄμφοιν παρθενίκαν ἔλων
σέμνωι] παρωστάκοισαν ἀγάλματι
ὕβρισσ᾽] ὁ Λ[ό]κρος, οὐδ᾽ ἔδεισε
παῖδα Δ]ίος πολέμω δότε[ρ]ραν.

And Ajax came in the grip of ruinous madness
into the temple of chaste Pallas, who
to sacrilegious mortals is by nature
most terrible of all the blessed gods;
and laying hold of the maiden with both hands
as she stood beside the holy statue,
he outraged her, that man from Lokros, and felt no fear
of Zeus's daughter, giver of war.[43]

Whether this scene can be regarded as the origin of the (later) tradition that any violence against a seer is a sacrilege is difficult to determine as the fragment from Alcaeus sees Ajax's act of sexual violence as an act against the goddess Athena. Beauty and violence reoccur when Apollo seeks to exchange the gift of prophecy for sexual favors. Cassandra's refusal of the god seals her fate but also asserts certain independence. She is now pictured as speaking of her own accord and not simple as a medium for

---

42. On the prominence of this scene in Greek art see Joan Breton Connelly, "Narrative and Image in Attic Vase Painting: Ajax and Cassandra at the Trojan Palladion," in *Narrative and Event in Ancient Art* (ed. Peter Holiday; Cambridge Studies in New Art History and Criticism; Cambridge: Cambridge University Press, 1993), 88–129.

43. Alcaeus, fr. S262 (Page). ET: Andrew M. Miller, *Greek Lyric: An Anthology in Translation* (Indianapolis: Hackett, 1996), 46.

Apollo. This independence, however, comes at a price as her prophecies are now regarded as false ecstasy and in turn generally ignored.

2. Manto

With the figure of Manto—the daughter of Teiresias—we remain in the literary sphere, though her character is quite different from Cassandra and Manto is also connected to an actual Greek sanctuary.[44] Cassandra was a unique figure who did not have a prophetic pedigree, being the only one from a royal family who became a seer. In contrast, Manto, the daughter of the blind seer Teiresias, is a good example that divination can be a trade that runs in the family.[45]

Teiresias is maybe the exemplary male seer in the Greek world. He was blinded by either Athena or Hera and in compensation given the gift of prophecy.[46] The special status of Teiresias is further highlighted by fact that he is only the soul in Hades who is endowed with intelligence:

---

44. Pausanias (3.19.6), however, mentions a sanctuary of Cassandra in Amyclae (καὶ ἀπ' ἐκείνου κώμη διαμένουσα θέας παρείχετο ἄξιον ἱερὸν 'Αλεξάνδρας καὶ ἄγαλμα· τὴν δὲ 'Αλεξάνδραν οἱ 'Αμυκλαιεῖς Κασσάνδραν τὴν Πριάμου φασὶν εἶναι) but does not state whether the cult is connected to mantic activity. Only in Plutarch, *Ag. Cleom.* 9.2, is Cassandra (now identified with Pasiphae) connected to an oracular shrine of Thalamai: ἱερὸν δὲ Πασιφάας καὶ μαντεῖον ἦν ἐν Θαλάμαις τιμώμενον, ἥν τινες μὲν ἱστοροῦσι τῶν 'Ατλαντίδων μίαν οὖσαν [τῶν] ἐκ Διὸς τὸν Ἄμμωνα τεκεῖν, τινὲς δὲ Κασάνδραν τὴν Πριάμου, τελευτήσασαν ἐνταῦθα καὶ διὰ τὸ πᾶσι φαίνειν τὰ μαντεῖα Πασιφάαν προσαγορευθεῖσαν. If Cassandra is seen as an independent seer/mantic, it is hardly surprising that we do not find many oracular shrines associated with her name, as oracular activity is intrinsically linked to Apollo in the Greek world.

45. Michael Attyah Flower, "The Iamidae: A Mantic Family and Its Public Image," in *Practitioners of the Divine: Greek Priests and Religious Officials from Homer to Heliodorus* (ed. Beate Dignas and Kai Trampedach; HellSt 30; Washington, D.C.: Center for Hellenic Studies, 2008), 187–206; A. Schachter, "The Seer Tisamenos and the Klytiadai," *CQ* 50 (2000): 292–95; Harris, *Aeschines and Athenian Politics*, 27.

46. On the figure of Teiresias, see Gherardo Ugolini, *Untersuchungen zur Figur des Tiresias* (Classica Monacensia 12; Tübingen: Narr, 1995); and Luc Brisson, *Le mythe de Tirésias: Essai d'analyse structurale* (Études préliminaires aux religions orientales dans l'empire Romain 55; Leiden: Brill, 1976). Two stories of how Teiresias became blind were in circulation in Antiquity: Ps.-Hesiod, fr. 275 W-M (cf. Ovid, *Met.* 3.316–350) states that Teiresias argues—after a double sex-change—that women enjoy sex more than men; this incenses Hera and she blinds him. As compensation Zeus gives him the gift of prophecy as well as a life-span of seven generations from Kadmos to the grandchildren of Oedipus (Ps.-Hesiod, fr. 276 W-M). Pherecydes of Athens (*FGH* 3,

ἀλλ' ἄλλην χρὴ πρῶτον ὁδὸν τελέσαι καὶ ἱκέσθαι
εἰς Ἀίδαο δόμους καὶ ἐπαινῆς Περσεφονείης,
ψυχῇ χρησομένους Θηβαίου Τειρεσίαο,
μάντηος ἀλαοῦ, τοῦ τε φρένες ἔμπεδοί εἰσι·
τῷ καὶ τεθνηῶτι νόον πόρε Περσεφόνεια
οἴῳ πεπνῦσθαι, τοὶ δὲ σκιαὶ ἀίσσουσιν.

but you must first complete another journey, and come to the house of Hades and dread Persephone, to seek prophecy from the ghost of Theban Teiresias, the blind seer, whose mind remains steadfast. To him even in death Persephone has granted reason, that he alone should have understanding, but the others flit about as shadows.[47]

In Greek literature Teiresias is connected to the city of Thebes and its rulers.

The close connection between Manto and her father is further stressed by the fact that Euripides reports that she guided her blind father.[48] This allows for some speculation that she learned her craft from him. According to Diodorus Siculus—who calls her Daphne instead of Manto—her gift of prophecy equaled her father's. In addition to her father, who only gave oral prophecies, she was able to write oracular responses and perfected that gift over the years, although this may already be a statement influenced by the practice of writing down oracles given at oracular shrines.

αὕτη δὲ τὴν μαντικὴν οὐχ ἧττον τοῦ πατρὸς εἰδυῖα, πολὺ μᾶλλον ἐν τοῖς Δελφοῖς διατρίψασα τὴν τέχνην ἐπηύξησε· φύσει δὲ θαυμαστῇ κεχορηγημένη χρησμοὺς ἔγραψε παντοδαπούς, διαφόρους ταῖς κατασκευαῖς·

---

fr. 92) reports that he saw Athena naked in the bath and that she in turn blinded him as well as made him a seer.

47. Homer, *Od.* 10.490–495; ET: Augustus Taber Murray and George E. Dimock, *Homer: The Odyssey* (2 vols.; 2nd ed.; LCL; London: Heinemann, 1995), 1:393, 395.

48. See Euripides, *Phoenissae* 834–835: ἡγοῦ πάροιθε, θύγατερ· ὡς τυφλῷ ποδὶ | ὀφθαλμὸς εἶ σύ, ναυβάταισιν ἄστρον ὥς; Sophocles, *Ant.* 1087; cf. *Oed. tyr.* 444, which states, however, that it is simply a young boy who acts as Teiresias's guide.

This maiden possessed no less knowledge of prophecy than her father, and in the course of her stay at Delphi she developed her skill to a far greater degree; moreover, by virtue of the employment of a marvellous natural gift, she also wrote oracular responses of every sort, excelling in their composition.[49]

According to Diodorus, Homer plagiarized several verses from her (παρ' ἧς φασι καὶ τὸν ποιητὴν Ὅμηρον πολλὰ τῶν ἐπῶν σφετερισάμενον κοσμῆσαι τὴν ἰδίαν ποίησιν), and Manto/Daphne is transformed into a Sybil, "for to be inspired in one's tongue is expressed by the word *sibyllainein*" (τὸ γὰρ ἐνθεάζειν κατὰ γλῶτταν ὑπάρχειν σιβυλλαίνειν).

Manto is mortal—unlike the first two female seers of Apollo, Themis and Phoebe, who were gods:

Πρῶτον μὲν εὐχῇ τῇδε πρεσβεύω θεῶν
τὴν πρωτόμαντιν Γαῖαν· ἐκ δὲ τῆς Θέμιν,
ἣ δὴ τὸ μητρὸς δευτέρα τόδ' ἕζετο
μαντεῖον, ὡς λόγος τις· ἐν δὲ τῷ τρίτῳ
λάχει, θελούσης, οὐδὲ πρὸς βίαν τινός,
Τιτανὶς ἄλλη παῖς Χθονὸς καθέζετο,
Φοίβη· δίδωσι δ' ἣ γενέθλιον δόσιν
Φοίβῳ· τὸ Φοίβης δ' ὄνομ' ἔχει παρώνυμον.
λιπὼν δὲ λίμνην Δηλίαν τε χοιράδα,
κέλσας ἐπ' ἀκτὰς ναυπόρους τὰς Παλλάδος,
εἰς τήνδε γαῖαν ἦλθε Παρνησσοῦ θ' ἕδρας.

First, in this prayer of mine, I give the place of highest honor among the gods to the first prophet, Earth; and after her to Themis, for she was the second to take this oracular seat of her mother, as legend tells. And in the third allotment, with Themis's consent and not by force, another Titan, child of Earth, Phoebe, took her seat here. She gave it as a birthday gift to Phoebus, who has his name from Phoebe. Leaving the lake and ridge of Delos, he landed on Pallas's ship-frequented shores, and came to this region and the dwelling places on Parnassus.[50]

---

49. Didorus Siculus 4.66.6; ET: Charles Henry Oldfather, *Diodorus of Sicily* (LCL; London: Heinemann, 1939), 3:29–31.

50. Aeschylus, *Eumenides* 1–10.

In the Greek world, her name is intrinsically linked to the oracular shrine at Claros in Asia Minor. It is reported in the *Epigoni* that after the capture of Thebes by the sons of the Seven they send part of their spoils as a tithe to Delphi. Among these were Teiresias, who died en route and was buried at Telephusa, and his daughter Manto. She became a gift to Apollo Pythios. The oracle at Delphi decreed that Manto was supposed to marry the first man she met after leaving the temple. This man is Rhacius son of Lebes from the city of Mycene. The newlywed couple travels to Asia Minor together. At Colophon miserable Manto is overcome by grief because of the fate and destruction of her native city and begins to cry. Using a far-fetched etymology, the place is therefore called Claros from the Greek word κλαίω, "to weep."

οἱ δὲ τὴν Θηβαΐδα γεγραφότες φασὶν ὅτε ὑπὸ τῶν Ἐπιγόνων ἀκροθίνιον ἀνετέθη Μαντὼ ἡ Τειρεσίου θυγάτηρ εἰς Δελφοὺς πεμφθεῖσα· καὶ κατὰ χρησμὸν Ἀπόλλωνος ἐξερχομένη περιέπεσε Ῥακίωι τῶι Λέβητος υἱῶι, Μυκηναίωι τὸ γένος. καὶ γημαμένη αὐτῶι (τοῦτο γὰρ περιεῖχε τὸ λόγιον, γαμεῖσθαι ὧι ἂν συναντήσηι), ἐλθοῦσα εἰς Κολοφῶνα καὶ ἐκεῖ δυσθυμήσασα ἐδάκυρσε διὰ τὴν τῆς πατρίδος πόρθησιν· διόπερ ὠνομάσθη Κλάρος ἀπὸ τῶν δακρύων. ἐποίησεν δὲ Ἀπόλλωνι ἱερόν.

The writers of the *Thebaid* say that Teiresias' daughter Manto was sent to Delphi by the Epigoni and dedicated as a tithe; and she went out in obedience to an oracle of Apollo and encountered Rhakios the son of Lebes, a Mycenaean by blood. She married him—this was part of the oracle, that she should marry the first man she met—and went to Colophon, and there, overcome by sorrow, she wept for the sack of her native city. Hence the place was named Claros, from her tears. And she established a shrine for Apollo.[51]

In the *Epitome* (6.2–6) to Apollodorus's Library Manto has a son with Apollo called Mopsos (Μόψου μάντεως ὃς Ἀπόλλωνος καὶ Μαντοῦς παῖς ὑπῆρχεν).[52] He is said to have wrangled with Calchas in the art of divina-

---

51. Epigonoi, fr. 3 (PEG) = Scholium ad Apollonius Rhod. 1.308b; ET: Martin L. West, *Greek Epic Fragments: From the Seventh to the Fifth Centuries BC* (LCL; Cambridge: Harvard University Press, 2003), 59.

52. Alternatively, Apollodorus, *Epitome* 3.7.7 refers to a lost play by Euripides

tion (οὗτος ὁ Μόψος περὶ μαντικῆς ἤρισε Κάλχαντι) and defeats him. As a result Calchas dies of a broken heart (ὧν γενομένων Κάλχας ἀθυμήσας τελευτᾷ). In the competition with Calchas, Mopsus uses his pedigree (i.e., being born of Apollo and Manto) to state that his predictions are truer/more precise than the one from Calchas:

ἐγὼ δ' Ἀπόλλωνος καὶ Μαντοῦς παῖς ὑπάρχων τῆς ἀκριβοῦς μαντείας τὴν ὀξυδορκίαν πάντως πλουτῶ.

but I, who am a son of Apollo and Manto, am richly provided with the clarity of vision that arises from exact divination.[53]

Thus the prophecy given to Calchas, that he would die were he to meet a prophet greater than himself, was fulfilled.[54]

We note that the figure of Manto is used to boost the status claims of the seers at Claros and that she serves as the link between the sanctuary in Asia Minor and mainland Greece.[55] The fictionality of her character can also be seen in her name, being simply a feminine form of the Greek word for "seer" (μάντις). We see that the person of a female seer functions as the founding myth for the Ionian sanctuary of Apollon Klarios in the territory of Colophon.[56] Here it is apparent that an oracular shrine that can use

---

where Manto has two childern with Alcmaeon named Amphilochus and Tisiphone: Εὐριπίδης δέ φησιν Ἀλκμαίωνα κατὰ τὸν τῆς μαννας χρόνον ἐκ Μαντοῦς Τειρεσίου παῖδας δύο γεννῆσαι, Ἀμφιλόχον καὶ θυγατέρα Τσιφόνην; see Euripides, fr. 73a, from the play *Alcmaeon in Corinth*: κἀγὼ μὲν ἄτεκνος ἐγενόμην κείνης ἄπο, | Ἀλκμέωνι δ' ἔτεκε δίδυμα τέκνα παρθένος.

53. *Epitome* 6.4. ET: Robin Hard, *Apollodorus: The Library of Greek Mythology: Apollodorus* (Oxford World's Classics; Oxford: Oxford University Press, 1997), 159.

54. On the different traditions of the Calchas-Mopsus encounter see Herbert W. Parke, *The Oracles of Apollo in Asia Minor* (London: Croom Helm, 1985), 114–15; and Flower, *Seer in Ancient Greece*, 44–45.

55. Claros is not mentioned in the Homeric epics but is attested in the Homeric Hymn to Apollo 1.40 (καὶ Κλάρος αἰγλήεσσα καὶ Αἰσαγένης ὄρος αἰπὺ) and in the Hymn to Artemis (9) 5 (ἐς Κλάρον ἀμπελόεσσαν, ὅθ' ἀργυρότοξος Ἀπόλλων); see also Strabo, *Geogr.* 14.1.27 (εἶτα τὸ Γαλλήσιον ὄρος καὶ ἡ Κολοφὼν πόλις Ἰωνικὴ καὶ τὸ πρὸ αὐτῆς ἄλσος τοῦ Κλαρίου Ἀπόλλωνος, ἐν ᾧ καὶ μαντεῖον ἦν ποτε παλαιόν); and Thucydides 3.33.

56. On the importance of Claros in the archaic and classical period see Parke, *Oracles of Apollo*, 112–24; for Hellenistic times see Christian Oesterheld, *Göttliche Botschaften für zweifelnde Menschen: Pragmatik und Orientierungsleistung der Apol-*

both Apollo, as god of oracles, and a member of a famous mantic family of Greece as part of its pedigree almost automatically belongs to the most important shrines of the larger Greek world.

In contrast to Cassandra, the literary figure of Manto is utilized to connect actual religious practice in the Greek world with a mythical past. As she never distances herself from Apollo as the god of oracles (and in some traditions even has a son by him), Manto's prophetic authority is not questioned. Her name can even be evoked in the struggle of Manto's descendants for authority with Calchas, the other most famous seer in the Greek world, who also received his prophetic gift from Apollo (ἥν διὰ μαντοσύνην, τήν οἱ πόρε Φοῖβος 'Απόλλων; *Il.* 1.72).

3. The Tradition of the Sibyl

The last female prophetic figure we will consider is the Sibyl.[57] Here we encounter a phenomenon that has also been connected with Manto, daughter of Teiresias—the importance of written prophecy that can be transmitted from generation to generation. Looking at the Sibyl means that we are ending our survey of the evidence with the interface of the pagan, Jewish, and Christian world in antiquity.[58]

The twelve books of the *Sibylline Oracles* known to us are all of either Jewish or Christian provenance. The phenomenon of the Sibyl, an aged women uttering ecstatic prophecies, however, is a pagan one, which was later adopted by Jewish writers, "modelling their works on the famous

---

Ion-Orakel von Klaros und Didyma in hellenistisch-römischer Zeit (Hypomnemata 174; Göttingen: Vandenhoeck & Ruprecht, 2008).

57. That the Sibyl was regarded as a seer/prophetess is made clear by the Suda: "*Sibylla* is a Roman word, interpreted as 'prophetess,' or rather 'seer' (*mantis*), hence female seers (*mantides*) were called by this one name" (quoted according to Flower, *Seer in Ancient Greece*, 24 n. 27). In the Jewish tradition things are different: here the Sibyl is called προφῆτις, not μάντις (Sib. Or. 3:818; cf. 3:582, 781)—this is in accordance with the use of the LXX, which avoids the standard Greek term for the prophets of Yahweh.

58. From a Christian perspective, Lactantius (*Epitome* 68.1) stresses that the Sibyl is a pagan figure. Thus she can be seen as an independent source that proclaims the truth of Christian faith: "Quare cum haec omnia vera er certa sint prophetarum omnium consona adnuntiatione praedicta, cum eadem Trismegistus, eadem Hystaspes, eadem Sibyllae cecinerint, dubitari non potest, quin spes omnis vitae er salutis in sola dei religione sit posita."

oracles."[59] As such the figure of the Sibyl is one of the elements that connects pagan, Jewish, and Christian antiquity.[60]

The earliest tradition of the Sibyl is in a fragment of the pre-Socratic philosopher Heraclitus (born ca. 545 B.C.E.) quoted in Plutarch:

Σίβυλλα δὲ μαινομένῳ στόματι ... ἀγέλαστα καὶ ἀκαλλώπιστα καὶ ἀμύριστα φθεγγομένη, χιλίων ἐτῶν ἐξικνεῖται τῇ φωνῇ διὰ τὸν θεόν.

But the Sibyl, "with frenzied lips, ... uttering words mirthless, unembellished, unperfumed, yet reaches to a thousand years with her voice through the god.[61]

In this quote we find the basis for the emerging tradition that the words of the Sibyl remain valid over centuries and that her prophecies are spoken in an ecstatic state, which guarantees that they are true and unmodified. The stress on the divine force that is responsible for the utterances is taken up in the beginning of book 3 of the *Sibylline Oracles*:

ἀλλὰ τί μοι κραδίη πάλι πάλλεται ἠδέ γε θυμός τυπτόμενος μάστιγι βιάζεται ἔνδοθεν αὐδήν ἀγγέλλειν πᾶσιν;

But why does my heart shake again? and why is my spirit lashed by a whip, compelled from within to proclaim an oracle to all?[62]

Unfortunately, Heraclitus does not tell us who is the god that drives the Sibyl, but the close connection between Apollo and oracular utterances allows us to speculate that it is Apollo who drives the Sibyl. We have to

---

59. James C. VanderKam, *An Introduction to Early Judaism* (Grand Rapids: Eerdmans, 2001), 107.

60. Thus Helmut Merkel, *Sibyllinen* (JSHRZ 5.8; Gütersloh: Gütersloher Verlagshaus, 1998), 1043.

61. Heraclitus, fr. B92 DK *apud* Plutarch, *Mor.* 397a; ET: Frank Cole Babbitt, *Plutarch's Moralia* (15 vols.; LCL; Cambridge: Harvard University Press, 1927–1969), 5:273.

62. Sib. Or. 3:4–6; ET: John J. Collins, "Sibylline Oracles," *OTP* 1:362; see also Sib. Or. 3:162–164 (καὶ τότε μοι μεγάλοιο θεοῦ φάτις ἐν στήθεσσιν | ἵστατο καί μ' ἐκέλευσε προφητεῦσαι κατὰ πᾶσαν | γαῖαν) and the repetition in 3:297–299; cf. 3:490–491 and 4:14; 5:52, 111, 286.

note, however, that only Ovid in his *Metamorphoses* makes an explicit connection between the (Cumean) Sibyl and Phoibos Apollo.⁶³

Already in the quote from Heraclitus we find many features of the Sibyl that will remain prevalent through the centuries, and that will also make her an ideal vehicle for the transportation of Jewish ideas. According to Pausanias, the Sibyl is a daughter of Zeus and Lamia and the first woman who sings oracles:

καὶ χρησμοῦς τε αὐτὴν γυναικῶν πρώτην ᾆσαι καὶ ὑπὸ τῶν Λιβύων Σίβυλλαν λέγουσιν ὀνομασθῆναι.

that she was the first woman to chant oracles, and that the name Sibyl was given to her by the Libyans.⁶⁴

Heracleides of Ponticus (ca. 360–325 B.C.E.) states that she is older than Orpheus, and in Jewish tradition she is said to be the daughter-in-law of Noah:

ὅτε γὰρ κατεκλύζετο κόσμος
ὕδασι, καί τις ἀνὴρ μόνος εὐδοκίμητος ἐλείφθη
ὑλοτόμῳ ἐνὶ οἴκῳ ἐπιπλώσας ὑδάτεσσιν
σὺν θηρσὶν πτηνοῖσί θ', ἵν' ἐμπλησθῇ πάλι κόσμος·
τοῦ μὲν ἐγὼ νύμφη καὶ ἀφ' αἵματος αὐτοῦ ἐτύχθην.

For when the world was deluged
with waters, and a certain single approved man was left
floating on the waters in a house of hewn wood
with beasts, and birds, so that the world might be filled again,
I was his daughter-in-law and I was of his blood.⁶⁵

---

63. Ovid, *Met.* 14.131–146. Clement of Alexandria (*Strom.* 1.21.108) states that the Sibyl is older than Orpheus and that she stands in conflict with Apollo: ὦ Δελφοί, θεράποντες ἑκηβόλου Ἀπόλλωνος | ἦλθον ἐγὼ χρήσουσα Διὸς νόον αἰγιόχοιο, | αὐτοκασιγνήτῳ κεχολωμένη Ἀπόλλωνι.

64. Pausanias 10.12.1. ET: W. H. S. Jones, *Pausanias: Description of Greece* (5 vols.; LCL; London: Heinemann, 1918–1935), 4:431.

65. Sib. Or. 3:823–827; ET: Collins, "Sibylline Oracles," 380.

PROPHETS MALE AND FEMALE

The tendency to connect the Sibyl with the mythical period takes into account that nothing is known about the origin of her prophecies. The Sibyl prophesies all over the world thus symbolizing a form of traveling prophecy,[66] which—due to that particular nature—can be expanded. In the course of history the one Sibyl known to Heraclitus, Aristophanes,[67] and Plato[68] multiplied during her travels from east to west and was transformed into a multitude of Sibyls that had to be carefully catalogued.[69] The most famous among these Sibyls were the ones located at Marpessos (Troad), Erythrae (Ionia), and Cumae (Italy).

The third book of the *Sibylline Oracles* takes up this traveling nature of the Sibyl when the colophon or sphargis of the third oracle not only explicitly names the figure of the Sibyl (in a fashion close to Sir 50:27) but stresses that she has traveled from Babylonia to Greece:

ταῦτά σοι Ἀσσυρίης Βαβυλώνια τείχεα μακρά
οἰστρομανὴς προλιποῦσα, ἐς Ἑλλάδα πεμπόμενον πῦρ
πᾶσι προφητεύουσα θεοῦ μηνίματα θνητοῖς
ὥστε προφητεῦσαί με βροτοῖς αἰνίγματα θεῖα.

(I say) these things to you, having left
the long Babylonian walls of Assyria, frenzied, a fire sent to Greece
prophesying the disclosures of God to all mortals,
so that I prophesy divine riddles to men.[70]

Naturally, that more than one place in antiquity claimed to be the home of the Sybil had to be addressed, and thus the colophon continues by linking her to the city of Erythrae in Asia Minor—a place long connected to Sibylline activities:

---

66. *IGR* IV 1540, πᾶσαν ἐπὶ χθον' ἔβην ("and I traveled all over the world" [second-century CE inscription from Erythrae]).

67. Aristophanes, *Peace* 1095, 1116.

68. Plato, *Phaedr.* 244b (καί, ἐὰν δὴ λέγωμεν Σίβυλλάν τε καὶ ἄλλους ὅσοι, μαντικῇ χρώμενοι ἐνθέῳ, πολλὰ δὴ πολλοῖς προλέγοντες εἰς τὸ μέλλον ὤρθωσαν, μηκύνοιμεν ἂν δῆλα παντὶ λέγοντες).

69. See Herbert W. Parke, *Sibyls and Sibylline Prophecy in Classical Antiquity* (London: Routledge, 1988), 125–35.

70. Sib. Or. 3:809–812; ET: Collins, "Sibylline Oracles," 380.

καὶ καλέσουσι βροτοί με καθ' Ἑλλάδα πατρίδος ἄλλης,
ἐξ Ἐρυθρῆς γεγαυῖαν ἀναιδέα· οἳ δέ με Κίρκης
μητρὸς καὶ Γνωστοῖο πατρὸς φήσουσι Σίβυλλαν
μαινομένην ψεύστειραν· ἐπὴν δὲ γένηται ἅπαντα,
τηνίκα μου μνήμην ποιήσετε κοὐκέτι μ' οὐδείς
μαινομένην φήσειε, θεοῦ μεγάλοιο προφῆτιν.

Throughout Greece mortals will say that I am of another country,
a shameless one, born of Erythrae. Some will say that
I am Sibylla born of Circe as mother and Gnostos as father,
a crazy liar. But when everything comes to pass,
then you will remember me and no longer will anyone
say that I am crazy, I who am a prophetess of the great God.[71]

These verses are a move to unite the plethora of Sibyls in antiquity in one single figure, who is simply referred to by different names. At the same time the problem of the reliability (i.e., the truth) of prophecies, so well known from the Bible and also problematized in the figure of Cassandra, is again addressed.

Here at the interface of pagan, Jewish, and Christian belief, we encounter a multifaceted prophetic figure that transmits oracles that are written down and preserved. Just as Cassandra and Manto whose antiquity or connection to the mythical past of Greek history is carefully emphasized, the Sibyl too is a figure of an old (and mythical) age. In the Jewish tradition, however, she seems to preceed the period of prophecy, which, according to Jewish tradition, lasts from Moses to Persian times. This early date depicts her as a true prophetic figure. Like the character of Enoch, who is born at the beginning of the historical period,[72] she is thus able to view the past *and* the future.[73] This unique setting of the Sibyl

---

71. Sib. Or. 3:813–818. ET: Collins, "Sibylline Oracles," 380.

72. 1 Enoch 93:3: "And Enoch took up his discourse and said: 'I was born the seventh in the first week and until my time righteousness endured'" (ET: George W. E. Nickelsburg, *1 Enoch 1: A Commentary on the Book of 1 Enoch, Chapters 1–36; 81–108* [Hermeneia; Minneapolis: Fortress, 2001], 434); see the comparison between the Sibyl and Enoch in J. L. Lightfoot, *The Sibylline Oracles: With Introduction, Translation, and Commentary on the First and Second Books* (Oxford: Oxford University Press, 2007), 70–77.

73. The literature on the *Sibylline Oracles* is legion; see the classic study by John J. Collins, *The Sibylline Oracles of Egyptian Judaism* (SBLDS 13; Missoula, Mont.: Society

enables the authors behind the prophetic figure to introduce their view of history and theology without opening it up to a historical or theological critique, since the figure who now utters the prophecies is from the distant (and ahistorical past). Again, a female person from the mythical past begins to shape the present.

Some Concluding Remarks

In the course of our survey we have looked at three female prophetic figures from the Greek world (Cassandra, Manto, and the Sibyl). All of them are characters from literary sources and were most likely created for the setting they now serve in. This said, however, I would argue that we are able to deduce certain features of female prophetic authority from the characters, since they were most likely modeled on certain traits occurring in historical figures.[74]

Like all prophetic figures, they are linked to Apollo, the primary god of oracles. Cassandra points us to the special attire worn by female seers as well as to the ongoing discussion about the evaluation of prophetic utterances. Manto, on the other hand, shows that the prophetic gift can run in a family and that it is not restricted to the male members of a kinship group. In the later traditions about the figure of Manto we also learn that the writing down of oracles and their collecting becomes an important factor.[75] This will be a significant feature of the oracular sayings of the

---

of Biblical Literature, 1974); and the magisterial contribution by Lightfoot, *Sibylline Oracles*. For recent contributions with references to the Hebrew Bible see Otto Kaiser, "Die Sibyllinischen Orakel und das Echo biblischer Ethik und Prophetie in ihrem Dritten Buch," in *Schriftprophetie. Festschrift für Jörg Jeremias zum 65. Geburtstag* (ed. Friedhelm Hartenstein, Jutta Krispenz, and Aaron Schart; Neukirchen-Vluyn: Neukirchener Verlag, 2004), 381–400; and Anselm C. Hagedorn, "'Über jedes Land der Sünder kommt einst ein Sausen': Überlegungen zu einigen Fremdvölkerworten der Sibyllinen," in *Orakel und Gebete: Interdisziplinäre Studien zur Sprache der Religion in Ägypten, Vorderasien und Griechenland in hellenistischer Zeit* (ed. Markus Witte and Johannes F. Diehl; FAT 2/38; Tübingen: Mohr Siebeck, 2009), 73–98.

74. See, e.g., the third-century B.C.E. epitaph from Larissa (Thessaly)—here a certain Satyra is mentioned who is called a seer (SEG 35.626 Σατύρα ἁ μαντίς); the inscription also shows that women were labeled seers, contra Robert Parker, *Polytheism and Society at Athens* (Oxford: Oxford University Press, 2005), 121, who suggests that the female equivalent to "seer" is always "priestess."

75. On this see Armin Lange, "Literary Prophecy and Oracle Collection: A Com-

Sibyl and will enable Hellenistic Jewish authors to cloak their message in a pagan garment. They are thus able to participate in a discourse on identity already found in the biblical prophetic books by using an "international" figure like the Sibyl to transport their idea of true prophecy. As a result, the Sibyl becomes the point where biblical and Greek traditions of (female) prophecy meet and can be fused; at the same time the actual "biography" of the Sibyl starts to fade into the background. Especially when comparing her to Cassandra, whose beauty and special garments make her an almost "real" person, it becomes clear that the Sibyl in her Jewish gestalt almost vanishes behind her message of an elected people who will be the leader of and example for all mortals.[76]

---

parison between Judah and Greece in Persian Times," in *Prophets, Prophecy, and Prophetic Texts in Second Temple Judaism* (ed. Michael H. Floyd and Robert D. Haak; LHBOTS 427; New York: T&T Clark, 2006), 248–75. Similar (written) preservation of oracular sayings can be observed for the Delphic oracle, but this is a topic for further investigation.

76. See, e.g., Sib. Or. 3:194–195.

Female Prophets among Montanists

Antti Marjanen

Introduction

A second-century Christian movement, called "Prophecy" by its own members and "Montanists" by later heresiologists, became known for three major features.[1] First of all, as the name of the movement indicates, its proclamation had a strong prophetic component. The Montanists believed that in the ecstatic utterances of the leaders of the movement, the Paraclete, whose coming was predicted by Jesus in John 16:12–13, was operative.[2] Second, the early leaders of the movement seemed to have

---

1. For an introduction to the Montanist movement, see Christine Trevett, *Montanism: Gender, Authority and the New Prophecy* (Cambridge: Cambridge University Press, 1996); Antti Marjanen, "Montanism: Egalitarian Ecstatic 'New Prophecy,'" in *A Companion to Second-Century Christian 'Heretics'* (ed. Antti Marjanen and Petri Luomanen; VCSup 76; Leiden: Brill, 2005), 185–212.
2. It has been debated whether the notion of the Paraclete as the source of prophetic inspiration among the Montanists characterized the very beginning of the movement in Phrygia (so Trevett, *Montanism*, 62–66; similarly Turid Karlsen Seim, "Johannine Echoes in Early Montanism," in *The Legacy of John: Second-Century Reception of the Fourth Gospel* [ed. Tuomas Rasimus; NovTSup 132; Leiden: Brill, 2010], 345–64) or whether it developed in Rome only some twenty or thirty years later, as Ronald Heine has argued ("The Role of the Gospel of John in the Montanist Controversy," *SecCent* 6 [1987/1988]: 1–19). I follow Trevett. The idea that Montanus and other earliest Montanist prophets acted as the mouthpieces of the Paraclete is set forth or presupposed in such various early sources as Irenaeus (*Haer.* 3.11.9), the report from the martyrs of Gaul quoted by Eusebius (*Hist. eccl.* 5.1.9–10), the early anti-Montanist source of Epiphanius (*Pan.* 48.11.5–8), Tertullian (*Jejun.* 1; *Pud.* 21; *Res.* 11; *Virg.* 1; *Prax.* 1; see also *Mon.* 2; 3), Hippolytus (*Haer.* 8.19.1), Pseudo-Tertullian (*Adv. omn. haer.* 7), and Origen (*Princ.* 2.7.3). Cf. also the later texts: Basil of Caesarea, *Epist.* 188; Jerome, *Epist.* 41.4; Pseudo-Dionysius of Tell Mahrē, *Chron.* Some fourth-

expected an imminent end that was later connected with chiliastic traits. Third, Montanism is one of the few early Christian movements in which women occupied a visible, even a leading, role. Women are especially connected with prophetic functions. It is this third feature that is the subject of the present article.

I will ask why women were able to assume such leading positions among Montanists. Is female advancement into the leadership of the movement to be explained by the personal character and strength of these women, or by a general understanding of prophecy as a female religious function, or by circumstances favorable to women becoming visible religious agents in the area where Montanism had its roots or by something else? Furthermore, what kind of impact did the visible role of women among Montanists have on the reception of the movement among other contemporary Christians? Did it contribute to its success or was it a decisive factor in Montanism's fall from favor, and eventual denouncement as heretical? Before discussing these questions I shall first present an overview of the material that deals with Montanist women. Since much of the evidence derives from heresiological sources, which are by their nature polemical, it is important to be critical when employing them for a historical reconstruction. With each individual text one has to ask whether the visibility of women serves other purposes than simply revealing a piece of historical data.

Evidence for Montanist Female Prophets

In addition to Montanus, after whom "Prophecy" was called "Montanism" by later heresiologists,[3] two women were mentioned by the earliest writers of the heresiological testimonia of Montanism to be the earliest proph-

---

century sources (Eusebius, *Hist. eccl.* 5.14; *Dialogue of a Montanist and an Orthodox* [see Pierre de Labriolle, *Les sources de l'histoire du Montanisme: Textes grecs, latins, syriaques publiés avec une introduction critique, une traduction française des notes et des "indices"* (Paris: Leroux, 1913), 97; see also 95]; Didymos, *Trin.* 3.41) suggest that Montanus himself said: "I am the Father, the Son, and the Paraclete." It is not certain, however, that this saying is authentic (so Trevett, *Montanism*, 79; but contra William Tabbernee, *Montanist Inscriptions and Testimonia: Epigraphic Sources Illustrating the History of Montanism* [North American Patristic Society Patristic Monograph Series 16; Macon, Ga.: Mercer University Press, 1997], 32–33).

3. The first known writer to use the term was Cyril of Jerusalem (d. 386) (*Catecheses illuminandorum* 16.8).

ets of the movement.[4] Eusebius cites an anonymous late-second-century presbyter who calls one of the women Maximilla (*Hist. eccl.* 5.16.13). Eusebius's other important, late-second-century or early-third-century source for Montanism, Apollonius, knows both women and refers to Priscilla by name (*Hist. eccl.* 5.18.3.). Hippolytus (*Haer.* 8.19; early third century), Tertullian (*Jejun.* 1; just after 200 C.E.), and an anonymous "Anti-Phrygian source"[5] (early third century) quoted by Epiphanius (*Pan.* 48.2.1–2) are other early writers who mention both Maximilla and Priscilla. Although the heresiological descriptions of the two women contain some polemical and inauthentic material,[6] the multiple, independent attestations of Maximilla and Priscilla as the early prophets of the Montanist movement confirm the historicity of the information beyond any reasonable doubt. But what exactly was their role as early prophets of the movement?

Based on the earliest accounts of the Montanist movement, one can conclude that, in addition to Montanus, Maximilla and Priscilla were teachers in the early movement.[7] The significant role the early prophets and teachers had in the Montanist movement supports the assumption that they were also the leaders and organizers of the movement. In the case of Montanus this is explicitly spelled out by Apollonius, who affirms that Montanus organized the meetings of the movement in Pepuza and Tymion, two Phrygian villages, which he chose to be the centers of Montanist activities, and that he appointed money collectors who provided salaries for those who preached "his doctrine" (Eusebius, *Hist. eccl.* 5.18.2). The female prophets are not credited with similar tasks in extant heresiological sources,[8] but many of the authentic Montanist prophetic oracles

---

4. For the sources and testimonia of Montanism, see Labriolle, *Sources de l'histoire du Montanisme*; Ronald E. Heine, *The Montanist Oracles and Testimonia* (Macon, Ga.: Mercer University Press, 1989); for Montanist inscriptions see Tabbernee, *Montanist Inscriptions and Testimonia*.

5. The title is coined by Laura Nasrallah, *An Ecstasy of Folly: Prophecy and Authority in Early Christianity* (HTS 52; Cambridge: Harvard University Press, 2003), 46–47. She also shows convincingly that Epiphanius has deployed a written source even if he does not explicitly refer to it (167–71).

6. Tertullian is an exception. Although being a heresiologist himself, he still has a favorable attitude both to the Montanist movement and Maximilla and Priscilla. See below.

7. An anonymous presbyter in Eusebius, *Hist. eccl.* 5.16.9; Hippolytus, *Haer.* 8.19.1; an anonymous Anti-Phrygian source in Epiphanius, *Pan.* 48.1.3.

8. Nevertheless, see Tertullian, *Jejun.* 1.

preserved in these texts are attributed to the women.[9] It is also remarkable that in those heresiological texts, which describe the attempts of bishops and other ecclesiastical leaders to exorcise the spirit they believed to be effective in Montanist prophets, their targets were the female prophets (Eusebius, *Hist. eccl.* 5.16.16; 5.18.13; 5.19.3). Together with Montanus, Maximilla and Priscilla were also reported to have composed books.[10]

In light of the visible role both Maximilla and Priscilla had according to authentic oracles and heresiological testimonia, Anne Jensen has even suggested that the real initiators and early leaders of Montanism were Maximilla and Priscilla, and Montanus was simply their advocate ("Paraclete"). According to her, only in later tradition did Montanus become the "Paraclete," the mouthpiece of the Spirit, which gave the heresy the male head it needed.[11] Jensen's thesis is intriguing but cannot be sustained in light of the evidence. That two of the earliest heresiological sources of Montanism (an anonymous presbyter cited by Eusebius [*Hist. eccl.* 5.16.7] and an early Anti-Phrygian source used by Epiphanius [*Pan.* 48.10.3–11.10]), independently confirm that Montanus was the first prophet and the leader of "Prophecy," makes it impossible to regard him as a mere advocate of the female prophets at the beginning of the movement. If these

---

9. It is debatable just how many of the prophetic oracles which the heresiologists introduce as quotations from Montanist sources are genuine. Kurt Aland ("Bemerkungen zum Montanismus und zur frühchristlichen Eschatologie," in *Kirchengeschichtliche Entwürfe: Alte Kirche, Reformation und Luthertum, Pietismus und Erweckungsbewegung* [ed. Kurt Aland; Gütersloh: Mohn, 1960], 105–48, esp. 143–48) lists sixteen, whereas Ronald Heine (*Montanist Oracles and Testimonia*) and Sheila E. McGinn ("The 'Montanist' Oracles and Prophetic Theology," in *Papers Presented at the Twelfth International Conference on Patristic Studies Held in Oxford, 1995* [vol. 3 of *Preaching, Second Century, Tertullian to Arnobius, Egypt before Nicaea*; ed. Elizabeth A. Livingstone; StPatr 31; Leuven: Peeters, 1997], 128–35) regard fourteen as authentic. Of these, seven are attributed to Maximilla and Priscilla, one to Quintilla (a later Montanist/Quintillianist woman prophet), and the rest to Montanus or to anonymous prophets.

10. Hippolytus, *Haer.* 8.19.1; *Dialogue of a Montanist and an Orthodox* (Labriolle, *Sources de l'histoire du Montanisme*, 106–7); possibly also Michael the Syrian, *Chronicle* (Tabbernee, *Montanist Inscriptions and Testimonia*, 38). Eusebius (*Hist. eccl.* 6.20.3) also mentions that Gaius in his refutation of a Montanist Proclus refers to new holy books Montanists had composed. Likewise, in his *Life of Constantine* Eusebius states that the Constantinian legislation demanded the burning of Montanist books (3.66).

11. Anne Jensen, *God's Self-Confident Daughters: Early Christianity and the Liberation of Women* (trans. O. C. Dean Jr.; Louisville: Westminster John Knox, 1996), 154.

anti-Montanist writers had known of the female initiators of the movement, they would most likely have utilized that information to attack even more the credibility of the "Prophecy," instead of inventing a male founder for the movement. Apollonius's description of Montanus as the organizer of the movement corroborates this conclusion (*Hist. eccl.* 5.18.2).[12] The prophetic oracles attributed to Montanus that contain his self-affirmation that he was "the father, the son, and the (holy) spirit/the Paraclete" also underline his leading position in the prophetic movement (*Dialogue of a Montanist and an Orthodox*; Didymus, *Trin.* 3.41). They indicate that he saw himself as the mouthpiece of the Trinity.[13]

The priority of Montanus as the first prophet, teacher, and leader of the Montanist movement does not reduce the value of the female prophets. Although Maximilla and Priscilla were recruited by Montanus and became his followers as prophets, they were also respected leaders and teachers of the movement. That representatives of other forms of Christianity tried to drive out evil spirits from these two women especially underlines their significance (Eusebius, *Hist. eccl.* 5.16.16; 5.18.13; 5.19.3). There is no reason to believe that ecclesiastical officials would have chosen inferior spiritual opponents as the targets of their exorcism.

Maximilla and Priscilla were not the only female prophets in the Montanist movement. When Maximilla's prediction of the imminent end following her death (Epiphanius, *Pan.* 48.2.4) did not materialize, new male and female prophets appeared and assumed leadership of the movement. Tertullian, who was well known for his pro-Montanist sympathies, refers to an anonymous (most likely Montanist[14]) female prophet, who was active

---

12. So also Trevett, *Montanism*, 160.
13. Labriolle, *Sources de l'histoire du Montanisme*, 97, 101, 103. Heine ("Role of Gospel of John") insists that these particular oracles are later theological constructions that have been created to make Montanus look like a Modalistic Monarchian. However, as Tabbernee (*Montanist Inscriptions and Testimonia*, 33) has pointed out, these oracles do not have to be seen as an attempt to formulate hypostatic equation of Father, Son, and Holy Spirit. Montanus states only that he sees himself as an instrument of prophetic speech that derives its authority from the Father, the Son, and the Spirit. The oracles do not actually deviate much from a similar oracle presented in a first-person form and preserved as a statement of Montanus in an early anti-Montanist source used by Epiphanius: "I am the Lord, the almighty God, who dwells in a human being" (*Pan.* 48.11.1).
14. To be sure, Tertullian does not explicitly identify this woman prophet as Montanist but he describes her as "favored with sundry gifts of revelation, which she

in a Christian church in Carthage (*An.* 9.4). She experienced revelations through ecstatic visions, in the course of which she conversed with angels and sometimes even with the Lord. According to Tertullian, she also had a special ability "to understand the hearts of the people," and therefore she could counsel those in need of spiritual remedies. After having her visions during worship services she reported what she had seen to a select group. In this way the truth of her communications was collectively examined. As an example of her visions, Tertullian points out that once she saw "a soul in bodily shape." Clearly, the female prophet was an influential member of the Christian community in Carthage and Tertullian approved of her actions. Compared to her predecessors in Phrygia, she did not exercise her prophetic activity in public but privately after and outside the worship services. This may explain why Tertullian, who otherwise was critical of women's involvement in public ecclesiastical tasks and roles (cf., e.g., *Praescr.* 41), gave his consent to this woman.[15] Even if Tertullian accepted female prophets (*Marc.* 5.8), including Maximilla and Priscilla (*Prax.* 1; *Jejun.* 1), he emphasized that women should not assume public ecclesiastical roles, which were manly functions (*Virg.* 9), but they should always act as "modesty's priestesses" (*Cult. fem.* 2.12).[16]

Another kind of female prophet was active in Caesarea in Cappadocia in the mid-third century. In his letter to Cyprian, Firmilian, the bishop of Caesarea, speaks of a female prophet who performed some miraculous acts and promised to cause the earth to be shaken (Cyprian, *Ep.* 75.10). Firmilian does not explicitly call the woman a Montanist, but that he describes her as acting in a state of ecstasy "as if filled with the Holy Spirit" suggests in the second quarter of the third century that she was at least a sympathizer of the "Prophecy."[17] To Firmilian's horror, the female prophet also administered baptisms and the Eucharist.

---

experiences in the Spirit by ecstatic vision." This suggests that she belonged to "the 'Montanist' circle at Carthage" as Tabbernee (*Montanist Inscriptions and Testimonia*, 54) characterizes that group of Christians who were favorably disposed to Montanist emphases even if they remained adherents of the Christian community in Carthage.

15. So also Trevett, *Montanism*, 173.

16. Indeed, it is clear that Maximilla and Priscilla did not act according to Tertullian's wish, but he never tackles this issue. Either he is not aware of their "real" prophetic activity or he prefers to overlook it. For the latter, note that Tertullian can portray the activity of Maximilla and Priscilla as "preaching God" (*Jejun.* 1).

17. Jensen (*God's Self-Confident Daughters*, 182–86) argues that during Firmilian's time a female Montanist prophet could no longer have received a leading position in a

The most prominent woman after Maximilla and Priscilla among the female prophets was Quintilla, a woman whom only Epiphanius mentions (*Pan.* 49.1.1–3.4). According to Epiphanius, Quintilla founded a special religious group that had its roots in the Montanist movement. Epiphanius's description of Quintilla and her followers is somewhat confusing, because on the one hand he emphasizes the independent identity of the group treating it separately in his heresiology, on the other hand he also identifies Quintillianists with Priscillianists. He is not even completely sure whether it is Quintilla or Priscilla who saw a dream in which Jesus appeared to her in Pepuza and imparted a revelation that had a great impact on the development of the Montanist thinking. The report of the female visionary quoted by Epiphanius describes the content of the dream: "Christ came to me dressed in a white robe in the form of a woman, imbued me with wisdom, and revealed to me that this place is holy, and that Jerusalem will descend from heaven here" (*Pan.* 49.1.3).[18] Since early Montanist sources associates only Montanus, not Priscilla, with the identification of Pepuza with Jerusalem (Apollonius in Eusebius, *Hist. eccl.* 5.18.2), and since early Montanist sources do not reveal any evidence for a future expectation of the descent of the heavenly Jerusalem in Pepuza,[19] it is most likely that the visionary is not Priscilla but Quintilla. The latter probably belonged to those second- and third-generation prophetic leaders who followed the primary triad of the Montanist prophets. Quintilla's male colleagues included at least Themiso (Eusebius, *Hist. eccl.* 5.16.17; 5.18.5), Miltiades (5.16.3), Alcibiades and Theodotus (5.3.4), as well as Proclus (6.20.3).

Quintilla's main contribution to Montanist thinking seems to have been the placement of Pepuza at the center of the eschatological fervor of the movement. After having been the place where the activities of the Montanist movement originated, it now also became a place where the future expectations found their home. According to Epiphanius, Pepuza

---

Christian church outside her own (Montanist) circle. Therefore Jensen does not regard her as a Montanist. Jensen may be right that the female prophet in Firmilian's church should not be seen as a professing Montanist, but she could be a sympathizer (cf. the adherents of the "Montanist" circle at Carthage; see n. 14 above) who wanted to introduce Montanist emphases to the life of Firmilian's church in Caesarea.

18. The translation of the oracle is derived from *The Panarion of Epiphanius of Salamis: Books II and III [Sects 47–80, De Fide]* (trans. Frank Williams; Nag Hammadi and Manichaean Studies 36; Leiden: Brill, 1994), 21.

19. For a more thorough discussion, see Marjanen, "Montanism," 204–6.

had meanwhile become a deserted place but—evidently with Quintilla's vision—it regained an important position as a place of pilgrimage and veneration among Montanists (Epiphanius, *Pan.* 48.14.1-2).

Another interesting feature that, according to Epiphanius, was typical of Quintillianists is that they ordained women as clergy. As scriptural support for this practice they referred to the fact that Moses' sister Miriam and the four daughters of Philip the Evangelist were prophets (*Pan.* 49.2.2). According to Epiphanius, they also had women bishops and presbyters,[20] since the apostle Paul states that "in Christ Jesus there is neither male nor female" (Gal 3:28; Epiphanius, *Pan.* 49.2.5).

In addition to these literary sources,[21] female prophets also appear in Montanist inscriptions. A fourth-century memorial stela, discovered in modern Akoluk in the region of the Phrygian highlands, is dedicated to a female prophet Nanas, the daughter or wife of Hermogenes, who had "angelic visitations and speech . . . in greatest measure."[22] Both the epithet "female prophet" and the way her ecstatic experience is described suggest a Montanist provenance for the stela. Female prophets were practically nonexistent in other Christian communities of the fourth century after the rejection of the "Prophecy" as a heretical movement, and "angelic visitations and speech" do not fit very well with a description of a pagan prophet.[23] The memorial stela does not give a clear picture of the role and the duties of Nanas as a prophet in the local Montanist community. The good quality of the stela and the lengthy epitaph, which mainly concentrates on the merits of Nanas and not on her late husband, who is only briefly mentioned in the memorial stone, nevertheless suggest that Nanas played a significant role as a prophet of the Montanist community. The memorial stela was thus erected as a sign of appreciation for her contribution among local Montanists.

---

20. There are also some Montanist tombstone inscriptions from the third century that mention female presbyters; for the evidence see Tabbernee, *Montanist Inscriptions and Testimonia*, 66–72, 80–82.

21. In addition to those literary references to Montanist female prophets mentioned above, Apollonius also refers to a female prophet whom he accuses of receiving gold, silver, and expensive clothes (Eusebius, *Hist. eccl.* 5.18.4). It is not clear, however, whether this woman is an anonymous female prophet and his contemporary or Priscilla who has been mentioned just above (*Hist. eccl.* 5.18.3).

22. Tabbernee, *Montanist Inscriptions and Testimonia*, 419–25.

23. Ibid., 424.

Another memorial stela dedicated to a female Montanist prophet has been found in Ankara.[24] It derives from the fifth or sixth century. Although the stela explicitly characterizes the woman, Stefania, not as a prophet but as a "lamp-bearing virgin," the latter expression was known to be an epithet for a female prophet among Montanists. In his description of Quintillianists, Epiphanius refers to "seven virgins with lamps, dressed in white" and prophesying to the people (*Pan.* 49.2.3–4).[25] Another task that Epiphanius ascribes to these women is that they encourage people to mourn and repent in preparation for the coming of the bridegroom, Christ. That the epitaph of Stefania calls her ἡγουμένη shows that she was the leader of this particular group of lamp-bearing virgins, that is, the main female prophet of the community.

What does it mean that these lamp-bearing prophets were explicitly called virgins? It is obvious that the Matthean wise, lamp-bearing virgins provide the background for the women, but is that all? Or were the prophets supposed to be unmarried? It has even been proposed that the visible role of women as ecclesiastical leaders among Montanists presupposed that they were celibate ascetics.[26] In the extant evidence of Montanism there seems to be no clear rule concerning the marital status of the people holding ecclesiastical offices. It is, for example, unclear whether Maximilla and Priscilla were married. Apollonius claims that they had been married but left their husbands after they had been filled with the Spirit (Eusebius, *Hist. eccl.* 5.18.3). It may be true that the women had undergone a divorce, but it may also be a polemical statement made to defame them.[27] What is of interest, though, is that in the same context Apollonius also stresses that Priscilla was certainly not a virgin even though she is called one (Eusebius, *Hist. eccl.* 5.18.3–4). This may imply that the role of a female prophet was usually combined with the idea that virginity made the institution of female prophets more acceptable. With that set of circumstances the

---

24. Ibid., 518–25.

25. That the Quintillianist tradition refers to seven lamp-bearing virgins may be due to the influence of the book of Revelation in which seven becomes the eschatological number (1:4, 11, 20); for this see Tabbernee, *Montanist Inscriptions and Testimonia*, 525.

26. For references see ibid., 523.

27. It is also possible that both Maximilla and Priscilla were married to unbelieving men who were unsympathetic to their Christian conviction. Thus the women divorced their husbands—simply following the guidance of Paul in 1 Cor 7:15.

"social and ecclesial disadvantages inherent in femaleness were negated," as William Tabbernee succinctly put it.[28] The later phenomenon of the lamp-bearing virgins presupposes the same idea. All this fits well together with a general appreciation of asceticism among Montanists. Some texts seem to suggest that the Montanist prophets held celibacy to be a preferable alternative in general. Montanus himself is accused of teaching the annulment of marriage, which may simply mean that he was in favor of unmarried life (Eusebius, *Hist. eccl.* 5.18.2).[29] Tertullian has preserved an oracle of a Montanist prophet that also advocates a strong spiritual commitment of women over against married life: "Do not seek to die on bridal beds, nor in miscarriages, nor in soft fevers, but seek to die the martyr's death, that He may be glorified who has suffered for you" (*Fug.* 9).

Nevertheless, the ascetic ideal, which some Montanist female prophets seem to have complied with, can hardly explain fully the favorable attitude of the movement toward them and women in other ecclesiastical offices. For example, Nanas, one of the female Montanist prophets, was indeed married. The same seems to be true with the two third-century women presbyters whose epitaphs present them together with their husbands (for the references see n. 20). Thus there are other reasons that account for the approval of the female prophets (and other ecclesiastical female leaders) and to those we turn in the next section.

Why Female Prophets?

Among the few oracles of the Montanist prophets that have been preserved, one attributed to Maximilla says: "The Lord has sent me to be adherent, revealer, and interpreter of this pain, covenant, and promise; he has compelled me, whether I want or not, to learn the knowledge of God" (Epiphanius, *Pan.* 48.13.1).[30] The oracle speaks about a divine calling and

---

28. Tabbernee, *Montanist Inscriptions and Testimonia*, 523.

29. To be sure, there are texts that suggest that Montanists also allowed ordinary family life. The early source of Epiphanius, for example, emphasizes that Montanists did not forbid marriage in general but only a second marriage after the death of the first spouse or after divorce (Epiphanius, *Pan.* 48.9.7; so also Tertullian, *Mon.* 1; 14; 15; *Pud.* 1; *Marc.* 1.29; Jerome, *Epist.* 41.3).

30. Somewhat surprisingly, the three Greek participle forms that have been translated "he has compelled me, whether I want or not," are masculine. This has led some to think that the oracle was not spoken by Maximilla but by a male prophet or the Paraclete. This conclusion is not necessary, however. The use of the masculine parti-

inner compulsion similar to that assigned to biblical prophets such as Jeremiah (Jer 20:9). But the inner burning to be a prophet is not enough.[31] The calling has to be recognized by others as well before it can be realized. What factors made it possible for women like Maximilla to be authorized as a prophet in a society where women were not normally allowed to have influential roles? Maximilla, Priscilla, and their female successors seem to have had the right set of skills in order to advance to a position, such as the one they had, in a patriarchal Mediterranean society. Even if our sources do not reveal any biographical data about their personal qualities and backgrounds, we have to assume that they had exceptional mental and spiritual capacity. They must also have had some kind of education at least in matters of their religion but probably also in other subjects. But this is certainly not enough to create the kind of spiritual career they had. Other external factors are needed to level out the difficulties women had in trying to become influential.

Some have suggested that the visible role women had in various ecclesiastical offices among Montanists can be explained by the impact of Phrygian native cults, such as the worship of Cybele, on the development of the "Prophecy."[32] There were, for example, lamenting lamp-bearers in Phrygian cults. To be sure, the familiarity with lamp bearers may have made it easier at some point to connect a Matthean theme with the idea of female prophets inviting people to repentance in the face of the coming Christ. Nevertheless, this interesting parallel cannot account for the immense popularity female prophets enjoyed already at the very beginning of the movement. The motif of lamp-bearers does not occur in the

---

ciples is probably due to the fact that Maximilla is described as "adherent, revealer, and interpreter," which are all masculine nouns.

31. Anthropological studies of spirit possession suggest that especially women may also unconsciously employ "possession as a means of insinuating their interests and demands in the face of male constraint" and can thus receive a social acknowledgment within their religious community by means of it (see I. M. Lewis, *Ecstatic Religion: An Anthropological Study of Spirit Possession and Shamanism* [Harmondsworth, Eng.: Penguin, 1971], 79). It is of course possible that this was also true with female Montanist prophets, but it is interesting that no anti-Montanist testimonia refer to this kind of motive in order to disparage the prophetic role of women. This also suggests that psychological factors do not wholly explain the prophetic activity of women.

32. E.g., Wilhelm Schepelern, *Der Montanismus und die phrygischen Kulte: Eine religionsgeschichtliche Untersuchung* (Tübingen: Mohr Siebeck, 1929), 127–28.

earliest sources of Montanism but only in connection with Quintillianists and other later sources.³³

I argue that the main reason why female prophets could reach such an influential position among Montanists was basically exegetical. The Montanists could refer to the Old Testament and to early Christian tradition to bolster their claim that even women could act as the mouthpieces of the Paraclete. Several texts among anti-Montanist testimonia show that all the possible biblical and ecclesiastical paragons of female prophecy were employed to legitimate the position of female Montanist prophets. Although none of them appears in the preserved Montanist oracles, the heresiologists give a rather clear picture of the texts dealing with female prophets and prophecy that played a role in debates between the Montanists and the representatives of other forms of Christianity.

The earliest anti-Montanist writer who implies that the representatives of the New Prophecy referred to biblical and early Christian examples to legitimate the prophetic activities of the Montanist women was the anonymous presbyter quoted by Eusebius (*Hist. eccl.* 5.17.3–4). It is noteworthy that the woman whom he explicitly mentions is Ammia of Philadelphia. That she is introduced to support the Montanists' claim for women's right to act as prophets is interesting in two ways. First, it demonstrates her importance; second, it only confirms what we know on the basis of other sources as well: there was not yet a generally accepted canon of authoritative writings to guide the decision making of Christian churches. Thus, although Ammia is not mentioned in the texts that eventually became canonical, she can be seen as a paradigmatic figure that can be used in the debate about female prophets. In his commentary on 1 Cor 14:36, Origen lists other women who have been included in the debates between the Montanists and other Christians concerning the role of female prophets

---

33. Another link between Montanists and the cult of Cybele has been seen in Jerome's characterization of Montanus as "castrated and emasculated" (*Epist.* 41.4). Based on this, it has been suggested that Montanus may have been a former priest of Cybele who had castrated himself (so, e.g., W. H. C. Frend, *The Rise of Christianity* [Philadelphia: Fortress, 1984], 253). No early source confirms this. Some fourth-century sources suggest that Montanus used to be a priest of an idol (Didymus the Blind, *Trin.* 3.41) or that of Apollo (*Dialogue of a Montanist and an Orthodox* [Labriolle, *Sources de l'histoire du Montanisme*, 103]), but not even they provide a link between Montanus and Cybele worship. And even if Montanus had been a eunuch, it does not yet make him a priest of Cybele. It is well known that even some Christians of other persuasions castrated themselves.

(*Fr. 1 Cor.* 14:36).[34] All the women of the Old Testament who were explicitly characterized as prophets (Miriam [Exod 15:20], Deborah [Judg 4:4], and Huldah [2 Kgs 22:14]) were obviously referred to by the Montanists as paragons of their female prophets. In addition, the most important female prophets in early Christian writings from the perspective of the Montanist prophets were, according to Origen, the four daughters of Philip (Acts 21:10). Another female prophet of the New Testament who seems to figure in the debates is Anna, the daughter of Phanuel (Luke 2:36). Even Mary, the mother of Jesus, appears in discussions.[35]

The only female prophet appearing in the texts that eventually formed the New Testament canon but not employed by the Montanists to strengthen their case was the female prophet in Rev 2:20, Jezebel, named after the pagan queen mentioned in 1 and 2 Kings. Because the text describes her as a woman who misguided her church members "to practice fornication and to eat food sacrificed to idols" (NRSV), it is understandable that the Montanists did not want to identify with her. Yet it is not surprising that in the heresiological literature Jezebel is seen as a prototype of female Montanist prophets. Epiphanius sees in the condemnation of Jezebel by the Son of God in the book of Revelation a prediction that materialized in the destiny of the female Montanist prophets: "Don't you people see that he means the women who are deceived by a false conception of prophecy, and will deceive many? I mean that he is speaking of Priscilla, Maximilla and Quintilla, whose imposture the Holy Spirit did not overlook" (*Pan.* 51.33.8–9).[36]

The Montanists not only used those texts that explicitly mentioned a female prophet to substantiate their claims, but they also seem to have been interested in 1 Cor 11:1–16, a text implying that even Paul allowed women to prophesy if they only did it with their heads veiled.[37] A further text that could have been useful in the argumentation of the Montanists is the eschatological prophecy of Joel 2:28, which, according to Luke, receives its fulfillment at Pentecost (Acts 2:17–18). Nevertheless, the egali-

---

34. For the text see Labriolle, *Sources de l'histoire du Montanisme*, 55–56.

35. The daughters of Philip, Deborah, and Mary, the mother of Jesus, are also mentioned in the *Dialogue of a Montanist and an Orthodox* (Labriolle, *Sources de l'histoire du Montanisme*, 105, 106).

36. The translation by Williams, *Panarion of Epiphanius of Salamis*, 21.

37. Tertullian, *Marc.* 5.8; see also *Dialogue of a Montanist and an Orthodox* (Labriolle, *Sources de l'histoire du Montanisme*, 105, 106).

tarian attitude with regard to the outpouring of the Spirit does not seem to have been employed by the Montanists to the extent one would expect, unless its traces have completely disappeared.[38]

The explicit references to female prophets in texts that were considered authoritative make the Montanist argument for their continued role within a Christian community a strong one. Based on that evidence, the Montanists claimed that their female prophets simply stand in a long line of ancient religious tradition and do not create anything new. Yet history shows that the gravity of the claim did not suffice for very long. What were the counterarguments? Were they weightier or was the battle decided on entirely different grounds?

How Did the Heresiologists React to the Montanist Claims?

As stated above, the main argument that the Montanists used to legitimize their prophetic activity was to regard it as a realization of Jesus' promise of the Paraclete in the Gospel of John (16:12–13). What was not yet revealed by Jesus himself to his own disciples was now being proclaimed by the Montanist prophets who guided Jesus' later followers "to all truth." This view was strongly criticized by Christians of other persuasions who could not accept any new revelation beyond the Old Testament Scriptures and apostolic testimonies. Even Tertullian, who strongly sympathized with Montanist views, did not espouse the idea that the new Montanist revelations would replace or improve the apostolic *regula fidei*. For all that, he readily admitted that the Montanist interpretation of the Johannine Paraclete passages well justified changes, useful and necessary in matters of church life and discipline (Tertullian, *Virg.* 1). Indeed, Tertullian can insist that the realization of the Johannine Paraclete passages illustrates a divine strategy against the devil:

> What kind of (supposition) is it, that, while the devil is always operating and adding daily to the ingenuities of iniquity, the work of God should

---

38. Nevertheless, see Tertullian, *Marc.* 5.8. The introductory chapter of the *Martyrdom of Saints Perpetua and Felicitas*, in which some scholars see a Montanist touch, refers to this text while speaking about the value of "new prophecies" and "new visions…, according to the promise" (for the text and the translation, see Herbert Musurillo, *The Acts of the Christian Martyrs* [Oxford Early Christian Texts; Oxford: Clarendon, 1972], 106–7).

either have ceased, or else have desisted from advancing? whereas the reason why the Lord sent the Paraclete was, that, since human mediocrity was unable to take in all things at once, discipline should, little by little, be directed, and ordained, and carried on to perfection, by that Vicar of the Lord, the Holy Spirit.[39]

Unlike Tertullian, many other early Christian theologians criticized this line of reasoning. A new prophetic revelation, which made claim for being more far-reaching than the Old Testament and the apostolic writings, could not be approved. Apollonius, for example, criticizes Themiso, a late-second-century or an early-third-century Montanist leader, for having "the audacity to compose a general letter in imitation of the apostle and to instruct those whose faith was better than his own, and with empty words to engage in fruitless disputation, to blaspheme against the Lord, and the apostles, and the holy church" (Eusebius, *Hist. eccl.* 5.15.5).[40]

Another argument adduced against the Montanist prophets had to do with the ecstatic character of their activity. The first anti-Montanist text that raises this issue is preserved by Eusebius (*Hist. eccl.* 5.17.1–14). It is written by an anonymous presbyter who himself quotes another anti-Montanist writer, Miltiades. In trying to prove that the Montanist prophets are false, Miltiades argues that the Montanists cannot place themselves in the long line of Old Testament and Christian prophetic succession since, unlike Montanist prophets, Old Testament and Christian prophets never spoke in ecstasy. Therefore, they are true prophets, whereas the Montanist prophets are false.

In the debate between Miltiades and the Montanists, the aspect of gender is not an issue. Origen refers to a similar debate that deals with the position of Montanism in Jewish-Christian prophetic succession but this time the role of women becomes a central topic (*Fr. 1 Cor.* 14:36).[41] Origen's discussion presupposes that the Montanists kept asking why their female prophets were not allowed to prophesy even though the four daughters of Philip were. Origen gives two reasons. First, he categorically

---

39. *Virg.* 1; ET: S. Thelwall, *Ante-Nicene Fathers* (ed. Alexander Roberts and James Donaldson; 10 vols.; 1885–1896; repr., Peabody, Mass.: Hendrickson, 1994), 4:27.

40. The translation is derived from William Tabbernee, *Fake Prophecy and Polluted Sacraments: Ecclesiastical and Imperial Reactions to Montanism* (VCSup 84; Leiden: Brill, 2007), 108, with some modifications.

41. For the text see Labriolle, *Sources de l'histoire du Montanisme*, 55–56.

states that the prophecy of the Montanist women have not come true. Here Origen follows Deut 13:1–5 and 18:21–22 that only the realization of a prediction legitimizes the prophet. Although he does not give any example of an unrealized prediction of the female Montanist prophets, some other early theologians do. For example, the Anti-Phrygian source of Epiphanius points out that Maximilla predicted that "the consummation would come after her, and no consummation has come yet" (*Pan.* 48.2.6). The same source not only underlines the fallacy of the Montanist prophecies but also emphasizes that the Montanist prophecies are obscure and useless to the extent that they remain incomprehensible (*Pan.* 48.3.11–4.2).

Origen's second argument is exegetical. He refers to all female biblical prophets, possibly already presented by the Montanists in their own argumentation, and shows that, unlike female Montanist prophets, none of them exercised their prophetic activity in public or tried to lead men. According to the biblical texts, the four daughters of Philip did not present their prophecies in public meetings of the church (Acts 21:9); Miriam, the sister of Aaron, was only a leader of women (Exod 15:20); and Deborah (Judg 4:4) and Huldah (2 Kgs 22:14) did not speak to the people but only to private individuals.

The arguments of Miltiades and Origen taken together actually summarize the entire debate about female prophecy between the Montanists and the representatives of other forms of Christianity in three points:

1. The Montanist prophecy in its entirety, including their female prophets, is false because it takes place in ecstasy (Miltiades). A similar argument is presented by the early Anti-Phrygian source of Epiphanius, which also claims that true prophets deliver their revelations "with sound mind and a rational intellect" (Epiphanius, *Pan.* 48.3.1). Nevertheless, the text goes further than Miltiades and distinguishes between two ecstasies. The one, which does not cloud one's reason, is acceptable. A good example of this kind of ecstasy is Peter's vision in Cornelius's house (Acts 10:10; *Pan.* 48.7.3). Another kind of ecstasy, represented by Montanists, does cloud the mind and thus makes their prophecy reprehensible. A similar differentiation is made by Didymus the Blind. According to him, divine ecstasy was a matter of sobriety, whereas Montanist ecstasy was a matter of mania.[42]

---

42. *Fr. 2 Cor* 5:12; for the text see Labriolle, *Sources de l'histoire du Montanisme*, 162–63. Interestingly, this goes against both Philo (*Her.* 263–265) and Tertullian (*An.* 45.3; cf. also *Marc.* 4.22.5), who see madness, the temporary absence of reason (Philo:

2. The female prophets of Montanism are not true prophets because their predictions do not come true. This claim is made by Origen. Nevertheless, he does not provide any concrete example of the unrealized prophecies of the Montanist prophets. Other heresiologists correct this defect as indicated above.

3. The female Montanist prophets are false because they, unlike their Old Testament and early Christian predecessors, prophesy in public and thus even try to lead men.[43]

The Consequences of Female Prophecy for the Parting of Ways

As far as we know, based on extant anti-Montanist sources, the central emphases of Montanist theology were not actually controversial from the perspective of other forms of Christianity. For example, according to Hippolytus, the Montanists had fully acceptable views of God as the Creator, of ecclesiology, and of Christology (*Haer.* 8.19.2). Epiphanius, a fourth-century heresiologist, also confirms that there is nothing wrong with the Montanists' notion of God, the Trinity, Christ, and the resurrection. Even the emphasis the Montanists laid on prophetic activity was not problematic as such. Many other contemporary Christians valued Old Testament and Christian prophets. Thus it was not *the fact that* the Montanists had prophets that was an issue. Rather it was the *way* the prophets acted that was a problem. It was the (wrong) ecstatic character of prophetic activity, their claim to new revelation, as well as the public appearance of female prophets that seem to have contributed in a decisive way to Montanism being eventually declared heretical.

---

mania; Tertullian: *amentia*), as the presupposition for the best form of ecstasy and the source of divine inspiration; for this see Nasrallah, *Ecstasy of Folly*, 36–44, 51–58. For the differentiation of various ecstasies, see Marjanen, "Montanism," 197.

43. So Origen; cf. also *Dialogue of a Montanist and an Orthodox*; for the text see Labriolle, *Sources de l'histoire du Montanisme*, 105–8.

Part 2
Prophecy in Biblical Texts

SPEAKING IN DREAMS:
THE FIGURE OF MIRIAM AND PROPHECY*

Hanna Tervanotko

INTRODUCTION

The prophetic role of the figure of Miriam remains a topic of discussion.[1] Often the views concerning Miriam's function are based on one text, Exod 15:20–21, that refers to Miriam as "the prophetess, the sister

---

* I am grateful to Professor Daniel E. Fleming for his mentoring while I was preparing this paper during my stay at the New York University. I equally wish to thank Professor Martti Nissinen for his helpful comments and Ms. Maureen Farrell-García for helping me to improve my English. Any mistakes that remain are my own.

1. The figure of Miriam has been studied in two monographs: Rita Burns, *Has the Lord Indeed Spoken Only through Moses? A Study of the Biblical Portrait of Miriam* (SBLDS 84; Atlanta: Scholars Press, 1987); Ursula Rapp, *Mirjam: Eine feministisch-rhetorische Lektüre der Mirjamtexte in der Hebräischen Bibel* (BZAW 317; Berlin: de Gruyter, 2002). In addition, a number of articles deal with Miriam, e.g., Phyllis Trible, "Bringing Miriam out of the Shadows," *BibRev* 5.1 (1989): 14–25; Rainer Kessler, "Mirjam und die Prophetie der Perserzeit," in *Gott an den Rändern: Sozialgeschichtliche Perspektiven auf die Bibel* (ed. Ulrike Bail und Renate Jost; Gütersloh: Kaiser, 1996), 64–72; Irmtraud Fischer, "The Authority of Miriam: A Feminist Rereading of Numbers 12 Prompted by Jewish Interpretation," in *Exodus to Deuteronomy* (ed. Athalya Brenner; FCB 2/5; Sheffield: Sheffield Academic Press, 2000), 159–73; idem, *Gotteskünderinnen: Zu einer geschlechterfairen Deutung des Phänomens der Prophetie und der Prophetinnen in der Hebräischen Bibel* (Stuttgart: Kohlhammer, 2002), 64–94; Susan Ackerman, "Why Is Miriam Also among the Prophets? (And Is Zipporah among the Priests?)," *JBL* 121 (2002): 47–80. What is common for all these publications is that they limit their discussion to the evidence preserved in the Hebrew Bible. Only Sidnie White Crawford, "Traditions about Miriam in the Qumran Scrolls," *Studies in Jewish Civilization* 14 (2003): 33–44, includes the nonbiblical texts in her analysis. For Miriam in patristic traditions see Agnethe Siquans, *Die alttestamentlichen Prophetin-*

of Aaron" (NRSV). This is the only text that clearly points to Miriam as a female prophet. Despite this title the short passage does not offer any explanation for her possible prophetic role. Raising a victory song in Exod 15:20-21 can hardly be interpreted as a sign of prophecy.[2] While a big part of the discussion has focused on this passage, other passages of the Hebrew Bible can shed light on Miriam's prophetic role too. Notably, in Num 12:2 Miriam and Aaron raise the question of Moses' exclusive prophecy. They ask, "Has the LORD spoken only through Moses? Has he not spoken through us also?" (Num 12:2). In Num 12:6-8 God answers that, while Moses gets to know the divine will "face to face" (i.e., directly), communication with prophets takes place in riddles and in dreams. This could be interpreted as an affirmation that Miriam and Aaron were also prophets even if neither of these verses offers any explanation regarding the nature of Miriam's prophecy.[3] Or do they?

Visions and dreams were central means of prophecy in antiquity.[4] People in ancient times thought that dreams could contain special messages. Dreams could be generally viewed as communication with the

---

nen in der patristischen Rezeption: Texte—Kontexte—Hermeneutik (HBS 65; Freiburg: Herder, 2011).

2. Burns (*Has the Lord Indeed Spoken*, 46), however, points out that music and dance were means to evoke ecstasy in the ancient Near East. Various prophets could have used them. According to 1 Sam 10:5 the drums together with other instruments accompanied the prophets who were in ecstasy. In contrast, Carol Meyers (*Exodus* [New Cambridge Bible Commentary; Cambridge: Cambridge University Press, 2005], 116–19) has convincingly demonstrated that the musical instruments were used for multiple purposes. Nothing of Exod 15:20-21 seems to indicate that Miriam was in ecstasy. Rather, keeping in mind what the several references to women's singing and dancing in celebrations indicate, the function of the song appears to be a victory celebration. See Martti Nissinen, "Biblical Prophecy from a Near Eastern Perspective: The Cases of Kingship and Divine Possession," in *Congress Volume Ljubljana 2007* (ed. André Lemaire; VTSup 133; Leiden: Brill, 2010), 441–68.

3. This has been previously argued by Wilda C. Gafney, *Daughters of Miriam: Women Prophets in Ancient Israel* (Minneapolis: Fortress, 2008), 82–83; Fischer, "Authority of Miriam," 167–68. Athalya Brenner (*The Israelite Woman: Social Role and Literary Type in Biblical Narrative* [BiSe 2; Sheffield; JSOT Press, 1985] 61) points out that Num 12 does not explicitly state that Miriam and Aaron are not prophets.

4. Martti Nissinen, "What Is Prophecy?" in *Inspired Speech: Prophecy in the Ancient Near East: Essays in Honor of Herbert B. Huffmon* (ed. John Kaltner and Louis Stulman; JSOTSup 378; London: T&T Clark, 2004), 20–22.

Divine.[5] This experience was open to both men and women in the ancient Near East, as is evident from texts that indicate women were connected to visions and dreams regularly. Moreover, there is also evidence that communication with the Divine was not designated to a particular office, but was accessible to different people: professional prophets and laypeople.[6] This evidence demonstrates that divine communication, including prophecy through dream revelations in the ancient Near East, was experienced by a wide variety of people, inclusive of both genders.

Given that ancient Near East prophecy was so inclusive, Miriam's role as a prophet needs reconsideration. In this study I focus on Miriam's function in Num 12. I will ask whether Num 12 could point to a tradition that attests to Miriam's dream. Supplementary evidence for this case is offered by texts deriving from the Second Temple period, such as the Visions of Amram[d] (4Q546) and Pseudo-Philo's *Liber antiquitatum biblicarum* (*L.A.B.*), which refer to Miriam's dreams more explicitly. After reading each passage separately, I will analyze the relationship between these texts. Did one of the texts use the other while creating a tradition of Miriam as a dreamer? In light of a comparative reading of the Hebrew Bible and the texts deriving from the Second Temple period, studied in chronological order, I will argue that Num 12 does present Miriam as a literary figure to whom was attributed dream visions in the ancient Jewish literature.

---

5. Sally A. L. Butler, *Mesopotamian Conceptions of Dreams and Dream Rituals* (AOAT 258; Münster: Ugarit-Verlag, 1998), 2; Jan Bergman, Magnus Ottoson, and G. Johannes Botterweck, "חלם," *TDOT* 4:421–32.

6. Meanwhile, female prophets appear also in other ancient Near East texts. See Butler, *Dreams*, 17. Also the Neo-Assyrian texts from Nineveh attest to women's prophetic acts. In other ancient Near East cultures women have other religious positions. See Simo Parpola, *Assyrian Prophecies* (SAA 9; Helsinki: Helsinki University Press, 1997); Hennie J. Marsman, *Women in Ugarit and in Israel: Their Social and Religious Position in the Context of the Ancient Near East* (OTS 49; Leiden: Brill, 2003), 517–18; Jonathan Stökl, "Ištar's Women, YHWH's Men? A Curious Gender-Bias in Neo-Assyrian and Biblical Prophecy," *ZAW* 121 (2009): 87–100; idem, "Female Prophets in the Ancient Near East," in *Prophecy and the Prophets in Ancient Israel: Proceedings of the Oxford Old Testament Seminar* (ed. John Day; LHBOTS 531; London: T&T Clark, 2010), 47–61. See also the contributions by Stökl and Nissinen in this volume.

Speaking in Dreams in the Hebrew Bible

Divine messages are often communicated in dreams in the Hebrew Bible.[7] Many dreams appear in the patriarchal narratives, where the heads of the families receive divine messages while sleeping. Abraham is sleeping when God speaks to him (Gen 15:12).[8] God also appears to and addresses Isaac and Jacob during the night (26:24; 28:12–15). At least one of the messages to Jacob is explicitly delivered in a dream (28:16). Apart from the earlier patriarchs, Joseph is also known to have dreams in Genesis. Unlike these heads of households who receive divine dreams at their adult age, Joseph has dreams already as a young boy (37:7, 9), which are later fulfilled. Joseph differs from the patriarchs because he not only has dreams, but he also interprets them. During his stay in Egypt his role changes from dreamer into interpreter of other people's dreams (40:8, 12–13, 18–19; 41:25–36). While Joseph interprets dreams, it is specified that he does not do it autonomously. Rather the text states explicitly that the interpretation of dreams comes from God (40:8; 41:16). Hence Joseph, who delivers explanations of dreams, receives his understanding from God. Joseph's dreams and his function as a dream interpreter witness that it was not only the patriarchs (i.e., the heads of the households) who accessed communication with God. Other prominent characters could also receive divine information.

Interestingly, the Genesis dreams appear to be related to a particular family, as the dreams connected to Abraham, Isaac, Jacob, and Joseph show. These are the only characters in Genesis who receive divine messages in dreams, but they are not the only figures who receive messages from God. Although the Pentateuch rarely attests to the divine plans revealed to women, it does sometimes happen. An angel appears to Hagar in 16:7–12 while she is escaping and reveals to her the future of her child and his relevance in the divine plan. In 25:23 God tells Rebekah that she will give birth to rival twins. The means of communication is not explicitly

---

7. I deal with the various texts here in their order of appearance in the HB. This order does not mirror their chronological order. Generally on this topic, see Jean-Marie Husser, *Dreams and Dream Narratives in the Biblical World* (BiSe 63; Sheffield: Sheffield Academic Press, 1999).

8. Abraham is referred to as a prophet in Gen 15:1, 4; 20:7. For the patriarchal dreams see Diana Lipton, *Revisions of the Night: Politics and Promises in the Patriarchal Dreams of Genesis* (JSOTSup 288; Sheffield: Sheffield Academic Press, 1999).

described. The passage simply states that Rebekah inquired of God. While these narratives can be interpreted as divine communication with women with promises for the future, they do not contain the particular features of the dreams that are connected to the patriarchs. The divine dreams of Genesis are notably revealed only to the male members of the families. Despite their direct communication with God, however, the patriarchs and Joseph are usually not described as prophets.

The Former and Latter Prophets contain a more detailed picture of dreams in relation to prophecy. Various passages that deal with prophetic communication with the Divine in the books of prophets mention that these acts were connected to *seeing*. For instance, 1 Sam 9:9 states that at an early period of Israel's history a prophet was called a seer.[9] This implies that many prophets were known to access divine knowledge visually, that is, in a dream. Furthermore, when Saul does not receive a message from God, he is distressed and complains that God does not answer him either by prophets or dreams (1 Sam 28:6, 15). This confirms the earlier notion regarding the patriarchs and other prominent people that prophets were not the only people who could communicate with the Divine in dreams. Other people who were in contact with God could have divine dreams too.

Not all of the dreams received by the prophets were received without difficulty. A true prophetic dream was understood as something more than just falling asleep and dreaming. Several Hebrew Bible texts reflect criticism against certain dreamers and their dreams, which are condemned as false (Deut 12:32b–13:5; Jer 23:25–28; 27:9; Zech 10:2). This "false prophecy" vis-à-vis "true prophecy" suggests that dreaming per se was not always a divine experience.[10] Polemics against false prophecy questioned the provenance of the dreams, asking which dreams *came* from God and which prophecies were false.

---

9. "Formerly in Israel, anyone who went to inquire of God would say, 'Come, let us go to the seer'; for the one who is now called a prophet was formerly called a seer."

10. For false prophecy see Robert R. Wilson, *Sociological Approaches to the Old Testament* (GBS; Philadelphia: Fortress, 1984), 67–80; Martti Nissinen, "Falsche Prophetie in neuassyrischer und deuteronomistischer Darstellung," in *Das Deuteronomium und seine Querbeziehungen* (ed. Timo Veijola; Schriften der Finnischen Exegetischen Gesellschaft 62; Göttingen: Vandenhoeck & Ruprecht, 1996), 172–95; Carolyn J. Sharp, *Prophecy and Ideology in Jeremiah: Struggles for Authority in the Deutero-Jeremianic Prose* (OTS; London: T&T Clark, 2003), 103–24. For analysis of Deut 13, see Juha Pakkala, *Intolerant Monolatry in the Deuteronomistic History* (Publications of the Finnish Exegetical Society 76; Göttingen: Vandenhoeck & Ruprecht, 1999), 20–50.

These examples demonstrate that divine messages were received in dreams throughout the Hebrew Bible.[11] Most of the people that communicate with God through dreams are called prophets in the Hebrew Bible. Some other people have divine dreams too (e.g., the patriarchs and Joseph). They can be characterized as distinguished ("selected") people, who might communicate also without their visions. Importantly, when the dreams preserved in the Hebrew Bible are compared with those of the ancient Near East it appears that they are limited to a more restricted group of people.[12] The dreamers are mostly men who are known as prophets or who have otherwise prominent positions, while the Hebrew Bible does not attest to the dreams of those women who are called prophets (נביאה).[13] This does not necessarily mean that women did not access this type of communication, as dreaming was probably not restricted to a particular group of people, but that it is not preserved in the Hebrew Bible.[14]

Miriam

After getting more familiar with the concept of dream visions and making a point of how they relate to women, we can now analyze the figure of Miriam more closely. First, we will consider Miriam's role and her possible visionary acts of Num 12. After that we move on to analyze the texts outside the Hebrew Bible that shed more light on her visions.

---

11. Frances Flannery-Dailey, *Dreamers, Scribes, and Priests: Jewish Dreams in the Hellenistic and Roman Eras* (JSJSup 90; Leiden: Brill, 2004), 38–56. On pp. 42–44 Flannery-Dailey provides an exhaustive table of dreams of the Hebrew Bible.

12. For literature concerning prophecy in the ancient Near East, see n. 6.

13. Miriam (Exod 15:20–21), Deborah (Judg 4–5), Huldah (2 Kgs 22:13–20; 2 Chr 34:22–28), and Noadiah (Neh 6:14). Burns (*Has the Lord Indeed Spoken*, 42–46), Brenner (*Israelite Woman*, 57–66), and Gafney (*Daughters of Miriam*, 76–119) discuss these characters in more detail. Tal Ilan ("Huldah, the Deuteronomic Prophetess in the Books of Kings," *lectio difficilior* 1 [2010]: 1–16 [online: http://www.lectio.unibe.ch/10_1/ilan.html]) identifies Huldah as the most powerful Deuteronomic prophet of her day. Notably, the rabbinic literature (e.g., b. Meg. 14a) includes more women in the list of female prophets.

14. Joel 2:28–29: "Then afterward I will pour out my spirit on all flesh; your sons and your daughters shall prophesy, your old men shall dream dreams, and your young men shall see visions. Even on the male and female slaves, in those days, I will pour out my spirit." This could indicate that dreaming included also women. See Gafney, *Daughters of Miriam*, 110.

Miriam in Numbers 12:1–15

Numbers 12:1–15 is not a coherent text. Several features indicate that this passage derives from various sources and periods and that it went through an extensive editorial process.[15] For instance, verses 1–2 present two different reasons for the conflict that occurs between the figures of Moses, Aaron, and Miriam in Num 12. Verse 1 mentions Miriam and Aaron (in that order) criticizing Moses for his Cushite wife, while the question regarding Moses' exclusive prophetic role is raised in verse 2. The rest of Num 12 does not explicitly refer to either of these arguments.[16]

Verses 6–8 consist of God's address to Miriam and Aaron regarding Moses' exclusive prophecy. Many scholars think that these verses constitute a separate unit from the rest of Num 12.[17] A close reading of this passage reveals that it indeed contains nothing that would evidently link it to

---

15. August Dillmann, *Die Bücher Numeri, Deuteronomium und Josua* (2nd ed.; Kurzgefasstes exegetisches Handbuch zum Alten Testament 13; Leipzig: Hirzel, 1886), 63–64; Paul Heinisch, *Das Buch Numeri* (Heilige Schrift des Alten Testaments 2.1; Bonn: Hanstein, 1936), 53–54; George Buchanan Gray, *A Critical and Exegetical Commentary on Numbers* (ICC; 1903; repr., Edinburgh: T&T Clark, 1965), 120–22; Martin Noth, *Numbers: A Commentary* (trans. James D. Martin; OTL; Philadelphia: Westminster, 1968), 4–11, 92–93; Burns, *Has the Lord Indeed Spoken*, 48–79; Baruch A. Levine, *Numbers 21–36* (AB 4A; New York: Doubleday, 2000), 338–43; Horst Seebass, *Numeri* (BKAT 4.2; Neukirchen-Vluyn: Neukirchener Verlag, 2003), 61. Despite the majority of scholars recognizing literary difficulties in this passage, others read Num 12:1–15 as a textual unity. Bernard P. Robinson ("The Jealousy of Miriam: A Note on Num 12," *ZAW* 101 [1989]: 428–32), Rolf P. Knierim and George W. Coats (*Numbers* [FOTL 4; Grand Rapids: Eerdmans, 2005], 179–81), and Rapp (*Mirjam*, 133–37) treat this passage as a literary unit.

16. See Hanna Tervanotko, "Miriam's Mistake: Numbers 12 Renarrated in *Demetrius the Chronographer*, 4Q377 (*Apocryphon Pentateuch b*), *Legum allegoriae* and the Pentateuchal Targumim," in *Embroidered Garments: Priests and Gender in Biblical Israel* (ed. Deborah W. Rooke; HBM 25; Kings College London Studies in the Bible and Gender 2; Sheffield: Sheffield Phoenix, 2009), 144–45. Meanwhile Jacob Milgrom (*Numbers* [JPSTC; Philadelphia: Jewish Publication Society of America, 1990], 94) views the criticism of the Cushite wife as a pretext employed by Miriam and Aaron in order to challenge the prophetic priority of Moses. For the Cushite wife see Karen Strand Winslow, "'For Moses Had Indeed Married a Cushite Woman': The LORD's Prophet Married Well," *lectio difficilior* 1 (2011): 8–11. Online: http://www.lectio.unibe.ch/11_1/inhalt_e.htm.

17. Burns, *Has the Lord Indeed Spoken*, 77–78; Baruch A. Levine, *Numbers 1–20* (AB 4; New York: Doubleday, 1993), 75.

the disputes of 12:1–2 or to 12:10–15 that deals with Miriam's punishment and צרעת.[18] Also stylistic remarks argue against textual unity with the rest of Num 12. For instance, the introductory formula "hear my words" (שמעו נא את דברי) that appears in 12:6 stands out in this context. As God has already spoken in this passage (12:4–5), it is peculiar that the listeners are addressed only here. Moreover, the present context makes clear that the addressees of the speech are Aaron and Miriam. Yet they are not mentioned anywhere in verses 6–8.[19] Hence some have suggested that verses 6–8 first circulated separately from the other material of Num 12 and that it was put together with the rest of the material only at a later stage.[20]

The theme of prophecy is prominent in Num 12. As pointed out already, in verses 6–8 God addresses this theme. Moreover, verses 13–14 function as a demonstration of Moses' prophetic role, since he communicates directly with God. Numbers 12 argues that Moses has access to direct communication with the Divine.[21] The prophetic role of Miriam and Aaron is addressed as well. Most notably, Miriam's question in 12:2 indicates her and Aaron's involvement in communicating with God. When she asks whether God has spoken through them too, it indicates that such a tradition was known.[22] Moreover, God's address in verses 6–8 does not

---

18. This term that is often translated as "leprosy"; see John F. A. Sawyer, "A Note on the Etymology of ṣāraʿat," *VT* 26 (1976): 241–45. Jacob Milgrom (*Leviticus 1–16* [AB 3; New York: Doubleday, 1991], 768–889) renders the term "scale decease."

19. See Noth, *Numbers*, 95–96. Burns (*Has the Lord Indeed Spoken*, 52–54) presents the evidence for the independent tradition in detail.

20. See n. 15. Several scholars find characteristics of Canaanite and early Hebrew poetry in vv. 6–8. See William Foxwell Albright, *Yahweh and the Gods of Canaan: A Historical Analysis of Two Contrasting Faiths* (Jordan Lectures in Comparative Religion 7; London: Athlone, 1968), 1–46; Frank Moore Cross, *Canaanite Myth and Hebrew Epic: Essays in the History of the Religion of Israel* (1973; repr., Cambridge: Harvard University Press, 1997), 234–35; John S. Kselman, "A Note on Numbers 12:6–8," *VT* 26 (1976): 503–4; Burns, *Has the Lord Indeed Spoken*, 52–53.

21. Robert R. Wilson, "Early Israelite Prophecy," *Int* 32 (1978): 12; George W. Coats, "Humility and Honor: A Moses Legend in Numbers 12," in *Art and Meaning: Rhetoric in Biblical Literature* (ed. David A. J. Clines, David M. Gunn, and Alan J. Hauser; JSOTSup 19; Sheffield: JSOT Press, 1982), 97–107; Levine, *Numbers 1–20*, 338–43.

22. Gafney (*Daughters of Miriam*, 82–83) and Rapp (*Mirjam*, 191–93) suggest that Miriam's function in this text is to represent a group that claimed inclusive prophecy in the Persian period in contrast to the group that promoted merely Moses (i.e., exclusive prophecy); see also Fischer, "Authority of Miriam," 167–68.

negate this communication. It only affirms that it was different from the communication with Moses.

God's response to Miriam and Aaron displays some inconsistencies. Despite the claim that the Divine speaks directly only with Moses (vv. 6–8), this communication with Aaron and Miriam does not happen in a dream either. Rather, God seems to speak to them directly by first calling them in verse 5 to go to the tent of meeting and then addressing them in verses 6–8. In spite of these multiple references to Miriam's direct communication with God, Num 12 does not give a clear depiction of Miriam's prophetic experiences of the Divine, other than that it differed from that of Moses.[23]

In light of the complicated literary history of Num 12, the date of this passage is not easily established. Some features of Num 12 suggest this passage has an early provenance. For instance, the mention of Moses' intermarriage (12:1), a detail that was later censored in various texts, could be a sign of an early date.[24] However, other details of the text point to a later date. For instance, the avoidance of an anthropomorphic portrayal of the Divine may indicate a postexilic date. Verse 5 narrates how God comes down in a pillar of cloud. Thus the text indicates that people could not see God despite communicating with the Divine. It is known that the Deuteronomistic editing usually deleted anthropomorphic features, evidence that could hint that God appeared in humanlike form.[25] Another sign of a postexilic date is reflected in the portrayal of Moses. Moses' role as the supreme prophet who communicates directly with God becomes a prominent theme in the postexilic period (e.g., Deut 34:10).[26] Therefore at least

---

23. Here my conclusions differ from those of Rapp and Fischer. See above.

24. For more early features see Levine, *Numbers 1–20*, 103–9.

25. Moshe Weinfeld, *Deuteronomy and the Deuteronomistic School* (Oxford: Clarendon, 1972), 191–93.

26. Various scholars think that the tradition that attests to Moses as the chief prophet should be attributed to the Dtr school and Dtr editing of the HB. See Noth, *Numbers*, 93; Lothar Perlitt, "Mose als Prophet," *EvT* 31 (1971): 588–608; repr. in idem, *Deuteronomium-Studien* (FAT 2/8; Tübingen: Mohr Siebeck, 1994), 1–19, esp. 6–8; Wilson, "Early Israelite Prophecy," 13–16; Thomas C. Römer, "L'école deutéronomiste et la formation de la Bible hébraïque," in *The Future of the Deuteronomistic History* (ed. Thomas Römer; BETL 147; Leuven: Leuven University Press, 2001), 190–91; Christophe Nihan, "Un prophète comme Moïse (Deutéronome 18:15): Genèse et relectures d'une construction Deutéronomiste," in *La construction de la figure de Moïse—The*

those passages of Num 12 that highlight Moses' high position in front of God vis-à-vis other prophets cannot be dated before the exile.

Moreover, Num 12 contains terminology that suggests it has an even later date than Deuteronomy. Most importantly, Num 12:10–15, which deals with Miriam's צרעת, mirrors impurity laws and priestly practices presented in Lev 13–14. It is unlikely that the story regarding Miriam's צרעת, and how it was received, was written before the rules of צרעת were known. Numbers 12:10–15 should be dated around the Persian period.[27] This indicates that the final form of Num 12 was probably put together around the same era.[28]

Whereas Exod 15:20–21 does not explain the use of the title "female prophet" when introducing Miriam, Num 12 clearly suggests Miriam had a role in the debate concerning Moses' position as the prophet. Micah 6:4 presents Miriam as an early leader, alongside Moses and Aaron. Presenting Miriam as one of those sent by God to lead others implies that she had some authority.[29] If Miriam was known as a character that engaged in prophecy, her role as prophetic leader could explain her presence in the debate concerning prophecy in Num 12 too.[30] Unfortunately, however, Mic 6:4 does not mention Miriam's prophetic role. Instead, one must take into consideration texts that engage this topic and Miriam's access to the Divine more explicitly.

Construction of the Figure of Moses (ed. Thomas C. Römer; Supplément à Transeuphratène 13; Paris: Gabalda, 2007), 75–76.

27. Römer ("L'école deutéronomiste," 191) argues that these verses (12:10–15) and 12:1 have nothing to do with Dtr thinking. Rather, they reflect a different stream of Judaism. Levine (*Numbers 1–20*, 333) argues that the seven-day period referred to in Num 12:13–14 reflects an ancient custom.

28. Noth, *Numbers*, 10; Levine, *Numbers 1–20*, 106–8; Römer, "L'école deutéronomiste," 188–89; Kessler, "Mirjam und die Prophetie," 64–72; Fischer, "Authority of Miriam," 165–66; Rapp, *Mirjam*, 191–93. Cf. Timothy R. Ashley (*The Book of Numbers* [NICOT; Grand Rapids: Eerdmans, 1993], 6–7), who refers to scholars who date the P source to the time before the exile (e.g., Kaufmann, Milgrom) and argues for a preexilic date.

29. See, e.g., Josh 24:5; 1 Sam 12:11; 25:32; Jer 35:15; Mal 3:23. In these verses being sent by God points to only prominent figures. They have a role in fulfilling divine plans. Moreover, that God sends also angels (Judg 13:8) strengthens the point. The "sent people" have a special role in God's plans.

30. Kessler, "Mirjam und die Prophetie," 64–72.

Miriam in the Visions of Amram

While the Hebrew Bible, despite introducing Miriam as a female prophet, does not portray her in an explicitly prophetic role, the wider ancient Jewish literature presents a richer picture of this character. This literature is characterized as "parabiblical" or "paratextual," because it continues the narrative preserved in the Pentateuch.[31] Nonetheless, this type of literature can also have elements that are independent from the Hebrew Bible. In what follows I will analyze two paratexts. They do not merely mention the figure of Miriam, but they also suggest that this character had visions.

The earliest reference to a Miriam tradition that goes beyond the narrative of the Hebrew Bible appears in a text called the Visions of Amram (4Q543–549) in the Qumran library. The editor of the Visions of Amram, Émile Puech, suggests that the text may go back to the third or even the fourth century B.C.E.[32] According to their paleographical date, the texts of 4Q543, 4Q544, and 4Q547 date the earliest. They were probably written in the early and mid-Hasmonean period, the second half of the second century B.C.E.[33] The other copies of the Visions of Amram also date to the Hasmo-

---

31. For the term *parabiblical* see Emanuel Tov, "Foreword," in *Qumran Cave 4.VIII: Parabiblical Texts, Part 1* (ed. Harold Attridge et al.; DJD 13; Oxford: Clarendon, 1994), ix. Subsequently the term has been used to designate a wide range of material. For instance, DSSR 3 is subtitled *Parabiblical Texts*, and it applies to texts that rework the "biblical" material in various ways. The problem with this term is that it implies that there was already a "Bible," while at that time there was no canon. Therefore, the term *paratextual* literature is more accurate. This term was originally introduced by Gérard Genette, *Palimpsestes: La littérature au second degré* (Collection poétique; Paris: Seuil, 1982). For the use of the term see also Philip Alexander, Armin Lange, and Renate Pillinger, eds., *In the Second Degree: Paratextual Literature in Ancient Near Eastern and Ancient Mediterranean Cultures and Its Reflections in Medieval Literature* (Leiden: Brill, 2010).

32. Émile Puech, "Visions de 'Amram," in *Qumran Grotte 4.XXII: Textes araméens, première partie: 4Q529–549* (ed. Émile Puech; DJD 31; Oxford: Clarendon, 2001), 287.

33. Ibid., 285–89; Devorah Dimant, "The Qumran Aramaic Texts and the Qumran Community," in *Flores Florentino: Dead Sea Scrolls and Other Early Jewish Studies in Honour of Florentino García Martínez* (ed. Anthony Hilhorst, Émile Puech, and Eibert J. C. Tigchelaar; JSJSup 122; Leiden: Brill, 2007), 197–205. Robert R. Duke (*The Social Location of the Visions of Amram: 4Q543–547* [StBL135; New York: Lang, 2010], 89–101) dates the Visions of Amram between 225 and ca. 150 B.C.E.

nean or the early Herodian period. Nonetheless, the term פרשגן (copy)[34] that appears in the beginning of the Visions of Amram (4Q544 1 1) signifies that the preserved text is itself copied.[35] This remark implies that the preserved manuscripts do not contain the autograph of the Visions of Amram and therefore the text is certainly earlier than the copies of the Qumran library. Whereas the fourth-century date suggested by Puech may be too early, there are good grounds to assign this text to a date in the third or the latest the second century B.C.E.[36] Similarities with other texts, most notably with the Aramaic Levi Document (ALD), support the given date.[37] Six or seven copies preserved in the Qumran library indicate that this text did not find itself there by accident, but rather that it was a well-known composition.[38]

In the Visions of Amram the head of the patriarchal house instructs his children from his deathbed, narrating the content of visions that he had years prior. Due to the fragmentary nature of the copies of the Visions of Amram, and the lack of a reconstruction that would make use of all copies, it is difficult to analyze the continuity of the text with certainty. In what follows we will merely focus on one passage of this text, 4Q546 12 6, which concerns Miriam's רח.

---

34. BDB (1109) explains that the term פרשגן is an Aramaic word that appears also in the HB (Ezra 4:11, 23; 5:6). The term was known also in other ancient Near East languages.

35. Henryk Drawnel, "The Initial Narrative of the *Visions of Amram* and Its Literary Characteristics," *RevQ* 24 (2010): 527.

36. Some have argued that this type of literature mirrors issues evident in the second century B.C.E. when the priestly office was contested. The threat against the priests would at least partly explain the focus on purity that is evident in the Visions of Amram; see Robert Kugler, "Testaments," *Encyclopedia of the Dead Sea Scrolls* (ed. Lawrence H. Schiffman and James C. VanderKam; 2 vols.; New York; Oxford University Press, 2000), 2:933–36. In her presentation to the International Organization for Qumran Studies conference in Helsinki 2010, Liora Goldman also favored a priestly origin for this text.

37. Jonas C. Greenfield, Michael E. Stone, and Esther Eshel, *Aramaic Levi Document: Edition, Translation, Commentary* (SVTP 19; Leiden: Brill, 2004), 19–22.

38. Not all scholars agree on the number of copies. Duke (*Social Location*, 35–42) and Liora Goldman ("Dualism in the Visions of Amram," *RevQ* 24 [2010]: 421–32) have questioned the status of 4Q548 and 4Q549. In my view 4Q549 is another copy of the Visions of Amram. My arguments will be detailed in my forthcoming thesis: Hanna Tervanotko, "Denying Her Voice: The Figure of Miriam in Ancient Jewish Literature" (PhD diss.; University of Helsinki, 2013).

In the Aramaic Jewish texts this term רז applies to divine knowledge.[39] Only people who are linked to רז access the mysteries, that is, information that is revealed for the selected ones.[40] The term רז already appears in Aramaic literature at least from the third century B.C.E. on,[41] while it is not used before the second century B.C.E. in Hebrew texts. The earliest Hebrew text where רז appears is Ben Sira, which is dated to the first quarter of the second century B.C.E.[42] Whereas in the Hebrew texts the term רז appears particularly in connection with wisdom literature (most prominently in 4QInstruction and 4QMysteries), the Aramaic texts found in the Qumran library link the term with several well-known figures of Second Temple literature. Enoch, Methuselah, and Noah are all connected to רז in the *Genesis Apocryphon* (1Q20 V, 20, 25; VI, 12). The figure of Aaron is linked to רז in the Visions of Amram (4Q545 4 16).[43] Notably Miriam is the only female figure that the preserved Dead Sea Scrolls attest to accessing רז.

Some figures dealing with רז feel compelled to share their vision. This happens at least with Enoch (1Q20 V, 20–21), who first makes רז known to Methuselah, who then interprets it for Lamech. One reason for this could be that רז needs to be interpreted.[44] A similar use of רז can be found also

---

39. *HALOT* (5:1980) defines this term as a secret that is sometimes revealed in the night. Moreover, it is God that reveals the secrets. According to Martti Nissinen, "Transmitting Divine Mysteries: The Prophetic Role of Wisdom Teachers in the Dead Sea Scrolls," in *Scripture in Transition: Essays on Septuagint, Hebrew Bible, and Dead Sea Scrolls in Honour of Raija Sollamo* (ed. Anssi Voitila and Jutta Jokiranta; JSJSup 126; Leiden: Brill, 2008), 529–30, "the word is of Persian etymology, but it corresponds to Akkadian *piristu* and *niṣirtu*, both denoting the secret lore and cosmic knowledge kept by gods and revealed to selected individuals."

40. Samuel I. Thomas, *The "Mysteries" of Qumran: Mystery, Secrecy, and Esotericism in the Dead Sea Scrolls* (SBLEJL 25; Atlanta: Society of Biblical Literature, 2009), 118–22.

41. Book of Daniel; 1 Enoch (4Q201 1 IV, 5); Birth of Noah pericope (4Q204 5 II, 26); Book of Giants (4Q203 9 3); Visions of Amram (4Q545 4 16; 4Q546 12 4); Genesis Apocryphon (1Q20) and the so-called Elect of God text (4Q534 1 I, 7–8; 4Q536 2I + 3 9, 12).

42. For the date of Ben Sira see John J. Collins, *Jewish Wisdom in the Hellenistic Age* (OTL; Louisville: Westminster John Knox, 1997), 24. For a list of the Hebrew texts, see Thomas, *"Mysteries" of Qumran*, 4–5.

43. Puech, "4QVisions d'Amramᶜ," 343.

44. Samuel I. Thomas, "'Riddled' with Guilt: The Mysteries of Transgression, Sealed Vision, and the Art of Interpretation in 4Q300 and Related Texts," *DSD* 15 (2008): 155–71.

in the Hebrew Bible where Daniel explains the mystery (רז) of the king's dream. The content of רז is revealed to Daniel in a vision during the night (Dan 2:19).[45]

For this study it is important to recognize that apart from individuals, certain families are connected with רז. In this case, several members of a single family have access to רז. The *Genesis Apocryphon* attests to Enoch, Methusaleh, Lamech, and Noah all accessing רז. Similarly to the patriarchal narratives of Genesis, in the *Genesis Apocryphon* the divine plans are notably revealed only to the male members of the families. Women's possible access to רז is not mentioned.

Such continuity could be explained if parents had a role in instructing their offspring into רז. For instance, Levi reports how he instructed his sons and their sons (4Q213 1 I, 5). Levi, who teaches his children wisdom, ensures that his descendants will access some special knowledge. The early Jewish literature attests that Levi's offspring are indeed connected to visions. The visions occur in each successive generation. Levi's dreams are preserved in *ALD* 4 and 11.[46] He foresees the significance of his son Qahat (11:5–6) and his grandson Amram (11:6; 12:4). Qahat's address to his son Amram is preserved in the Testament of Qahat. Finally, the Visions of Amram narrates Amram's visions and his testament. The text refers to his vision at least four times (4Q544 1 10–11; 4Q546 9 2; 14 5; 4Q547 9 8).[47]

The Visions of Amram[c] 4, 15–16, where Aaron is linked to רז, deals with Aaron's significance. Amram explains that the secret (רז) of Aaron's work is that he is a holy priest and his descendants will be sacred. In the same text the importance of Moses is communicated to Amram in a vision. 4Q545 3 2–4 reads: "I will show you the mystery [רז] of his service: He is

---

45. Daniel is not called a prophet in the book, but "chief prefect over all the wise men of Babylon" (2:48). Yet his visionary acts indicate also a prophetic role. In addition, Daniel is considered a prophet in several early Jewish texts, e.g., 4Q174; Josephus, *Ant.* 10.263-281; *L.A.B.* 4:6, 8. For Daniel and mysteries, see Benjamin L. Gladd, *Revealing the Mysterion: The Use of Mystery in Daniel and Second Temple Judaism and Its Bearing on First Corinthians* (BZNW 160; Berlin: de Gruyter, 2009), 7–50.

46. Cf. the visions preserved in T. Levi 2:6–12. There the angel speaks to Levi and tells him that he will be a high priest and shall tell of God's mysteries; in T. Levi 8 the vision includes men dressed in white who bring the message. Here the prophecy concerns the significance of his offspring, while Levi does not tell this vision to anyone. Levi is told to instruct his children in the knowledge and he does so.

47. See Pieter van der Horst, "Moses' Father Speaks Out," in Hilhorst, Puech, and Tigchelaar, *Flores Florentino*, 491–98.

a holy judge."⁴⁸ The structures of these messages regarding the importance and future of Aaron and Moses resemble each other. A heavenly messenger announces and reveals the mystery (רז) of their ministry to their father prior to their birth.⁴⁹

Unexpectedly רז is likewise linked with the figure of Miriam in Amram's vision. In this case, רז appears both prior to her birth and in the middle of her father's vision. The text reads: "and the secret of Miriam he made for them."⁵⁰ Unfortunately the passage that discusses רז connected to Miriam is even more fragmentary than the ones concerning Moses and Aaron. Apparently, something about Miriam was revealed to Amram, just as in the cases of Moses and Aaron. As this text clearly deals with Amram's three children, my suggestion is that this line of the text follows the same as the lines on Aaron and Moses.⁵¹ Regarding Moses and Aaron, the term רז seems to point to their significance. Miriam's future and especially her importance could be interpreted similarly. Furthermore, that the term רז appears in this context suggests that the significance of Miriam that was announced to her father contained Miriam's access to divine knowledge. All three of Amram's children, Aaron, Moses, and Miriam, were connected with רז.

All in all, the use of רז differs from earlier prophecy in Jewish literature. It is not linked to a profession or a title. Rather access to רז was characteristic of certain family lines in Second Temple literature. While general conclusions regarding women and רז cannot be certain due to lack of evidence, what can be said is that, according to the interpretation preserved in the Visions of Amram, Miriam communicated with the Divine. As רז

---

48. My translation. Similarly Edward Cook, "4QVisions of Amramᵈ ar," *DSSR* 3:427.

49. Drawnel, "Initial Narrative," 531–32.

50. Puech, "Visions d'Amramᵈ ar," 364–65: 4Q546 12, 4: ורז מרים עבד לה[ון], "et le secret de Maryam lui/le[ur *fit*]."

51. I am aware that the order of the fragments of 4Q546 is not certain. Puech ("4QVisions d'Amramᵈ," 365–68) places fr. 12 at the top of col. VIII and fr. 14 in col. IX. If his placement is correct it would indicate that Miriam's רז appears in Amram's dream, i.e., Miriam's future was revealed to her father. Duke (*Social Location*, 33) thinks the location of 4Q546 12 cannot be identified. Klaus Beyer (*Die aramäischen Texte vom Toten Meer*, vol. 2 [Göttingen: Vandenhoeck & Ruprecht, 2004], 123–24) also does not place this text anywhere in his reconstruction of the text of the Visions of Amram.

often points to dream visions, it is possible that the Visions of Amram implies that Miriam had dream visions.

Miriam in *Liber Antiquitatum Biblicarum* 9:10

The most obvious link between Miriam and dream visions appears in *L.A.B.* 9:10.[52] Pseudo-Philo's *Liber antiquitatum biblicarum* is a first-century C.E. paratext that has survived in Latin.[53] The preserved text renarrates major events of the Pentateuch, from the creation of Adam to the death of Saul, singling out some of the most prominent events and characters of this history. Pseudo-Philo's treatment of biblical female figures stands out particularly from ancient Jewish literature. For instance, while the first-century writer Josephus reduces and even removes passages with female characters from his renarrations, Pseudo-Philo adds to some of them.[54] Pseudo-Philo refers to the figure of Miriam twice (9:10 and 20:8). The first passage narrates Miriam's dream vision.

---

52. Fundamental studies on Pseudo-Philo include Leopold Cohn, "An Apocryphal Work Ascribed to Philo of Alexandria," *JQR* 10 (1898): 277–332; Guido Kisch, *Pseudo-Philo's Liber Antiquitatum Biblicarum* (Publications in Medieval Studies 10; Notre Dame, Ind.: University of Notre Dame Press, 1949); M. R. James, *The Biblical Antiquities of Philo* (repr., with a new prolegomenon by Louis H. Feldman; Library of Biblical Studies; New York: Ktav, 1971); Charles Perrot and Pierre-Maurice Bogaert, *Introduction littéraire, commentaire et index* (vol. 2 of *Les antiquités bibliques*; SC 230; Paris: Cerf, 1976); Frederick J. Murphy, *Pseudo-Philo: Rewriting the Bible* (New York: Oxford University Press, 1993); Howard Jacobson, *A Commentary on Pseudo-Philo's Liber Antiquitatum Biblicarum with Latin Text and English Translation* (2 vols.; AGJU 31; Leiden: Brill, 1996); Bruce Norman Fisk, *Do You Not Remember? Scripture, Story and Exegesis in the Rewritten Bible of Pseudo-Philo* (JSPSup 37; Sheffield: Sheffield Academic Press, 2001).

53. For a more complete discussion on the nature of Pseudo-Philo see the literature quoted above. Also Daniel J. Harrington, "Pseudo-Philo," *OTP* 2:297–303; and, most recently, Tal Ilan, "The Torah of the Jews of Ancient Rome," *JSQ* 16 (2009): 363–95.

54. Perrot and Bogaert, *Introduction littéraire*. Perrot (*Introduction littéraire*, 52) discusses "the feminism of Pseudo-Philo." He observes that the author does not lack moments to talk about women. The term employed by Perrot, "Pseudo-Philo's feminism" (my trans.), has been accepted by later scholars. See Pieter van der Horst, "Portraits of Biblical Women in Pseudo-Philo's *Liber Antiquitatum Biblicarum*," *JSP* 5 (1989): 29–46; idem, "Tamar in Pseudo-Philo's Biblical History," in *Feminist Companion to Genesis* (ed. Athalya Brenner; FCB 2; Sheffield: Sheffield Academic Press, 1997), 300–305; Betsy Halpern-Amaru, "Portraits of Women in Pseudo-Philo's *Bib-*

Pseudo-Philo tells us that a Jewish man called Amram lives in Egypt. He marries a woman of his own tribe (Levi) and he has two children: Aaron and Miriam (Maria). One night Miriam has a dream where a man asks her to give her parents the following message: "I had a vision this night, and behold a man was standing in a linen garment and he said to me. 'Go and say to your parents, "Behold the child who will be born of you will be cast forth into the water; likewise through him the water will be dried up. And I will work signs through him and save my people, and he will exercise leadership always."'"[55] Miriam shares her dream with her parents, who do not believe her. It is clear that Miriam's vision represents communication with the Divine. The passage says in the beginning that one night the spirit of God comes to Miriam, that her vision includes an angelic figure, and that it reveals the future. Later it becomes clear that Miriam's dream was not a false vision since it is fulfilled.[56]

On the one hand, Miriam's vision preserved in Pseudo-Philo resembles closely a prophetic dream that reveals future events. On the other hand, these elements are also used to describe those accessing divine knowledge; hence the description in *L.A.B.* 9:10 is somewhat close to how people receive רה. Could Pseudo-Philo and Visions of Amram share a common tradition that attested to Miriam's dream vision?

The texts do contain similarities. First, they both narrate events from Amram's life and affirm his role in the pentateuchal narrative.

---

lical Antiquities," in *"Women Like This": New Perspectives on Jewish Women in the Greco-Roman World* (ed. Amy-Jill Levine; SBLEJL 1; Atlanta: Scholars Press, 1991), 83–106; Murphy, *Pseudo-Philo*, 258–59. Cf. Jacobson, *Commentary*, 1:250–51, who thinks that studies arguing that Pseudo-Philo is well disposed to women are "well-intentioned but perhaps a bit generous." Jacobson equally points out that the Pseudo-Philo does not, for instance, deal with the matriarchs. For Jacobson this appears as a sign of uneven treatment. I do not agree with his view. In contrast to ancient Jewish texts where the emphasis on particular women is not even present, a lack of some specific characters in Pseudo-Philo cannot be taken as a sign of a general style. For instance, in Pseudo-Philo the renarration of Judg 4–5 focusing on Deborah is four times longer than in the HB. Pseudo-Philo dedicates four chapters (30–33) entirely to Deborah. Tamar's pregnancy (Gen 38) is outlined in Pseudo-Philo, and Tamar is given an honorary title "our mother" in *L.A.B.* 9:5.

55. Translation by Jacobson, *Commentary*, 1:105.

56. Flannery (*Dreams in Hellenistic Judaism*, 120) points out that the fact that her parents do not believe her ridicules the figure of Miriam. Meanwhile, men's dreams are not mocked in Hellenistic Jewish texts.

Second, they emphasize endogamic marriages. Endogamy plays an important role in Visions of Amram. The figures of the Levitical family are married to members of the same family. The protagonist of this text, Amram, maintains (4Q544 1 8) that while he was away from home for forty-one years he did not take another wife but that, during those years away from home, he stayed faithful to his wife, Jochebed. In Pseudo-Philo Amram speaks against intermarriage, and according to Pseudo-Philo he "takes a woman from his own tribe" (9:9). Jochebed appears in this text in 9:12. Hence this text also outlines the union between Amram and Jochebed. Moreover, in 9:5 Amram praises Tamar for having a child with her father-in-law and hence not having a relationship with Gentiles.

Third, that both texts ascribe to Miriam access to divine knowledge reflects their positive treatment of female figures in general. In Visions of Amram, Amram's decision not to take another wife from local Canaanite women is not merely a question of negligence of intermarriage but seemingly due to his feelings for Jochebed, as his expression of longing to look upon "the face of my wife" reveals.[57] Outside this text, Amram mentions his wife several times, at least twice by name (4Q544 I, 5, 7). This is remarkable given that the name of Jochebed does not appear in those narrations of the Hebrew Bible where one could expect to find her (Exod 2; Num 26:59; 1 Chr 5:29).[58] Even if the text of Visions of Amram is preserved only in fragments, these few examples suggest that the figure of Jochebed was given more attention in this text than in the Hebrew Bible.[59]

In contrast to the Hebrew Bible, Visions of Amram and Pseudo-Philo present a distinguished image of Miriam as a visionary. The thematic similarities that these texts share suggest that they go back to a common tradition. A more thorough analysis that would take into consideration all the texts must be a subject of another study.

---

57. Similarly, Betsy Halpern-Amaru, "Burying the Fathers: Exegetical Strategies and Source Traditions in Jubilees 46," in *Reworking the Bible: Apocryphal and Related Texts at Qumran* (ed. Esther G. Chazon, Devorah Dimant, and Ruth A. Clements; STDJ 58; Leiden: Brill, 2005), 149; William Loader, *The Dead Sea Scrolls on Sexuality: Attitudes towards Sexuality in Sectarian and Related Literature at Qumran* (Grand Rapids: Eerdmans, 2009), 324–25.

58. This may be due to the consanguineous marriage between Amram and Jochebed, which was unacceptable for many.

59. For Pseudo-Philo's dealing with women see above, n. 54.

Comparative Reading of the Texts

After analyzing the texts attesting to Miriam's dream visions individually, and concluding that Visions of Amram and Pseudo-Philo may elaborate a common tradition, it is time to ask whether there can be any connection between the tradition that recognized Miriam as a visionary and Num 12, which implies that Miriam communicated with God. While discussing the nature of Visions of Amram, I argued that this text presents Miriam not as a female prophet (i.e., a character that regularly consulted the Divine) but as a prominent figure who, similar to others, had divine visions. Pseudo-Philo makes this tradition more evident.[60] Hence Miriam's dream was known at least in the first century C.E., but such a tradition could be earlier.

In the previous discussion on Num 12 I concluded that this passage was probably compiled around the Persian period. If this hypothesis regarding the date of Num 12 is accepted, the date comes rather close to the suggested time of Visions of Amram, which goes back to the early Hellenistic era. This text connects Miriam with רֹה and argues that her significance, similar to the other children of Amram, was announced to Amram in a vision. If Visions of Amram was not composed much later than Num 12, it is indeed possible that the compiler of the latter was aware of a tradition that connected Miriam with visions.

Date is not the only argument that favors the theory that Num 12 knew about Miriam's visionary acts. The content and in particular the internal inconsistencies of Num 12 suggest that a tradition that attested to Miriam as a visionary could have existed by the time of its compilation.[61] Miriam asks in Num 12:2 whether God did not speak through her as well. Such a question would be rather nonsensical if no tradition attested to such communication. Moreover, as noted earlier, the Divine's affirmation of Moses' role in Num 12:6–8 does not exclude the possibility of communication with others. On the contrary, people had dreams in which God appeared to them. Ancient Jewish literature witnesses that divine information was indeed transferred to Miriam in dreams. Reading Num 12 in the light of Miriam's role as a visionary makes it more understandable.

---

60. Later Jewish literature demonstrates that Miriam's dream continued to be of interest. It is preserved in b. Meg. 14a; Soṭ. 12b–13a; and in Exodus Mekilta by Rabbi Shimon ben Yohai.

61. Burns (*Has the Lord Indeed Spoken*, 78–79) thinks that in Num 12:2–9 Miriam represents a priestly, not a prophetic, group.

Hence Num 12 as it is preserved can be read as a debate concerning prophecy. While the later texts may have aimed at filling the gap in the Hebrew Bible concerning Miriam's lack of an explicit mention of visions, they do not depend on the narration of Num 12 directly. Visions of Amram and Pseudo-Philo do not present Miriam's visions in the same framework (wilderness) as Num 12. Nor do they reflect the conflict tone present in Num 12. The Visions of Amram presents Miriam as one of Amram's well-known children who equally to them accessed רז. Pseudo-Philo elaborates Exod 2 by asserting that Miriam's prophecies took place before the Israelites' departure from Egypt, when Miriam was still a young girl. Since the later texts do not continue renarrating Num 12, which is set in a very different context, they should not be read only as later attempts to explain what remains ambiguous in the Hebrew Bible, namely Miriam's prophetic role. Rather, all three texts present a different framework for Miriam's role as a female prophet. These texts all suggest that Miriam was known as a visionary and that her prophetic role may have been associated with that visionary context. The visionary function was depicted in various compositions, even though they elaborated it differently.

Conclusions

The Hebrew Bible offers only glimpses of what it means to be a female prophet in Miriam's case. In this paper I have focused on Miriam's prophetic role in light of Num 12. This text depicts Miriam as playing a prominent role while discussing prophecy. The challenge is that despite Miriam's presence in the text, it does not explicitly claim that Miriam was one of the prophets who received dreams and visions.

Some ancient Jewish literature fills in that gap by its portrayal of Miriam as a prophet. Visions of Amram and Pseudo-Philo demonstrate that a tradition that assigned Miriam a prophetic role existed in the Second Temple era and that this tradition was more developed than what remains in the Hebrew Bible. The traditions preserved in Visions of Amram and Pseudo-Philo explicate that Miriam's prophetic function was connected to dreams in which she received divine information.

In light of these texts, we should reconsider Miriam's role in Num 12. As it is difficult to build a definitive link between Num 12 and the interpretation of Miriam's dreams preserved in Visions of Amram and Pseudo-Philo, we have to consider two different possibilities for the mention of both Miriam and dream revelation in Num 12:2 and 6–8. One option is that Num 12 deals with Moses' preeminent prophetic role. In this context, the figure of Miriam serves to initiate the discussion in 12:2 and to demonstrate in 12:13–14 that Moses indeed spoke with God directly. This option assumes that Miriam's own prophetic role is not addressed in Num 12.

The other possibility, one that I find more likely in light of other evidence from the Persian period, is that the person or persons who arranged the material of Num 12 had in mind Miriam's role as a visionary. Hence it is no coincidence that Miriam initiates the discussion concerning prophecy and that God addresses her about this matter. In doing so, her own relationship with God is dealt with. This reading of Num 12 offers an explanation for a number of problems that occur in the passage, notably for the question Miriam raises in 12:2, God's address regarding divine dreams in 12:6–8, and the assertion of Moses' supreme position in front of the Divine in 12:10–15. The later texts that recognize Miriam as a dreamer who communicated with the Divine give further evidence that Num 12 in its present form addresses the question of a hierarchy of prophecy and Miriam's role as a female prophet.

CHILDLESS FEMALE DIVINERS IN THE BIBLE AND BEYOND

Esther J. Hamori

Recent scholarship has recognized that the long-assumed dichotomy between "prophecy" and "divination" is polemical, outdated, and not to be accepted as objectively factual any more than the emic presentations of "religion" and "magic" more broadly. While there is always room to focus on biblical "prophets" as diviners of a particular kind, or more accurately with a particular title, we should also consider what the broader range of divinatory roles looks like as a whole, including but not limited to prophecy. The present essay comes out of my work on the fuller picture of women's divination in the Hebrew Bible, including prophecy, necromancy, technical "inquiry," and more.

I will focus here on women who have divinatory titles or who are otherwise described in primarily divinatory roles.[1] Five biblical women are given the title נביאה: Miriam, Deborah, Huldah, Noadiah, and the unnamed woman of Isa 8:3. A group of women in Ezek 13:17–23 are said to prophesy (מתנבאות), though it is the odd description of their divinatory activity that is particularly intriguing. There is another brief poetic reference to daughters prophesying in Joel 3:1, with quite a different tone. The necromancer of Endor accesses a divine message through her divinatory art of raising the dead. The "wise women" of Tekoa and Abel have roles similar to those of the "wise men" in other texts who are advisors to kings and are associated with a range of activities.

In most ways these depictions of women's divination have no more in common than the range of texts describing men's divination. I have,

---

1. For discussion of other female characters who are portrayed as engaging in divination, see Esther J. Hamori, *Women's Divination in Biblical Literature: Prophecy, Necromancy, and Other Arts of Knowledge* (AYBRL; New Haven: Yale University Press, forthcoming).

however, observed one surprising commonality throughout this range of portrayals—virtually none of these women are said to have children. This stands in stark contrast to male characters who engage in divination, as well as to the majority of other female characters, including women whose offspring are not relevant to the story of Israel's lineage. In biblical traditions, divine favor to a woman is commonly manifested through her becoming a mother. We thus see mention of women as mothers even when this is not pivotal to the story. Consider, for instance, the midwives rewarded with children in Exod 1:21, or the tradition that "redeems" Naomi by making her the surrogate mother to Ruth's child (Ruth 4:16–17).

Before continuing, I will emphasize that I am interested here in the literary portrayal of women engaging in divination. Whichever of these women actually existed, there is clearly no hope of knowing more about their lives than their stories tell. What we can know is that the biblical texts do not portray these characters as mothers—and as literary figures, they exist only in these stories in which they are not mothers. In other words, a character's hypothetical life outside the text is not relevant: my point relates precisely to what the texts actually say. In addition, I do not claim that the writers consciously set out to create childless characters, but only that there is an observable pattern of female diviners not also being depicted as mothers. In the discussion that follows, I will at times refer to a character as not having children, or not being a mother. This should throughout be taken as a description of the character's place in the pattern of women whose literary portrayals do not include motherhood. This pattern seemed to me initially to be an odd coincidence, but a coincidence nonetheless. After a discussion of the relevant biblical character portrayals, I will present some evidence—first literary, then anthropological—that has led me to conclude that it is unlikely to be coincidental.

The Pattern within the Hebrew Bible

I will begin with the four women who are given both a personal name and the title נביאה, none of whom are said to have children. In Exod 15:20 Miriam is referred to as "Miriam the prophet [הנביאה], the sister of Aaron." We read of her siblings, her song, and her skin disease, but never of any offspring—not in or around the poetry of Exod 15, not in the narrative of Num 12, nor in the genealogies (Num 26:58–60 and 1 Chr 5:29 [Eng. 6:3]). Her childlessness is not a punishment; that is covered by the skin disease. (In contrast, Aaron, who is rebuked alongside his sister in Num 12, has four sons.) Rather, her childlessness is simply not mentioned.

Deborah too is called a prophet (אשה נביאה, Judg 4:4), though we see her only sitting as a judge, giving military orders in the name of Yahweh, and singing with Barak. The text informs us of the name of her husband, but she is never said to have children. She is, however, called "a mother in Israel" (אם בישׂראל, 5:7) despite the fact that she has no offspring. The phrase is recognizably metaphorical, though scholars differ on precisely what the metaphor expresses. It occurs one other time, in the speech of the wise woman of Abel (2 Sam 20:18), where it is sometimes taken as a description of the city, but more straightforwardly should refer to the woman herself, as I will discuss later. Both Susan Ackerman, in her work on Deborah, and Claudia Camp, in her work on the "wise women," assess the phrase אם בישׂראל. Although they both understand it in 2 Samuel to refer to Abel itself as a town where people would seek advice, rather than to the wise woman, they do demonstrate that the term "a mother in Israel" is metaphorical, conveying some kind of advisory role.[2]

In light of the pattern of childlessness among female prophets, the use of the expression "a mother in Israel" to refer to an advisory role is especially intriguing. I would suggest that it is not merely that Deborah happens to be called "a mother in Israel" in spite of the fact that she has no children. Given her role as advisor, and moreover prophet, she is "a mother in Israel" specifically as opposed to being a mother of children. In other words, it may not be coincidental that the idiom "a mother in Israel" twice describes a woman's advisory role, and the named female prophets are not mothers. It just may be that, rather than being merely an interesting idiom, this is an expression of the particular sense in which the female prophet is a mother.[3]

In 2 Kgs 22:14 we come to the prophet Huldah. She is introduced as Huldah the prophet (הנביאה), the wife of Shallum. Unlike in the case of Miriam, where we hear of her parents, her siblings, and her siblings' children, or in the case of Deborah, where we hear of her husband, in this text we learn of Huldah's husband, his father and grandfather, her

---

2. Susan Ackerman, *Warrior, Dancer, Seductress, Queen: Women in Judges and Biblical Israel* (ABRL; New York: Doubleday, 1998), 38–43; Claudia V. Camp, "The Wise Women of 2 Samuel: A Role Model for Women in Early Israel," *CBQ* 43 (1981): 26–29.

3. We might compare the Catholic use of the title "Father" here.

husband's job, and their home in Jerusalem in the Mishneh. Once again, however, we hear nothing of children. With the amount of information that we are given regarding Huldah's home and family, this is a noteworthy silence.

The last named female prophet, Noadiah הנביאה, appears only in passing in Neh 6:14. There is no mention of her having children, though no significance should be attached to this, given the one verse that makes up her story.

There is a fifth woman who is called a הנביאה, but she is not given a name. This is the woman who bears Isaiah's child. This nameless woman is then the only female prophet who is said to be a mother. While the activities that qualify Miriam and Deborah as prophets are unclear, we can at least surmise that their words are somehow relevant. Not so in this text. The woman of Isa 8 is not a prophet who prophesies. What she does in the story, she does only through her reproductive capacity: she bears a sign-child. This woman literally delivers an oracle.

I should note that some have suggested that this woman is not a prophet at all, but Isaiah's wife. Ackerman understands the term הנביאה here to be an "honorific, derived from her husband, as the wife of a king is called a queen."[4] I would tend to see her instead as a prophet who embodies her message, in a rather significant commitment to the prophetic sign-act. The text overtly describes the birth of the sign-child as prophetic symbolic action, and, not to put too fine a point on it, most of this action is hers. I understand the woman's sign-act together with her title to indicate that she is indeed a prophet. However, even assuming that she is meant to be a prophet and is an exception to the pattern I observe, the reason for Ackerman's skepticism is clear: the woman does nothing but bear Isaiah's sign-child. Thus none of the named female prophets have children, and the unnamed woman who has a child does not prophesy; she does not even speak. (Even Noadiah, though never quoted, at least tries to intimidate Nehemiah.) Only Isaiah speaks here. He is the one who gives the child his prophetic name, in contrast with the many stories of mothers giving their children meaningful names. In literary terms, the two categories of women having children and verbally prophesying still do not come into contact.

---

4. Susan Ackerman, "Isaiah," in *Women's Bible Commentary* (ed. Carol A. Newsom and Sharon H. Ringe; expanded ed.; Louisville: Westminster John Knox, 1998), 173; but see, e.g., Alfred Jepsen, "Die Nebiah in Jes 8, 3," *ZAW* 72 (1960): 267–68.

The medium of Endor, about whom we have a whole chapter of narrative set in her home, is not said to have children. Unlike the women who are identified by their husbands, including Deborah and Huldah, the necromancer, אשת בעלת־אב, is identified only by her relationship to the spirits of the dead.[5] The woman is not a mother, and children figure nowhere in the story. Nonetheless, interpreters frequently describe her preparation of a meal for Saul as a "maternal" act.[6] Presumably women prepared meals for men regularly, including wives for husbands, and servants for masters. It would be an obvious choice to read this scene straightforwardly as a subject-royal dynamic, related to that of servant-master, or if figuratively, at least as compared to adults, as in the wife-husband dynamic; but the instinct to depict the medium as motherly is strong. Such interpretations making the medium a mother in spirit only emphasize that the text does not make her a mother in fact.

The two "wise women" of 2 Sam 14 and 20 are also not portrayed as mothers. They are often referred to as "the woman of Tekoa" and "the woman of Abel"—which is peculiar, given that the texts introduce each as "a wise woman" (אשה חכמה), and only later refers to their towns. The term should be understood as the female counterpart to "wise man" (איש חכם and the like), as in Gen 41:8; Isa 19:11–12; 44:25; and throughout Dan 2, 4, and 5 (in Aramaic). As we see in those texts and others, the "wise man" is a type of diviner, sometimes so called for his skill, and sometimes apparently as a professional title.[7] The feminine form of the male

---

5. For full discussion of the difficult term, see Esther J. Hamori, "The Prophet and the Necromancer: Women's Divination for Kings," *JBL* (forthcoming).

6. E.g., J. P. Fokkelman on "the woman's motherly care" (*The Crossing Fates* [vol. 2 of *Narrative Art and Poetry in the Books of Samuel*; Studia semitica Neerlandica 23; Assen: Van Gorcum, 1986], 620); cf. Sarah Nicholson, *Three Faces of Saul: An Intertextual Approach to Biblical Tragedy* (JSOTSup 339; Sheffield: Sheffield Academic Press, 2002), 229; Leila Leah Bronner, *Stories of Biblical Mothers: Maternal Power in the Hebrew Bible* (Lanham, Md.: University Press of America, 2004), 91.

7. On חכמים as a professional class of wise magicians, including discussion of several of these "wise men" texts and others, see Ann Jeffers, *Magic and Divination in Ancient Palestine and Syria* (SHCANE 8; Leiden: Brill, 1996), 40–44. (She does not discuss the "wise women" of 2 Samuel.) As Jeffers observes, the "wise men" are often referenced in tandem with other types of diviners, or with magicians, and their function may shift. One might compare (though not extrapolate from) the combined skills of the "magi" or "wise men" of Matt 2:1–2, who believe a significant birth has occurred on the basis of astronomical divination.

divinatory term in combination with the women's actions demonstrates the appropriateness of such an interpretation. Such use of the feminine divinatory title אשה חכמה (whether professional or not, as with men) is highlighted when seen in contrast with the description of Abigail as an "intelligent woman," אשה טובת־שׂכל (1 Sam 25:3).

The "wise woman" of Tekoa, who, much in the style of Nathan, delivers a parable in response to which the king condemns himself, is not literally a mother. Her parable, however, is entirely and explicitly about a crisis of motherhood. She had two sons, and a fight broke out between them in the field, and one killed the other; now the whole clan wants to put the surviving son to death! "They will extinguish my [only] remaining coal," she laments (וְכִבּוּ אֶת־גַּחַלְתִּי אֲשֶׁר נִשְׁאָרָה, 2 Sam 14:7). She continues by framing this in terms of the family line, as her late husband will be left without name or remnant on the face of the earth; but we know that this is not the primary issue at stake. The parable, of course, is about David being reconciled to his son—Absalom, Absalom!—over whom he has a poignantly emotional crisis of fatherhood.

The second "wise woman," who takes a rather tough stance with Joab—ordering the people to tell him to approach so she can speak to him, then telling him to listen to her, and finally responding to his request for Sheba ben Bichri by agreeing to hand over at least the man's head—is also not a mother. She does, however, call herself (and not the city, as some assume) "a mother in Israel" (2 Sam 20:19). This expression reflects an advisory role here, as it does in reference to Deborah in Judg 5:7. She rebukes Joab: "I am among the peaceable and faithful of Israel; you are seeking to kill off a city and a mother in Israel [להמית עיר ואם בישראל]."

The use of the verb "to kill" indicates that עיר stands for the people of the city (cf. 1 Sam 5:12), and so both objects of the verb are human, as one would expect. One might also argue that because the verb להמית is doing double duty, the first object could be inanimate: "to destroy a city and kill a mother in Israel." It is too convoluted, though, to imagine either that the verb "to kill" would take two inanimate objects ("to kill a city, a mother-town") or that the first object would refer metaphorically to the people and the second object would refer metaphorically to the first ("to kill the people of the city, a mother in Israel"). The simplest explanation is that the woman, who has just described herself as peaceable and faithful, refers to herself as "a mother in Israel." On the basis of this text alone the phrase should be understood to refer to the "wise woman." The additional use of the same phrase to refer to Deborah renders alternatives unnecessarily contrived.

In the narrative accounts of titled female diviners, we thus have four named prophets, none of whom is a mother; one anonymous prophet who bears a child, but does not utter a word; a necromancer who is not a mother; and two "wise women" who do not have children, but the first is a mother in parable and the second "a mother in Israel."

We come then to the two poetic texts addressing women's divination. The "daughters of your people who prophesy" in Ezek 13 do many mysterious things, things involving bands and veils and hunting souls, but one thing they do not do is have children. As with all of the women under discussion, the point here is not to suggest that any actual women involved in this type of divination (to whatever extent it is historically based) could not have been mothers, or that the author of this text intentionally created childless characters; but that here, in poetry as in prose, the tradition does not reflect a notion of these female diviners as mothers. The absence of any reference to motherhood in a poetic indictment is less significant than in a prose narrative, but the passage may usefully be contrasted with Ezekiel's other poetic indictments that do refer to offspring, those of both metaphorical female idolaters and actual male diviners (but not female diviners, actual or metaphorical). These include the invective against Jerusalem personified as an idolatrous woman, whose religious abominations include sacrificing her sons and daughters (16:20–21); the horrifying oracle against Oholah and Oholibah (Samaria and Jerusalem), who are idolaters guilty of cultic crimes such as desecrating the Sabbath, and who also sacrifice their children (23:37); and the oracle following that of the "daughters of your people who prophesy," which refers repeatedly to the hypothetical sons and daughters of Daniel, Noah, and Job (14:13–23).

The oracle of Joel 3:1–2 paints a provocative picture. When God pours out his spirit on all flesh, the prophet says, people of all kinds will be inspired—that is, almost all kinds. "Your sons and your daughters will prophesy," Joel proclaims; "your old men will dream dreams; your young men will see visions." He carries on, "I will pour out my spirit even on male and female servants in those days!" So we have male and female children, the old men, the young men, and "even" servants of both sexes. Where are the old women? The old men in this oracle are not explicitly fathers, but the juxtaposition of generations—the sons and the daughters, and the old men—is suggestive. With regard to old women, the potential mothers, there is no ambiguity—they are nowhere to be found.

Despite the glimmers of the notion that titled female diviners could theoretically have children (as seen in Isa 8:3), almost none of these women in the Hebrew Bible do. Male characters are another story. They are depicted as having many different types of families. There are men with religiously insignificant children, men with sign-children, men without children. A good number of the books named for (male) prophets are only collections of oracles, written as the words of the prophets, and thus cannot be considered in regard to literary portrayal of the prophets themselves (i.e., Joel, Obadiah, Micah, Nahum, Habakkuk, Zephaniah, and Malachi; others are discussed below). However, many narrative texts mention men called prophets, seers, and men of God—many more than those mentioning such women. There is in these texts a notable variety in the portrayal of the men's familial status. Many of the men who are called נביאים have children, including Abraham, Moses, Samuel, the old prophet of 1 Kgs 13, and Isaiah; Hosea, not explicitly called a prophet but clearly presented as one, does as well.[8] Shemaiah, who prophesies in Jer 29:31, is likely the father of Uriah ben Shemaiah, who prophesies in Jer 26:20. The musicians Heman, Jeduthun, and Asaph—all also called seers in various places—all have children.[9] The three musician-seers are explicitly said to prophesy, and their sons prophesy alongside them to musical accompaniment (1 Chr 25:1-8). Hanani the seer (2 Chr 16:7) has a son, the prophet Jehu ben Hanani (1 Kgs 16:7; 2 Chr 19:2). In these last five cases, the prophets and seers have sons who follow in the family business.[10]

There may be references to children of three more men with the title נביא, Hananiah, Nathan, and Oded, though each name is presumably common. Hananiah famously opposes Jeremiah (Jer 28); there is a Zedekiah ben Hananiah in Jer 36:12, and more interestingly an Irijah ben Shelemiah ben Hananiah who arrests Jeremiah, raising the possibility of a family feud (Jer 37:13). Nathan is one of David's court prophets, and Aza-

---

8. I am not including Aaron in this list, as the text calls him a prophet of Moses, not of God (Exod 7:1). If he is to be considered a diviner of sorts, he too is in the category of those with children.

9. The three are called "seers" in 1 Chr 25:5; 35:15; and 2 Chr 29:30, respectively. Their children are named in the passage discussed here, and in 2 Chr 29:13-14.

10. We see the expectation of fathers training sons as apprentices in divination in Mesopotamia as well (W. G. Lambert, "The Qualifications of Babylonian Diviners," in *Festschrift für Rykle Borger zu seinem 65. Geburtstag am 24. Mai 1994: Tikip santakki mala basmu* [ed. Stefan M. Maul; CM 10; Groningen: Styx, 1998], 141–58), and in the mantic families of ancient Greece (Michael Attyah Flower, *The Seer in Ancient Greece* [Joan Palevsky Imprint in Classical Literature; Berkeley: University of California Press, 2008], 37–50).

riah and Zabud, both sons of Nathan, serve in Solomon's court (1 Kgs 4:5). There is also an Igal ben Nathan named as one of David's military chiefs (2 Sam 23:36). There is some confusion between a prophet Oded and a prophet Azariah ben Oded (2 Chr 15:1-8); this could be a scribal error (there is another Azariah in v. 12), or an indication of another father-son line of prophets.[11]

The prophets, seers, and men of God who are not said to have children include a good number of those whose eponymous books include narrative—Jeremiah, Ezekiel, Amos, Jonah, Haggai, and Zechariah—as well as Gad, Eldad and Medad, the anonymous prophets of 1 Kgs 20 and 2 Chr 25:15-16, Micaiah, Elijah and Elisha, Jehu ben Hanani, Iddo the seer (2 Chr 9:29), and another Shemaiah (from the time of Rehoboam, called a man of God in 1 Kgs 12:22 and 2 Chr 11:2, and a prophet in 2 Chr 12:5, 15).

Of the men who explicitly engage in other forms of divination—Joseph, who has "significant" dreams (in the technical sense), interprets the dreams of others, and uses a divining cup; David, who "inquires" and uses an ephod for divination; Saul, who prophesies, "inquires," and attempts to divine through אורים and dreams; Jacob and Solomon, assuming they incubate their dreams;[12] and Daniel, who interprets dreams and divine writing—every one but the last certainly has children, and several verses in Ezekiel suggest a tradition of Daniel as having children as well.[13] It is doubtful that Job's activity in demanding God to appear and explain himself should be considered divination (the theophanic communication signals a different genre of religious phenomenon), but insofar as God

---

11. Lastly, there are too many men named Ahijah to tell whether the prophet of 1 Kgs 11 has children.

12. On Near Eastern perspectives regarding types of dreams, see Sally A. L. Butler, *Mesopotamian Conceptions of Dreams and Dream Rituals* (AOAT 258; Münster: Ugarit-Verlag, 1998), 15-41; and on dream incubation, 217-39; and Annette Zgoll, *Traum und Welterleben im antiken Mesopotamien: Traumtheorie und Traumpraxis im 3.-1. Jahrtausend v. Chr. als Horizont einer Kulturgeschichte des Träumens* (AOAT 333; Münster: Ugarit-Verlag, 2006).

13. The reference to the children of Daniel (and Noah and Job), repeated three times in Ezek 14:12-20, is prophetic rhetoric and does not constitute a portrayal of fatherhood, but implies an assumption that Daniel had children. For any historical reconstruction, such poetic rhetoric would be irrelevant; in an examination of biblical literature regarding traditions according to which diviners had children, it is relevant.

responds to Job's demand by revealing hidden knowledge, it shares a certain family resemblance; Job also has children.

Although in a very few cases the mentions of male and female diviners with no reference to children are equally insignificant for establishing a pattern, as with Iddo and Noadiah, the difference between the broader pictures of men and women is evident. In any single story, it would be a stretch to read anything into the lack of personal information; what is significant is the pattern. The great majority of female characters in the Hebrew Bible have children; almost none of the female diviners do. Portrayals of male diviners, in contrast, exhibit a range in familial status. There are also minor female characters whose brief appearances relate to things other than their own families, but who are said to have children anyway (e.g., the midwives of Exod 1:21). We would not necessarily expect to see the mention of children in any individual story; however, this is presumably part of why the pattern of not seeing them in so many stories of this one type has not previously been observed.

A claim that any one character must be childless simply because no child is mentioned in the text would be an argument from silence (and would beg the question of what constitutes the extratextual life of a character). I claim, rather, that what is significant is the pattern of the absence of children through the literary portrayals of virtually all of the female diviners in biblical texts. The literary construction of female diviners in the Hebrew Bible reflects a discomfort with the intersection of traditional female roles and prophetic, visionary, and other divinatory roles. Most women with special access to divine knowledge are depicted as living outside other social norms as well.

THE PATTERN BEYOND THE HEBREW BIBLE

Historical and anthropological evidence suggests that the association we have seen in biblical literature between unusual access to the spirit world and nonnormative social position conforms to observable social reality. This takes many forms, from the social location of both male and female shamans to the celibate male priesthood of Catholicism. As seen in women in particular, the relationship between special knowledge and fringe status is often expressed through unconventional family structures, such as marital role reversal (as understood within a given culture), or the lack of children. We find examples of this in the ancient, medieval, and modern worlds.

The most immediate point of comparison—that is, the one context that might have a direct bearing on our interpretation of the Israelite texts—is unfortunately somewhat opaque. The divinatory practices of women elsewhere in the ancient Near East, and ideas about them as reflected in literature, could provide more information about assumptions possibly behind the Israelite texts as well. There has not yet been any study of women's divination in the ancient Near East. The work of a specialist in this area would be most welcome. Without claiming to be exhaustive on the topic of women's divination in Mesopotamia, I will discuss a few literary figures and written reports.

Three female characters in Mesopotamian literature are depicted as especially skilled in dream interpretation: Ninsunna, Nanše, and Geštinanna. The first two are divine themselves, which rather rules them out of direct comparison to women accessing divine knowledge. The remaining case, Geštinanna, is human—utterly so—and as it happens, childless. Her brother Dumuzi had failed to mourn Inana, his lover, after her descent to the underworld. When Inana sees this, her choice of whom to send to the underworld in her place is easily made: "She looked at him, it was the look of death. She spoke to him (?), it was the speech of anger. She shouted at him (?), it was the shout of heavy guilt: 'How much longer? Take him away.'"[14] Geštinanna mourns her brother and offers to go to the underworld in his place, an offer that the lovers apparently both accept, and she is fated to spend half of every year there. Though he is to spend the other half of the year in the underworld, Dumuzi is still primarily known in relation to his lover, Inana. Geštinanna, physically banished from the human world, is associated only with one man: Dumuzi.

Among records of actual female diviners, most notable are the female prophets and dreamers from Mari, and the female prophets behind many of the Neo-Assyrian oracles from a millennium later. There is not sufficient evidence regarding the lives of almost any of these women to comment about them. The historical-literary distinction here is key: as a literary figure, a character only exists where she is described in the text, and so the decision (however conscious) not to portray a character as a mother is worth comment. In the genre of an oracle report, such as a letter to Zimri-Lim, we know that the letter is meant to report only this particular infor-

---

14. Jeremy Black, Graham Cunningham, Eleanor Robson, and Gábor Zólyomi, "Inanna's Descent to the Underworld," in *The Literature of Ancient Sumer* (Oxford: Oxford University Press, 2004), 75, lines 354–357; ETCSL 1.4.3.

mation, and the fact that the family status of the woman is not mentioned is not significant for our understanding of the contextual view of women's divination. The Neo-Assyrian texts are almost entirely the reports of the oracles themselves, with no additional information.

With this said, one aspect of the view of female diviners in the Mari letters is worth noting here, if only to dispel the belief that these key sources on Near Eastern women's divination depict an acceptance of women's oracles equal to that of men's. While the divination of women—from untitled women to professional diviners and women of the royal court—was reported, we have evidence that it was seen as less reliable than the divination of men. Some prophets and dreamers submitted a clipping of their hair and a fringe of their garment for the purposes of ritual verification. These enclosures are made significantly more frequently in the reports of women's oracles, even those of the royal women.[15]

Comparisons to contexts a bit further afield, when seen in combination, may be informative as well. The Pythia, prophet of Apollo at Delphi, gives us a clear picture of the separation between female divinatory and common familial roles. The early tradition required the Pythia to be a virgin upon taking office, and to remain so throughout her service (a lifetime appointment). Later, at least by the mid-fifth century, a woman who had already had children or even grandchildren could become the Pythia—that is, a postmenopausal woman who would be "pure" from that time on.[16] This restriction of the divinatory role to virgins and postmenopausal women, but not childbearing women, is seen elsewhere as well. The independent seers (μαντεῖς), in contrast, worked under no such restrictions, and tended to be men with families.[17] The Pythia was also at a physical remove: though the Delphic Oracle was a large complex that served huge numbers of visitors, it was located partway up a mountain, and the Pythia would remain there, presented in literature as seated on a tripod over a chasm (though archaeological evidence would indicate nothing more than fissures in the bedrock).[18]

---

15. Esther J. Hamori, "Gender and the Verification of Prophecy at Mari," *WO* 42 (2012): 1–22.

16. Sarah Iles Johnston, *Ancient Greek Divination* (Malden, Mass.: Blackwell, 2008), 38–44.

17. Ibid., 110–18; Flower, *Seer in Ancient Greece*, 37–50.

18. Johnston, *Ancient Greek Divination*, 33–50.

Sarah Iles Johnston sees the expectation of "purity" in the myth of Cassandra as well. Apollo initially gives Cassandra the gift of prophecy with the understanding that she will give him her virginity in return; when she refuses, he curses her with the disbelief of all who hear her prophecy. Johnston notes that the story provides an explanation for the unlikely juxtaposition of the potent god Apollo bestowing special favor on a woman who remains celibate (as seen for instance at the Delphic Oracle).[19]

A variety of expressions of unease with women's overlapping family and divinatory roles can be seen cross-culturally, but the span of examples indicates that in a wide range of contexts, women's divinatory roles—or, more properly, lower status divinatory roles, which are the type to which women tend to have more access—are associated with nonnormative gender roles. In the following examples, each culture's own constructions of gender are taken into account. It is the separation of roles *as understood within each context* that is key.

In medieval Christianity, what made it possible for a woman to be accepted as a visionary was generally to be an ascetic. Some women were "enclosed" ascetics—that is, literally shut up in solitary confinement in a monastic cell—and others lived as ascetics in the world. Both options would tend to effectively separate the roles of mother and visionary.[20] The former is reminiscent of the virginal and physically remote Pythia. The latter is more radical: in order to live as ascetics among men (and perhaps to do so safely), it was necessary to embody the rejection of traditional female roles. Some women, now commonly called the "transvestite saints," dressed and lived as men, including Pelagia, Marina, Athanasia, Wilgefortis (also called by the masculine names Pelagius, Marinus, Athanasius, and Uncumber), Hildegard of Bingen, Catherine of Siena, Margery Kempe, and others.[21] Though apparently some "transvestite saints" were not identified as female until they died, most were seen to be transcend-

---

19. Ibid., 42–43, on the best-known version of the myth, as found in Aeschylus, *Agamemnon* 1200–1212.

20. These women at times claimed to have visions of suckling the baby Jesus, which bears an intriguing resemblance to the replacement language and imagery of the knowing woman (wise or prophet) as a "mother in Israel."

21. Sabrina Petra Ramet, ed., *Gender Reversals and Gender Cultures: Anthropological and Historical Perspectives* (London: Routledge, 1996), 5. See also Vern L. Bullough and Bonnie Bullough, *Cross Dressing, Sex, and Gender* (Philadelphia: University of Pennsylvania Press, 1993), 51–54, on various stories of female saints who lived as men.

ing their womanhood. Eugenia, for example (who became Eugenius), was told by a bishop, "You are rightly called Eugenius ... for you act in a manly [courageous] way."[22] This has much earlier roots in the literary tradition of female saints: in the *Acts of Thecla*, after Thecla has cut off her hair and taken on male dress and appearance in order to go teach, she survives attempts on her life, but wants to continue. It is Paul himself who gives his approval in the story: "Go and teach the word of God!"[23]

Such stories—and there are many of them—assume an authority that comes with the male body. We see this both in the women's embodiment of male religious activity through taking on male identity to teach or preach, and in responses such as Paul's to Thecla and the bishop's to Eugenia/us. As Karen Jo Torjesen frames it, "The female body suffered in the hands of male hagiographers for whom the effacing of female sexuality also represented the transition from sin to holiness." In addition to the women cutting off their hair, wearing male garb, and vowing chastity, their biographers distanced the pious women from the "femaleness" of their bodies, at times through the ascetic disciplines themselves: they remark that Pelagia's body was no longer recognizably female due to her fasting, Demetria's tears were said to wash away her beauty, Syncletica went without bathing, and so on.[24]

The creation of distance between divinatory and mainstream maternal female roles is evident in these ancient and medieval contexts in a variety of ways, including through the virginity of the divining woman, through her advanced age (postmenopause), through enforced physical separation from men (in the underworld, the oracle, or a monastic cell), and through symbolically shedding femininity altogether in preference for taking on male identity, or virtual embodiment. I have been surprised to discover that, while by no means universal, the same phenomena are found in many modern societies as well.[25]

---

22. John Ansom, "The Female Transvestite in Early Monasticism: The Origin and Development of a Motif," *Viator—Medieval and Renaissance Studies* 5 (1974): 22.

23. J. L. Welch, "Cross-Dressing and Cross-Purposes: Gender Possibilities in the Acts of Thecla," in Ramet, *Gender Reversals and Gender Cultures*, 68–69.

24. Karen Jo Torjesen, "Martyrs, Ascetics, and Gnostics: Gender-Crossing in Early Christianity," in Ramet, *Gender Reversals and Gender Cultures*, 86.

25. On the methodological validity of cross-cultural comparison of gender roles in religious groups, see Susan Starr Sered, who notes that as an anthropologist she would not expect to find universals in most areas of religious belief and practice, but that we do find gendered patterns in religion, because "there are cross-culturally relevant

The most clearly divinatory roles for women in many cultures today, and the roles that in some ways are most relevant to the discussion of biblical divination, are those of shamans.[26] Such roles take many forms; the word *shaman* itself indicates different things in different places, and there is even variety within a given culture. There is enough overlap, however, to warrant discussing such roles together.[27] I will not address broader cross-cultural issues regarding the shaman, diviner, or prophet, including other gender issues, for which readers may refer to any number of previous works.[28] I will restrict myself here to the issue of the distancing of female diviners from traditional female roles, as expressed in a variety of ways.

In addition to the phenomenological relevance of shamanism (consider, e.g., "the spirit of Yahweh fell on so-and-so"), shamans are particularly sociologically relevant to this study. In a patriarchal context such as the "face" of Israelite religion (i.e., the majority of ideas and practices that were written down, passed on, and drawn together), women's religious roles would likely be marginal, and thus more comparable to most shamanic roles than to technical diviners or male priests.[29] Shamans and

---

social patterns in women's lives." Moreover, the primary pattern that Sered identifies as a cross-cultural social reality for women, and thus not a coincidental influence on women's religious experience, is the centrality of concerns surrounding motherhood (*Priestess, Mother, Sacred Sister: Religions Dominated by Women* [Oxford: Oxford University Press, 1994], 71–72). See also Mary Keller, *The Hammer and the Flute: Women, Power, and Spirit Possession* (Baltimore: Johns Hopkins University Press, 2002).

26. On the relevance of shamanism and spirit divination for biblical prophecy, see Lester L. Grabbe, *Priests, Prophets, Diviners, Sages: A Socio-Historical Study of Religious Specialists in Ancient Israel* (Valley Forge, Pa.: Trinity Press International, 1995), 107–12, 135–51; idem, "Shaman, Preacher, or Spirit Medium? The Israelite Prophet in the Light of Anthropological Models," in *Prophecy and Prophets in Ancient Israel* (ed. John Day; Proceedings of the Oxford Old Testament Seminar; LHBOTS 531; New York: T&T Clark, 2010), 117–32. For cross-cultural comparison of female shamanic figures, see esp. Keller, *Hammer and Flute*.

27. E.g., the roles of the Korean shamans *mansin* and *mudang*, on which see Brian Wilson, "The Korean Shaman: Image and Reality," in *Korean Women: View from the Inner Room* (ed. Laurel Kendall and Mark Peterson; New Haven: East Rock Press, 1983), 113–28; Laurel Kendall, *Shamans, Housewives, and Other Restless Spirits: Women in Korean Ritual Life* (Studies of the East Asian Institute; Honolulu: University of Hawaii Press, 1985), 61.

28. See esp. Thomas W. Overholt, *Cultural Anthropology and the Old Testament* (GBS; Minneapolis: Fortress, 1996).

29. It should be noted that "patriarchy" is not the black-and-white issue it was

other marginal religious figures, both male and female, frequently also occupy nonnormative social positions in regard to gender expectations and gender performance, including in familial structure or status.

It is commonly understood in the study of shamanism that shamans, cross-culturally, cross gender boundaries. As early as 1914—long before it became (relatively) common to discuss the multiplicity of gender identities—the anthropologist Marie Antoinette Czaplicka noted many ways in which the Chukchi shamans of Siberia appear and function not as male or female, but as a third category all their own. This role includes cross-dressing, and at times same-sex marriage (culturally distinct from that in modern, Western, first-world societies).[30] The gender role transformation of shamans among the Siberian Chukchi is well known, and has become the classic scholarly example of shamanic gender crossing, but the phenomenon is also well known more broadly.[31] There are similar practices,

---

treated as for a long time. Recognizing the complexity of a culture's many interacting and intersecting parts, we see that issues of race, class, age, health, and other factors also critically influence power structures. Household religion might have been significantly less patriarchal than much of what we see in biblical texts. See, e.g., Carol L. Meyers, "Contesting the Notion of Patriarchy: Anthropology and the Theorizing of Gender in Ancient Israel," in *A Question of Sex? Gender and Difference in the Hebrew Bible and Beyond* (ed. Deborah W. Rooke; HBM 14; Sheffield: Sheffield Phoenix, 2007), 83–105. With this said, in systems dominated by men, women's access to (what their cultures view as) divine knowledge and divine contact will be subject to limitations that men's access is not. In her overtly methodologically focused work on women's spirit possession and social power structures, Keller summarizes, "The agency of women in general and the instrumental agency of possessed women in particular always exists in relation to the structures of power in which they live" (*Hammer and Flute*, 161).

30. Marie Antoinette Czaplicka, *Aboriginal Siberia: A Study in Social Anthropology* (Oxford: Clarendon, 1914), 249–53. Her terminology, "third class," should not be mistaken for the equivalent of modern terms such as "third sex" and "third gender." (John Pairman Brown uses the heading "third sex" in his brief 1981 discussion of Czaplicka, but the sense has changed since then as well; "The Mediterranean Seer and Shamanism," *ZAW* 93 [1981]: 376–77.)

31. Marjorie Mandelstam Balzer, "Sacred Genders in Siberia: Shamans, Bear Festivals, and Androgyny," in Ramet, *Gender Reversals and Gender Cultures*, 164–82. Gender transformation is also well documented among other peoples of northeastern Siberia, including the Koryak, Itelmen (Kamchadal), and Siberian Eskimo (Iupik) (165).

for instance, among Native American shamans, particularly within the Plains groups but also the Navaho, Hopi, and others.[32]

Long before the dawn of modern gender studies, the practice of gender transformation among shamans was recognized as common to many religious groups. As in anthropology (and other fields) more broadly, this was seen for some time as a universal phenomenon, and cultural specificity was blurred by the sweeping stroke of the structuralists. More recently, a key goal in cross-cultural studies has been to walk the line, as much as one can, in full recognition of environmental particularity, observe practices with correlatives in other cultures, and learn something about ideas that may extend beyond a given culture. Throughout this discussion, I take for granted that "shaman" has a variety of culturally specific meanings, what anthropologists refer to as shamanic "gender transformation" looks different in each context, and so on. These significant differences notwithstanding, female shamanic figures in many societies do not conform to their culture's standards of normative familial roles. Where female shamans do live in a home with children, anthropologists often describe a sharp reversal of gender roles. More frequently, however, societies show a preference for either prepubescent girls or postmenopausal women.

In Korea, today as in the past, most shamans are female. Both male and female shamans at times engage in gender role transformation, through cross-dressing and otherwise; male shamans were generally expected to wear women's clothing, at least until recently.[33] For female shamans (*mansin, mudang*), some of these role reversals are longer lasting, most germanely those relating to family life. In traditional Korean society, the roles of housekeeping and childcare on the one hand, and working many hours outside the home for pay on the other, are highly gendered. In the family of a married female shaman, these roles are typically reversed. She

---

32. Walter L. Williams, *The Spirit and the Flesh: Sexual Diversity in American Indian Culture* (2nd ed.; Boston: Beacon, 1992); note comparison in Balzer, "Sacred Genders in Siberia," 177.

33. Youngsook Kim Harvey, "Possession Sickness and Women Shamans in Korea," in *Unspoken Worlds: Women's Religious Lives* (ed. Nancy Auer Falk and Rita M. Gross; 3rd ed.; Belmont, Calif.: Wadsworth, 2001), 65. Laurel Kendall and Hien Thi Nguyen, "Dressing up the Spirits: Costumes, Cross-Dressing, and Incarnation in Korea and Vietnam," in *Women and Indigenous Religions* (ed. Sylvia Marcos; Santa Barbara, Calif.: Praeger, 2010), 93–114. Many of the anthropological studies I discuss here utilize the classics of gender theory, such as Judith Butler, *Gender Trouble: Feminism and the Subversion of Identity* (New York: Routledge, 1990).

becomes the head of the household, while her husband cleans the home and takes care of the children.[34] In addition, the work of female shamans requires women to sing and dance in private homes, which in the cultural context rings of another profession entirely. The negative views of these features of a female shaman's private life often result in women and their families not wanting this professional calling in the first place; when a woman does become a shaman, some do not marry, and many marriages do not last. It is pertinent to the discussion of biblical portrayals of gender roles to note that this involves the combination of both cultural judgments regarding what actually happens in shamans' families, and assumptions about what must be happening. The anthropologists Laurel Kendall and Hien Thi Nguyen observe: "By cultural stereotype, the shaman's husband is a man who lives off of money earned by his wife, in effect a kept man, and a *mansin*'s work requires both days and nights away from home, provoking suspicion"; thus, given the collection of difficulties and negative associations, "marriage is usually a casualty of the *mansin* profession."[35]

In his work on traditional Chinese religions, Randall Nadeau compares the entranced speech of Seng-fa, a Buddhist girl who was active in 499–505 C.E. when she was nine to sixteen years old, to the modern "spirit writing" of "Heavenly Savants" (*T'ien-ts'ai*) of the Unity Sect (*I Kuan Tao*) in Taiwan, where eight- to fifteen-year-old girls "are chosen by gods and spirits to compose scriptures."[36] According to the sectarian manual, a Heavenly Savant must be "pure in thought," of unquestionable character, and unmarried (as well as uneducated, so she cannot be thought to have written without divine inspiration).[37]

Nadeau witnesses the shamanic performance of Aiyun, a 16-year-old girl who had become her community's spirit-writing Heavenly Savant two years earlier, after her first shamanic trance. "Soon," he notes, "she will be replaced by one of the younger girls, as she is nearing the age when

---

34. Harvey, "Possession Sickness," 65; Kendall and Nguyen, "Dressing up the Spirits," 96.

35. Kendall and Nguyen, "Dressing up the Spirits," 96–97. See also Kendall, *Shamans, Housewives*, esp. 54–85.

36. Randall L. Nadeau, "Harmonizing Family and Cosmos: Shamanic Women in Chinese Religions," in Falk and Gross, *Unspoken Worlds*, 70–71.

37. Ibid., 72.

her powers will diminish," that is, when she will become less likely to be "pure."[38]

These young, "pure," unmarried girls are not the only shamans in the village. There are also old women, the so-called grandmothers who speak to spirits. Nadeau asks Aiyun's father about these old women "who ply a nightly trade of shamanic intercession with ghosts and ancestors in village and neighborhood temples." The father replies, "Oh, they really are low-class. They can't read and write at all, and they're just a mouthpiece for minor spirits, with all that guttural groaning and spitting. Our Savants are courtly and refined, and they have to be pure."[39]

In addition to describing a perceived class difference, Aiyun's father suggests that the old women are not "pure." Anthropologist Jack Potter has observed a pattern of women becoming "grandmothers who speak to spirits" in the New Territories of Hong Kong after their children have died. He notes that these women "know how to recapture the souls of sick village children ... take care of the souls of girls who die before marriage, and protect the life and health of village children by serving as ... fictive mothers."[40] Neither the prepubescent and adolescent girls nor the "grandmothers who speak to spirits" are in their childbearing years. The symbolic "mother" role is intriguing, then, given the discussion of the "mother in Israel" above.

Nadeau notes the ambivalent attitude toward Chinese female shamans. Although they have an important role, "shamanesses are largely invisible, operating in liminal spaces and times: in small temples or rural settings, late at night." As he summarizes: "Herein lies the central paradox for Chinese female shamans. Culture wants them in the inner chambers but the spirits want them out. This paradox is resolved both by severely marginalizing female shamans, who are even more ostracized than their male counterparts," and by valuing their role in restoring harmony to others, as with the "grandmothers" mentioned above who are marginalized but esteemed for interceding for sick children.[41] This contradiction is seen, for instance, in the mixed reputation of Seng-fa, whose inspired

---

38. Ibid., 72–73.
39. Ibid., 73.
40. Jack M. Potter, "Cantonese Shamanism," in *Studies in Chinese Society* (ed. Arthur P. Wolf; Stanford: Stanford University Press, 1978), 321–45; as quoted by Nadeau, "Harmonizing Family and Cosmos," 73.
41. Nadeau, "Harmonizing Family and Cosmos," 75–78.

speeches were written down and preserved, but were listed in the "Registry of Doubtful Scriptures" by the Buddhist monk Seng-yu.[42]

We see a similar type of discomfort with the intersection of religious activity and potentially childbearing women in Eastern Indian *habisha* rituals (involving vows). The women who perform these rituals are not shamans, but the rituals are seen to endow the vow maker with "great spiritual power," and are "remarkable for the intense religious fervor they inspire."[43] The women are supposed to be postmenopausal. This is consciously an issue of menstruation and impurity, as the women of the village in Orissa, India, explained to anthropologist James Freeman.[44] According to Freeman, other possible factors include that "public singing and dancing are considered particularly inappropriate, if not scandalous, behaviors for young women. By contrast, women beyond the age of childbearing are allowed much greater freedom in speech and action." He notes in addition that the rituals are quite time-consuming, so young women with children are less able to participate.[45] He summarizes, "Menopause gives a woman greater ritual purity (absence of pollution) and frees her from the numerous ritual proscriptions place on women of childbearing age.... [Postmenopausal women are] released from many social obligations required of younger women. They enjoy the highest degree of domestic, social, and ritual freedom that any adult Hindu woman ever knows."[46] Concepts of the holiness of prepubescent girls and the impurity of women after puberty are known elsewhere in India as well.[47]

A more explicit distancing of spiritual insight from the fertile female body is present in religious literature as well. According to Cynthia Ann Humes, "some Hindu and Buddhist soteriological texts ... argue the necessity of females to adopt male bodies before complete emancipation can be reached ... women are specifically admonished to purge themselves of 'women's' characteristics and 'become male' in gender orientation to

---

42. Ibid., 70.

43. James M. Freeman, "The Ladies of Lord Krishna: Rituals of Middle-Aged Women in Eastern India," in Falk and Gross, *Unspoken Worlds*, 114–15.

44. Ibid., 116–17.

45. Ibid., 122–23.

46. Ibid., 123.

47. Janet Chawla, "The Not-So-Subtle Body in Dais' Birth Imagery," in Marcos, *Women and Indigenous Religions*, 127–41, esp. 137.

become enlightened."[48] Some of the Upanishads, for instance, include the view that women's fertility "would obstruct that path to enlightenment" because of the connection to female sexuality.[49]

Such ideas are in no way restricted to the various Asian contexts above. The Mapuche shamans (*machi*) of Chile also embody gender transformation in a variety of ways, several of which we have seen in the above examples as well. As with the previous examples, the performance of gender among these shamans rests on crossing the traditional boundaries of their own culture (rather than happening not to correspond to mainstream North American expectations). This includes short-term outward signs, such as cross-dressing, and the more encompassing enactment of gender role reversal in family life. In her work with the Mapuche, Ana Mariella Bacigalupo observed (as had previous anthropologists) that "Mapuche often view female *machi* as masculine and their husbands as feminine" and "subservient," and that "Mapuche tend to perceive female *machi* as masculine because they transgress ordinary Mapuche women's gender roles."[50]

Mapuche views of *machi* motherhood are said to be paradoxical. On the one hand, most female *machi* do become mothers, and at times use metaphors of motherhood in ritual or attribute some of their insight to their role as a mother. On the other hand, the Mapuche see "marriage, sexuality, and mothering as interfering with female *machi*'s healing practices and as lessening their healing powers.... Female *machi* who receive a shamanic calling before menarche and those who are older and no longer fertile or sexually active are considered the most powerful. Single female *machi*, those who are not mothers, and those who have older children hold an advantage over fertile female *machi* with young children who distract them from their healing endeavors."[51] Some *machi* women are thus expected not to have children, and must at times choose between being a *machi* and being a mother. Throughout her work, Bacigalupo refers repeatedly to three particular female shamans, Machi Rocío, Machi Pamela, and

---

48. Cynthia Ann Humes, "Becoming Male: Salvation through Gender Modification in Hinduism and Buddhism," in Ramet, *Gender Reversals and Gender Cultures*, 123.
49. Ibid., 126.
50. Ana Mariella Bacigalupo, *Shamans of the Foye Tree: Gender, Power and Healing Among Chilean Mapuche* (Austin: University of Texas Press, 2007), 225–26.
51. Ibid., 227.

Machi Fresia. They each have different experiences of the conflicts over motherhood: Rocío became a *machi* later in life and her children were already adults; Pamela "struggled to rear her children and heal while her husband rejected her *machi* practice; she reacted by giving precedence to her *machi* spirit over her husband and children"; and Fresia found that "her machi practice was, in effect, incompatible with marriage and motherhood," and she "chose to break away from *machi*-hood in order to become a wife and mother."[52]

Similar patterns—in spite of the many cultural differences—are also found among rituals of the Garífuna (Black Carib) women of Belize, for instance, in which older women in particular participate; in indigenous Australian religion, where only postmenopausal women are initiated into the men's rituals; and in the Shona religion of Zimbabwe, where it is explicitly the case that spirit mediums (Nehanda *mhondoro*) must be postmenopausal.[53]

In his cross-cultural study of shamanism, I. M. Lewis already identified the large numbers of older women among shamans and attributed it to fertility issues, in that they are either postmenopausal or infertile.[54] In some of the contexts discussed above, the particular presence of postmenopausal women (at Delphi, among Chinese shamans, etc.) is apparently connected to issues of "purity." In other contexts, it is said to be a matter of access to time or money. Whatever the combination of factors in each social location, the frequency of the phenomenon is apparent.

We thus find that cross-culturally, it is not uncommon to see a separation between maternal and divinatory roles, and also more broadly for women in traditional childbearing roles to be restricted from rituals understood to invoke divine presence. This takes forms quite similar to those seen in the ancient and medieval examples, including the require-

---

52. Ibid., 229–30.

53. Virginia Kerns, "Garífuna Women and the Work of Mourning (Central America)," in Falk and Gross, *Unspoken Worlds*, 130–33; Rita M. Gross, "Menstruation and Childbirth as Ritual and Religious Experience among Native Australians," in Falk and Gross, *Unspoken Worlds*, 306; Keller, *Hammer and Flute*, 155–56 (based on the work of David Lan, *Guns and Rain: Guerrillas and Spirit Mediums in Zimbabwe* [London: James Currey, 1985], 93–94).

54. I. M. Lewis, *Ecstatic Religion: A Study of Shamanism and Spirit Possession* (3rd ed.; London: Routledge, 2003), 85–86; however, one might take issue with Lewis's fuller description of this, which reflects perspectives on women and marriage more common when the book was first published in 1971.

ment for virginity, the preference for postmenopausal women, and the enacting of roles culturally understood as male, or other demonstrations of the theological preference for the male body.[55]

Conclusion

The conclusion I draw from this research is that the pattern evident in the Hebrew Bible is unlikely to be coincidental. We see almost exclusively portrayals of female diviners who are childless. The exception, the description of the anonymous woman of Isa 8:3 who bears a sign-child, does not include prophecy or speech of any kind. There is nothing in between: there are many women in divinatory roles who do not have children, and one woman who delivers an oracle-child. There is no biblical tradition of any female diviner who just happens to have offspring. Whether this literary depiction was a conscious choice on the part of any of the writers is impossible to judge. It is easy to imagine that at times it was conscious, as perhaps in the case of Miriam, whose lineage the tradition would likely have considered at some point. If in any cases there was a historical woman behind the narrative, I would tend to think that she is so far behind it (i.e., the literary construction is so far removed) that the historical figure's actual family status is irrelevant. Whether in more general terms such portrayals reflected the realities of life on the ground—that is, whether female diviners actually tended to be childless—is also beyond our ability to conclude based on the evidence available. Perhaps such portrayals grew out of historical realities, perhaps they were consciously drawn, or perhaps both. However, even if neither of these is the case—if actual female diviners did not tend to be childless, and if the writers did not consciously portray women without children—perhaps these depictions are themselves a result of the same factors that create this cross-cultural social trend. It is conceivable that the literary construct itself is Israel's expression of the widespread instinct to separate female divinatory and traditional maternal roles. The biblical writers overwhelmingly depict female diviners in a way that coincides with the pattern we see in ancient, medieval, and modern societies, and it seems increasingly improbable that this is all coincidence.

---

55. The additional element of male shamans frequently cross-dressing demonstrates that this is part of a broader pattern of gender boundary transgression, and cannot be assumed always to have a patriarchal undertone.

"Misogyny" in Service of Theocentricity: Legitimate or Not?

Dale Launderville

The prophet Ezekiel challenges his exilic audience in the early sixth century B.C.E. to take responsibility for their deportation by claiming that their conduct had been "like the impurity of a menstruating woman" (כְּטֻמְאַת הַנִּדָּה, Ezek 36:17).[1] The ill effects of their deeds were contagious, multiplying in various directions to the point of defiling the whole land. Those exiles schooled in the Priestly rules for distinguishing the sacred and the profane would most likely have reacted with disgust to the image of menstrual blood spreading widely through the land. Ezekiel often uses shocking, outrageous imagery in order to provoke the members of his audience to reflect upon their relationship with Yhwh and to come to greater self-awareness (e.g., Ezek 16:25, 39–41; 23:8, 20). The effect of Ezekiel's rhetoric depends not only upon the words he uses and the message he conveys but also upon the way that the hearer receives these images and meanings. I argue that even though Ezekiel uses imagery that can be seen as portraying Woman as the dangerous Other or as a symbol of evil, he challenges his audience to adopt a theocentric perspective on their covenantal life that will move them beyond misogyny.[2]

To explain this instance of Ezekiel's education of the emotions of his audience, I will examine the following four questions: (1) Is disgust at menstrual purity a bodily sensation cultivated by the system of Priestly purity in Lev 12–15? (2) Is disgust at idolatry a bodily sensation that Ezekiel wants to cultivate in his audience? (3) Is Priestly attention to men-

---

1. Moshe Greenberg, *Ezekiel 21–37* (AB 22A; New York: Doubleday, 1997), 727.
2. For a comparison of a feminist with a theocentric perspective, see S. Tamar Kamionkowski, *Gender Reversal and Cosmic Chaos: A Study of the Book of Ezekiel* (JSOTSup 368; London: Sheffield Academic Press, 2003), 41.

strual cycles a way to honor women's bodies or oppress them? (4) Are disgust and shame emotions to be channeled or eliminated from individuals and communities committed to worshipping Yhwh? Threading its way through these four questions is the rhetorical and ethical issue that Ezekiel simply uses this feminine imagery without much concern for its potentially misogynistic consequences. I contend that Ezekiel provokes these misogynistic attitudes only to call them into question.

Among feminist biblical critics, Fokkelien van Dijk-Hemmes argues that Ezekiel uses the image of Woman as city in order to include both genders within this image.[3] As the image is used in Ezek 16, 23, and 36, it conveys extreme humiliation through its gender-specific metaphorical language. Van Dijk-Hemmes contends that the male audience of the Ezekiel text has the option of escaping from this humiliation. She notes that in Ezek 23:45 "righteous" male "judges" declare Oholah (Samaria) and Oholibah (Jerusalem) as wives of Yhwh to be guilty of adultery and homicide. Ezekiel 23:48, which Walther Zimmerli regards as redactional,[4] emphasizes that "all women" should take warning from the fate of these two cities.

The tendency to project blame, to denigrate, and to hate the feminine Other in the patriarchal society of ancient Israel was strong, and the prophet Ezekiel uses traditional wife-city imagery in a provocative, offensive way. The males in Ezekiel's audience—both his immediate audience and those in subsequent generations—would probably have tried to evade their identification as wife Jerusalem. Yet such an identification is, I contend, the cutting edge of Ezekiel's use of the image of Jerusalem/Israel as a defiant menstruating woman. Ezekiel was not aiming to denigrate women but rather to move the men and women of Jerusalem to accept the humiliation they received from the Babylonians as caused by their own sinfulness. In particular, Ezekiel exhorts the males in his audience to grow in their acceptance of collective responsibility as covenant partners with Yhwh.[5]

---

3. Fokkelien van Dijk-Hemmes, "The Metaphorization of Woman in Prophetic Speech: An Analysis of Ezekiel 23," in *A Feminist Companion to the Latter Prophets* (ed. Athalya Brenner; FCB 8; Sheffield: Sheffield Academic, 1995),254.

4. Walther Zimmerli, *Ezekiel 1: A Commentary on the Book of the Prophet Ezekiel, Chapters 1–24* (trans. Ronald E. Clements; Hermeneia; Philadelphia: Fortress, 1979), 492.

5. Pamela Milne ("Labouring with Abusive Biblical Texts: Tracing Trajectories of Misogyny," in *The Labour of Reading: Desire, Alienation, and Biblical Interpretation*

To be sure, as J. Cheryl Exum has pointed out, this imagery of judgment as informed by the feminine personification of Jerusalem is done at the expense of female sexuality—a fact that intensifies the complicated hermeneutical task of reading a text like Ezek 36:17.[6] However, the more basic opposition in this theological text of Yhwh judging the people of Jerusalem is the divine versus the human rather than male versus female. If the reader, particularly the male reader, refuses to accept this identification with wife Jerusalem, then he or she, from Ezekiel's perspective, will not be able to come to terms with the violence done by the Babylonians to the city of Jerusalem in the sixth century B.C.E. and the resulting trauma.[7] By identifying the Israelites of Jerusalem as a defiant menstruous woman in Ezek 36:17, Ezekiel challenges his male audience both to accept their negligence in embracing the feminine dimension of the covenant relationship and to feel disgust for their idolatrous behavior. Those feminist interpreters who criticize and resist these troubling texts but refrain from jettisoning them serve Ezekiel's intention of bringing his male audience to honest assessment of their identity and the ways they have sinned against Yhwh and others in the covenant relationship.[8]

[ed. Fiona C. Black, Roland Boer, and Erin Runions; SemeiaSt 36; Atlanta: Society of Biblical Literature, 1999], 279–80) contends that the probability of a misogynistic reading of these texts is too high for an informed resistant feminist reading to neutralize. In her critique of feminist scholars who tend to treat issues of gender bias ahistorically, Alice Keefe (*Woman's Body and Social Body in Hosea* [JSOTSup 338; GCT 10; Sheffield: Sheffield Academic Press, 2001], 154) summarizes the views of resistant readers to troubling passages on feminine sexuality in the Bible: "Hosea, then, is not only patriarchal literature which presupposes male rights to control female sexuality, but it is misogynistic literature which assumes and depends upon a view of female sexuality as something intrinsically negative, inferior and symbolically 'other' to the identity of the Israelite community." Jacqueline E. Lapsley (*Whispering the Word: Hearing Women's Stories in the Old Testament* [Louisville: Westminster John Knox, 2005], 3) distinguishes "revisionist" feminist biblical scholars from "rejectionists" in that the former search biblical passages for muted voices and traditions and do not reject the Bible as authoritative simply on the basis of its patriarchal bias.

6. J. Cheryl Exum, *Plotted, Shot, and Painted: Cultural Representations of Biblical Women* (JSOTSup 215; GCT 3; Sheffield: Sheffield Academic Press, 1996), 119–22.

7. On the contextualization of the trauma experienced by Ezekiel and the exiles, see Gale Yee, *Poor Banished Children of Eve: Woman as Evil in the Hebrew Bible* (Minneapolis: Fortress, 2003), 111–34.

8. Kathleen M. O'Connor, "The Feminist Movement Meets the Old Testament: One Woman's Perspective," in *Engaging the Bible in a Gendered World: An Introduc-*

Disgust over Genital Emissions: A Reaction to Impurity or Sin?

Ezekiel addresses an audience whose members seem drawn to him as an authority (20:1) but can dismiss him as a mere entertainer (33:30–33). Perhaps they have come to expect outlandish images and eccentric behavior from him. Yet Ezekiel seems to use the image of menstrual impurity before a Priestly audience in order to provoke disgust (7:19–20).[9] For Israelite priests, the avoidance of sexual intercourse during a woman's menstrual period was a serious concern. The penalty according to the Holiness Code was to be "cut off" (כרת) from the people (Lev 20:18). Because the Israelite priests were socialized to regard menstrual blood as a dangerous pollutant, they would probably have been more disposed than the average male to have a visceral reaction to the idea of this potent blood.[10] Disgust has been described as "one of the most violent affections of the human perceptual system. … Everything seems at risk in the experience of disgust. It is a state of alarm and emergency, an acute crisis of self-preservation in the face of an unassimilable otherness, a convulsive struggle."[11] Ezekiel seems intent on evoking this sensation so that he might involve his audience emotionally as well as rationally in the theological message about the dynamics of the covenant relationship.

The blood discarded during a woman's menses (נִדָּה) is regarded by the priests as a potent substance close to the sources of life and death.[12] Etymologically, נִדָּה can be derived from the root נדד, which in the qal

---

tion to Feminist Biblical Interpretation in Honor of Katharine Doob Sakenfeld (ed. Linda Day and Carolyn Pressler; Louisville: Westminster John Knox, 2006), 21; Lapsley, *Whispering the Word*, 4–9.

9. Tarja S. Philip, *Menstruation and Childbirth in the Bible: Fertility and Impurity* (StBL 88; New York: Lang, 2006), 66; Karel van der Toorn, *From Her Cradle to Her Grave: The Role of Religion in the Life of the Israelite and the Babylonian Woman* (trans. Sara J. Denning-Bolle; BiSe 23; Sheffield: JSOT Press, 1994), 51–54.

10. Jacob Milgrom (*Leviticus 1–16* [AB 3; New York: Doubleday, 1991], 952) notes with reference to Ezek 7:19–20; Lam 1:17; and Ezra 9:11: "The menstruant, therefore, is a metaphor for extreme pollution, ultimate revulsion."

11. Winfried Menninghaus, *Disgust: The Theory and History of a Strong Sensation* (trans. Howard Eiland and Joel Golb; Albany: State University of New York Press, 2003), 1.

12. Philip, *Menstruation and Childbirth*, 9–11. Milgrom (*Leviticus 1–16*, 46) notes that "[semen and menstrual blood] represent the life force; their loss represents death."

means "to escape, flee," and in the hiphil "to expel, drive away";[13] or from the root נדה, which in the piel means "to exclude, drive out, push aside."[14] According to Baruch Levine, the blood itself discharged from the womb is not impure, but rather the result of its being discharged is impure.[15] Menstrual blood itself is aptly labeled "the blood of life";[16] however, since it is discharged from the womb, it can be seen as a "failed conception."[17] Thus menstrual blood symbolizes both life and death: life prior to discharge, and death upon discharge.[18] The priests, as boundary keepers between the sacred and the profane, were charged with keeping the impure separate from the holy (Lev 10:10; Ezek 22:26). One of their tasks would have been instructing women and the members of their households on their obligations regarding genital emissions.[19]

The Priestly world is androcentric and hierarchical.[20] Thus it is noteworthy that the symmetry of the structure of Lev 15 treats the genital

---

13. Cf. *HALOT* 2:672; BDB 622.

14. Cf. *HALOT* 2:672–73; BDB 622; Baruch Levine, *Leviticus* (JPSTC; Philadelphia: Jewish Publication Society of America, 1989), 97.

15. Levine (*Leviticus*, 97) explains that נִדָּה "does not connote impurity in and of itself but, rather, describes the physiological process of the flow of blood."

16. Anne-Marie Korte, "Female Blood Rituals: Cultural-Anthropological Findings and Feminist-Theological Reflections," in *Wholly Woman, Holy Blood: A Feminist Critique of Purity and Impurity* (ed. Kristin De Troyer, Judith A. Herbert, Judith Ann Johnson, and Anne-Marie Korte; SAC; Harrisburg, Pa.: Trinity Press International, 2003), 205.

17. Kathleen O'Grady, "The Semantics of Taboo: Menstrual Prohibitions in the Hebrew Bible," in De Troyer, Herbert, Johnson, and Korte, *Wholly Woman, Holy Blood*, 8.

18. O'Grady (ibid., 2) explains the ambiguity of the taboo (i.e., as something marked off from the ordinary) as follows: "*Tapu* is a complex linguistic configuration that fuses together particular concepts—sanctity and uncleanness—in the same verbal structure."

19. Adriana Destro, "The Witness of Times: An Anthropological Reading of Niddah," in *Reading Leviticus: A Conversation with Mary Douglas* (ed. John F. A. Sawyer; JSOTSup 227; Sheffield: Sheffield Academic Press, 1996), 125–26; Philip, *Menstruation and Childbirth*, 51. Charlotte Elisheva Fonrobert (*Menstrual Purity: Rabbinic and Christian Reconstructions of Biblical Gender* [Conversations; Stanford: Stanford University Press, 2000], 70–74) surfaces countervoices within the talmudic tradition that the woman senses the beginning of her menstrual flow and thus plays a key role in distinguishing the pure from the impure.

20. Philip, *Menstruation and Childbirth*, 70. Korte ("Female Blood Rituals," 169) notes: "While a range of identities can describe women's alternating positions within

emissions of men and women with a measure of equality.[21] In the first half of the chapter, verses 2–15 deal with an unhealthy male discharge followed by a normal male discharge (vv. 16–18); the second half of the chapter begins with a discussion of a normal female discharge in verses 19–24 followed by a treatment of an unhealthy female discharge (vv. 25–30). This inverse parallelism attests that the genital emissions of both male and female symbolize life and death and so are not a matter of indifference.[22] Both Gordon Wenham and Jacob Milgrom identify this structure of Lev 15 as a chiasm by shifting verse 18 from the section on male genital emissions to a section of its own; as the midpoint of the chiasm, verse 18 deals with the defiling effect of sexual intercourse between male and female.[23] Here the complementarity of male and female in the reproductive process echoes the picture of Gen 1:26-28 in which humanity, consisting of male and female, is to be fruitful and multiply.

Against this backdrop of relatively evenhanded treatment of male and female genital emissions, signs of androcentric bias surface in the chapter. The male genital emissions are treated first, which then seems to influence the way the female emissions are read. If the potency of the impurity is measured by the type of purification required,[24] then the unhealthy male discharge (i.e., gonorrhea) and the unhealthy female discharge (i.e., menorrhagia) are equally dangerous, as indicated by the following shared directives: once the discharge stops, both male (v. 13) and female (v. 28) must wait seven days; then on the eighth day each must offer two turtledoves or two pigeons to a priest as a purification offering and a burnt offering (vv. 14-15, 29-30). However, the normal female discharge (i.e., menstruation) is regarded as more potent than the normal male discharge (i.e., seminal emission): once a woman recognizes the discharge of blood from her womb, she must regard herself as in a state of impurity for seven days (v. 19); when a man has a seminal emission, he must bathe and regard

---

familial relationships (daughter, sister, wife, co-wife, mother, grandmother, aunt, cousin, or niece), in female-dominated religions women receive attention primarily as mothers, grandmothers, and sisters. This is in marked contrast to male-dominated religions, which deal with and define women predominantly as wives and daughters, that is to say, in their roles most directly affecting male space and interest."

21. Gordon Wenham, *The Book of Leviticus* (NICOT; Grand Rapids: Eerdmans, 1979), 216-17; Philip, *Menstruation and Childbirth*, 45-47.

22. Milgrom, *Leviticus 1-16*, 46, 767; Philip, *Menstruation and Childbirth*, 46-47.

23. Wenham, *Book of Leviticus*, 217-19; Milgrom, *Leviticus 1-16*, 904-5, 930-31.

24. Milgrom, *Leviticus 1-16*, 986-1000.

himself as in a state of impurity until evening. Because the male emission is episodic rather than durative, the measures taken to contain it are less involved.[25] The man who has an emission must take care to wash any object made of cloth or skin tainted by his semen (v. 17). But menstrual blood is more contagious. The woman during her period must limit the objects that her menstrual blood touches, for whoever touches an object tainted with her blood is obliged to launder one's clothes, bathe, and remain in a state of impurity until evening (vv. 20–23). The key issue for the Priestly legislators is that the contagious impure genital substance be kept from contact with other people and objects as much as possible; for the more that impurity spreads in the community, the greater the likelihood of the defilement of sancta.[26]

One consequence of these Priestly regulations is that they tend to promote hygiene and etiquette within the community.[27] Neither male nor female is quarantined for a genital emission, as would be the case with a scaly skin disease (Lev 14:3–8). The menstruating woman is encouraged to carry on her normal life within the household but to take special care that her menstrual blood is contained.[28] Yet the following directive may seem too restrictive: "whoever touches her shall be unclean until evening" (Lev 15:19). If this directive intends to "build a fence around the woman" so as to prevent menstrual sex, then it would stand in accord with the seriousness of this prohibition as stated in the Holiness Code (Lev 18:19; 20:18).[29] However, in the Priestly system of impurities (Lev 12–15), menstrual sex is not categorized as a sin meriting כרת but rather as an act in

---

25. Ibid., 927, 936–37; Fonrobert, *Menstrual Purity*, 45–46.

26. Milgrom, *Leviticus 1–16*, 980–81.

27. Levine, *Leviticus*, 92–93; van der Toorn, *From Her Cradle*, 49; Thomas Kazen, "Dirt and Disgust: Body and Morality in Biblical Purity Laws," in *Perspectives on Purity and Purification in the Bible* (ed. Baruch J. Schwartz, David P. Wright, Jeffrey Stackert, and Naphtali S. Meshel; LHBOTS 474; New York: T&T Clark, 2008), 55–56.

28. Rahel Wasserfall ("Introduction: Menstrual Blood into Jewish Blood," in *Women and Water: Menstruation in Jewish Life and Law* [ed. Rahel Wasserfall; Brandeis Series on Jewish Women; Hanover, N.H.: University Press of New England for Brandeis University Press, 1999], 5) notes that during the Second Temple period women were secluded in "houses of impurity," were not allowed to use cosmetics or jewelry, were expected to eat alone, and could not carry out their household duties.

29. David P. Wright, "The Spectrum of Priestly Impurity," in *Priesthood and Cult in Ancient Israel* (ed. Gary Anderson and Saul Olyan; JSOTSup 125; Sheffield: JSOT Press, 1991), 176–78.

which the man becomes impure by contact with the menstrual blood of the woman (15:24); this man, like the menstruating woman, remains in a state of impurity for seven days. Even though the prohibition on touching a menstruating woman has the potential for generating hateful prejudice, the point of the prohibition is to highlight the potency of reproductive blood.[30] The Priestly system of impurities in Lev 12–15 is more intent on promoting fertility and maximizing the reproductive potential of the community than in singling out menstrual blood as a defiling force in the community.[31] The Priestly legislator even regards heterosexual intercourse as defiling; here the reason that both the man and the woman must bathe and refrain from visiting the sanctuary until evening is due to contact with discharged semen (15:18).[32] For the Priestly legislator, the key issue is the containment of genital substances. Since perfect containment is impossible and not desirable, it is essential that the members of households practice the prescribed methods of purification so as to respect sacred space and observe proper etiquette toward Yhwh.[33]

In Ezek 36:17–18 the prophet juxtaposes menstrual impurity with bloodshed on the land and idolatry. Menstrual impurity here may be a symbol for forbidden sexual sins that defile the land (Lev 18:6–29). If so, these verses restate the three major types of sins that defile the land: certain sexual sins, homicide, and idolatry.[34] Ezekiel's use of the image of menstrual impurity here shifts from the cultic understanding of menstrual impurity mapped out in Lev 15 to one in which the ethical understanding predominates.[35] Influenced by the Holiness Code (Lev 18:19;

---

30. Philip, *Menstruation and Childbirth*, 8, 68–69; Martha C. Nussbaum, *Hiding from Humanity: Disgust, Shame, and the Law* (Princeton: Princeton University Press, 2004), 93. Fonrobert (*Menstrual Purity*, 29) notes that the phrase "I am unclean" (אני טמאה) means "I am menstruating" and am unavailable for sexual intercourse; in post-temple halakah, the menstruating woman is "not a source of impurity to other people" even though she is labeled impure.

31. Milgrom, *Leviticus: A Book of Ritual and Ethics* (CC; Minneapolis: Fortress, 2004), 12–13.

32. Philip, *Menstruation and Childbirth*, 50.

33. Van der Toorn, *From Her Cradle*, 49–53; cf. Milgrom, *Leviticus 1–16*, 931–34, 941, 1002; Dale Launderville, *Spirit and Reason: The Embodied Character of Ezekiel's Symbolic Thinking* (Waco, Tex.: Baylor University Press, 2007), 96.

34. Daniel I. Block, *The Book of Ezekiel: Chapters 25–48* (NICOT; Grand Rapids: Eerdmans, 1998), 345.

35. Philip, *Menstruation and Childbirth*, 64.

20:18), Ezekiel regards menstrual impurity as a sin with both ethical and cultic ramifications. It is as if wherever menstrual discharge is not treated with the prescribed Priestly purificatory procedures, such impurity is to be categorized as menstrual sex. One could argue that if Israelite women disregarded the purificatory measures for normal menstruation, then they would have increased the likelihood for menstrual sex, which carried the penalty of כרת. However, by merging the cultic and ethical categories of menstrual impurity, Ezekiel creates the impression that neglect of the purificatory procedures for menstrual discharge is an offense that poses serious dangers to the fabric of the community and its relations with Yhwh. Since Ezekiel compares the sinfulness of the Israelites' conduct with menstrual impurity, it almost seems as if the image of the menstruating woman who ignores the Priestly purification procedures becomes the primary way of picturing sinful Israel—the feminine Other is seen as a dangerous force corrupting the covenantal community.[36]

Neglect of Purity Regulations as a Step Toward Idolatry

Ezekiel seems to select the image of menstrual impurity because it not only serves to explain the exile but also raises the question of the negligence of the Israelites toward Yhwh. The exiles are now a defiled people in a foreign land without a temple. They have no means of purifying themselves from major transgressions, yet it would seem that after the purging of the exile they would need to be attentive to the purity regulations once again (Ezek 44:23; 45:18–24; 46:3, 9).[37] This new start would seem already in the exile to have been an issue for Ezekiel, who claimed that Yhwh was a "little

---

36. Julie Galambush, *Jerusalem in the Book of Ezekiel* (SBLDS 130; Atlanta: Scholars Press, 1992), 7. Korte ("Female Blood Rituals, 176) explains: "Many male-dominated religions affirm menstrual and childbirth pollution and use it to explain women's 'otherness'. This affirmation of pollution frequently results in the exclusion of women from religious places and from religious practices like prayer, fasting, studying holy texts, or attending religious services." Gerburgis Feld ("'. . . Wie es eben Frauen ergeht' (Gen 31:35): Kulturgeschichtliche Überlegungen zum gegenwärtigen Umgang mit der Menstruation der Frau in Gesellschaft und Theologie," in *Von der Wurzel getragen: Christlich-feministische Exegese in Auseinandersetzung mit Antijudaismus* [ed. Luise Schottroff and Marie-Theres Wacker; BIS 17; Leiden: Brill, 1996], 35–37) argues that the origin of menstrual taboos and rites are not examined historically and anthropologically but are communicated via male-authored theological texts.

37. Milgrom, *Leviticus: Book of Ritual*, 148; Walther Zimmerli, *Ezekiel 2: A Com-*

sanctuary" (מקדש מעט) in their midst (Ezek 11:16).[38] If Yhwh were there with them in Babylon, then they should be thinking about how to respond to this divine presence in their individual and family lives.[39]

The purity regulations of Lev 15 are communally mandated but reach into the affairs of the household. As such, they resemble many of the ethical and cultic regulations in Lev 18–20 as part of the Holiness Code in which the holiness of the sanctuary depends upon the purity of the land of Israel.[40] Already in Lev 15, the Priestly legislators make clear that what happens in the household has an impact on the sanctuary; the public and the private spheres are not totally separate. Thus the Holiness Code provides an example of how some purity regulations increase in seriousness by carrying an ethical dimension in addition to the cultic: menstrual sex is a sin and not simply a breach in etiquette for a people in covenant with Yhwh (Lev 18:19; 20:18).[41]

Ezekiel warns that certain sexual transgressions need to be guarded against and implies that a disaster in which people are "vomited" from the land (Ezek 22:10, 15; 36:16–20; Lev 18:28–29; 20:5, 22; cf. Ezra 9:10–15) will be the consequence. Ezekiel uses the ambiguous image of menstrual blood (i.e., a sign of a missed opportunity for new life) in order to accent the fact that substances with mysterious power can point beyond themselves to Yhwh as the life-giver, or they can become ends in themselves. Thus the disregard of Yhwh that leads to having sex with a woman in her menstrual period is portrayed in Ezek 36:17–18 as having an affinity to idolatry, in which a reality separate from Yhwh is regarded as giving life.[42]

---

mentary on the Book of the Prophet Ezekiel, Chapters 25–48 (trans. James D. Martin; Hermeneia; Philadelphia: Fortress, 1983), 486, 493.

38. Paul Joyce, "Dislocation and Adaptation in the Exilic Age and After," in *After the Exile: Essays in Honour of Rex Mason* (ed. John Barton and David J. Reimer; Macon, Ga.: Mercer University Press, 1996), 50.

39. Philip, *Menstruation and Childbirth*, 71.

40. Jan Joosten, *People and Land in the Holiness Code: An Exegetical Study of the Ideational Framework of the Law in Leviticus 17–26* (VTSup 67; Leiden: Brill, 1996), 178, 184. Milgrom (*Leviticus: Book of Ritual*, 139) notes that the Bible does not refer to the land as "the holy land," for "Israel's behavior alone will sanctify the land or defile it."

41. Philip, *Menstruation and Childbirth*, 58–59.

42. Greenberg, *Ezekiel 21–37*, 727–28; Milgrom, *Leviticus 1–16*, 931–34, 941, 1002.

To these idols (גלולים, "shit-gods")[43] the Israelites gave their offerings, including their children who "passed through fire" (20:31; 36:18).[44] Thus they defiled themselves (נטמאים, 20:31). So the apparent rationale for Ezekiel's regarding menstrual sex as a sin—and it seems by implication also the other regulations on genital emissions in Lev 15—is that greater mindfulness of the link between individual and family purity and the covenant relationship with Yhwh will prevent the snowballing effect of sexual transgressions in which the generative power of sexuality narrows to the point that the erotic becomes an end in itself (e.g., pornography).[45] From the theocentric perspective of the priest-prophet Ezekiel, a distinct advantage of observing the purity regulations is that they impinge on the daily lives of the people and help them to be mindful of the covenant relationship with Yhwh (cf. Ezek 20:19–20, 30–31; 22:10–11; 23:43–48).

The central theological message of Ezek 36:16–38 is that Yhwh will restore the exiles to their homeland and make the land abundantly fruitful in order to vindicate his reputation as Israel's God in the eyes of the nations.[46] Yhwh is emphatic in 36:22–23 and 32 that he is not acting out of pity for the Israelites. The coldness of this statement is startling and so should lead the reader to see how much emphasis Ezekiel places upon the otherness of Yhwh.[47] This otherness and uniqueness of Yhwh have been overlooked by Israel in its idolatrous ways. But the announced restoration does not simply promise a return to the status quo. Rather because Yhwh's honor is at stake, Yhwh will give Israel a heart transplant and will place his Spirit within them so that they will obey his statutes and ordinances (36:26–27; cf. Ps 51:13).[48] On their own, the Israelites will not be able to obey.

---

43. Daniel Bodi, "Les *gillûlim* chez Ézéchiel et dans L'Ancien Testament, et les différentes pratiques cultuelles associées à ce terme," *RB* 100 (1993): 509–10.

44. Moshe Greenberg, *Ezekiel 1–20* (AB 22; Garden City, N.Y.: Doubleday, 1983), 369–70; Daniel I. Block, *The Book of Ezekiel: Chapters 1–24* (NICOT; Grand Rapids: Eerdmans, 1997), 636–37; Zimmerli, *Ezekiel 1*, 411; John Day, *Molech: A God of Human Sacrifice in the Old Testament* (Cambridge Oriental Publications 41; Cambridge: Cambridge University Press, 1989), 65–71.

45. James B. Nelson, *Embodiment: An Approach to Sexuality and Christian Theology* (Minneapolis: Augsburg, 1978), 17–18.

46. Block, *Ezekiel 25–48*, 347–52.

47. Ibid., 351.

48. Launderville, *Spirit and Reason*, 44.

By placing his Spirit within the Israelites, Yhwh seems to bridge the distance between his transcendent otherness and the lowly humanity of the Israelites.[49] This promise is a dramatic development from the proclamation that Yhwh is a "little sanctuary" among the exiles (Ezek 11:16), but yet it is continuous with it in the sense that Yhwh is making his presence known among the people outside the land of Israel and outside the temple. Yhwh is the actor who will change the external and internal conditions of the exiles and thus create a new standing place from which they are to relate to him. He will return them to the land and remove all their uncleanness and their idols (36:24–25). Under such circumstances, Yhwh says: "you shall be my people, and I will be your God" (36:28). Yhwh intends to show forth his holiness through the Israelites in the sight of the nations (36:23). Because impurity and holiness are incompatible, Yhwh intends to remove the impurities from Israel.[50] Such a promise would support the continuing relevance of a Priestly mentality and set of practices in which the distinction between the sacred and the profane is to be maintained (22:26).

Rhetorically, Ezekiel aimed to challenge his exilic audience with the image of menstrual impurity to come to a new awareness of how much they had dishonored Yhwh by their idolatrous ways and their unmindfulness of his claim upon their lives through the covenant. Such waywardness, as assessed by Ezekiel, fed upon itself as if it were a contagious substance or a virus that infected an entire body. As members of the covenant community, the individual bodies of the Israelites had an impact on one another in their households and in their cities (22:6–12). For the book of Ezekiel, if these relationships were not ordered according to the covenant relationship with Yhwh, the Israelites would try to find security and power with false gods and in unethical ways. These errant ways were like a potent defiling substance that corrupted the entire body; thus the remedy was to expel the body from the land (22:17–22; Lev 18:25–30). Ezekiel demanded that Israel not regard itself as a victim but rather take responsibility for the exile. The shocking image of menstrual impurity seems to have been selected in order to get the attention of the exiled priests and their compatriots and bring them to honest self-examination.[51]

---

49. Greenberg, *Ezekiel 21–37*, 737.

50. Milgrom, *Leviticus 1–16*, 732–33; Zimmerli, *Ezekiel 2*, 249.

51. On rhetoric as "a form of mental and emotional energy," see George A. Kennedy, *Comparative Rhetoric: An Historical and Cross-Cultural Introduction* (New York: Oxford University Press, 1998), 3.

Ezekiel's Use of the Image of Menstrual Impurity: Misogynistic or Realistic?

Did the image of menstrual impurity offer the males in Ezekiel's exilic audience a way of deflecting responsibility away from themselves and blaming women or the feminine Other within the community? As discussed earlier, the Priestly set of practices for dealing with genital emissions, despite its androcentric starting point, recognizes that semen can be as defiling as menstrual blood. The key difference is that menstrual blood lasts longer and is more abundant. Nevertheless, the potency or mysterious power in menstrual blood is categorized as defiling, that is, death dealing.[52] The efforts to contain menstrual blood may well overlook the fact that it is also the blood of life when it is in the womb (Lev 12:4–5).[53] Analogously, Israel's unmindfulness of its covenant relationship with Yhwh plays itself out in its blindness not only to the defiling effects of its misdeeds but also to the life-giving potential of Yhwh's gifts. But there is a risk in Ezekiel's rhetoric: by identifying menstrual blood as a negative potency, a male audience may identify women as the source of their woes.[54] Such projection would allow these men to shirk responsibility and continue to live in a dreamworld in which they perceive themselves as victims.

One positive consequence of the Priestly system in Lev 15 is that it pays attention to the woman's body and its central role within the household and community.[55] Later rabbinic treatises on נִדָּה pay close attention to the woman's identifying her menstrual cycle, which she then can communicate to her household.[56] Her observance of ritual baths is one practice by which she acknowledges that the blood flows that are given to her by nature are occurrences not only beyond her control but also of significance to the household and community.[57] When the temple is no longer intact as the primary sacred space in a Jewish community in the exile, in

---

52. Milgrom, *Leviticus 1–16*, 46.
53. Ibid., 749–50, 1002.
54. Van Dijk-Hemmes, "Metaphorization of Woman," 254; Nussbaum, *Hiding from Humanity*, 111, 120.
55. Destro, "Witness of Times," 132–33; Philip, *Menstruation and Childbirth*, 65.
56. For a discussion of the feminist view that this Priestly set of regulations as interpreted in the talmudic tradition objectifies and instrumentalizes woman's body, see Fonrobert, *Menstrual Purity*, 63–67.
57. Destro, "Witness of Times," 132–33.

the Diaspora, and after the destruction of the Second Temple in 70 C.E., then the woman's body substitutes for the temple in the realm of family purity as the site for distinguishing the pure from the impure.[58] Is such attention an example of the oppression of women by a patriarchal system? Or is it a way of honoring the central importance of the woman's body to the communal well-being?

At first glance, Ezekiel's use of the image of menstrual impurity would seem an instance of misogynistic rhetoric in which Ezekiel and his male audience identify the woman as the source of the waywardness of the people.[59] But this possible interpretation of his rhetoric has credibility only because of the vital position of the woman to the integrity and sustainability of the household.[60] Ezekiel argues that cultic and ethical transgressions have progressively defiled the land such that the land has reached the saturation point and must vomit out the inhabitants. But by raising up household relationships as integral to the covenant with Yhwh, Ezekiel is recognizing the key role that the woman plays in the marriage metaphor for the covenant relationship. In this metaphor, she emphasizes the human, embodied element of the divine-human relationship. If she follows the practices enjoined by the Priestly purity system, she will be attentive to the mysterious power within her menstrual blood as a divine force essential to the life of the household.[61] By listening to the movements of this life force and recognizing that she is not in control of it but rather is watching over it as the gift of life, she is playing an indispensible role in the re-creation

---

58. Tirzah Meacham, "An Abbreviated History of the Development of the Jewish Menstrual Laws," in Wasserfall, *Women and Water*, 23–39. Philip (*Menstruation and Childbirth*, 65) notes: "The female body was, indeed, a site into which it was convenient to tie obedience to the laws guarding the sanctity of the family." For post-70 C.E. identification of the family as a site for carrying out impurity laws in place of the temple, see Lesley A. Cook, "Body Language: Women's Rituals of Purification in the Bible and Mishnah," in Wasserfall, *Women and Water*, 40–59; see also Fonrobert, *Menstrual Purity*, 29.

59. Van Dijk-Hemmes, "Metaphorization of Woman," 254–55; Exum, *Plotted, Shot, and Painted*, 108–10, 117.

60. Carol Meyers, "The Family in Early Israel," in *Families in Ancient Israel* (ed. Leo Perdue, Joseph Blenkinsopp, John J. Collins, and Carol Meyers; Family, Religion and Culture; Louisville: Westminster John Knox, 1997), 28–32; Saul M. Olyan, *Rites and Rank: Hierarchy in Biblical Representations of Cult* (Princeton: Princeton University Press, 2000), 85–86.

61. Destro, "Witness of Times," 132–33; Korte, "Female Blood Rituals," 178–80, 186.

of the household. This attitude of watchfulness and receptivity is one that Ezekiel is called to cultivate in his role as sentinel (Ezek 3:16–21; 33:1–9). In 36:17 the metaphor of the defiant menstruous woman refers primarily to the male audience, many of whom were probably priests. Ezekiel called them to recognize how they had failed to embrace their corporate identity as a feminine reality depicted as the wife of Yhwh.

The purity regulations protect the mysterious power of menstrual blood so that it is constructive of household relations rather than dispersed with powerful unintended consequences on the relationships of the community. The matrix of household relationships is central to the Israelite community in preexilic, exilic, and postexilic contexts.[62] Ezekiel explains the central role of the woman in the covenant relationship when he depicts Jerusalem as the wife of Yhwh and claims that her promiscuous ways have defiled Jerusalem and led to its destruction. But the image of wife Jerusalem locates the defilement in her body, which can be seen as an analogue to the temple.[63] Even though the term נִדָּה is not used in Ezek 16, it may be that דָּמָיִךְ in 16:9 refers to menstrual blood. Here Yhwh bathes, washes, and anoints woman Jerusalem as she becomes his covenant partner or wife. But then in 16:15–53 Ezekiel describes her promiscuous ways and Yhwh's judgment against her because she has not been faithful to the exclusive character of the covenant relationship. The mysterious power within her for new life has taken the form of "lust" (נְחֻשְׁתֵּךְ, v. 36) that has been poured out before her lovers. How the woman/wife supports the relationships within the household is essential to its well-being. Purity regulations have as their goal the promotion of right relationships within the household of Yhwh, of which individual Israelite households are parts or analogous subsets. The mysterious power of menstrual blood is a force for life when it supports these household relationships but a force for death when it defiles them.

Does Ezekiel's emphasis on menstrual blood and the waywardness of woman Jerusalem allow Ezekiel's male audience to exonerate themselves and shift the blame for the exile to women? I argue that this is not Ezekiel's intent, even though the reference in 23:45 and 48 to "righteous

---

62. Jon L. Berquist, *Controlling Corporeality: The Body and the Household in Ancient Israel* (New Brunswick, N.J.: Rutgers University Press, 2002), 64–65; Dale Launderville, *Celibacy in the Ancient World: Its Ideal and Practice in Pre-Hellenistic Israel, Mesopotamia, and Greece* (Collegeville, Minn.: Liturgical Press, 2010), 80–91.

63. Galambush, *Jerusalem in Ezekiel*, 87.

judges" condemning wife Samaria and wife Jerusalem for adultery and homicide with "all women" being admonished thereby would indicate that such patriarchal scapegoating was ready-to-hand.[64] Much more radically, Ezekiel calls the exiles as a whole to identify with woman Jerusalem and to recognize their part in these infidelities and defilements (16:35–43; 18:21–32).[65] For the males in the audience to identify with woman Jerusalem, particularly as she is stripped and exposed to her foreign lovers in 16:37–41, means that they would have experienced a measure of gender reversal.[66] For the male heads of exilic households to see themselves as wives who have been punished for infidelity means that they would interpret their position of diminished power as one that would have come not only from a historical disaster brought by foreign invaders but also by a sociological shift in which they are answerable to a higher male authority within the household structure.[67] This experience of gender inversion would help Ezekiel's male audience see that from a theocentric perspective their authority in the household is derived from Yhwh. Disregard of this divine source of their authority could only result in disaster for the household and the community. Instead of blaming Woman as a mysterious force in undermining the community, the men are called to relinquish their control over the household in the sense that they are above all to be attentive to the power of Yhwh active in their midst and exercising authority over their lives.

Those men with misogynistic predispositions would probably hear Ezekiel's use of feminine images for the Israelites' shortcomings as a reason to blame women.[68] But this response will only remove these men from Ezekiel's message that they are to identify with woman Jerusalem and to

---

64. The "women" in Ezek 23:48b (cf. 16:41) figuratively refer to the other nations; thus, on a literal level, the "women" refer to both the men and the women of these nations. See Leslie C. Allen, *Ezekiel 20–48* (WBC 29; Nashville: Nelson, 1990), 51.

65. Jacqueline E. Lapsley, "Shame and Self-Knowledge: The Positive Role of Shame in Ezekiel's View of the Moral Self," in *The Book of Ezekiel: Theological and Anthropological Perspectives* (ed. Margaret Odell and John Strong; SBLSymS 9; Atlanta: Scholars Press, 2000), 172.

66. Kamionkowski, *Gender Reversal and Cosmic Chaos*, 7–8, 92, 132; Galambush, *Jerusalem in Ezekiel*, 101–2.

67. Kamionkowski, *Gender Reversal and Cosmic Chaos*, 60–67.

68. Nussbaum (*Hiding from Humanity*, 111) notes: "the locus classicus of group-directed projective disgust is the female body."

see her idolatrous ways as their own ways (16:35–43; 18:21–32).[69] The efforts of the Judeans to act autonomously outside the covenant relationship are not to be attributed to a personified collective entity called woman Jerusalem apart from the individuals who constitute this collective entity. In order to live out the covenant relationship, they must be attentive and obedient to the demands of this relationship. Their transgressions function like menstrual blood defiling the land in geometrical fashion once it is unleashed and not countered.

The Role of Disgust and Shame in Ethics and Theology

Among those men with misogynistic predispositions, the image of menstrual impurity was likely to stir disgust. As noted earlier, this sensation mobilizes the entire nervous system to protect a person from a dangerous, foreign substance. The fear of being corrupted by this "disgusting" reality would provoke strong protective reactions in Ezekiel's audience.[70] For a priest to hear about menstrual blood unleashed in the community, the sight of spilled blood and the smell of rotting decay would trigger a sense of revulsion as if it were a decaying corpse. This revulsion has been associated with the sense of smell, taste, and touch, but the sight of something repulsive or the hearing about it can trigger the primary sensation of disgust.[71] This defensive reaction aims to prevent the ingestion, inhaling, or incorporation of this corpse-like matter. To the extent that the cultic distinction between clean and unclean is linked with bodily sensations, the reaction of disgust would signal the presence of something unclean: a substance perceived not only as unpleasant but also as threatening.[72]

The priest-prophet Ezekiel continues his primary task of instructing the exiles on the sin of idolatry with his use of the image of menstrual impurity. He recognizes that his audience—most likely composed primarily of males and priests—has already been socialized to have a strong

---

69. Kamionkowski, *Gender Reversal and Cosmic Chaos*, 58–61; Galambush, *Jerusalem in Ezekiel*, 31, 102, 132; cf. Greenberg, *Ezekiel 1–20*, 298–99.

70. Allen, *Ezekiel 20–48*, 178; Philips, *Menstruation and Childbirth*, 10, 66; Kazen, "Dirt and Disgust," 58.

71. William Ian Miller, *The Anatomy of Disgust* (Cambridge: Harvard University Press, 1997), 134; Kazen, "Dirt and Disgust," 52–54.

72. Kazen, "Dirt and Disgust," 54.

visceral reaction to menstrual blood.⁷³ So he likens their idolatrous and unethical behavior to that of menstrual impurity; he hopes to educate his audience to feel disgust toward their sins as they would feel toward decaying matter. The term *abomination* is used in the Holiness Code (e.g., Lev 18:22, 26, 27, 29, 30; 20:13), Deuteronomy (12:31; 13:15; 14:3), and Ezekiel (e.g., 8:6, 9, 13, 15, 17) to describe those moral and cultic realities that should evoke this visceral sensation of disgust.⁷⁴ Disgust is both a physical and emotional feeling.⁷⁵ As an emotion, this feeling has a rational component that can be shaped by socialization and education.⁷⁶ Ezekiel calls his audience to task for not recognizing idols as disgusting. He refers to such idols as "shit-gods" (גלולים, 20:7, 8 [39 of 48 OT occurrences in Ezekiel]) and "detestable things" (שקוצים, 20:7, 8, 30), so that the Israelites' ingrained tendency to worship idols, which Ezekiel shows in his description of their long history of engaging in such a practice (20:7–39), might be countered by a sense of revulsion.⁷⁷ Ezekiel's efforts to cultivate a sense of disgust in his audience toward idols is his frequent use of the term תועבה, "abomination"; of the 117 occurrences of this term in the Hebrew Bible/Old Testament, Ezekiel uses it 43 times.⁷⁸ His effort to educate his people's deeply felt emotions is central to their capacity to come into right relationship with Yhwh.

Ezekiel claims that the exiles will only realize the full extent of their sinful, disgusting behavior when they are restored to the land, which will

---

73. Ibid. Nussbaum (*Hiding from Humanity*, 113) notes: "women become vehicles for the expression of male loathing of the physical and the potentially decaying. Taboos surrounding sex, birth, menstruation—all these express the desire to ward off something that is too physical, that partakes too much of the secretions of the body."

74. Block, *Ezekiel 1–24*, 203.

75. Kazen, "Dirt and Disgust," 60.

76. Nussbaum, *Hiding from Humanity*, 35.

77. O'Grady ("Semantics of Taboo," 25–26) notes that "within the sensation of disgust, there is this ambiguous reaction of both repulsion and attraction to the revolting object—at least distantly analogous to the experience of being drawn and repelled by an encounter with 'the holy.'" Carolyn Korsmeyer and Barry Smith ("Visceral Values: Aurel Kolnai on Disgust," in *On Disgust*, by Aurel Kolnai [ed. Carolyn Korsmeyer and Barry Smith; Chicago: Open Court, 2004], 9) state concerning the riveting attention given to a revolting object: "This character of the intentionality of disgust imparts a complex, Janus-faced feel to the emotion, one that almost savors its object at the same time that it is revolted by it."

78. Zimmerli, *Ezekiel 1*, 190.

then produce abundant fruit (20:42–44; 36:25–31). He notes: "Then you shall remember your evil ways, and your dealings that were not good; and you shall loathe yourselves [נקטתם] for your iniquities and your abominable deeds [תועבותכם]" (36:31). Ezekiel has explained at length how the Israelites were simply not able to obey Yhwh's statutes and ordinances and thereby grow in knowledge of him and how they were to understand themselves in relation to him (20:8, 13, 16, 21, 24). This growth in self-awareness required that they go through the crucible of the exile. Only in light of the gift of Yhwh's restoration of them would they be the new creatures who could understand the enormity of their transgressions. This inability to "think big" about God could be remedied only by Yhwh's placing a new heart and a new spirit in the returning exiles (36:26–27). Now they would have the capacity to understand themselves properly in relationship with Yhwh.[79]

Ezekiel notes in his story about woman Jerusalem (Ezek 16) that the Israelites previously were able—almost by genetics— to loathe others in their family. He says of woman Jerusalem in relation to her Hittite mother and to her sisters Sodom and Samaria: "Like mother, like daughter. You are the daughter of your mother, who loathed [גאלת] her husband and her children; and you are the sister of your sisters, who loathed [גאלו] their husbands and their children" (16:44–45). He directs woman Jerusalem to compare herself to her sisters whom she has looked down upon and exhorts her: "Be ashamed [בושי] and bear your disgrace [כלמתך] because your sisters are more upright than you" (16:52). But the end of this account in Ezek 16 voices the same promise as occurs in 36:31: when Jerusalem is restored to the covenantal status that she experienced in her youth, she will become aware of her sinful ways and will be ashamed (בוש) as a result of Yhwh's atoning action (כפר, 16:63).[80] Here self-loathing and shame point to the same emotion; for humans, it is a feeling essential to honest self-assessment.[81]

---

79. Lapsley, "Shame and Self-Knowledge," 159.
80. Lapsley, "Shame and Self-Knowledge," 165; Margaret Odell, "An Exploratory Study of Shame and Dependence in the Bible and Selected Near Eastern Parallels," in *The Biblical Canon in Comparative Perspective* (vol. 4 of *Scripture in Context*; ed. K. Lawson Younger Jr., William W. Hallo, and Bernard F. Batto; Ancient Near Eastern Texts and Studies 11; Lewiston, N.Y.: Mellen, 1991), 228–29.
81. Lapsley, "Shame and Self-Knowledge," 153, 159.

Ezekiel wants his exilic audience to feel shame over past disgraceful, abominable deeds. The sensation of disgust is seen as contributing to a feeling of shame that will constructively lead to greater self-awareness. But these inner feelings of disgust and shame are not merely primordial states that dictate how one should honestly feel and act. These feelings have a rational component; they are shaped by a communal context and so are "self-conscious emotions" rather than "primary emotional states."[82] Thus, for Ezekiel's audience to hear that their worship of other deities is like menstrual impurity, the feeling of disgust that he hopes to generate in them is not automatic. How the exiles feel about menstrual impurity probably depends on their gender and family context: if from a priestly family, menstrual impurity probably took on the character of a taboo; but if from a family like that of Jacob and Rachel, it probably was a reality talked about and acknowledged as a sign of fertility.[83] Ezekiel hopes to tap into a feeling of disgust his audience should have over the mindless spread of menstrual impurity throughout the community. It is not menstruation per se that is defiling; rather it is the mindless proliferation of menstrual impurity over which Ezekiel hopes that his audience feels disgust. If they feel this disgust, then he urges them to see that their sinful and idolatrous ways have generated disgust in the sight of Yhwh like that of menstrual impurity spreading throughout the community. The feeling of disgust is a visceral emotion that can bring to bear one's best energies in combating a threat and so can support the values of a community.[84] But disgust is an emotion that is appropriate only to the extent that the person feeling it recognizes that it

---

82. Ibid., 151.

83. Philip, *Menstruation and Childbirth*, 22–25; Nussbaum, *Hiding from Humanity*, 120. Elissa Stein and Susan Kim (*Flow: The Cultural Story of Menstruation* [New York: St. Martin's Griffin, 2009], 15) note: "We know that for nearly all women, menstruation is a normal, if wildly variable and profoundly subjective, life experience. Another thing we know is that it seems to involve not just our uteruses, ovaries, and vaginas, but much of the rest of our bodies, as well: our brains, glands, hearts, and other organs. What's more, no matter how old we are, if we're female, we're actually menstrual our entire lives: either pre-, menstrual, peri-, menopausal, or post-. And the stages of our lives are in a sense defined by where we are on the menstrual time line."

84. Miller, *Anatomy of Disgust*, 178–80. Nussbaum (*Hiding from Humanity*, 115) dismisses Miller's view that a society is more advanced if it recognizes more things as disgusting because his focus is simply on bodily things, e.g., the cleansing of slime, filth, and bodily products.

has been shaped through socialization and needs to be rationally tested so that it is in accord with its context and a higher sense of fairness.[85]

Conclusion

In trying to generate a sense of disgust in his audience over their idolatrous and sinful behavior, is Ezekiel guilty of misogyny in his use of the image of menstrual impurity? Ezekiel recognizes that the exiles will come to greater self-awareness only by going through the exile and being restored from exile. It is this stripping away and giving back that will make the exiles aware of Yhwh's governance of their lives but most especially of his overwhelming power and transcendence. They and their ancestors have tried to treat him as one God among others who can be manipulated. Such transformed self-awareness cannot be gained merely by words but requires practice. There must be an engagement with others and an environment larger than one can manage in order for growth in self-knowledge.[86] Ezekiel's provocative and at times outrageous rhetoric aims to move his audience to self-examination. It is in this process of self-reflection that the sensation of disgust elicited by the image of menstrual impurity can be properly gauged. If the persons reflecting are calling themselves to account and taking responsibility for their part in the troubles besetting the community, they will avoid setting up women as the source of their suffering. The sensation of disgust can shape a person's self-understanding and attitude toward others. If this sensation is not regularly monitored and called into question, it can be a source of great injustice to others. Likewise, the emotion of shame has potential to make one realize the wide difference between God and humans and so assist the Israelites in coming into right relationship with Yhwh as their covenant partner.

The Priestly system of purity was androcentric and hierarchical, but it was not misogynistic. As a system, it fostered deeply held emotions to be mobilized to defend the community against outside threats. These threats entered the community through the choices that the Israelites made. The bias of the Priestly system of impurity toward the well-being of the house-

---

85. Nussbaum, *Hiding from Humanity*, 35, 116.
86. Jacqueline E. Lapsley, *Can These Bones Live? The Problem of the Moral Self in Ezekiel* (BZAW 301; New York: de Gruyter, 2000) 103, 109, 171; Greenberg, *Ezekiel 21–37*, 737; Launderville, *Spirit and Reason*, 60.

hold can be seen as supporting a social structure that honors women as vital to its functioning and reconstituting itself.

Spermatic Spluttering Pens: Concerning the Construction and Breakdown of Prophetic Masculinity

Roland Boer

This study is an exercise in uncovering (and I use the word deliberately) the earthiness and indeed crudity of the biblical language of prophetic masculinities. It is all very well in the polite circles of (usually religiously driven) academia to speak of the dominant patriarchies of the Bible or of the masculinities that saturate many of its texts, but these are convenient abstractions, a relieved stride toward the euphemisms that enable us to avoid the earthiness of those texts. So, for the sake of avoiding such euphemisms, I seek to be as crude as the biblical texts themselves, with no apology given apart from the need to be forthright in our interpretation.

The following study has two sections: one—organizing the sausage-fest—concerning the construction of the prophetic universe, particularly in terms of the power claimed through the act of writing; the other—too many dicks—showing how that world breaks down through its own impossibility. The focus is that provocatively crude prophetic text known as Ezekiel. However, in order to situate that argument, a few theoretical observations are in order, dealing with ideology, hegemony, and semantic fields. More theory will follow later in the study, but these are sufficient as an opening.

Ideology, Hegemony, and Semantic Fields

My theoretical starting point is that the workings of language provide an unwitting insight into ideology. In brief, I take ideology in the classic Marxist sense as unfolding in two related directions: it designates false consciousness, specific beliefs or opinions concerning a vital matter (privilege, wealth, etc.) that are not only mistaken but support an unjust status quo. But ideology is also—and more neutrally—a way of mediating the complex reality of the world and our places within it.[1] If the first type of ideology can be dispensed with, the second is here to stay. And if the first requires critique, the second needs description and understanding.[2]

How, then, does language provide a window into ideology? I do not mean the oft-repeated assertion that the way to understand a people and a culture is through their language. Or rather, I take this self-evident truth and give it a twist: it is not the content of the language that counts, the ideas and beliefs it seeks to express directly, but the forms and structures—or what I call the machinery and workings—of language that provide unwitting insights into the deeper patterns of ideology, precisely those that everyone assumes to be natural. This is where the analogy with architecture is illuminating: in the same way that the form—the patterns, lines, and fashions—of architecture express most directly the zeitgeist of an age,[3] so also does the form of language give voice to the structuring ideological assumptions of those who deploy it.

With these basic positions concerning ideology in place, it is now possible to add some complexity via the theory of hegemony, which is itself a Marxist development of the theory of ideology. It has become a standard if somewhat banal point that masculinity is by no means an eternal, static, and singular quality inherent to men, but that it is constructed, performed, multiple, fluid, and subject to historical change.[4] Masculinities may be constructed discursively, socially, or economically; they may be consti-

---

1. See Michèle Barrett, *The Politics of Truth: From Marx to Foucault* (Stanford: Stanford University Press, 1991), 18–34; Louis Dupré, *Marx's Social Critique of Culture* (New Haven: Yale University Press, 1983), 238–44; Jorge Larrain, "Ideology," in *A Dictionary of Marxist Thought* (ed. Tom Bottomore; Oxford: Blackwell, 1983); Jorge Larrain, *Marxism and Ideology* (Contemporary Social Theory; London: Macmillan, 1983).

2. Terry Eagleton, *Ideology: An Introduction* (London: Verso, 1991); Fredric Jameson, *Valences of the Dialectic* (London: Verso, 2009), 315–63. See further Slavoj Žižek, ed., *Mapping Ideology* (London: Verso, 1994).

3. Fredric Jameson, *The Cultural Turn: Selected Writings on the Postmodern, 1983-1998* (London: Verso, 1998), 162–89; Fredric Jameson, *Postmodernism, or, the Cultural Logic of Late Capitalism* (Postcontemporary Inteventions; Durham, N.C.: Duke University Press, 1991), 97–129.

4. See, e.g., Raewyn W. Connell, *Maculinities* (2nd ed.; Berkeley: University of California Press, 2005); Charlotte Hooper, *Manly States: Masculinities, International Relations, and Gender Politics* (New York: Columbia University Press, 2001), 17–76.

tuted through performance; they may be fluid and constantly shifting. The multiplicity of masculinities is a feature of any historical period, and masculinities change over time, are created, die, and are recreated again and again. Apart from the obligatory theoretical touchstones of Foucault, Butler, Haraway, and a host of lesser lights, another who makes a regular appearance in studies of gender and masculinity is Antonio Gramsci. Or rather, a bowdlerised version of Gramsci's theory of hegemony that owes much to Edward Said's misreading usually turns up. According to this perception of hegemony, it designates the dominant position, the one of the ruling class or race or gender.[5] It is reinforced by force (police, both secret and not so secret, law courts, and army) and persuasion (propaganda in the media, education, and argument).

There is some limited truth in this perception. However, a careful reading of the many treatments of hegemony in Gramsci's notebooks[6] reveals that such an interpretation is superficial.[7] Instead, Gramsci's purpose in developing the theory of hegemony (a reworking of the Marxist theory of ideology) was to find a way to overthrow those in power, to explore how a new, liberating hegemony might develop. A corollary to this purpose is the argument that the ruling hegemony is inherently uncertain and shaky. So also with the Bible: despite the effort in the Bible to present a series of overlapping ruling and dominating perspectives, all the way from social organization to sexuality, not to mention religion, they are very shaky indeed. Or to put it even more forcefully, the very act of asserting dominance is inherently unstable. Subversion lurks in every murky doorway and under every bed. Hegemony is continually undermined from within and without. A major reason why the dominant hegemony is unstable is that it must constantly deal with insurrection—in politics, social movements, ideas, personal beliefs, and so on. After all, the reason Gramsci, the Communist, developed the notion of hegemony was to find a way to

---

5. See Connell, *Masculinities*, 77–78; Hooper, *Manly States*, 40.
6. Antonio Gramsci, *Prison Notebooks* (ed. Joseph A. Buttigieg; trans. Joseph A. Buttigieg and Antonio Callari; 3 vols.; New York: Columbia University Press, 1992–2007); idem, *Selections from the Prison Notebooks* (ed. and trans. Quintin Hoare and Geoffrey Nowell Smith; London: Lawrence & Wishart, 1971).
7. Roland Boer, *Criticism of Heaven: On Marxism and Theology* (HM 18; Leiden: Brill, 2007), 215–74. See esp. Benedetto Fontana, *Hegemony and Power: On the Relation Between Gramsci and Machiavelli* (Minneapolis: University of Minnesota Press, 1993); Peter Thomas, *The Gramscian Moment: Philosophy, Hegemony and Marxism* (HM 24; Leiden: Brill, 2009).

overcome the dominance of the fascist state under Mussolini and capitalism more generally.

To this account of Gramsci's theory I would like to add Louis Althusser's argument concerning what he calls "Ideological State Apparatuses"—a term that adds some economic and social depth to what are usually called institutions.[8] For Althusser, Ideological State Apparatuses include education, religion, family, politics, the legal system, and culture. But the important point for my analysis is that while these apparatuses are zones where the ruling ideas seek to be inculcated, they are also *sites of ideological struggle*.[9] And these struggles take place *within* the apparatuses. Although the ruling class attempts to dominate and control the Ideological State Apparatuses, their hold is unstable and contested—a point Althusser owes to Gramsci's notion of hegemony. Ideological struggles take place in these institutions. This is precisely what I seek to uncover in my reading of the texts of Ezekiel, for here too the effort to construct a dominant form of scribal masculinity is notable for its instability and tendency to undermine itself. These texts too are sites of ideological struggle.

The third theoretical point concerns semantic fields. Words never operate in isolation; they are part of semantic fields that produce both the richness of language and difficulties for translators (at a microlevel). The idea of semantic fields works in two directions. A semantic field may be described as a clan of meaning, in which a word sharing the same root belongs to the same clan. This is particularly true of Hebrew, where often verb, noun, and adjective may share the same consonantal root and thereby belong to the same clan. Second, semantic fields operate in a situation where the same word may be used for a range of (although not always clearly) related meanings. In this case, these various senses are obviously

---

8. Louis Althusser, *Lenin and Philosophy and Other Essays* (trans. Ben Brewster; London: New Left Books, 1971), 121–73; Louis Althusser, *Sur la reproduction* (Actuel Marx confrontation; Paris: Presses universitaires de France, 1995), 269–314.

9. Althusser famously defines "Ideology" as the representation of the imaginary (understood in Lacan's sense via the distinction between the imaginary, symbolic, and Real) relationship of individuals to their real conditions of existence, thereby revolutionizing Marxist approaches to ideology (it is not simply false consciousness). It is not the *imaginary relationship* itself that is ideology—for instance, an illusion such as belief in justice, or God, or the honesty of one's rulers. It is not, in other words, a deliberate concealment of the truth by a conspiracy of priests and the powerful. Rather, ideology is the way this imaginary relation is *represented*. It operates at a second remove from reality.

connected, but one applies—or so goes the advice to budding translators—the most appropriate sense depending on the literary context. In what follows I operate with a somewhat different assumption, namely that whenever a word is used it evokes, however implicitly, the other senses of its semantic range or cluster. That is, I am interested not in the sparseness of meaning but in its richness and fullness. At least a couple of implications flow from these points: the idea of semantic fields illuminates the perpetual problem of lack of fit in translations, for what we have so often is a partial overlap between two semantic fields rather than a tight fit.[10] Further, semantic fields also lead to the delectable uncertainty of translation, the sense that one can never be absolutely sure that this word is the best one for a translation.

Organizing the Sausage-Fest

With these initial theoretical points under our belts, it is now possible to move to specific textual analysis, which begins with the way masculinity, prophets, and power center on the act of writing and the one who writes. I seek the construction of a masculine hegemony, the way the sausage-fest is organized. In order to do so, I engage initially in some textual analysis followed by a wad of theory.

Spermatic Spluttering Pen(ise)s

Our opening text is Ezek 9, especially verses 2–3 and 11, where we find an extraordinarily curious phrase: קסת הספר במתניו. Commentators are not keen to make much of it, usually rendering it something like "a writing case at his side," or perhaps "a writing kit at his loins."[11] Let us take a

---

10. As one example, the Danish word *køre* refers to both driving a car (or truck or bus) and riding a bicycle. Danes will often speak of driving a bicycle, or simply "driving" to somewhere when they mean riding a bicycle. To an English speaker it sounds odd, since the semantic field of "drive" does not include bicycles.

11. Commentators are spectacular in missing the importance of this verse, perhaps because its claims are unremarkable for the male guild of biblical scholars: George A. Cooke, *A Critical and Exegetical Commentary on the Book of Ezekiel* (ICC; 1936; repr., Edinburgh: T&T Clark, 1985), 104; Walther Eichrodt, *Ezekiel: A Commentary* (trans. Cosslett Quin; OTL; Philadelphia: Westminster, 1970), 130–31; Moshe Greenberg, *Ezekiel 1–20* (AB 22; Garden City, N.Y.: Doubleday, 1983), 176; Walther Zimmerli, *Ezekiel 1: A Commentary on the Book of the Prophet Ezekiel, Chap-*

moment to see what it actually means, for it will become a key marker for my argument concerning masculinity in prophetic texts.

As for Ezek 9, קסת is one of those Ezekelian *hapax legomena*, to which commentators a little too rapidly attribute the meaning of—perhaps—a writing case or inkpot or tablet, albeit with the flimsiest of evidence. It may be worth asking why commentators make nothing of this text, preferring a neutral sense for a *hapax legomenon* like קסת, when in other cases—such as the explicit texts of Ezek 16 and 22–23—the overwhelmingly male coterie of biblical scholars is all too ready to espy in *hapax legomena* references to women's genitals. Is it because sexualizing the textual bodies of women is a way of objectifying and thereby disempowering them, while the textual bodies of men must not be so treated? If so, then my reading is an explicit attempt to sexualize, objectify, and thereby disempower textual male bodies.[12] So, in light of what follows, I suggest that here we have a tool, or more specifically a stylus, of the one who follows. And he is the ספר, simply a scribe, one who writes texts and does things with numbers; the word is the Qal present participle of the verb ספר, "to write, number." קסת ספר is then the tool of the writer, the scribal stylus.[13]

But what about במתניו? The preposition ב is obvious, but let us stay with its basic sense of "on" or even "in." The ending יו- on מתניו is the masculine singular possessive on מתנים. Note the dual form, for that will soon become important. מתנים is supposed, according to lexica, to designate the muscles binding the abdomen to the lower limbs—abs, as we

---

ters 1–24 (trans. Ronald E. Clements; Hermeneia; Philadelphia: Fortress, 1979), 248. If any comment is made, it involves one of the commentator's favorite moves: repeat a speculative point made by another, but now as a thoroughly verifiable statement. In this case it involves a loose etymological connection with an Egyptian (!) word, *gšt(y)*, perhaps a dubious picture, and thereby it is established that scribes would carry their horns somewhere in the nether regions.

12. Thanks to Stefanie Schön for this observation when she responded to an early version of this chapter presented to a seminar at the Centre for Gender Research at the University of Oslo, Oct. 15, 2010.

13. Or, as Greenberg unwittingly and ambiguously puts it, "a scribe's kit" (*Ezekiel 1–20*, 176). Cooke's "a writer's inkhorn" (Cooke, *Ezekiel*, 104) and Zimmerli's "a scribe's instrument" (Zimmerli, *Ezekiel 1*, 224) come close to such a scrotal wordplay. For Zimmerli the English is far more telling than the German "original," which has "Schreibzeug des Schreibers" (*Ezechiel 1, I. Teilband* [BKAT 13.1; Neukirchen-Vluyn: Neukirchener Verlag, 1979], 188).

might call them in our parlance. In this respect, it is a parallel term to חלצים, the section of the body between the ribs and the hip bones. But there is one curious, usually unexplained feature of both terms, hinted at in the brilliant older translation as "loins": both words end in the rare dual form. As any student of introductory Hebrew knows, two classes of dual forms remain, one less obvious (waters, heavens, Egypt, Jerusalem), the other far more obvious, for they refer to natural pairs relating to the body: eyes, ears, hands, feet, lips, (but also shoes, horns, and wings). A question springs forth: why are the terms usually rendered loins or abs in the dual form? We are, I would suggest, in the realm of testicles, nuts, the family jewels.[14] Indeed, one cannot help wondering whether the Bible is engaged in emphatic overkill, for not only do we have the rare dual forms for חלצים and מתנים, but we also have two terms that mean the same thing—as the parallelism in Isa 11:5 shows all too well.[15] Is this a case of naming each of the twins with a name that evokes its brother, like tweedledum and tweedledee?

The implication: קסת הספר במתניו may well mean "the scribal pen(is) on his testicles." Perhaps the King James Version edges closest with "a writer's inkhorn by his side," but even here the translators quailed before the direct reference to balls and the scribal penis. As if to firm up my reading, Isa 8:1 comes to my aid, for there we find the prophet instructed to write בחרת אנוש, "with the stylus of a man" or with "the manly stylus"[16]—hopefully it would be iron or even diamond hard, as is Jeremiah's "pen of iron" (עט ברזל in Jer 17:1). Hebrew too is fully aware of the elision between pen and penis. Needless to say, this phrase from Ezek 9 (backed up by Isa 8:1)

---

14. Of course, I am stressing this point here and wish to go beyond a metonymic meaning toward a denotative sense. That most of the cognates tend to be understood as "rope" or "string" highlights the avoidance of this sense.

15. "Righteousness shall be the girdle of his balls [במתניו]; and faithfulness the girdle of his nuts [חלציו]."

16. The argument that אנוש is a generic term for humanity is about as persuasive as that concerning "man." To suggest it merely means the "common script" or "with an ordinary pen" conveniently misses the simple sense of this stylus—so Willem A. M. Beuken, *Jesaja 1–12* (trans. Ulrich Berges; HTKAT; Freiburg: Herder, 2003), 213; and Brevard Childs, *Isaiah: A Commentary* (OTL; Louisville: Westminster John Knox, 2001), 70. Misleading as well is Wildberger's "'Unheilsgriffel'" and Watts's "stylus of disaster." See John D. W. Watts, *Isaiah 1–33* (WBC; Waco, Tex.: Word, 1985), 148; Hans Wildberger, *Jesaja 1–12* (BKAT 10.1; Neukirchen-Vluyn: Neukirchener Verlag, 1972), 311–12.

has profound implications for understanding the ideological function of writing, of the scribe, of the writing prophet, of masculinity, and of the text we now read, which is the product of those scribes. Above all, it shows how closely power, writing, and masculinity are tied together in the biblical material we are considering.

Let us now widen the analysis and consider these verses in their literary context. Ezekiel 9 follows the fetid and nightmarish vision of corrupt worship and fertility practices of chapter 8, offering an apocalyptic scenario of divinely sanctioned mass slaughter. The agents of that massacre are six men, each with a "weapon of annihilation" (כלי משחתו, v. 1). They will be the ones who go out under divine directive to fill Israel and Judah with the corpses of the slain; but there is a seventh character, "the man clothed in linen" (v. 2). He it is who has the spermatic spluttering penis, the scribal stylus nestled on his nuts.

However, two features of the man stand out, apart from his formidable stylus. The first is the curious phrase איש אחד. Now, this phrase may simply mean "a man," as most translations would have it, but אחד often stresses the word with which it likes to associate: so he is a singular man, one who stands apart, a distinct individual. Yet there is another, related sense that I would like to pick up: אחד means "first and foremost." In other words, the full semantic range or field of the term designates a man who stands out from the crowd and is superior to it. Of course, the image of this man, dressed in linen and favoring a scribal dong, would set him apart from the macho men around him. *His* weapon or tool (כלי) is far more potent than theirs.

How so? He has the power of life and death, for he is to go out into the city of Jerusalem and write a ת on the foreheads of all those who groan and

sigh about the way things have gone, that is, those who cannot abide by what is happening but feel helpless. Picture, if you will, a man going about with his scribal pen, daubing the foreheads of the men of the city who will be saved—not with the Hebrew letter with which we familiar, but with a Paleo-Hebrew ת that looks like a ragged cross, perhaps the mark on a treasure map.

Do they kneel so he can reach their foreheads with his spluttering penis? Or is it so formidable that it can simply reach their foreheads without assistance? And what, precisely, is the ink this überman uses? Perhaps his own semen, for he may already have known what Sir George Mansfield Cumming-Smith, the head of the British spy service (1909–1926), was to discover much later: when he heard that semen is an excellent invisible ink, Cumming-Smith (!) observed, "every man his own stylo."

The results of our initial foray into the strange world of Ezek 9 has yielded a few secrets: this first or überman is far more powerful than the others, for his tool is not a simple weapon of annihilation but a scribal pen(is) firmly based on his testicles. With that pen(is) he designates salvation and destruction—the key of heaven, if you will. In the hierarchy of the text, he is next to God. In other words, masculinity and power are determined by one's phallic ability to write. Even more, the scribe is not merely the one who has such power due to his unique abilities; no, he is the one who constructs masculine power in the first place with his spermatic spluttering pen(is).

The Writing Lesson, or, the Construction of Scribal Class Identity

However, in order to see precisely how that works, let me dip into some more theory for a few moments. I engage, in sequence, Claude Lévi-Strauss and then Christina Petterson. One of the essays in Lévi-Strauss's extraordinary *Tristes Tropiques* (part memoir, part theoretical development, it was written by an older man, bedecked with honors and recognition in metropolitan Paris, recalling with a good deal of longing the forays and discoveries of his youth in the jungles of Brazil) is called "The Writing Lesson."[17] It recounts an incident on one of Lévi-Strauss's forays into the central highlands of the Brazilian jungle in which he sought to determine precisely how many subgroups of the Nambikwara tribe remained. He persuaded the chief of the group to which he was attached to arrange a rendezvous of all the groups some distance away. And in order to entice everyone to turn up, Lévi-Strauss and his companions arranged for a number of oxen to carry the gifts for exchange. The situation was not without its tensions, since the chief had assumed the Frenchmen would supply all of them with food by shooting game. Further, not all the groups saw eye to eye and they were not necessarily pleased at having been called together for an apparently useless purpose. Tense and fractious—think of the late-night delay in an area where you know you should not be, the

---

17. Claude Lévi-Strauss, *Tristes Tropiques* (trans. John Weightman and Doreen Weightman; 1973; repr., Picador Classics; London: Pan, 1989), 385–99.

spark of alpha-male chest beating suddenly filling the air with the sulphur and ozone of human thunder—the chief seized upon a novel way to assert his authority: he read some writing on a page. Since he had already determined that writing was a desirable attribute, providing Lévi-Strauss on earlier occasions with pages full of wavy lines in response to his questions, the chief now resorted to writing to assert his power. From the collection of gifts he pulled out a piece of paper full of wavy lines, with hills and hollows, bumps and curves. As Lévi-Strauss writes:

> As soon as he had got the company together, he took from a basket a piece of paper covered with wavy lines and made a show of reading it, pretending to hesitate as he checked on it the list of objects I was to give in exchange for the presents offered me: so-and-so was to have a chopper in exchange for a bow and arrows, someone else beads in exchange for his necklaces.... This farce went on for two hours.[18]

According to the only account available of the incident—that of our intrepid anthropologist—writing won the chief some breathing space. The text written may have been nonsensical according to any linguistic code—a point Lévi-Strauss is keen to assert—but it was understood by the chief and those around as a code of power.

Lévi-Strauss's account suffers, as Jacques Derrida was to point out (in his effort to leapfrog over his own mentor, a version, perhaps, of honoring the father by killing him) in *Of Grammatology,* of an excess dose of Western rationality, as well as voicing an ethnocentrism that disguises itself as anti-ethnocentrism.[19] With observations like "This farce went on for two hours" or "this piece of humbug,"[20] Derrida has a point. But Lévi-Strauss has also stumbled across a crucial insight: writing, understood as a complex socioeconomic phenomenon, means power. This is particularly applicable in social situations in which the scribe is not only the odd one out, but especially one who makes the exception central and thereby carves out structures of power. As Lévi-Strauss writes: "The only phenomenon with which writing has always been concomitant is the creation of cities

---

18. Ibid., 388.

19. Jacques Derrida, *Of Grammatology* (trans. Gayatri Chakravorty Spivak; Baltimore: Johns Hopkins University Press, 1976), 118–40.

20. Lévi-Strauss, *Tristes Tropiques*, 388, 389.

and empires, that is, the integration of large numbers of individuals into a political system and their grading into castes or classes."²¹

Lévi-Strauss's account may now be enhanced by the perceptive recent study of Christina Petterson,²² who explores the way the indigenous catechist in the Danish mission to Greenland became instrumental in shaping the new class structures of the colony. Catechists were drawn from mixed parentage (a group called called *blandinger*), with a Danish father and Greenlandic mother, since they were both part of the language, culture, and economy of Greenland and yet separate from it. They were paid by the Danish government (less, of course, than the missionaries themselves) and underwent a lengthy process of training in the arts of writing, at times in Denmark. A central feature involved the daily keeping of diaries, which gradually changed within the life spans of most catechists from an obvious discomfort with the new medium of self-reflection to a greater ease and loquaciousness. The diaries were written in both Greenlandic and Danish (a mark of their in-between status), although the Danish diaries tended to be written by those who had been educated in Denmark. Initially, the catechists were the eyes, ears, and mouth of the Danish missionaries; but eventually they became, argues Petterson, the new Greenlandic ruling class. How so? As the first scribes, the catechists began the process of developing a literate culture in Greenland. Eventually, their heirs would be in charge of the first printing press, the newspaper(s), book production, and thereby the scribal production of Greenlandic society.

At the center of this production of a Greenlandic literate culture is the vital process of constructing new categories of masculinity and class— the two are inextricably tied together. While the hunter was constructed as the privileged one outside the Danish colonial presence, as the ideal and idealized male Greenlander who lived through his ancient skills, the abject masculinities of the riffraff were constructed in order to account for the menial tasks of the majority of Greenlanders under Danish rule (essentially the colonial working class). But what about the catechists? Their heirs became the new supermasculine intellectuals,²³ the ones in

---

21. Ibid., 392.

22. Christina Petterson, *The Missionary, the Catechist and the Hunter: Governmentality and Masculinites in Greenland* (Leiden: Brill, 2013).

23. We need to be careful about making a leap across different cultural constructions of masculinity here, for in the ancient Near East at least two forms of masculinity may be discerned, one a warlike warrior-king masculinity and the other a priestly

control of the reins of power: they constitute the Greenlandic ruling class of today, who have positioned themselves in the ambivalent position of seeking, initially, equality with and, later, independence from Denmark, a convoluted process that also grants them superiority over other Greenlanders. In sum: as with prophetic masculinity, the ability to use a pen(is) involves the production of masculinity itself, specifically a superior masculinity over against others that is simultaneously an assertion of class superiority. What we have is a self-referential construction of masculinity that makes one's own masculinity superior—so also with prophets like Ezekiel and Jeremiah.

Thus from Lévi-Strauss we gain some theoretical depth to the assertion that writing means power and from Petterson the point that writing is a crucial means for constructing a masculine-class complex. It should come as no surprise, then, that the scribe of Ezek 9 seems to have dipped his pen(is) in steroids, for in the act of writing he asserts a masculine power that challenges that of chiefs, princes, and kings.

Is it possible that the phallic scribe has acquired the virile power once ascribed openly to Yahweh, power that certainly attached to El? As the Ugaritic poem would have it:

> [El walks (?)] the shore of the sea,
> And strides the shore of the deep.
> [El takes (?)] two torches,
> Two torches from the top of the fire.
> Now they are low, now they rise.
> Now they cry "Daddy, daddy,"
> and now they cry "Mama, mama."
> El's "hand" grows long as the sea,
> El's "hand" as the flood.
> Long is El's "hand" as the sea,
> El's "hand" as the flood.
> El takes the two torches,
> The two torches from the top of the fire,
> He takes and puts in his house.
> El, his rod sinks.

---

perfect-male masculinity. I would suggest that both forms are part of ruling-class constructions and thereby not unrelated. Many thanks to Jonathan Stökl for this point.

El, his love-staff droops.
He raises, he shoots skyward.
He shoots a bird in the sky;
He plucks it and puts it on the coals.[24]

Given the creative power of the scribe, he may well have quietly assumed such a role. So we have a situation where the scribe's cock is his very firm, iron-like pen, the implement that rests on his balls and constructs the world of the text. That pen(is) is the implement of power, a power that is inescapably masculine due to the very identity of the pen(is) itself. Rigid, solid, unchallengeable, is it not?

Too Many Dicks

I have left one crucial feature until now, for it opens up the possibility that the scribal dong may wilt under pressure, the pen becoming uselessly soft in one's hand: the issue of auto-referentiality. In the accounts I have considered thus far—Ezek 9 and Jer 36—we find scribes doing their thing: they write, challenge, dominate, and disseminate. But who tells such stories of spermatic scribes? The scribes themselves, of course. In other words, these accounts are auto-referential, which is really another way of saying they are masturbatory.

Scribal Auto-referentiality

Before I tease out that last point, one more dip into theory, now—symptomatically—my own earlier work on scribal self-referentiality, by which I write myself explicitly into my own text. In *Jameson and Jeroboam*[25] I spent a reasonable amount of time analyzing the insomnia-curing regnal formulae of the books of Kings and Chronicles—for example, the formula at the close of the reign of Jeroboam:

---

24. Translation modified from Howard Eilberg-Schwartz, *God's Phallus and Other Problems for Men and Monotheism* (Boston: Beacon, 1994), 107–8. The text is KTU 1.23, lines 30–39.

25. Roland Boer, *Jameson and Jeroboam* (SemeiaSt 30; Atlanta: Scholars Press, 1996).

> As for the rest of the affairs of Jeroboam, how he warred and how he reigned, they are indeed written in the book of the daily affairs of the Kings of Israel. The time that Jeroboam reigned was twenty-two years, and he slept with his ancestors, and Nadab his son reigned instead of him. (1 Kgs 14:19–20)

The pattern continues throughout Kings and Chronicles, marking births, deaths, and transitions from one reign to another. These formulae became a mine of formal information regarding class and economics, but here I wish to stress two features of my reading. First, the formulae exhibit what may be described as a literary self-consciousness: the scribes responsible for the text write themselves into the text through reference to—largely fictitious—sources.[26] That is, in referring to a book of the daily affairs of the kings of Israel, or the book of the acts of Solomon, and so on, the scribes provide their own covert signature, or they reinscribe their social authority by citing other scribal products as authoritative. The reference to others writing is actually a reference to their own writing.

Second, when we get to Chronicles the prophets become prime sources to which the reader is referred. For instance, compare the texts of 1 Kgs 11:41 and 2 Chr 9:29:

> As for the rest of the affairs of Solomon, and all that he did and his wisdom, are they not written in the book of the affairs of Solomon?

> As for the remaining affairs of Solomon, the first and the last, are they not written in the records of Nathan the prophet, and in the prophecy of Ahijah the Shilonite, and in the visions of Iddo the seer concerning Jeroboam son of Nebat?

Quite a shift, is it not, especially in the midst of passages that are otherwise almost identical between the two texts? The prophets have largely disappeared from the actual narrative (in Kings we have the cycles of Elijah and Elisha, for instance) only to camp themselves in the formulae that frame the narrative. More importantly, the gaggle of prophets peering over the edge of the balcony that contains the regnal formulae is a greater assertion of their writing presence. Ahijah, Iddo, Nathan, and the range of other

---

26. Katie Stott, *Why Did They Write This Way? Reflections on References to Written Documents in the Hebrew Bible and Ancient Literature* (LHBOTS 492; London: T&T Clark, 2008).

names, often dragged out of the narrative and relocated here—have all become writers, joining the well-known "writing prophets," Isaiah, Jeremiah, and Ezekiel.

The last point is already a development in the direction of my argument here, so let me now push the relevance further. To begin with, the elision of scribe and prophet is a crucial move. In Kings we may get away with the impression that scribe and prophet are distinct characters, the former writing about the latter, even with the auto-referential function of the regnal formulae. In Ezek 9 the catatonic prophet[27] witnesses the central and chilling role of the scribe, while in Jer 36 the scribe becomes the crucial medium for the prophetic words. However, Chronicles marks the fully fledged outcome of a process already marked, as we saw earlier, in the texts of the "writing" prophets: scribe and prophet have merged into an even more potent figure.[28] By now it should be obvious that this über-scribe is the most powerful figure in the text—a fact that he is keen to let us know. The scribe is, after all, the one who writes the text, allots roles to all its characters—even Yahweh—and thereby creates the universe of the text itself.

Now we can fold back to my earlier theoretical deliberations and pick up the point that these scribes also occupy a distinct class position. Writing, especially in a context where it is a unique craft, is not powerful in and of itself, for that would be to take an idealist position. Writing includes complex structures of economics, politics, and family, the creation of necessary time and tools to learn the craft. It also produces a paradox of marginalization, since the scribe is removed from direct political and military activity characteristic of other elements of the ruling class. Yet, precisely through this marginalization, scribes are able not only to identify as a class faction, but to put themselves in a position of immense power through

---

27. Roland Boer, "Ezekiel's Axl, or Anarchism and Ecstasy," in *Violence, Utopia, and the Kingdom of God* (ed. Tina Pippin and George Aichele; New York: Routledge, 1998), 24–46.

28. One might extend this argument to suggest that the scribal class appropriates prophetic power and authority, or indeed that writing was always a prophetic act since written words had power, as one sees in execration texts, curses, and so on. That is, if writing and literacy had a kind of "magical power" simply by their existence, then they already feel quite close to the power of words in prophetic oracles. Many thanks to Corrine Carvalho for this observation.

being the ones who record, write, represent, and preserve a certain image of the world.

With this argument for auto-referentiality of scribal production under our belts and zipped in place, it becomes possible to read all of the references to scribal activity as precisely a reference to its own activity. Thus far I have used but one text and some theory to make my argument. A telling text it is, but can the argument be sustained across other prophetic references to writing? In order to insure the rugged firmness of my argument, I offer the necessary scholarly chatter of supplementary references in a brief survey. I have already noted the "manly stylus" of Isa 8:1, which becomes useful when Isaiah is to "write [כתב] upon a tablet" and "carve [חקק] upon a book [ספר]" (Isa 30:8). But now we can add Moses, the prophet before all prophets, who is instructed on Sinai by none less than Yahweh: "Write [כתב] these words; in accordance with these words I have made a covenant with you and with Israel" (Exod 34:27). And in being a writer, a "carver," or "chiseler" (כתב), Moses emulates the divine scribe himself who writes upon the chunks of stone (Exod 34:1). Writing seems to have a power in itself, creating history (Ezek 24:2) and even a whole new world centered on a new temple (Ezek 43:11), rendering a man childless (Jer 22:30), causing oppression and destruction (Isa 10:1; Jer 25:13), marking the covenant on one's heart (Jer 31:33), and giving life itself (Isa 4:3; Jer 17:13). And one cannot avoid Jer 36, in which the prophet may have been instructed to write down all the words that Yahweh had spoken to him (Jer 30:2), even with a stylus of iron (עט ברזל in Jer 17:1); but when it came to the crunch, he resorted to Baruch, the scribe. A close reading of the story—which I cannot undertake here[29]—would note that the phallic scroll (מגלה, from the semantic field of גלל, which includes the senses of rolling, flowing, and befouling, and is cognate with גליל, "rod," and גלול, "idol") itself becomes the main character, being written upon, read from on a number of occasions (twice by Baruch and once to the king himself by Jehudi), carved up and burned, and then recreated in Baruch's hands at the dictation of Jeremiah. Except that now it has many words added to it, the rod-like scroll swelling in size in response to the king's effort to destroy it, so much so that its divinely sourced words make it equivalent in size to the Torah.[30]

---

29. See the fine interpretation by Robert Carroll, *Jeremiah: A Commentary* (OTL; Philadelphia: Westminster, 1986), 656–68.

30. Philip R. Davies, *Scribes and Schools: The Canonization of the Hebrew Scriptures* (Library of Ancient Israel; Louisville: Westminster John Knox, 1998), 120.

Each moment in the brief survey I have just provided is now a moment of auto-referentiality, whether Moses, Isaiah, Jeremiah, or Ezekiel, and even Dan 5, where the writer is also a reader, for he is the only one who can read and thereby interpret the writing on the wall, written by a detached human hand during one of King Belshazzar's opulent banquets. Now I would like to push auto-referentiality to its logical and masturbatory extreme, for such an exercise of auto-creation can ultimately only become self-serving and icky (to borrow a phrase from Alice Bach in reference to my own work some time ago[31]). Let me offer two telling moments in the jerky logic of prophetic production.

BESTIAL OBSESSIONS

The first moment comes with our very queer[32] Ezekiel, yet again, who was apparently fascinated by masturbation. For instance, he accuses Oholibah (Jerusalem) in Ezek 23 of lusting not merely after "horsemen riding on horses" (Exod 23:12), but after donkey-sized and horse-like cocks that shower cum on all in their path. As Ezek 23:20 reads, "She was horny [תעגבה] for her toyboys [פלגשיהם], whose cocks [בְּשָׂרָם] were the size of donkey schlongs [חמורים-בסר] and whose ejaculations [זרמתם] were like horse cum [זרמת סוסים]."[33] Jeremiah too was fascinated by horse cocks

---

31. Alice Bach, "On the Road between Birmingham and Jerusalem," *Semeia* 82 (1998): 303.

32. Teresa Hornsby, "Ezekiel," in *The Queer Bible Commentary* (ed. Deryn Guest; London: SCM, 2006), 412–26.

33. I must thank N. T. Wrong for alerting me to this verse and offering the translation, which is much closer to the Hebrew. While Edwardes has "whose meat was like the meat of asses, and whose jitting was like the jitting of stallions" (*Erotica Judaica: A Sexual History of the Jews* [New York: Julian, 1967], 90), the RSV has, lamely, "and doted upon her paramours there, whose members were like those of asses, and whose issue was like that of horses." Van Dijk-Hemmes offers a slightly better but still very tame translation: "She lusted after the paramours there, whose organs are like the organs of asses and whose ejaculation is like the ejaculation of stallions" ("The Metaphorization of Woman in Prophetic Speech: An Analysis of Ezekiel 23," in *A Feminist Companion to the Latter Prophets* [ed. Athalya Brenner; FCB 8; Sheffield: Sheffield Academic Press, 1995], 252). Runions and Halperin also note the fascination with mega-cocks: David J. Halperin, *Seeking Ezekiel: Text and Psychology* (University Park: Pennsylvania State University Press, 1993), 117, 146; Erin Runions, "Violence and the Economy of Desire in Ezekiel 16:1–45," in *Prophets and Daniel* (ed. Athalya Brenner; FCB 2/8; Sheffield:: Sheffield Academic Press, 2001), 166 n. 27.

and their loads of jism: in Jer 5:8 he observes that the Jerusalemites are "horny [מיזנים] stallions with massive balls [משכים]."³⁴ Indeed, the text I quoted from Ezekiel provides a spattered wordplay, for זרמה—ejaculation—comes from זרם: to pour or overwhelm, with the noun, זֶרֶם, meaning a downpour or a rainstorm. So what Ezek 23:20 is really saying is that Jerusalem longs for an equine cum-storm, a zoological זרמה, if I may coin a phrase, or bestial *bukkake*,³⁵ as it is known in the business.

Prophetic Auto-fellatio

All of which provides a very different angle on the famous eating of the scroll in Ezek 2–3. Here we go beyond the masturbatory logic of scribal self-production to a moment of what can only be called auto-fellatio, replete with the cum-shot and swallowing. Indeed, Ezekiel outdoes the conventional categories of porn, with its standard blow job and cum-shot,

---

34. One soon becomes accustomed to an image of polite translators squirming over such passages and thereby producing limp offerings such as "well-fed lusty stallions" or "sleek and lusty." So John Bright, *Jeremiah* (AB 21; Garden City, N.Y.: Doubleday, 1965), 36. Not unexpectedly, Carroll has some fun with the difficulties of commentators, suggesting "well hung" for משכים (Carroll, *Jeremiah*, 178). To his credit, McKane gives the verse some space, even if he ends up offering the flat and properly scientific translation "with big testicles"; William McKane, *Introduction and Commentary on Jeremiah I–XXV* (vol. 1 of *A Critical and Exegetical Commentary on Jeremiah*; ICC; Edinburgh: T&T Clark, 1986), 119. Edwardes (*Erotica Judaica*, 95), of course, goes the whole hog, suggesting, "They were big-ball'd horses, well-hung stallions." The word מיזנים offers us an insight into perceptions of Yahweh. מיזנים is a pual participle of יזן, which means to be in heat, horny, dying for a hump. That would suggest that the name Jezaniah, יזניהו (Jer 40:8 and 42:1), means not, as some as have argued, "Yahweh hears" but "Yahweh is raging for a hump." I should note William Holladay's effort to deny, after a lengthy discussion, any sexual or testicular meaning at all! See William L. Holladay, *Jeremiah 1: A Commentary on the Book of the Prophet Jeremiah, Chapters 1–25* (Hermeneia; Philadelphia: Fortress, 1986), 180–81.

35. "Bukkake" is a far more appropriate translation of זרמה than it at first seems to be. Bukkake is the noun form of the Japanese verb *bukkakeru* (ぶっ掛ける, dash or splash water), and means "to dash," "splash," or "heavy splash." The word *bukkake* is often used in Japanese to describe pouring out water with sufficient momentum to cause splashing or spilling. Indeed, *bukkake* is used in Japan to describe a type of dish where the broth is poured on top of noodles, as in *bukkake-udon* and *bukkake-soba*. In pornography it describes a scene where a number of men ejaculate on a woman. It is a form of hygrophilia, sexual arousal from contact with bodily secretions. So I would suggest a formula: zoological זרמה :: bestial *bukkake*.

either with swallowing or the full facial on the male or female administering fellatio. No, Ezekiel presents an image where he sucks his own cock and swallows his own cum. The text reads: "And when I looked, behold, a hand was stretched [יד שלוחה] out to me, and, lo, a written scroll [מגלת ספר] was in it" (Ezek 2:9). A few terms are crucial here: יד שלוחה means not merely a hand extended, but also a cock at full muster (יד of course being a euphemism for a schlong and שלח exciting a range of meanings that include sending out, giving free reign, and unleashing). And מגלת ספר is not simply a "written scroll" but a "scroll of writing." מגלה is, as I noted earlier, part of the semantic field of גלל, with the overlapping sense of rolling about, flowing, and befouling. The image one gains from this intriguing word is of rolling about or writhing in bed and befouling it with, for instance, the flow of one's own onanistic splatter. Needless to say, the closely related גליל, "rod," only enhances the phallic nature of the rolled-up scroll. And סֵפֶר: should it not set our radar singing? Here is the same term used for the spermatic pen(is) in chapter 9. Now, we may read Ezek 2:9 in two ways: either we take the image of the hand literally, stretched out and filled with a massive scribal schlong; or we may take this text as an example of parallelism, in which the stretched-out hand and the scroll-cum-phallus are one and the same. Rather than decide one way or another, I prefer it both ways. And in either case, Ezekiel is to take his über-dong into his own mouth.

Now, one may object that the one handing the dong-like scroll to Ezekiel to eat is Yahweh, indeed that Ezekiel sucks Yahweh off, a reverse of the scene in Ezek 8:17, in which the apostate worshippers are putting "the branch to my nose" (emended from "their nose"), that is, offering their cocks to God for fellatio.[36] No great threat to my reading, I would suggest, except that in the all-powerful world of scribal creation, Yahweh too is the product of the writer's pen(is).

In an anticipation of what is to come, this schlong is itself written up, for the scroll was inscribed with many words, full of mourning and lamentation and woe (Ezek 2:10). Not unlike the doppelgänger pole or stick (עץ) in 37:16 upon which Ezekiel must write, this is a tattooed scribal implement, a cock covered with its own inscriptions. The text (2:8–3:3) now

---

36. Halperin, *Seeking Ezekiel*, 131–34. Of the commentators I have consulted, only Halperin sees the full possibilities of oral sex in Ezek 2–3. The remainder simply miss it entirely. See Cooke, *Ezekiel*, 30–38; Eichrodt, *Ezekiel*, 59–65; Greenberg, *Ezekiel 1–20*, 60–81; Zimmerli, *Ezekiel 1*, 91–93, 106–7.

follows a repetitive pattern: twice does Yahweh speak to him; thrice is his mouth mentioned, four times is the scroll mentioned; six times is the word *eat* repeated. The regular, stroking rhythm of auto-fellatio, one that would have made Saint Onan proud, until the climax: "it was in my mouth like honey for sweetness" (3:3). What threatened to be bitter (2:10) turned out to be like honey. Ezekiel has come in his own mouth.

Conclusion: Five-Finger Fantasies and Beyond

The comprehensive world of prophetic masculine power, of scribal class superiority, has become at least a masturbatory fantasy, if not a case of pure auto-fellatio in which the only outcome is that the all-powerful prophet sucks off his own spermatic spluttering pen(is) and comes in his own mouth. No matter how sweet it might be, the image is both an idealist fantasy and a drearily common one. The prophetic scribe may think that he has the power of heaven and hell, the ability to create the universe and even Yahweh, but it is pure fantasy, a grand idea that makes little difference to the material reality of the world.

His soul mate may well be the Egyptian god Atum-Ra, who creates the universe through an almighty tug-off: "The Ennead of Atum came into being by his semen and his fingers."[37] As Edwardes observes,

> Egyptian *coffin texts* reveal how Atum-Ra, the *causa causans*, created the universe when he "frigged with his fist and took the pleasure of emission." Memphite theology, in referring to "the seed and the hands of Atum," ceremonialized the myth that First Great Cause gave birth to the gods "through the action of his hands in the pleasure of ejaculation."[38]

Yet perhaps the scribal prophet has more in common with another version of the Egyptian myth of creation. In a moment of fine theological distinctions, one may differentiate between the five-finger theology of Memphis (see above) and the more intriguing auto-fellatial theology of Heliopolis.[39]

---

37. James B. Pritchard, ed., *Ancient Near Eastern Texts Relating to the Old Testament* (3rd ed. Princeton: Princeton University Press, 1969), 5.

38. Edwardes, *Erotica Judaica*, 11.

39. It would be intriguing to ponder the liturgical forms taken by such a theological distinction, especially if Egyptian religion had become a world religion.

I suspect that the Hebrew prophets may well have more in common with the latter.

Geb, the father of the gods and creator. British Museum image AN1162559001 © Trustees of the British Museum. Permission granted for reproduction.

Sex and the Single Prophet: Marital Status and Gender in Jeremiah and Ezekiel

Corrine L. Carvalho

The word of Yahweh came to me, saying, "Do not take a wife for yourself. Do not have sons or daughters in this place." (Jer 16:1)[1]

O mortal one, note: I am taking the one whom your eyes desire from you in a slaughter, but do not wail, do not weep, and do not bring forth your tears. (Ezek 24:16)

In the midst of the devastation that looms as background to the books of Jeremiah and Ezekiel, the redactors of each book enact a scene where the prophet's marital status functions as a metaphor for the city's fate. In Jeremiah God commands the lamenting prophet not to marry, while in Ezekiel the exiled priest becomes a tearless widower as the city is ravished by its enemy. Although the unmarried state of both prophets is quite different in form and function, nevertheless each text uses this element of the prophets' lives as an appropriate vehicle for the messages of their scrolls.[2]

There have been a number of comparisons of the books of Jeremiah and Ezekiel.[3] Both books, for example, refute the same adage about inter-

---

[1]. All translations are mine unless otherwise noted; all verse numbering follows the Hebrew text. I would like to thank the Old Testament Colloquium and Chris Franke for their helpful comments on this paper. All shortcomings in the paper are solely my own responsibility.

[2]. See also Esther Hamori's essay in this volume.

[3]. See, e.g., Thomas M. Raitt, *A Theology of Exile: Judgment/Deliverance in Jeremiah and Ezekiel* (Philadelphia: Fortress, 1977); Dieter Vieweger, *Die literarischen Beziehungen zwischen den Büchern Jeremia und Ezechiel* (BEATAJ 26; Frankfurt: Lang,

generational punishment (Jer 31:29; Ezek 18:2). Both collections contain poems that personify the city as an adulterous wife (Jer 2:2–4:2; 13:20–27; Ezek 16; 23). Both books portray restoration as involving a change of "heart" for the people (Jer 24:7; 32:29; Ezek 11:19; 36:16). Classic studies of these books focus on the question of literary borrowing and redaction, but more recently scholars assume that each book reflects language and motifs popular at the time of the scrolls' production. In this light, the question that I ask in this study is this: How do the notices about the prophets' marital status, read through the lens of gender, advance the theological program of each book?[4]

Marriage was a public arena through which people expressed their gendered identity.[5] "Spouses" were not undifferentiated partners, but rather individuals legally contracted to create distinct social units through which each person played a specific role defined by their gender. Women's gender identity was often determined by marital and sexual status. Because Israelite marriage defined whether their sexual activities were licit or "harlotry,"[6] women enacted their gender primarily through their marital status.

1993), esp. 55–57; Kelvin G. Friebel, *Jeremiah's and Ezekiels's Sign-Acts: Rhetorical Nonverbal Communication* (JSOTSup 283; Sheffield: Sheffield Academic Press, 1999); Hendrik Leene, "Blowing the Same Shofar: An Intertextual Comparison of Representations of the Prophetic Role in Jeremiah and Ezekiel," in *The Elusive Prophet: The Prophet as a Historical Person, Literary Character and Anonymous Artist* (ed. Johannes C. de Moor; OTS 45; Leiden: Brill, 2001), 175–98; Lawrence E. Boadt, "Do Jeremiah and Ezekiel Share a Common View of the Exile?" in *Uprooting and Planting: Essays on Jeremiah for Leslie Allen* (ed. John Goldingay; LHBOTS 459; London: T&T Clark, 2007), 14–31.

4. Moshe Greenberg notes parallels between Ezek 24:15–27 and Jer 16:1–9, but does not focus on the rhetoric of gender (*Ezekiel 21–37* [AB 22A; New York: Doubleday, 1997], 514–15. See also Walther Zimmerli, *Ezekiel 1: A Commentary on the Book of the Prophet Ezekiel, Chapters 1–24* (trans. Ronald E. Clements; Hermeneia; Philadelphia: Fortress, 1979), 506; Diana Lipton, "Early Mourning? Petitionary Versus Posthumous Ritual in Ezekiel XXIV," *VT* 56 (2006): 189–91.

5. By gender, I mean the socialized expression of one's gender identity. I distinguish *gender* from *sex* (one's biological determination of gender) and *sexual identity* (often called "orientation").

6. I follow Gerlinde Baumann (*Love and Violence: Marriage as Metaphor for the Relationship between YHWH and Israel in the Prophetic Books* [Collegeville, Minn.: Liturgical Press, 2003], 39–56) in defining זנה as any type of illicit female sexual activity.

Marriage also served as an important arena for the performance of masculinity.[7] It was often within the context of marriage that the question was answered, "What makes a man a man?"[8] While the structures of this gender performance may be more easily detected in the proverbial literature, there are certainly narrative texts in which the assumptions about masculine family roles are at play. Pharaoh's inability to control the daughter who brings home a Hebrew baby, and Ahab's failure to "rule over" Jezebel, for instance, serve the narrators' larger purposes by portraying both men as less than "manly." There is no text in the Hebrew Bible outside of Jeremiah where a man who is not a eunuch is characterized as permanently single.[9]

---

7. The study of masculinity in the Bible is growing. In addition to the discussion and bibliography in T. M. Lemos, "'They Have Become Women': Judean Diaspora and Postcolonial Theories of Gender and Migration," in *Social Theory and the Study of Israelite Religion: Essays in Retrospect and Prospect* (ed. Saul M. Olyan; SBLRBS 71; Atlanta: Society of Biblical Literature, 2012), 81–109; see, e.g., John Goldingay, "Hosea 1–3, Genesis 1–4, and Masculist Interpretation," *HBT* 17 (1995): 37–44; David J. A. Clines, *Interested Parties: The Ideology of Writers and Readers of the Hebrew Bible* (JSOTSup 205; GCT 1; Sheffield: Sheffield Academic Press, 1995), esp. 212–43; idem, "He-Prophets: Masculinity as a Problem for the Hebrew Prophets and Their Interpreters," in *Sense and Sensitivity: Essays on Reading the Bible in Memory of Robert Carroll* (ed. Alistair G. Hunter and Philip R. Davies; JSOTSup 348; Sheffield: Sheffield Academic Press, 2002), 311–28; Harold C. Washington, "Violence and the Construction of Gender in the Hebrew Bible: A New Historicist Approach," *BibInt* 54 (1997): 324–63; Dennis T. Olson, "Untying the Knot? Masculinity, Violence, and the Creation-Fall Story of Genesis 2–4," in *Engaging the Bible in a Gendered World: An Introduction to Feminist Biblical Interpretation in Honor of Katherine Doob Sakenfeld* (ed. Linda Day and Carolyn Pressler; Louisville: Westminster John Knox, 2006), 73–86; Ken Stone, "Gender Criticism: The Un-Manning of Abimelech," in *Judges and Method: New Approaches in Biblical Studies* (ed. Gale A. Yee; Minneapolis: Fortress, 2007), 183–201; Lori Hope Lefkovitz, *In Scripture: The First Stories of Jewish Sexual Identities* (Landham, Md.: Rowman & Littlefield, 2010). On the application of queer theory to the construct of masculinity, see Roland Boer, *Knockin' on Heaven's Door: The Bible and Popular Culture* (London: Routledge, 1999), esp. 13–32; Stuart Macwilliam, "Ideologies of Male Beauty and the Hebrew Bible," *BibInt* 17 (2009): 265–87; the essays in Ovidiu Creangă, ed., *Men and Masculinity in the Hebrew Bible and Beyond* (BMW 33; Sheffield: Sheffield Phoenix, 2010); Susan E. Haddox, *Metaphor and Masculinity in Hosea* (StBL 141; New York: Lang, 2011).

8. Ken Stone, "Gender and Homosexuality in Judges 19: Subject-Honor, Object-Shame?" *JSOT* 67 (1995): 87–107.

9. I hesitate to use the term *celibate* here, since men's sexual activity was not

When these observations are applied to the marital statuses of Jeremiah and Ezekiel, the answer to my initial question seems easy. Both prophets are depicted as unmarried because such a state represents social collapse. The command to Jeremiah ties his marital prohibition to the hopelessness of the city's future.[10] The severing of Ezekiel's marital relationship symbolizes the significance of the destruction of the temple.[11] While these conclusions are true, they do not address the fact that these are singularly gendered metaphors that engage expectations of gender performance as they turn each prophet's private life into a public metaphor. As Cynthia Chapman has noted, gender in the ancient Near East, especially masculinity, is performed in a variety of social contexts.[12] Each book's rhetorical engagement of gendered discourse serves the larger purpose of that book's particular theological agenda. I will explore the ways in which marital relationships and gender performances are woven throughout both books to reveal different strategies in their engagement with gender.

In this paper I will examine the rhetorical function of divinely induced singleness within each of these prophetic corpora. I presume

---

limited to marriage. However, Dale F. Launderville assumes, perhaps correctly, that joining this to the prohibition of procreation does connote celibacy (*Celibacy in the Ancient World: Its Ideal and Practice in Pre-Hellenistic Israel, Mesopotamia, and Greece* [Collegeville, Minn.: Liturgical Press, 2010], 374–75).

10. William L. Holladay, *Jeremiah 1: A Commentary on the Book of the Prophet Jeremiah, Chapters 1–25* (Hermeneia; Philadelphia: Fortress, 1986), 466–73; Jack R. Lundbom, *Jeremiah 1–20* (AB 21A; New York: Doubleday, 1999), 752–61; Friebel, *Jeremiah's and Ezekiel's Sign-Acts*, 82–99; Terence E. Fretheim, *Jeremiah* (SHBC; Macon, Ga.: Smyth & Helwys, 2002), 247–50; Louis Stulman, *Jeremiah* (Abingdon Old Testament Commentaries; Nashville: Abingdon, 2005), 161–63.

11. Walther Eichrodt, *Ezekiel: A Commentary* (trans. Cosslett Quin; OTL; Philadelphia: Westminster, 1970), 340–50; Zimmerli, *Ezekiel 1*, 502–9; Ronald M. Hals, *Ezekiel* (FOTL 19; Grand Rapids: Eerdmans, 1989), 173–77; Joseph Blenkinsopp, *Ezekiel* (IBC; Louisville: John Knox, 1990), 104–5; Daniel I. Block, *The Book of Ezekiel: Chapters 1–24* (NICOT; Grand Rapids: Eerdmans, 1997), 783–98; Greenberg, *Ezekiel 21–37*, 505–16; Katheryn Pfisterer Darr, "The Book of Ezekiel: Introduction, Commentary, and Reflections," *NIB* 6:1340–46; Karl-Friedrich Pohlmann, *Das Buch des Propheten Hesekiel (Ezechiel): Kapitel 20–48* (ATD 22.2; Göttingen: Vandenhoeck & Ruprecht, 2001), 358–63; Paul M. Joyce, *Ezekiel: A Commentary* (LHBOTS 482; London: T&T Clark, 2007), 166–69; Tyler D. Mayfield, *Literary Structure and Setting in Ezekiel* (FAT 2/43; Tübingen: Mohr Siebeck, 2010), 141–50.

12. Cynthia R. Chapman, *The Gendered Language of Warfare in the Israelite-Assyrian Encounter* (HSM 62; Winona Lake, Ind.: Eisenbrauns, 2004), esp. 20–59.

that both books function within the gender assumptions of their ancient context. Hetero-normativity is never questioned. The books reflect elite male privilege, seen most blatantly in the equation of corporate sin and female promiscuity. Beyond those givens, however, further questions can be asked. How do these passages conceive of gender roles? How does the subversion of gender function as a metaphor or sign for political loss and corporate identity? To what extent does the single status of each prophet introduce issues of gender bending or sexual indeterminacy as a way to depict the undoing of world order? How does the resulting gender interruption fit with how each book conceives of the relationship between prophet and God?

Elite Ezekiel Eschews Effeminacy

I start with the book of Ezekiel because its treatment of gender conforms more closely to what a contemporary audience, even a scholarly one, expects of a prophetic treatment of gender. In other words, its gendered agenda more overtly reaffirms patriarchal privilege.[13] The book of Ezekiel is fully patriarchal. For example, Julie Galambush has shown that the book is primarily concerned with the fate of landowning males.[14] Ezekiel's characterization as doubly privileged (both as a male and as a priest) serves as the lens through which the book is read.[15] The book's recurrent intonation

---

13. I define *patriarchy* as a system of unearned privilege based first on gender, but then secondarily on things such as ethnicity, lineage, economics, age, able-bodiedness or purity, etc. I use the term purposefully because it recognizes that this system unduly affects both men and women, and it reveals the intersection of various structures of privilege. I am avowedly not interested in the ways in which contemporary sexism has affected biblical scholarship as if only male scholars are responsible for sexism. I am not interested in sexism as an isolated social reality, either, because a focus on sexism only continues to mask the insidious strength of patriarchy.

14. "God's Land and Mine: Creation as Property in the Book of Ezekiel," in *Ezekiel's Hierarchical World: Wrestling with a Tiered Reality* (ed. Stephen L. Cook and Corrine L. Patton; SBLSymS 31; Atlanta: Society of Biblical Literature, 2004), 91–108. See the discussion of masculinity in these texts by T. M. Lemos, "Emasculation of Exile: Hypermasculinity and Feminization in the Book of Ezekiel," in *Interpreting Exile: Displacement and Deportation in Biblical and Modern Contexts* (ed. Brad E. Kelle, Frank Ritchel Ames, and Jacob L. Wright; SBLAIL 10; Atlanta: Society of Biblical Literature, 2011), 377–93.

15. I view the characterization of Ezekiel in the book as a literary construct that may or may not have any relationship to an historical person. For further discussion

of purity and abomination activate the hierarchical purity system as the only functional explanation for devastation and loss.[16] The ways in which its use of the marriage metaphor in chapters 16 and 23 both utilize and promote patriarchal privilege have been clearly demonstrated.[17]

Aside from the gendered metaphors of Ezek 16 and 23, women appear rarely in this book. Beyond the mention of Mrs. Ezekiel, the only other women are those weeping for Tammuz in 8:14, the female prophets in chapter 13,[18] and the maternal metaphor in 19:17-23.[19] Nowhere do women speak for themselves. Even Ezekiel's wife, the only nonnegative portrayal of a woman, is given no agency, no personality, not even a name. She is solely defined in terms of her husband's experience of her: she is the one whom *his* eyes desire.[20] To be sure, Ezekiel's negative view of women matches the negative treatment of most social groups in the book as a whole, including the prophets.[21] The characterization of women as at best

---

of this reading, see my earlier essay, Corrine L. Patton, "Priest, Prophet, and Exile: Ezekiel as a Literary Construct," in Cook and Patton, *Ezekiel's Hierarchical World*, 73–89.

16. See, e.g., Saul M. Olyan, *Rites and Rank: Hierarchy in Biblical Representations of Cult* (Princeton: Princeton University Press, 2000).

17. For treatments of these texts, see my earlier work, Corrine L. Patton, "'Should Our Sister Be Treated Like a Whore?': A Response to Feminist Critiques of Ezekiel 23," in *The Book of Ezekiel: Theological and Anthropological Perspectives* (ed. Margaret S. Odell and John T. Strong; SBLSymS 9; Atlanta: Society of Biblical Literature, 2000), 221–28; as well as the bibliography in Gale A. Yee, *Poor Banished Children of Eve: Woman as Evil in the Hebrew Bible* (Minneapolis: Fortress, 2003). On these texts as anti-Yahwistic, see Roland Boer, *Marxist Criticism of the Bible* (London: T&T Clark, 2003), esp. 133–57.

18. For a feminist critique of this passage, see Nancy R. Bowen, "The Daughters of Your People: Female Prophets in Ezekiel 13:17–23," *JBL* 118 (1999): 417–33; Esther Fuchs, "Prophecy and the Construction of Women: Inscription and Erasure"; and Renate Jost, "The Daughters of Your People Prophesy," both in *Prophets and Daniel* (ed. Athalya Brenner; FCB 2/8; Sheffield: Sheffield Academic Press, 2001), 66–68 and 70–76, respectively.

19. See Corrine L. Carvalho, "Putting the Mother Back in the Center: Metaphor and Multivalence in Ezekiel 19," in *Thus Says the Lord: Essays on the Former and Latter Prophets in Honor of Robert R. Wilson* (ed. John J. Ahn and Stephen L. Cook; LHBOTS 502; London: T&T Clark, 2009), 208–21.

20. Baumann asserts that the prophet's marriage in ch. 24 does not connote a positive view of marriage (*Love and Violence*, 163–65).

21. For the condemnation of the prophets, see ch. 13. The only groups that might be viewed positively are the Davidic kings (although not Zedekiah, whom the book roundly criticizes) and the Zadokites in ch. 44, a view at odds with the rest of the book.

ineffectual and at worst actively evil fits the book's overall representation of the people of Jerusalem.

Ezekiel's marriage is mentioned only in chapter 24. Verses 15–27 describe two significant parallel events, the destruction of the temple and the death of the prophet's wife.[22] God commands both prophet and people not to mourn either event, explicitly stating that the prophet's lack of mourning will be a "sign" (מופת) for the people.[23] The meaning of the symbolic act is explained in verses 19–23: the wife represents the destroyed temple, which also should not be mourned. These verses make clear that the marriage described in chapter 24 has an explicit metaphoric or symbolic function.

Ezekiel's wife is introduced solely in order to kill her off. She has no persona and even her death has significance only for the male chorus, which is supposed to identify with the prophet. It is significant that she is not called Ezekiel's "beloved." In fact, she is not even called his wife until verse 18. Rather, she is introduced as the object of his coveting or lust; the word here (מחמד), often politely translated as "delight," comes from the verbal root of coveting that is found in the Ten Commandments. The only

---

The debates about Ezekiel's view of the monarchy have been discussed in a number of works, including Jon D. Levenson, *Theology of the Program of Restoration of Ezekiel 40–48* (HSM 10; Atlanta: Scholars Press, 1976), 55–107; Steven S. Tuell, *The Law of the Temple in Ezekiel 40–48* (HSM 49; Atlanta: Scholars Press, 1992), 103–20; Iain M. Duguid, *Ezekiel and the Leaders of Israel* (VTSup 56; Leiden: Brill, 1994); Paul M. Joyce, "King and Messiah in Ezekiel," in *King and Messiah in Israel and the Ancient Near East: Proceedings of the Oxford Old Testament Seminar* (ed. John Day; JSOTSup 270; Sheffield: Sheffield Academic Press, 1998), 323–37; Michael Konkel, *Architektonik des Heiligen: Studien zur zweiten Tempelvision Ezechiels (Ez 40–48)* (BBB 129; Berlin: Philo, 2001); Daniel I. Block, "Transformation of Royal Ideology in Ezekiel," in *Transforming Visions: Transformations of Text, Tradition, and Theology in Ezechiel* (ed. William A. Tooman and Michael A. Lyons; PrTMS 127; Eugene, Or.: Wipf & Stock, 2010), 208–46.

22. On the differences between the MT and LXX versions of this passage, see Johan Lust, "The Delight of Ezekiel's Eyes: Ez 24:15–24 in Hebrew and in Greek," in *X Congress of the International Organization for Septuagint and Cognate Studies, Oslo, 1998* (ed. Bernard A. Taylor; SBLSCS 51; Atlanta: Society of Biblical Literature, 2001), 1–26.

23. Margaret Odell suggests that the actions God commands Ezekiel to perform require him to dress as a bridegroom at the very time he should be mourning his wife ("Genre and Persona in Ezekiel 24:15–24," in Odell and Strong, *Book of Ezekiel*, 205–8). While I find the notion intriguing, the speech that makes Ezekiel a sign does not focus on the reversal of mourning into rejoicing.

other place that this noun is used to describe feelings toward a partner is in Song 5:16. The use of the word in Ezek 24:18 characterizes Ezekiel as a man who finds his wife desirable.[24]

The equation of wife and sanctuary plays on the use of the term "delight" (מחמד) found in other biblical books.[25] Of its fourteen occurrences, all but one refers to something lost in the downfall of a city. Out of those thirteen uses, nine refer to objects, not people; when those objects are identified, they are temples (Isa 64:10; Lam 1:10), objects made of precious metals (i.e., temple vessels: 2 Chr 36:19; Hos 9:6), or items displayed in the enemy's temple (Joel 4:5). In Ezek 24:21 the word is also used to describe the destroyed temple. The book of Ezekiel chooses an epithet to describe the wife whose polyvalence engages the literature related to the destruction of a temple.

The text makes clear that the vehicle for this metaphor is God's command not to mourn the wife.[26] Ezekiel's widowhood allies him with many other male exiles who probably also lost wives in the city's siege and fall. The metaphor rhetorically engages the social meanings of public mourning.[27] This is a sign that depends in part on gender expectations within the context of ritual mourning. The metaphor is not about private feelings, but rather the public enactment of gender roles at the point of death.

The ritual mourning that factors largely in DH's portray of David exposes some of the ways that public mourning functioned within gender expectations.[28] There are five acts of public mourning or lament in these

---

24. Friebel, *Jeremiah's and Ezekiel's Sign-Acts*, 338–39. While it might be tempting to conclude that this one notice of a "happy" marriage undercuts feminist observations of the patriarchal function of ancient marriage, that Ezekiel happened to take pleasure in his wife does not mean that this was a constituent part of all Israelite marriages. Indeed, the oddity of this relationship is what makes the symbolic act work. It is only when the community notices that Ezekiel is not mourning that the symbol is engaged.

25. See Julie Galambush, *Jerusalem in the Book of Ezekiel: The City as Yahweh's Wife* (SBLDS 130; Atlanta: Scholars Press, 1992), 140–41; Darr, "Book of Ezekiel," 1343.

26. I follow Greenberg in his explanation of how Ezekiel's priestly status was not the issue (*Ezekiel 21–37*, 509–10).

27. See Thomas Renz, *The Rhetorical Function of the Book of Ezekiel* (VTSup 76; Boston: Brill, 2002) 91–92; Margaret S. Odell, *Ezekiel* (SHBC; Macon, Ga.: Smyth & Helwys, 2005), 317.

28. See Gary A. Anderson, *A Time to Mourn, a Time to Dance: The Expression of Grief and Joy in Israelite Religion* (University Park, Pa.: Pennsylvania State University

narratives: David mourns the deaths of Saul and Jonathan (2 Sam 2); Paltiel weeps after Michal (3:16); Bathsheba mourns Uriah (11:26); David laments his dying child (12:16, 21–22) and David mourns Absalom (18:33). In all of these passages, honor or shame is ascribed both to the mourner and to the one being mourned.[29] The contrast between the shameful nature of the public mourning for Absalom and the honorable nature of the public lament for Saul shows that honor and shame are ascribed to the dead through the act of lamentation. Public mourning also accords honor or shame to the person who is doing the mourning. In the passages involving spouses, the actions of both Paltiel and Bathsheba mark them as doing the honorable thing.[30]

Perhaps the most telling examples of the social significance of mourning are the two times David is faced with the death of a child. In the first instance, the death of Bathsheba's child, his failure to mourn is literally remarkable.[31] Those around him find the behavior, at best, strange, but certainly inappropriate (2 Sam 12:21). In contrast, his mourning of the death of Absalom is equally inappropriate, an action for which Joab must chastise him. David's failure to mourn the death of an innocent child, as well as his lament at the death of a rebellious child, are both shameful acts. This interplay of death and mourning in the David cycle reveals that public mourning is a function of one's relationship to the person who has

---

Press, 1991); Saul M. Olyan, *Biblical Mourning: Ritual and Social Dimensions* (Oxford: Oxford University Press, 2004); Stephen L. Cook, "Death, Kinship, and Community: Afterlife and the חסד Ideal in Israel," in *The Family in Life and in Death: The Family in Ancient Israel: Sociological and Archaeological Perspectives* (ed. Patricia Dutcher-Walls; LHBOTS 504; London: T&T Clark, 2009), 106–21.

29. Odell, "Genre and Persona," 200.

30. The mourning also complicates the story, adding even more time before she marries David and can legitimately be impregnated by him. This means that a full-term child must have looked rather odd to midwives expecting a premature baby. Why would David allow her to delay unless the interruption of her public mourning would have been even more of a scandal?

31. Lipton ("Early Mourning?" 194–96) and Friebel (*Jeremiah's and Ezekiel's Sign-Acts*, 342–45) use the Davidic parallel to argue that Ezekiel views postmortem mourning as inappropriate, in contrast to premortem repentance. Such conclusions, however, do not accord well with the details of the metaphor in this section (the text does not suggest that Ezekiel's wife died for unrepented sins), nor with the later notice that the lack of mourning is itself a punishment (implying that postmortem mourning itself was good).

died, and is coded as either honorable or shameful depending on a complex matrix of gender and status.[32]

The public mourning of a wife accords her honor.[33] Concomitantly, it accords the husband honor as well if his wife had enacted her gendered role in an honorable manner prior to her death. The act of not mourning a wife shames her. Such public shaming also shames the husband in one of two ways. If she deserved no public mourning (perhaps due to adultery, outspokenness, public disobedience of her husband's commands, etc.), the husband has already been shamed by her actions. If she had been an honorable woman, though, the man himself acts in a shameful manner by not mourning her.

The command to Ezekiel not to mourn his wife's death in chapter 24 is set in contrast to her designation as his delight. His public actions do not correspond with his equally public performance of his marriage.[34] Lack of mourning suggests that, for him, life was supposed to go on as if it were just another day. He was not to change the way he dressed, weep, or attend any funerary meals for her. While these would be (non)actions that the husband of a philandering woman might perform, it was certainly not honorable behavior for the husband of a "delightful" wife. For such a husband to simply ignore his wife's death would have shamed him.[35]

In chapter 24 God commands the exiles to follow Ezekiel's lead and not mourn the destruction of the temple, and along with the temple, the slaughter of their families (24:21). If this command had been separated from the depiction of Ezekiel's marriage, a reader might conclude that

---

32. There are numerous studies on the honor-shame system within the ancient biblical world. I am influenced by Saul M. Olyan, "Honor, Shame, and Covenant Relations in Ancient Israel and Its Environment," *JBL* 115 (1996): 201–18. See also Ken Stone, *Sex, Honor, and Power in the Deuteronomistic History* (JSOTSup 234; Sheffield: Sheffield Academic Press, 1996).

33. Dale F. Launderville, *Spirit and Reason: The Embodied Character of Ezekiel's Symbolic Thinking* (Waco, Tex.: Baylor University Press, 2007), 290–92.

34. On the distinction between emotion and public action in this passage, see Odell, "Genre and Persona," 198–202; and Stephen S. Tuell, "Should Ezekiel Go to Rehab? The Method to Ezekiel's 'Madness,'" *PRSt* 36 (2009): 289–302. For a reading that combines the two, see Friebel, *Jeremiah's and Ezekiel's Sign-Acts*, 345–49.

35. For an analysis of its ethical meaning, see Jacqueline Lapsley, "A Feeling for God: Emotions and Moral Formation in Ezekiel 24:15–27," in *Character Ethics and the Old Testament: Moral Dimensions of Scripture* (ed. Mark Daniel Carroll R. and Jacqueline Lapsley; Louisville: Westminster John Knox, 2007), 93–102.

the temple's destruction should not be mourned because it was deserved, especially if read in conjunction with the depiction of the abominations performed in the temple in chapters 8–11. But when the command is paralleled with a husband not mourning a wife he found "delightful," then it becomes clear that the lack of mourning is a shameful (non)activity. Read in conjunction with its metaphoric parallel, the elite male audience, whose temple has been destroyed, is commanded to act shamefully in response to this event. This prohibition against mourning is announced as an essential element of the punishment for their iniquities (24:23).[36]

The marriage metaphor of chapter 24, however, should not be completely separated from the two other marriage metaphors in the book, Ezek 16 and 23. In these chapters, marital shame is a prominent image. Ezekiel 16 and 23 use a marriage metaphor to depict the kind of wife it would not be shameful not to mourn. In this metaphoric marriage the wife's promiscuous behavior, serial shaming of her spouse, and selfish neglect of her children justify her divine husband's assault on her. Neither Yahweh nor the audience is expected to mourn her execution (23:45–47).

The shift of the metaphor between chapters 23 and 24, however, is significant. When chapters 23 and 24 are read in concert with each other, the interplay of gendered metaphors becomes more complex. In these back-to-back chapters, the male audience of the book is required to flip who they should identify with: in chapter 23, they are identified with the wife, while in chapter 24 they are the nonmourning husband.[37] The two chapters are rhetorically linked through the repetition of words from the root חמד. While chapter 24 features the word מחמד ("delight"), one of the words that is repeated 4 times in chapter 23 is חמד (vv. 6, 12 [bis], and 23). This segholate noun only appears in Ezek 23, and it is used for the sisters' arousal at the sight of foreign, hypervirile men.[38] The interplay with the prophet's lust for his wife in chapter 24 is noteworthy: the male

---

36. Launderville, *Spirit and Reason*, 291.

37. While Stuart Macwilliam uses queer theory to examine similar unstable gender identities in Jer 2 ("Queering Jeremiah," *BibInt* 10 [2002]: 384–404), the fluidity is even more evident in Ezek 23–24. On feminization in the Hebrew Bible, see Howard Eilberg-Schwartz, *God's Phallus and Other Problems for Men and Monotheism* (Boston: Beacon, 1994).

38. S. Tamar Kamionkowski, *Gender Reversal and Cosmic Chaos: A Study of the Book of Ezekiel* (JSOTSup 368; London: Sheffield Academic Press, 2003), 134–49; Yee, *Poor Banished Children of Eve*, 127–29.

audience, who in chapter 23 is supposed to see their feminized selves as having an improper lust, is punished in chapter 24 by being commanded not to mourn the loss of the temple/wife whom they properly desired as male "husbands" or caretakers. The text plays with gender confusion as the city crumbles around the chorus of Ezekiel's compatriots.

The details in chapter 24 subvert any resistance by a male audience to identifying with a nonmourning Ezekiel. The audience of chapter 24 may initially identify with the unmourned wife, first because they were the "wives" in the previous metaphor, and second because the notion of a slain beloved is more honorable than a husband acting in a shameful way. The text tells them, however, that Ezekiel's lack of mourning is a sign (מופת) that, not only should they not identify with the wife in this metaphor, but they have no right to mourn what was once their pride and joy.[39] In addition, 24:21 explicitly assigns the death of the temple to God. [40] "Note, it is I who am profaning my own sanctuary, the pride of *your* manliness, the delight of *your* eyes, the thing that *your* inner selves pity." God's command to Ezekiel not to mourn his wife, who is *not* portrayed in a negative light, shames the prophet, just as not mourning the temple's destruction shames the Judean leadership. These males have been kept from performing their gendered status in an honorable way by the very deity who has taken their delight from them.

Throughout the book of Ezekiel shame is equated with restoration.[41] Gendered behavior factors strongly within this system.[42] A man who acts as a woman, even a woman who is honorable, brings shame on himself and his family by such behavior. Yet one of the theological strategies of the book of Ezekiel is to undercut male honor codes by casting the male audience as subservient, and therefore honorably shamed, in relationship to God. The rhetorical strategy of chapters 16 and 23 of gender-bending

---

39. Jacqueline E. Lapsley, *Can These Bones Live? The Problem of the Moral Self in the Book of Ezekiel* (BZAW 301; Berlin: de Gruyter, 2000), 115–16; Joyce, *Ezekiel: A Commentary*, 168.

40. Joyce, *Ezekiel: A Commentary*, 168.

41. Jacqueline E. Lapsley, "Shame and Self-Knowledge: The Positive Role of Shame in Ezekiel's View of the Moral Self," in Odell and Strong, *Book of Ezekiel*, 143–73.

42. See Kamionkowski, *Gender Reversal*, 58–91. I reject the idea that women are always "shamed." While that may be true from our contemporary perspective, those who exist within an honor-shame culture would accept the possibility of honorable women, servants, slaves, foreigners, etc. They simply apply different criteria for "honor" in these cases, one of which is always deference.

the male audience so that they act in the role of a woman is one part of this larger program.⁴³ In chapter 24 the same goal is achieved by refusing men their gendered mourning so that they shame themselves by not mourning the loss of what they had once lusted for. Men coded as men are as shameful as men coded as women.

The irony is that the same absence of mourning that shames Ezekiel's audience serves to exalt the transcendence of the prophet's God. In the book, God is not depicted as anguished about the fall of the city.⁴⁴ In chapters 8–11 God has purposefully abandoned the temple because of the impurities built up by the ruling elite; he is not chased out by Israel's enemies or by any kind of defeat. In this chapter, Babylon does not profane the temple or kill wives—God does. Therefore, it is not shameful for God not to mourn the temple.⁴⁵ The only theologically proper response for the male audience, the only one that demonstrates that they "get it," is for them also not to mourn loss of temple, wives, or any source of what made them honorable men.

Chapter 24 depicts the fall and its subsequent exile as decidedly *not* social collapse, but rather as business as usual.⁴⁶ It is wholly expected: wives die, cities collapse. God takes them both. Jerusalem's fall has no cosmic ramifications. The sign of Ezekiel's marital status reinforces this interpretation of the fall of Jerusalem. This lack of emotion does not shame this male-coded God, because his relationship to the city is one that does not call into question his divine status. He has no obligation to mourn for something that had once been pleasurable but was no longer essential to his own status. Instead, it is the audience who feels shamed, cast in the role of both uncaring husband and unloved wife. They are the ones who find no one at their funeral, no eulogy spoken, no lament sung. They are

---

43. On the question of female metaphors applied to males in the book of Ezekiel, see Dale Launderville's essay in this volume.

44. Joyce notes that mourning the destruction of the temple would imply that the destruction was unwarranted (*Ezekiel: A Commentary*, 168).

45. This program fits the overall depiction of God within the book as the divine one who does not "love" Israel, as Baruch J. Schwartz has shown in "Ezekiel's Dim View of Israel's Restoration," in Odell and Strong, *Book of Ezekiel*, 43–67, esp. 52–53. See also Paul Joyce, *Divine Initiative and Human Response in Ezekiel* (JSOTSup 51; Sheffield: Sheffield Academic Press, 1989), 100; and Darr, "Ezekiel," 1340.

46. Teresa Hornsby, "Ezekiel," in *The Queer Bible Commentary* (ed. Deryn Guest; London: SCM, 2006), 421. For the opposite conclusion, see S. Tamar Kamionkowski, "Gender Reversal in Ezekiel 16," in Brenner, *Prophets and Daniel*, 170–85.

the ones told to remain silent and sing no songs. They have died and life carries on, business as usual, while Ezekiel, their singer of love songs, gives voice to no lament.

Jeremiah Jeers Jehovah

Incoherence is one of the marked literary features of the book of Jeremiah, a feature that, as Kathleen O'Connor notes, reflects the message of chaos that the book struggles to communicate.[47] Unlike Ezekiel, "incoherence" might also be ascribed to the gender program of the book's final form. While Jeremiah, like Ezekiel, operates within a system of unquestioned patriarchy and hetero-normativity, it does so with a fuller range of gender performance displayed throughout the text. Even in those texts that use gendered metaphors, the system of representation is more confused and chaotic than that found in the book of Ezekiel.

The prevailing patriarchy of the book has been demonstrated in a number of ways. The book assumes the normativity of elite male control. It symbolizes sin with the figure of a promiscuous woman.[48] Even metaphors

---

47. "The Book of Jeremiah: Reconstructing Community after Disaster," in Carroll R., *Character Ethics*, 89; idem, "Terror All Around: Confusion as Meaning-Making," in *Jeremiah (Dis)Placed: New Directions in Writing/Reading Jeremiah* (ed. A. R. Pete Diamond and Louis Stulman; LHBOTS 529; London: T&T Clark, 2011), 67–79.

48. The secondary literature on the figure of the metaphor of female promiscuity is extensive and significant. My assumptions about the book's patriarchy are founded on these studies, including, but not limited to, Athalya Brenner and Fokkelien van Dijk-Hemmes, *On Gendering Texts: Female and Male Voices in the Hebrew Bible* (BIS 1; Leiden: Brill, 1993), 178–93; Athalya Brenner, "On Prophetic Propaganda and the Politics of 'Love': The Case of Jeremiah," in *A Feminist Companion to the Latter Prophets* (ed. Athalya Brenner; FCB 8; Sheffield: Sheffield Academic Press, 1995), 256–74; J. Cheryl Exum, "The Ethics of Biblical Violence against Women," in *The Bible in Ethics: The Second Sheffield Colloquium* (ed. John W. Rogerson, Margaret Davies, and Mark Daniel Carroll R.; JSOTSup 207; Sheffield: Sheffield Academic Press, 1995), 248–71; Mary E. Shields, "Circumcision of the Prostitute: Gender, Sexuality, and the Call to Repentance in Jeremiah 3:1–4:4," *BibInt* 3 (1995): 61–74; A. R. Pete Diamond and Kathleen M. O'Connor, "Unfaithful Passions: Coding Women Coding Men in Jeremiah 2–3 (4:2)," *BibInt* 4 (1996): 288–310; Angela Bauer, "Dressed to Be Killed: Jeremiah 4.29–31 as an Example for the Functions of Female Imagery in Jeremiah," in *Troubling Jeremiah* (ed. A. R. Pete Diamond, Kathleen M. O'Connor, and Louis Stulman; JSOTSup 260; Sheffield: Sheffield Academic Press, 1999), 293–305; idem, *Gender in the Book of Jeremiah: A Feminist-Literary Reading* (StBL 5; 1999; repr., New

employing positive female figures (Daughter Zion and Rachel, for instance) do not generally challenge the system of gender privilege. But within those patriarchal assumptions, gender analysis of the book of Jeremiah is still more complex than that found in Ezekiel.

Gendered discourse is part of a larger strategy within the book to portray the world as chaotic and in the process of social collapse.[49] The book of Jeremiah lends itself to deconstructionist readings because it engages multiple rhetorical strategies to undercut social norms.[50] One example of this is the book's chaotic structure.[51] Within that chaos, gender issues are queered, meaning that the construction of gender in the book challenges assumptions about a discrete and stable gender dichotomy. For example, the gender program of chapters 1–10 follows that found throughout the prophetic tradition. When female metaphors are used, as in 2:1–4:2, they utilize the prophetic tradition of equating the sinful city with a sexually promiscuous wife. Males perform their male gender, displaying anxiety about status and patriarchal privilege. Similarly, in the prose narratives about Jeremiah in chapters 36–45, the point of tension is male authority. It is in the material harder to date that one finds a more creative, or less expected, use of gender symbols. These are found most clearly in the prophet's "confessions" or lamenting songs, in God's dialogues with the prophet, and in the so-called Book of Consolation.[52]

York: Lang, 2003); Christl M. Maier, *Daughter Zion, Mother Zion: Gender, Space, and the Sacred in Ancient Israel* (Minneapolis: Fortress, 2008), 103–10; Amy Kalmonofsky, "The Monstrous-Feminine in the Book of Jeremiah," in Diamond and Stulman, *Jeremiah (Dis)Placed*, 190–208. See also the critiques by Robert P. Carroll, "Desire under the Terebinths: On Pornographic Representation in the Prophets: A Response," in Brenner, *Feminist Companion to the Latter Prophets*, 275–307; Baumann, *Love and Violence*, esp. 105–34.

49. A. R. Pete Diamond, "Deceiving Hope: The Ironies of Metaphorical Beauty and Ideological Terror in Jeremiah," *SJOT* 17 (2003): 34–48.

50. For a discussion of the multivalence of the book, see Louis Stulman, "Jeremiah as a Polyphonic Response to Suffering," in *Inspired Speech: Prophecy in the Ancient Near East: Essays in Honor of Herbert B. Huffmon* (ed. John Kaltner and Louis Stulman; JSOTSup 378; London: T&T Clark, 2004), 302–18.

51. However, see Louis Stulman, *Order amid Chaos: Jeremiah as Symbolic Tapestry* (BiSe 57; Sheffield: Sheffield Academic Press, 1998). For discussions of the book's literary structure, see the essays in Martin Kessler, ed., *Reading the Book of Jeremiah: A Search for Coherence* (Winona Lake, Ind.: Eisenbrauns, 2004).

52. Bauer lists all of the references to women in her book *Gender in Jeremiah*.

Because the gender imagery in parts of Jeremiah undercuts patriarchal structures of power, application of queer theory can help reveal the extent to which these portions of the text depict male privilege as a sham. By queer theory, I mean an approach to gender that is deconstructionist in its aims; it is not simply criticism conducted through the lens of gender, but a criticism of those very gender categories.[53] Queer theory rejects the objective reality of sexual dichotomy functioning within patriarchy.[54] It addresses the social location of the modern reader, but attempts to undercut the assumptions that biological sex comes in two discrete versions (male and female) and that sexual desire is either only heterosexual or homosexual.[55] To give a brief example, it would reject the assertion that there are only two ways to interpret Jeremiah's single status: either that it is a heavy burden for a heterosexual male or that it is evidence that he was homosexual. Instead, it would prefer to view his gendered persona as fluid, that is, simultaneously changeable and often ambiguous. By resisting the gender dichotomy of Jeremiah's setting, the reader creates space within which gender ambiguity is both recognized in the text and allowed a positive function within the broader rhetorical strategies of the book.

In contrast to the book of Ezekiel, where the rhetoric of gender reversal more clearly reinforces gender dichotomies,[56] the treatment of gender in

---

However, I find it misleading to limit a discussion of gender to only those passages related to women.

53. Note how this definition of queer theory differs from that of Jonathan Stökl in this volume. Ken Stone notes that attention to the full spectrum of gender possibilities, including the differentiation among same-gendered characters as more or less "manly," pushes toward queer theory ("Gender Criticism," esp. 183–84 and 189–90).

54. Ken Stone, "Homosexuality and the Bible or Queer Reading? A Response to Martti Nissinen," *Theology and Sexuality* 14 (2001): 107–18; idem, *Practicing Safer Texts: Food, Sex and Bible in Queer Perspective* (Queering Theology; London: T&T Clark, 2005), esp. 135–49. On the sexual politics at stake with queer theory, see Macwilliam, "Queering Jeremiah," 384–88.

55. This differs from the definition of Stephen D. Moore, *God's Beauty Parlor: And Other Queer Spaces in and around the Bible* (Stanford: Stanford University Press, 2001); although see Hornsby, "Ezekiel," 412–26. For a survey of references to homosexuality in the ancient world, see Martti Nissinen, *Homoeroticism in the Biblical World: A Historical Perspective* (Minneapolis: Fortress, 1998).

56. On gender reversal as reinforcing gender dichotomies, see the discussion of Judg 4–5 in Deryn Guest, "From Gender Reversal to Genderfuck: Reading Jael through a Lesbian Lens," in *Bible Trouble: Queer Reading at the Boundaries of Biblical Scholarship* (ed. Teresa J. Hornsby and Ken Stone; SemeiaSt 67; Atlanta: Society of Bib-

Jeremiah is far more ambiguous and potentially subversive. Stone defines queer readings "as a diverse set of approaches to biblical interpretation that take as their point of departure a critical interrogation, or active contestation, of the ways in which the Bible is read to support hetero-normative and normalizing configurations of sexual and gender practices and sexual and gender identities."[57] Following Stone, I explore how the literary presentation of Jeremiah in the book invites a more fluid reading strategy, one that allows for ambiguity or polyvalence.[58] The text projects Jeremiah as a liminal figure,[59] one who transgresses boundaries and resides in a place of dis-resolution,[60] and that this liminality mirrors the situation of the ideal readers of the text: refugees of the war with Babylon.

Jeremiah's marital status (16:2) plays a less prominent role in the book as a whole than does the widowhood of Ezekiel.[61] It occurs as part

---

lical Literature, 2011), 12–20. See also Athalya Brenner, *The Intercourse of Knowledge: On Gendering Desire and "Sexuality" in the Hebrew Bible* (BIS 26; Leiden: Brill, 1997), esp. 139–52; Anthony Heacock, *Jonathan Loved David: Manly Love in the Bible and the Hermeneutics of Sex* (BMW 22; Sheffield: Sheffield Phoenix, 2011).

57. Ken Stone, "Queer Reading between Bible and Film: *Paris Is Burning* and the 'Legendary Houses' of David and Saul," in Hornsby and Stone, *Bible Trouble*, 94.

58. On the character of Jeremiah as a literary construct, see my earlier essay, Corrine L. Patton, "Layers of Meaning: Priesthood in Jeremiah MT," in *The Priests in the Prophets: The Portrayal of Priests, Prophets and Other Religious Specialists in the Latter Prophets* (ed. Lester L. Grabbe and Alice Ogden Bellis; JSOTSup 408; Sheffield: Sheffield Academic Press, 2004), 149–76. See also Pauline A. Viviano, "Characterizing Jeremiah," *WW* 22 (2002): 361–68; Joep Dubbink, "Getting Closer to Jeremiah: The Word of Yнwн and the Literary-Theological Person of a Prophet"; and Louis Stulman, "Jeremiah the Prophet: Astride Two Worlds," both in Kessler, *Reading the Book of Jeremiah*, 25–39 and 41–56, respectively; and John D. W. Watts, "Two Studies in Isaiah," in *Biblical Studies in Honor of Simon John De Vries* (vol. 1 of *God's Word for Our World*; ed. J. Harold Ellens, Deborah L. Ellens, Rolf P. Knierim, and Isaac Kalimi; JSOTSup 388; London: T&T Clark, 2004), 135–46. On God as a character in the book, see Mark E. Biddle, "Contingency, God, and the Babylonians: Jeremiah on the Complexity of Repentance," *Review and Expositor* 101 (2004): 247–66.

59. On liminality and pathos in Jeremiah, see Mary E. Mills, *Alterity, Pain, and Suffering in Isaiah, Jeremiah, and Ezekiel* (LHBOTS 479; London: T&T Clark, 2007), 111–16. On liminality and power, see Janet S. Everhart, "Jezebel: Framed by Eunuchs?" *CBQ* 72 (2010): 688–98.

60. Bauer-Levesque entertains how the gendered texts in Jeremiah "dislocate" binary conceptions ("Jeremiah," 389).

61. Moshe A. Zipor reads it within the context of other views of marriage in the book ("'Scenes from a Marriage'—According to Jeremiah," *JSOT* 65 [1995]: 83–91).

of a longer oracle where the prophet is cut off from many of the standard vehicles for social interaction. On the one hand, the brief reference to the prophet's single status is most unremarkable. It is not clear from this text if the command was supposed to last a lifetime, nor is the marital prohibition explicitly reinforced in any other part of the book. The passage quickly passes from the prohibition on Jeremiah's love life to focus on the issue of progeny (vv. 3-4). Why shouldn't he marry? Because, it assumes, the purpose of marriage is to produce children. And why shouldn't he procreate? Because, in such troubled times, the destruction of children only brings more sorrow. From this topic the book moves to prohibitions on weddings and funerals (vv. 5-9). Taken by itself, then, Jeremiah's perhaps temporary singlehood is not very interesting. However, when read within the gender performances that saturate the book as a whole, his marital status takes on added significance.

The book of Jeremiah has a fuller repertoire of female gender performance in both its metaphors and in its depiction of women than is found in the book of Ezekiel. On the metaphoric plane the city is both זונה (2:20; 3:1-10; 5:7-8; 13:27) and daughter (4:31; 6:2, 23-26; 8:11, 19-23; 9:6; 14:17; 31:21-22).[62] In addition, Jerusalem is called God's beloved (11:15; 12:7), and is likened to Rachel weeping for her children (31:15-17).[63] Therefore, some of the female metaphors personify the city in a way that elicits the audience's empathy.

Gender is also performed by a number of characters in the book. The book notes the presence of female professional mourners (9:16). Jeremiah speaks of his mother (15:10; 20:14-18). Men and women worship the Queen of Heaven (7:18; 44:15-19). But gender performance also factors in texts that do not mention women. This is most obvious in the prose sections that focus on clashes over male authority. The king,[64] other male

---

62. Foreign nations are also personified as daughters (46:11, 19, 24; 48:18; 49:2, 3, 4; 50:42; 51:33).

63. Susan E. Brown-Gutoff asserts that the metaphoric female "grows up" in this book into an adult mother, Rachel, weeping for her children ("The Voice of Rachel in Jeremiah 31: A Calling to 'Something New,'" *USQR* 45 [1991]: 177-90).

64. Hermann-Josef Stipp, "Zedekiah in the Book of Jeremiah: On the Formation of a Biblical Character," *CBQ* 58 (1996): 627-48; Alex Varughese, "The Royal Family in the Jeremiah Tradition," in Kaltner and Stulman, *Inspired Speech*, 319-28; Elena di Pede, "Jérémie et les rois de Juda, Sédécias et Joaqim," *VT* 56 (2006): 452-69. For a redactional analysis of the book based on the view of the monarchy, see John B. Job, *Jeremiah's Kings: A Study of the Monarchy in Jeremiah* (SOTSMS; Aldershot: Ashgate, 2006).

prophets, and the priests all challenge Jeremiah's prophetic authority.[65] In various places in the book, gender reversals reinforce hetero-normativity, as men are subjected to gender-shaming. The king becomes a sexually assaulted woman in 13:20–27. Warriors are compared to women giving birth (30:6).[66] Shaved men appear on stage in 41:4 representing those who are defeated on the battlefield. The Babylonians are turned into women (50:37; 51:30).[67] Prophets are accused of adultery, a crime applicable to women (23:14).[68] Kings, officials, priests, and prophets are not able to play the role of protector of women and children (e.g., 2:26–28).[69] Even the diatribe against their false idol worship confuses the gender of stone and tree (3:9).[70]

The characterization of Jeremiah takes shape against this gendered backdrop. In many ways the book depicts him as a marginalized prophet, especially as it explores the contours of true and false prophecy. I have argued elsewhere[71] that his characterization as a priest from Anathoth directs the reader to view him as outside the Jerusalem power grid. The unpopularity of his message also marginalizes him. In the prose section of the book, Jeremiah's clash with male authority is connected with his confinement and eventual imprisonment in a pit. He is quite literally cut

---

65. See, e.g., ch. 26.

66. On the distinction between the metaphor of childbirth and that of becoming a woman, see Claudia Bergmann, "We Have Seen the Enemy and He Is Only a 'She': The Portrayal of Warriors as Women," *CBQ* 69 (2007): 651–72. Amy Kalmanofsky uses horror theory to explore how the gender reversal in this motif shames the male audience (*Terror All Around: Horror, Monsters, and Theology in the Book of Jeremiah* [LHBOTS 390; London: T&T Clark, 2008], 20–29).

67. T. M. Lemos, "Shame and Mutilation of Enemies in the Hebrew Bible," *JBL* 125 (2006): 235–36.

68. Christina Niessen, "Schuld, Strafe und Geschlecht: Die Auswirkungen der Genderkonstruktionen auf Schuldzuweisungen und Gerichtsankündigungen in Jer 23,9–32 und Jer 13,20–27," *BZ* 48 (2004): 86–96.

69. See Chapman, *Gendered Language of Warfare*; idem, "Sculpted Warriors: Sexuality and the Sacred in the Depiction of Warfare in the Assyrian Palace Reliefs and in Ezekiel 23:14–17," in *The Aesthetics of Violence in the Prophets* (ed. Julia M. O'Brien and Chris Franke; LHBOTS 517; London: T&T Clark, 2010), 1–17.

70. Wilfred G. E. Watson, "Symmetry of Stanza in Jeremiah 2,2b–3," *JSOT* 19 (1981): 107–10; Saul M. Olyan, "The Cultic Confessions of Jer 2,27a," *ZAW* 99 (1987): 254–59.

71. See my "Layers of Meaning: Priesthood in Jeremiah MT," in *The Priests in the Prophets*.

off from human society. Gender performance is just one more tool used to mark the book's main character as marginal.

Jeremiah is often an ambiguous character in the book as well. In the book's first ten chapters, where hetero-normative assumptions are more prevalent, Jeremiah's very presence in various scenes is ambiguous. On the one hand, these chapters are presented as a collection of his oracles, which presumes that the whole thing is his speech. On the other hand, the book identifies the speaker of most of the oracles as God.[72] At first the gender of the addressee is not stated (4:8; 6:26), but as God's frustration with the community mounts, the command eventually becomes more gendered: God calls on mourning women to lament in 9:17–22.[73] In 4:8 it is clear that the purpose of the lament is to avert the disaster that bears down on them. God acts as both destroyer and foreign affairs advisor as the Babylonian war machine rolls closer.

There also seems to be a third voice in 4:19–22; 8:18–21; 10:19–21; and maybe 8:22–9:1 and 9:10–11 whose identity is wholly ambiguous. I agree with those scholars who find here the voice of the city, because of the references to the speaker's tents, curtains, and other urban items. Within this narrative flow, the ambiguous voice of the only figure that does lament in 4:19–22; 8:18–21; and 10:19–21 becomes more clearly the city,[74] since it cannot be the people who continue to fail to lament. Yet this city is unable to avert the disaster, just as Ištar in the Curse of Agade could not stop the fall of that city.

---

72. Mark E. Biddle, *Polyphony and Symphony in Prophetic Literature: Rereading Jeremiah 7–20* (Studies in Old Testament Interpretation 2; Macon, Ga.: Mercer University Press, 1996); Else K. Holt, "Word of Jeremiah—Word of God: Structures of Authority in the Book of Jeremiah," in Goldingay, *Uprooting and Planting*, 172–82. For a different analysis of "voice" in these chapters, see Nancy C. Lee, "Prophet and Singer in the Fray: The Book of Jeremiah," in Goldingay, *Uprooting and Planting*, 190–209.

73. See Fokkelien van Dijk-Hemmes, "Laments and Rituals of Lament," in *On Gendering Texts: Female and Male Voices in the Hebrew Bible* (ed. Athalya Brenner and Fokkelien van Dijk-Hemmes; BIS 1; Leiden: Brill, 1993), 83–90; Gerlinde Baumann, "Jeremia, die Weisen und die Weisheit: Eine Untersuchung von Jer 9,22f," *ZAW* 114 (2002): 59–79; Bauer, "Death, Grief, Agony, and a New Creation: Re-reading Gender in Jeremiah after September 11," *WW* 22 (2002): 378–86.

74. Nancy C. Lee reads 4:3–31; 8:18–9:1 (Eng. 2); and 10:17–25 as the voice of Daughter Zion who sings in dialogue with the prophet (*The Singers of Lamentations: Cities under Siege, from Ur to Jerusalem to Sarajevo* [BIS 60; Leiden: Brill, 2002], 47–73).

Jeremiah's voice is only explicitly identified twice: in 1:6 (plus vv. 11, 13), when he objects to his call because he is only an underling (נער);[75] and in 4:10, when he accuses God of deception. Yet this collection as a whole is presented as his speeches. The audience is required to imagine a male prophet speaking as God and speaking as a city, the latter of which is regularly personified as female. Is the reader to imagine that he would have performed these pieces in different voices to indicate different identities?[76] For example, were some of these songs sung in a falsetto to indicate a change of persona?[77] Or were these oracles delivered as they are presented: an undifferentiated mass of confusion? Even in this more gender-conforming section of the book, the gendered voices blur patriarchal dichotomies.

While Jeremiah is an indefinable figure in chapters 1–10, his characterization plays a prominent role in those chapters that feature his laments, 11–20.[78] These personal laments, which express the marginalization of the prophet, should be placed against the background of the first ten chapters. In chapters 1–10, God calls on various parts of the community to lament. These laments over his personal life come only after this demand-refusal pattern of city lament in the first ten chapters. Jeremiah's lamenting poems begin as a response to the opposition mounting against him, a situation that God condones. Many of Jeremiah's laments do not bemoan the fate of the city, but rather focus on the status of the male speaker who has lost his authoritative voice. In chapter 11, which is a transition into the section that contains Jeremiah's laments, God mandates the failure of

---

75. Brent A. Strawn, "Jeremiah's In/Effective Plea: Another Look at נער in Jeremiah I 6," *VT* 55 (2005): 366–77.

76. On the question of performance, see Friebel, *Jeremiah's and Ezekiel's Sign-Acts*, 20–34.

77. This question of gendered speaker in Jeremiah is raised in Barbara B. Kaiser's article on Lamentations, "Poet as 'Female Impersonator': The Image of Daughter Zion as Speaker in Biblical Poems of Suffering," *JR* 67 (1987): 164–82, esp. 166–74. See also Bauer, *Gender in Jeremiah*, esp. 63–66.

78. See Kathleen M. O'Connor, *The Confessions of Jeremiah: Their Interpretation and Role in Chapters 1–25* (SBLDS 94; Atlanta: Scholars Press, 1988); Mark S. Smith, *The Laments of Jeremiah and Their Contexts: A Literary and Redactional Study of Jeremiah 11–20* (SBLMS 42; Atlanta: Scholars Press, 1990). See also Biddle, *Polyphony and Symphony*; Mary Chilton Callaway, "The Lamenting Prophet and the Modern Self: On the Origins of Contemporary Readings of Jeremiah," in Kaltner and Stulman, *Inspired Speech*, 48–62.

such intercession: "*You*: do not pray on behalf of this people, and do not lift up a wail or a prayer on their behalf, because I am not listening when they call out to me on account of their wickedness" (11:14). Jeremiah, who cannot pray for the city, is reduced to lamenting his own status. The contrast between the professional female mourners who might be able to avert the disaster bearing down on the city in 9:17–22 and the ineffectual male lamenter complaining about his lack of power and authority is ironic. The gendered nature of these laments reveals anxiety over the loss of patriarchal privilege.

Chapters 14–15 focus the readers' attention on the efficacy of ritual prayer and lament. The community laments twice in chapter 14, once after notice of a drought that extends into the steppe (vv. 7–9) and again after a description of military defeat (vv. 19–22). Both times God responds by telling the prophet that their lamentation is useless. In both cases God specifically rejects the efficacy of prophetic intervention. In 14:11 Yahweh forbids Jeremiah to intercede, while in 15:1 God states that even the intercessions of Moses and Samuel would be insufficient. The ritual context of these prayers is emphasized in two ways. First, in 14:12 God states that their sacrifices will also be rejected. Second, the word used for prayer here is the same one used in Solomon's speech at the dedication of the temple to describe the intercessory function of this type of prayer.

Although Jeremiah's laments have often endeared him to many contemporary readers, rhetorically they function as a sign of his own failure.[79] Interspersed in these chapters are questions about lies and deception, a recurring theme in the book of Jeremiah. Chapter 14 describes the prophets who have been prophesying "peace" as deceitful. In addition, God's "truth" or reliability is questioned. In the first lament, the people state that he acts like a warrior who cannot save anyone (14:9), at which point God refuses to accept their laments, their sacrifices, or any intercessions on their behalf. In 15:18 Jeremiah describes God as a "deceitful brook" (אכזב). This time God tells Jeremiah that he can repent, the result of which will be that he becomes God's "mouth," forced to deliver God's messages. In other words, in both cases God rejects the claim that Yahweh deceives, first by stating that God is deliberately rejecting the people, and later by literally forcing the truth down the throat of this prophet. The

---

79. For the history of the interpretation of this feature of the book, see Callaway, "Lamenting Prophet."

laments themselves weave their way through these texts that focus on deceit.

In the Hebrew Bible, lament settings are themselves polyvalent.[80] Lamenting evokes a liminal experience,[81] a meeting with death/chaos at the crossroads, armed with a sitar rather than a sickle. This common motif explains the way that the form does not fit neatly into our contemporary discrete options for its setting. It is alternatively and sometimes simultaneously cultic prayer, dirge, a prayer for an individual, and even a plea for the community. This genre confusion is not only a contemporary problem: David's pleas for his dying child, set within rituals of mourning in 2 Sam 12:16–17, demonstrate that the polyvalent setting is part of the genre. The scene also highlights how the purpose of singing the lament was to ease a transition: from illness to health, from punishment to forgiveness, or from life to death.

Jeremiah's laments locate him within that liminal space. He laments his very liminality, angry that his prophetic authority has not been placed front and center. The laments not only contribute to the marginalization of the prophet, but they do so in a gendered way. Within the book of Jeremiah, the people credited with the skill (or literally "wisdom") in lamenting are women. In ancient Near Eastern poems describing the destruction of major cities, the weeping voice is that of the goddess. While Jeremiah's own laments partly fall within the genre of male priestly psalmic literature, his portrayal as the weeping prophet has him performing his gender in a gender-ambiguous role.

---

80. One approach to Jeremiah's laments is that they are meant to mirror or illustrate God's laments. See Terence E. Fretheim, "The Character of God in Jeremiah," in *Character and Scripture: Moral Formation, Community and Biblical Interpretation* (ed. William P. Brown; Grand Rapids: Eerdmans, 2002), 211–30. Kathleen M. O'Connor views him as the "ideal exile" ("The Book of Jeremiah: Reconstructing Community after Disaster," in Carroll R. and Lapsley, *Character Ethics,* 81–92). Jeremiah's suffering is actually polyvalent. Stulman says that he represents both the people and God (*Jeremiah*, 17 and 23–25). I would add that at various points he is also aligned with the suffering of the "poor," women, or forced exiles. There is not enough space, however, to tease this out here. See Louis Stulman, "Jeremiah as Polyphonic Response"; Dubbink, "Getting Closer to Jeremiah."

81. Mills sees Jeremiah's suffering as effecting that liminality (*Alterity, Pain, and Suffering,* 110–34).

The notice of Jeremiah's singleness appears in this section of the book.[82] Read within the context of Jeremiah's struggle with his own liminal identity, the prohibition serves to further marginalize him.[83] Indeed, it marks a significant shift in the book's presentation of the prophet's persona. In 11:5 Jeremiah speaks directly to God for only the third time in the book. In the midst of a prose sermon on the guilt of the people, Jeremiah merely says, "Amen/So be it." This great "amen" marks the beginning of his travails with God. He has moved from someone who, like the people, is incredulous about impending disaster, to someone who finally "gets" the inevitability and vastness of God's mounting wrath. With the sign of the loincloth in 13:1–11 Jeremiah enacts the inevitable disaster that looms. Jeremiah's intercession will not save them (14:11–12); the oracles of other prophets are false (14:13–16); not even Moses or Samuel could change Jerusalem's fate (15:1–2). The marginalization builds when Jeremiah is the only one allowed to "turn back" to God, thus becoming both divine mouthpiece (15:19) and an unbreachable bronze wall (15:20) against his foes.

Immediately after this promise to deliver Jeremiah alone, God tells him not to marry, nor to have children (16:1–2). He is even forbidden to participate in anyone's wedding or funeral (16:5).[84] This is more than just a symbol of hopelessness; it is part of his gendered persona. An honorable man would have had an honorable family. He would have attended the weddings of the people in his family, or among his social network. He would have lamented at the funerals of his friends, colleagues, and superiors. He would have drunk wine at the *marzēaḥs* and shaved when family died.[85] He would have attempted to identify an heir to his property.

---

82. See the discussion in Launderville, *Celibacy in the Ancient World*, 374–84, on which this analysis depends. See also Stulman, *Order amid Chaos*, 151–52.

83. See Holt, "Word of Jeremiah," 181–82.

84. Friebel, *Jeremiah's and Ezekiel's Sign-Acts*, 82–99. For the intertwining of marriage and death in this chapter, see Christl Maier and Ernst Michael Dörrfuss, "'Um mit ihnen zu sitzen, zu essen und zu trinken': Am 6,7; Jer 16,5 und die Bedeutung von marze͑ah," *ZAW* 111 (1999): 45–57; and John L. McLaughlin, *The marzeaḥ in the Prophetic Literature: References and Allusions in Light of the Extra-Biblical Evidence* (VTSup 86; Leiden: Brill, 2001), esp. 185–95.

85. On shaving as a mourning ritual, see Saul M. Olyan, "What Do Shaving Rites Accomplish and What Do They Signal in Biblical Ritual Texts?" *JBL* 117 (1998): 611–22; idem, "The Biblical Prohibition of the Mourning Rites of Shaving and Laceration: Several Proposals," in *"A Wise and Discerning Mind": Essays in Honor of Burke O. Long* (ed. Saul M. Olyan and Robert C. Culley; BJS 325; Providence: Brown Judaic Studies,

Jeremiah's inability to participate in these gender performances calls his own gender identity into question. Is he, as a male, claiming a status he does not have by refusing to participate in certain social functions? Is he renouncing his own gender identity by behaving like a woman (assuming that women could only attend certain social functions, and only when attached to some male figure)? Jeremiah's behavior is not just about the fact that marriages might be pointless. It also functions to undercut the expectations of the performance of masculinity. This subversion of his gender also raises questions, then, about his prophetic message. Does he advise surrender because he is insufficiently brave, and fears like a woman? Within a patriarchal system, once one aspect of a man's gendered identity comes under scrutiny, no single instance of acting male can negate it.

Chapter 20, which closes the focus on the weeping, single prophet, explores Jeremiah's singular relationship to God, engaging both themes of deception and sexuality. This chapter is set during and immediately after his first punishment as a criminal (20:4–5), an event that marks the completion of his social marginalization.[86] Jeremiah's last lament expresses the ultimate end point of God's systematic removal of Jeremiah from Judean society: Jeremiah's inability to be anything but God's little mouthpiece. The lament opens with his accusation that God has seduced him. While Bauer asserts that God has raped him,[87] this is a meaning found more prevalently in other stems of the verb פתה. This Hebrew verb in the Niphal, found also in Job 31:9, contains a sense of deception, of being enticed by false promises.[88] It implies that Jeremiah was tricked into thinking that God cared for him. The horrible result for which Jeremiah curses those who did not kill him before his birth is that he is now merely God's puppet, unable to do anything else but speak what God commands. The root chosen here has overtones of both deception and seduction, engaging both divine reliability and gender instability found throughout this section of the book.[89]

2000), 181–89. On the *marzēaḥ* see also Stefan Schorch, "Die Propheten und der Karneval: Marzeach—Maioumas—Maimuna," *VT* 53 (2003): 397–415.

86. Fretheim, *Jeremiah*, 289–90.

87. *Gender in Jeremiah*, 113–17; also O'Connor, *Confessions of Jeremiah*, 70–72; and Stulman, *Jeremiah*, 198–200. See the fuller discussion of the verb's meanings in Fretheim, *Jeremiah*, 290–92.

88. On possible connections between Jeremiah and Job, see Edward L. Greenstein, "Jeremiah as an Inspiration to the Poet of Job," in Kaltner and Stulman, *Inspired Speech*, 98–110.

89. Bauer, who reads 4:19–21 as the words of the prophet, concludes that Jer-

Whether seduced or raped, Jeremiah ends up "screwed."[90] This depiction of gender is not one that supports normative gender performance.[91] Jeremiah, though male, takes on the passive, acted upon, female role.[92] God overpowers the prophet, turning him into an object of social mockery. Although God will shame Jeremiah's enemies, who are also trying to seduce him, Jeremiah ends his laments in the position he claimed he was in during his speech in chapter 1. He is nothing but God's נער forced to do his bidding.[93] He is no man. He is no husband, warrior, elder. Cursing the day that his father heard he had a male child (20:15), he ultimately wishes he had been entombed in his mother's womb (20:17), an ending that further subverts the prevailing function of the gendered tropes of male progeny and female fertility.[94]

Throughout chapters 1–20, Jeremiah moves away from his own gender-regulating society and becomes increasingly marginalized, but he does so as he becomes more and more identified with a terrifying deity, whose secrets only he seems to know.[95] The more he is identified with God, the more he is viewed as a threat to Judean society. God represents the "terror" (מגור) that surrounds the city,[96] a horror explicitly played out in the image of parents eating their children (19:8–9). This divine terror is often presented in gendered terms, that is, as attacks on and rapes of a feminized

---

emiah is feminized in ch. 4 as well as in the divine seduction of 20:7 ("Death, Grief, Agony").

90. Although I am intrigued by the question of whether the categories of "genderfuck" (Guest, "From Gender Reversal to Genderfuck," 22–26) and hybridity (Stone, "Queer Reading," 77–80) capture the gendered rhetoric of ch. 20, I do not think either category exactly fits this particular text.

91. See the discussion of Rahab's heterosexual but nonnormative sexuality in Erin Runions, "From Disgust to Humor: Rahab's Queer Affect," in Hornsby and Stone, *Bible Trouble*, 47.

92. Clines, "He-Prophets."

93. Stulman notes how the womb becomes a place for both life and death in chs. 1 and 20 ("Jeremiah the Prophet"). On the use of the term נער see Strawn, "Jeremiah's In/Effective Plea."

94. See Bauer, *Gender in Jeremiah*; Stulman, "Jeremiah the Prophet," 41–56.

95. Launderville's recent book demonstrates the ways in which sexual restraint and celibacy in the ancient world functioned within the realm of union with the divine (*Celibacy in the Ancient World*).

96. Adrian H. W. Curtis, "Terror on Every Side!" in *The Book of Jeremiah and Its Reception* (ed. Adrian H. W. Curtis and Thomas Römer; BETL 128; Leuven: Peeters, 1999), 11–18. Kalmanofsky's book, *Terror All Around*, focuses on Jer 6.

victim (in chs. 2–3, 6, and 13).⁹⁷ As Jeremiah becomes more ambiguously gendered, he also comes to be more clearly identified with a terrible God whose mysteries he (unfortunately) fathoms. ⁹⁸ The restriction that he remain unmarried highlights God's exclusive claim on Jeremiah. The relationship between God and Jeremiah is not sexualized,⁹⁹ but the legal claim is still the same. Jeremiah would have committed "adultery" against God by ignoring his command, and thus he becomes functionally impotent as a symbol of God's exclusive claim on him.

The unique contours of Jeremiah's relationship with God, then, ask the reader to reexamine the theological function of Jeremiah's gender within the book. When the notice about Jeremiah's single status is coupled with the way that God's characterization becomes increasingly dangerous to the established human order, it reads as a deliberate rhetorical strategy to unsettle the categories of the monarchic world. Jeremiah is cut off from the public performance of his gender; he cannot marry, rule a wife, produce heirs. He is confined, arrested, and imprisoned so he cannot fight, rule, or harvest. When he is finally allowed to buy a piece of land that could serve as something his progeny could inherit (32:2–12), he is already terminally single, and the city itself is about to be demolished so that this land serves

---

97. See Kathleen M. O'Connor, "Reclaiming Jeremiah's Violence," in *O'Brien and Franke, Aesthetics of Violence*, 37–49, esp. 43–46. See also Maier, *Daughter Zion, Mother Zion*, esp. 82–93.

98. For a relatively recent review of the theology of the book, see Georg Fischer, *Jeremia: Der Stand der theologischen Diskussion* (Darmstadt: Wissenschaftliche Buchgesellschaft, 2007).

99. The text does not depict anything that could be interpreted as a "sacred marriage" between prophet and divinity, in part due to the biblical tradition's restraint from oversexualizing God. However, the language of seduction does add a layer of meaning that triggers a sexualized relationship. The existence of a ritual "sacred marriage" is still hotly debated, and too complex to enter into here. For those who uphold an historical sacred marriage ritual that served as a cultic union with a god, see Pirjo Lapinkivi, "The Sumerian Sacred Marriage and Its Aftermath in Later Sources"; Beate Pongratz-Leisten, "Sacred Marriage and the Transfer of Divine Knowledge: Alliances between the Gods and the King in Ancient Mesopotamia"; and Martti Nissinen, "Song of Songs and Sacred Marriage," all in *Sacred Marriages: The Divine-Human Sexual Metaphor from Sumer to Early Christianity* (ed. Martti Nissinen and Risto Uro; Winona Lake, Ind.: Eisenbrauns, 2008), 7–41, 43–73, and 173–218, respectively. My point here is that, even if such a ritual existed, there is no reflection of it in Jeremiah.

no function in restoring his manhood.¹⁰⁰ At the same time, God becomes a deceptive deity, a terror to "his" own people, the agent of social upheaval.

The question remains, then, does the gender-bending of the character of Jeremiah actually reinforce gender dichotomies by utilizing deviance from that norm as a marker of disorder? While such a conclusion may be the safest one to reach, the book's vision of restoration gives me pause. That the gender-bending of prophet, people, and city is a conscious ideological aim of the book is, for me, confirmed in Jer 31:22 with the enigmatic gender symbol of the new utopia: a woman "surrounding" a man. Although there are a variety of explanations given for this phrase,¹⁰¹ it should be read within the context of the other gendered elements of this section of the book. Jeremiah 30:6 raises the issue whether men can give birth. This rhetorical question, meant to elicit a negative response, sets the reader up first to identify the defeated warriors as reduced to female activity (grabbing the bellies in pain), and second to wonder at the new creation of chapter 31, which apparently also involves gender inversion.¹⁰² I agree with those scholars who conclude that whatever the text's exact meaning, it clearly views gender "disorder" as a mark of an ideal society.¹⁰³

---

100. Walter Brueggemann sees this passage as conveying the unexpected and unmotivated character of God's restoration ("A 'Characteristic' Reflection on What Comes Next (Jeremiah 32.16-44)," in *Prophets and Paradigms: Essays in Honor of Gene M. Tucker* [ed. Stephen Breck Reid; JSOTSup 229; Sheffield: Sheffield Academic Press, 1996], 16–32).

101. Among others, see the review of literature in Bauer, *Gender in Jeremiah*, esp. 145; and Bob Becking, *Between Fear and Freedom: Essays on the Interpretation of Jeremiah 30–31* (OTS 51; Leiden: Brill, 2004), 221–24; as well as Hendrik Leene, "Jeremiah 31,23-26 and the Redaction of the Book of Comfort," *ZAW* 104 (1992): 349–64; Deborah F. Sawyer, "Gender-Play and Sacred Text: A Scene from Jeremiah," *JSOT* 83 (1999): 99–111; Jack R. Lundbom, *Jeremiah 21–36* (AB 21B; New York: Doubleday, 2004), 448–53; Dorothea Erbele-Küster, "'Kann denn ein Männliches gebären?' (Jer 30,6): Noch einmal *gender trouble* im Alten Testament," in *"Du hast mich aus meiner Mutter Leib gezogen": Beiträge zur Geburt im Alten Testament* (ed. Detlef Dieckmann and Dorothea Erbele-Küster; Biblisch-theologische Studien 75; Neukirchen-Vluyn: Neukirchener Verlag, 2006), 39–54; Alice Ogden Bellis, "Jeremiah 31:22b: An Intentionally Ambiguous, Multivalent Riddle-Text," in Goldingay, *Uprooting and Planting*, 5–13; Paul A. Kruger, "A Woman Will 'Encompass' a Man: On Gender Reversal in Jer 31,22b," *Bib* 89 (2008): 380–88.

102. Fretheim, *Jeremiah*, 437–38.

103. See, e.g., Lundbom, *Jeremiah 21–36*, 451–52; Sawyer, "Gender-Play and Sacred Text"; and Bauer, "Death, Grief, Agony."

The text is intriguing in its ambiguity. The phrase evokes images that are both ascribed as "feminine" such as comforting and welcoming, as well as the literal surrounding that a woman's vagina does during intercourse to those gendered "masculine": protecting either as a male or as a city with walls. The text suggests that social disorder, or the blurring of the categories associated with social stability, is not only the marker of loss and destruction, but also characterizes the world that the book hopes for. The presentation of gender inversion as a sign of God's "new thing" that comforts a weeping feminized city and offers a vision of restoration for a male audience does not reinforce the patriarchal assumptions found in other parts of the book. It subverts it.

The narratives of chapters 26–52 remove most of the gender ambiguity of the first part of the book.[104] But even within this return to patriarchy, male power is depicted as ineffectual. From the manly kings who cannot control the subversive Jeremiah to the husbands of the exiles who join their wives in the worship of the Queen of Heaven (ch. 44),[105] male patriarchal privilege is a delusion in the human world, even if it is still intact in the divine realm. This section of the book ends where the book began: Jeremiah announcing that Israel is the nation that God plucks up and breaks down; only the lamenting prophet will be saved.[106] The text begins and ends with God as the central focus of the book, not the prophet.[107] God controls Judah's inevitable, horrible history, one scene at a time.

---

104. Robert R. Wilson argues that the "C" prose material clarifies the intended ambiguities of the poetic material ("Poetry and Prose in the Book of Jeremiah," in *Ki Baruch Hu: Ancient Near Eastern, Biblical, and Judaic Studies in Honor of Baruch A. Levine* [ed. Robert Chazan, William W. Hallo and Lawrence H. Schiffman; Winona Lake, Ind.: Eisenbrauns, 1999], 413–27). On how to read chs. 26–45, see Gary E. Yates, "Narrative Parallelism and the 'Jehoiakim Frame': A Reading Strategy for Jeremiah 26–45," *JETS* 48 (2005): 263–81.

105. On Jer 44 see Saul M. Olyan, "Some Observations Concerning the Identity of the Queen of Heaven," *UF* 19 (1987): 161–74; William McKane, "Worship of the Queen of Heaven (Jer 44)," in *"Wer ist wie Du, Herr, unter den Göttern?" Studien zur Theologie und Religionsgeschichte Israels für Otto Kaiser zum 70. Geburtstag* (ed. Ingo Kottsieper et al.; Göttingen: Vandenhoeck & Ruprecht, 1994), 318–24; Judith M. Hadley, "The Queen of Heaven—Who Is She?" in *Prophets and Daniel* (ed. Athalya Brenner; FCB 2/8; Sheffield: Sheffield Academic Press, 2001), 30–51.

106. On the way that the view of suffering in the rest of the book is undermined in chs. 36–45, see Stulman, "Jeremiah as a Polyphonic Response."

107. The ultimate ambiguity of the book lies in the placement of the poems of vengeance: is the slaying of Israel's enemies a necessary prerequisite for a vision of

Conclusion

For the male exilic audience the image of an unmarried male, one who has either lost his wife or one whose expectations for marriage have been dashed, served as an appropriate metaphor by which to express their experience of the fall of Jerusalem. Although the gender strategies in both Ezekiel and Jeremiah usually pushed the audience to view how loss of power, prestige, and privilege feminized them, in these notices about marriage they are called to see how they have failed to perform their gender in an honorable way.

For Ezekiel the prohibition to mourn one's personal and political losses reinforces the view that even the most honorable man needs to accept shame with respect to this God. The male audience takes on the status of a woman by how they are allowed to react to God's actions as sovereign male. The prohibition to mourn is able to place them in that position of shame even while utilizing a metaphor that enacts male gender.

The gender strategies in Jeremiah are more complex. The book routinely depicts the fall of the city as involving total social collapse. Part of this strategy is the way that the text questions the gender performance of all social groups in the city. Like Ezekiel, the representation of sinful males as sexually promiscuous females simultaneously shames and indicts its male audience.[108] The laments of men are assigned to women. The biographical section depicts tensions over male authority figures.

The queering of gender performance corresponds to a number of ways that the book as a whole queers other social dichotomies. Jeremiah's society is depicted as one where the world's social dichotomies have become at best ambiguous, or perhaps destructively chaotic. For example, the question of reliability, deception, and truth permeates the book, creating a society forced to deal with rampant ambiguity. Robert Carroll traces the way that the book questions the reliability of written and oral traditions.[109] Ter-

---

hope (LXX), or are they signs that, even though Judah has not changed, God remains in control (MT)? Either way, the focus remains on God.

108. On shame in Jeremiah see Johanna Stiebert, *The Construction of Shame in the Hebrew Bible: The Prophetic Contribution* (JSOTSup 346; Sheffield: Sheffield Academic Press, 2002).

109. Robert P. Carroll, "Inscribing the Covenant: Writing and the Written in Jeremiah," in *Understanding Poets and Prophets: Essays in Honour of George Wishart Anderson* (ed. Graeme A. Auld; JSOTSup 152; Sheffield: JSOT Press, 1993), 61–76. See

ence Fretheim notes the way that 32:27 calls into question God's power.[110] Kathleen O'Connor studies the collapse of language as part of the experience of tragedy.[111] The blurring of gender categories contributes to the representation of Jeremiah's world as one in the midst of social collapse: it shows that human society has broken down even at its most intimate roots. Even so, what is often missed is that this dissolution of social categories marks restoration as well as devastation. The chaos belies divine reality that both unsettles human delusions of power and realigns the human world where inversion is associated with comfort.

In the end, the gender strategies found in the both Ezekiel and Jeremiah serve to characterize God as divine. For Ezekiel God is untouched by the threat of shame or dishonor. In Jeremiah the gender ambiguity marks God as a dangerous divinity, capable of turning men into women, transgressing boundaries, and producing a new social order. Gender is a rhetorical category utilized by exilic poets to reimagine divinity in a world turned upside down.

---

also Yair Hoffman, "Aetiology, Redaction and Historicity in Jeremiah XXXVI," *VT* 46 (1996): 179–89; Karel van der Toorn, "From the Mouth of the Prophet: The Literary Fixation of Jeremiah's Prophecies in the Ancient Near East," in Kaltner and Stulman, *Inspired Speech,* 191–202; Joachim Schaper, "Exilic and Post-Exilic Prophecy and the Orality/Literacy Problem," *VT* 55 (2005): 324–42.

110. "Is Anything Too Hard for God? (Jeremiah 32:27)," *CBQ* 66 (2004): 232–36.

111. "The Tears of God and Divine Character in Jeremiah 2–9," in *God in the Fray: A Tribute to Walter Brueggemann* (ed. Tod Linafelt and Timothy K. Beal; Minneapolis: Fortress, 1998), 172–85; idem, *Lamentations and the Tears of the World* (Maryknoll, N.Y.: Orbis, 2002).

Bibliography

Abrahami, Philippe. "Masculine and Feminine Personal Determinatives before Women's Names at Nuzi: A Gender Indicator of Social or Economic Independence?" *CDLI Bulletin* 1 (2011). Online: http://cdli.ucla.edu/pubs/cdlb/2011/cdlb2011_2001.html.

Ackerman, Susan. "Isaiah." Pages 169–77 in *Women's Bible Commentary*. Edited by Carol A. Newsom and Sharon H. Ringe. Expanded ed. Louisville: Westminster John Knox, 1998.

———. *Warrior, Dancer, Seductress, Queen: Women in Judges and Biblical Israel*. ABRL. New York: Doubleday, 1998.

———. "Why Is Miriam Also among the Prophets? (And Is Zipporah among the Priests?)." *JBL* 121 (2002): 47–80.

Acosta-Hughes, Benjamin, Elizabeth Kosmetatou, and Manuel Baumbach, eds. *Labored in Papyrus Leaves: Perspectives on an Epigram Collection Attributed to Posidippus (P.Mil.Vogl. VIII 309)*. HellSt 2. Washington, D.C.: Center for Hellenic Studies, 2004.

Aland, Kurt. "Bemerkungen zum Montanismus und zur frühchristlichen Eschatologie." Pages 105–48 in *Kirchengeschichtliche Entwürfe: Alte Kirche, Reformation und Luthertum, Pietismus und Erweckungsbewegung*. Edited by Kurt Aland. Gütersloh: Gütersloher Verlagshaus, 1960.

Albright, William Foxwell. *Yahweh and the Gods of Canaan: A Historical Analysis of Two Contrasting Faiths*. Jordan Lectures in Comparative Religion 7. London: Athlone Press; Garden City, N.Y.: Doubleday, 1968.

Alexander, Philip, Armin Lange and Renate Pillinger, eds. *In the Second Degree: Paratextual Literature in Ancient Near Eastern and Ancient Mediterranean Culture and Its Reflections in Medieval Literature*. Leiden: Brill, 2010.

Allen, Leslie C. *Ezekiel 20–48*. WBC 29. Nashville: Nelson, 1990.

Alsop, Rachel, Annette Fitzsimons, and Kathleen Lennon. *Theorizing Gender*. Cambridge: Polity, 2002.

Althusser, Louis. *Lenin and Philosophy, and Other Essays.* Translated by Ben Brewster. London: New Left Books, 1971.

———. *Sur la reproduction.* Actuel Marx confrontation. Paris: Presses universitaires de France, 1995.

Anderson, Gary A. *A Time to Mourn, a Time to Dance: The Expression of Grief and Joy in Israelite Religion.* University Park: Pennsylvania State University Press, 1991.

Ansom, John. "The Female Transvestite in Early Monasticism: The Origin and Development of a Motif." *Viator—Medieval and Renaissance Studies* 5 (1974), 1–32.

Aristides, Aelius. *Panathenaic Oration and In Defence of Oratory.* Vol. 1 of *Aristides in Four Volumes.* [Only this volume was published.] Translated by Charles Allison Behr. LCL. Cambridge: Harvard University Press, 1973.

Asher-Greve, Julia M. "Decisive Sex, Essential Gender." Pages 11–26 in *Sex and Gender in the Ancient Near East: Proceedings of the 47th Rencontre Assyriologique Internationale, Helsinki, July 2–6, 2001.* Edited by Simo Parpola and Robert M. Whiting. CRAAI 47. Helsinki: Neo-Assyrian Text Corpus Project, 2002.

———. "The Essential Body: Mesopotamian Conceptions of the Gendered Body." *Gender and History* 9 (1997): 432–61.

———. "Images of Men, Gender Regimes, and Social Stratification in the Late Uruk Period." Pages 119–71 in *Gender through Time in the Ancient Near East.* Edited by Diane Bolger. GAS. Lanham, Md.: AltaMira, 2008.

Ashley, Timothy R. *The Book of Numbers.* NICOT. Grand Rapids: Eerdmans, 1993.

Assante, Julia. "Bad Girls and Kinky Boys? The Modern Prostituting of Ishtar, Her Clergy and Her Cults." Pages 23–54 in *Tempelprostitution im Altertum: Fakten und Fiktionen.* Edited by Tanja S. Scheer. Oikumene 6. Berlin: Antike, 2009.

———. "From Whores to Hierodules: The Historiographic Invention of Mesopotamian Female Sex Professionals." Pages 13–47 in *Ancient Art and Its Historiography.* Edited by A. A. Donohue and Mark D. Fullerton. Cambridge: Cambridge University Press, 2003.

———. "The kar.kid/*ḫarimtu*, Prostitute or Single Woman? A Reconsideration of the Evidence." *UF* 30 (1998): 5–96.

———. "What Makes a 'Prostitute' a Prostitute? Modern Definitions and Ancient Meanings." *Historiae* 4 (2007): 117–32.

Attridge, Harold, Torleif Elgvin, J. T. Milik, Saul Olyan, John Strugnell, Emanuel Tov, James VanderKam, and Sidnie White. *Qumran Cave 4.VIII: Parabiblical Texts, Part 1*. DJD 13. Oxford: Clarendon, 1994.

Bach, Alice. "On the Road Between Birmingham and Jerusalem." *Semeia* 82 (1998): 297–306.

Bacigalupo, Ana Mariella. *Shamans of the Foye Tree: Gender, Power and Healing among Chilean Mapuche*. Austin: University of Texas Press, 2007.

Bahrani, Zainab. *Women of Babylon: Gender and Representation in Mesopotamia*. London: Routledge, 2001.

Balzer, Marjorie Mandelstam. "Sacred Genders in Siberia: Shamans, Bear Festivals, and Androgyny." Pages 164–82 in *Gender Reversals and Gender Cultures: Anthropological and Historical Perspectives*. Edited by Sabrina Petra Ramet. London: Routledge, 1996.

Barrett, Michèle. *The Politics of Truth: From Marx to Foucault*. Stanford: Stanford University Press, 1991.

Batto, Bernard F. *Studies on Women at Mari*. JHNES 5. Baltimore: Johns Hopkins University Press, 1974.

Bauer, Angela. "Death, Grief, Agony, and a New Creation: Re-reading Gender in Jeremiah after September 11," *WW* 22 (2002): 378–86.

———. "Dressed to Be Killed: Jeremiah 4.29–31 as an Example for the Functions of Female Imagery in Jeremiah." Pages 293–305 in *Troubling Jeremiah*. Edited by A. R. Pete Diamond, Kathleen M. O'Connor, and Louis Stulman. JSOTSup 260. Sheffield: Sheffield Academic Press, 1999.

———. *Gender in the Book of Jeremiah: A Feminist-Literary Reading*. StBL 5. 1999. Repr., New York: Lang, 2003.

Bauer, Angela. *See also* Bauer-Levesque, Angela.

Bauer-Levesque, Angela. "Jeremiah." Pages 386–93 in *The Queer Bible Commentary*. Edited by Deryn Guest. London: SCM, 2006.

Baumann, Gerlinde. "Jeremia, die Weisen und die Weisheit: Eine Untersuchung von Jer 9,22f." *ZAW* 114 (2002): 59–79.

———. *Love and Violence: Marriage as Metaphor for the Relationship between YHWH and Israel in the Prophetic Books*. Translated by Linda M. Maloney. Collegeville, Minn.: Liturgical Press, 2003.

Becking, Bob. *Between Fear and Freedom: Essays on the Interpretation of Jeremiah 30–31*. OTS 51. Leiden: Brill, 2004.

Beentjes, Pancratius C. "What about Apocalypticism in the Book of Ben Sira?" Pages 207–27 in *Congress Volume Helsinki 2010*. Edited by Martti Nissinen. VTSup 148. Leiden: Brill, 2012.

Behrend, Heike. "Power to Heal, Power to Kill: Spirit Possession and War in Northern Uganda (1986–1994)." Pages 20–33 in *Spirit Possession, Modernity, and Power in Africa*. Edited by Heike Behrend and Ute Luig. Oxford: James Currey, 1999.

———. *Alice Lakwena and the Holy Spirits: War in Northern Uganda 1985–97*. Eastern Africa Studies. Oxford: James Currey, 1999.

Bellis, Alice Ogden. "Jeremiah 31:22b: An Intentionally Ambiguous, Multivalent Riddle-Text." Pages 5–13 in *Uprooting and Planting: Essays on Jeremiah for Leslie Allen*. Edited by John Goldingay. LHBOTS 459. New York: T&T Clark, 2007.

Bergmann, Claudia. "We Have Seen the Enemy and He Is Only a 'She': The Portrayal of Warriors as Women." *CBQ* 69 (2007): 651–72.

Berquist, Jon L. *Controlling Corporeality: The Body and the Household in Ancient Israel*. New Brunswick, N.J.: Rutgers University Press, 2002.

Beuken, Willem A. M. *Jesaja 1–12*. Translated by Ulrich Berges. HTKAT. Freiburg: Herder, 2003.

Beyer, Klaus. *Die aramäischen Texte vom Toten Meer*. Vol. 2. Göttingen: Vandenhoeck & Ruprecht, 2004.

Biddle, Mark E. "Contingency, God, and the Babylonians: Jeremiah on the Complexity of Repentance." *Review and Expositor* 101 (2004): 247–66.

———. *Polyphony and Symphony in Prophetic Literature: Rereading Jeremiah 7–20*. Studies in Old Testament Interpretation 2. Macon, Ga.: Mercer University Press, 1996.

Bird, Phyllis A. "The End of the Male Cult Prostitute: A Literary-Historical and Sociological Analysis of Hebrew *Qādēš-Qědēšîm*." Pages 37–80 in *Congress Volume: Cambridge, 1995*. Edited by John A. Emerton. VTSup 66. Leiden: Brill, 1997.

Black, Jeremy, Graham Cunningham, Eleanor Robson, and Gábor Zólyomi. *The Literature of Ancient Sumer*. Oxford: Oxford University Press, 2004.

Blenkinsopp, Joseph. *Ezekiel*. IBC. Louisville: John Knox, 1990.

———. *A History of Prophecy in Israel*. Rev. ed. Louisville: Westminster John Knox, 1996.

Block, Daniel I. *The Book of Ezekiel: Chapters 1–24*. NICOT. Grand Rapids: Eerdmans, 1997.

———. *The Book of Ezekiel: Chapters 25–48*. NICOT. Grand Rapids: Eerdmans, 1998.

———. "Transformation of Royal Ideology in Ezekiel." Pages 208–46 in *Transforming Visions: Transformations of Text, Tradition, and Theol-*

ogy in Ezekiel. Edited by William A. Tooman and Michael A. Lyons. PrTMS 127. Eugene, Or.: Pickwick, 2010.

Boadt, Lawrence E. "Do Jeremiah and Ezekiel Share a Common View of the Exile?" Pages 14–31 in *Uprooting and Planting: Essays on Jeremiah for Leslie Allen*. Edited by John Goldingay. LHBOTS 459. New York: T&T Clark, 2007.

Böck, Barbara. "Überlegungen zu einem Kultfest der altmesopotamischen Göttin Inanna." *Numen* 51 (2004): 20–46.

Bodi, Daniel. "Les gillûlîm chez Ézéchiel et dans l'Ancien Testament, et les différentes pratiques cultuelles associées à ce terme." *RB* 100 (1993): 481–510.

Boer, Roland. *Criticism of Heaven: On Marxism and Theology*. HM 18. Leiden: Brill, 2007.

———. "Ezekiel's Axl, or Anarchism and Ecstasy." Pages 24–46 in *Violence, Utopia, and the Kingdom of God: Fantasy and Ideology in the Bible*. Edited by Tina Pippin and George Aichele. New York: Routledge, 1998.

———. *Jameson and Jeroboam*. SemeiaSt 30. Atlanta: Scholars Press, 1996.

———. *Knockin' on Heaven's Door: The Bible and Popular Culture*. London: Routledge, 1999.

———. *Marxist Criticism of the Bible*. London: T&T Clark, 2003.

Böhl, F. M. Th. de Liagre. "Hymnen an Nergal, den Gott der Unterwelt." *BiOr* 6 (1949): 165–70.

Borger, Rykle. *Beiträge zum Inschriftenwerk Assurbanipals: Die Prismenklassen A, B, C = K, D, E, F, G, H, J und T sowie andere Inschriften*. Wiesbaden: Harrassowitz, 1996.

Botterweck, Johannes, Helmer Ringgren, and Heinz-Josef Fabry, eds. *Theological Dictionary of the Old Testament*. 15 vols. Translated by John T. Willis, Geoffrey W. Bromiley, and David E. Green. Grand Rapids: Eerdmans, 1974–2006.

Bowden, Hugh. *Classical Athens and the Delphic Oracle: Divination and Democracy*. Cambridge: Cambridge University Press, 2005.

———. "Oracles for Sale." Pages 256–74 in *Herodotus and His World: Essays from a Conference in Memory of George Forrest*. Edited by Peter Derow and Robert Parker. Oxford: Oxford University Press, 2003.

Bowen, Nancy R. "The Daughters of Your People: Female Prophets in Ezekiel 13:17–23." *JBL* 118 (1999): 417–33.

Brenner, Athalya. *The Intercourse of Knowledge: On Gendering Desire and "Sexuality" in the Hebrew Bible*. BIS 26. Leiden: Brill, 1997.

———. *The Israelite Woman: Social Role and Literary Type in Biblical Narrative*. BiSe 2. Sheffield: JSOT Press, 1985.

———. "On Prophetic Propaganda and the Politics of 'Love': The Case of Jeremiah." Pages 256–74 in *A Feminist Companion to the Latter Prophets*. Edited by Athalya Brenner. FCB 8. Sheffield: Sheffield Academic Press, 1995.

Brenner, Athalya, and Fokkelien van Dijk-Hemmes. *On Gendering Texts: Female and Male Voices in the Hebrew Bible*. BIS 1. 1993. Repr., Leiden: Brill, 1996.

Bright, John. *Jeremiah*. AB 21. Garden City, N.Y.: Doubleday, 1965.

Brinkman, John A. "Masculine or Feminine? The Case of Conflicting Gender Determinatives for Middle Babylonian Personal Names." Pages 1–10 in *Studies Presented to Robert D. Biggs*. Edited by Martha T. Roth, Walter Farber, Matthew W. Stolper, and Paula von Bechtolsheim. From the Workshop of the Chicago Assyrian Dictionary 2. AS 27. Chicago: Oriental Institute of the University of Chicago, 2007.

Brisson, Luc. *Le mythe de Tirésias: Essai d'analyse structurale*. Études préliminaires aux religions orientales dans l'Empire romain 55. Leiden: Brill, 1976.

———. *Sexual Ambivalence: Androgyny and Hermaphroditism in Graeco-Roman Antiquity*. Translated by Janet Lloyd. Berkeley: University of California Press, 2002.

Bronner, Leila Leah. *Stories of Biblical Mothers: Maternal Power in the Hebrew Bible*. Lanham, Md.: University Press of America, 2004.

Brown, John Pairman. "The Mediterranean Seer and Shamanism." *ZAW* 93 (1981): 374–400.

Brown-Gutoff, Susan E. "The Voice of Rachel in Jeremiah 31: A Calling to 'Something New.'" *USQR* 45 (1991): 177–90.

Brueggeman, Walter. "A 'Characteristic' Reflection on What Comes Next (Jeremiah 32.16–44)." Pages 16–32 in *Prophets and Paradigms: Essays in Honor of Gene M. Tucker*. Edited by Stephen Breck Reid. JSOTSup 229. Sheffield: Sheffield Academic Press, 1996.

Budin, Stephanie Lynn. *The Myth of Sacred Prostitution in Antiquity*. Cambridge: Cambridge University Press, 2008.

Buitenwerf, Rieuwerd. *Book III of the Sibylline Oracles and Its Social Setting with an Introduction, Translation, and Commentary*. SVTP 17. Leiden: Brill, 2003.

Bullough, Vern L., and Bonnie Bullough. *Cross Dressing, Sex, and Gender*. Philadelphia: University of Pennsylvania Press, 1993.

Burkert, Walter. "Signs, Commands, and Knowledge: Ancient Divination between Enigma and Epiphany." Pages 29–49 in *Mantikê: Studies in Ancient Divination*. Edited by Sarah Iles Johnston and Peter T. Struck. RGRW 155. Leiden: Brill, 2005.

Burns, John Barclay. "Devotee or Deviate: The 'Dog' (*keleb*) in Ancient Israel as a Symbol of Male Passivity and Perversion." *Journal of Religion and Society* 2 (2000). Online: http://moses.creighton.edu/jrs/toc/2000.html.

Burns, Rita. *Has the Lord Indeed Spoken Only through Moses? A Study of the Biblical Portrait of Miriam*. SBLDS 84. Atlanta: Scholars Press, 1987.

Busine, Aude. *Paroles d'Apollon: Pratiques et traditions oraculaires dans l'Antiquité tardive (IIe–VIe siècles)*. RGRW 156. Leiden: Brill, 2005.

Butler, Judith. *Bodies That Matter: On the Discursive Limits of "Sex."* New York: Routledge, 1993.

———. *Gender Trouble: Feminism and the Subversion of Identity*. New York: Routledge, 1990.

———. *Undoing Gender*. New York: Routledge, 2004.

Butler, Sally A. L. *Mesopotamian Conceptions of Dreams and Dream Rituals*. AOAT 258. Münster: Ugarit-Verlag, 1998.

Buttrick, George Arthur, ed. *The Interpreter's Dictionary of the Bible*. 4 vols. Nashville: Abingdon, 1962.

Cagni, Luigi. *L'epopea di Erra*. Studi semitici 34. Roma: Istituto di Studi del Vicino Oriente dell'Università, 1969.

———. *Das Erra-Epos: Keilschrifttext*. StP 5. Rome: Päpstliches Bibelinstitut, 1970.

Calame, Claude. *Choruses of Young Women in Ancient Greece: Their Morphology, Religious Role, and Social Function*. Greek Studies: Interdisciplinary Approaches. Lanham, Md.: Rowman & Littlefield, 1997.

Callaway, Mary Chilton. "The Lamenting Prophet and the Modern Self: On the Origins of Contemporary Readings of Jeremiah." Pages 48–62 in *Inspired Speech: Prophecy in the Ancient Near East: Essays in Honor of Herbert B. Huffmon*. Edited by John Kaltner and Louis Stulman. JSOTSup 378. London: T&T Clark, 2004.

Camp, Claudia V. "The Wise Women of 2 Samuel: A Role Model for Women in Early Israel." *CBQ* 43 (1981): 14–29.

Carroll, Robert P. "Desire under the Terebinths: On Pornographic Representation in the Prophets—A Response." Pages 275–307 in *A Feminist Companion to the Latter Prophets*. Edited by Athalya Brenner. FCB 8. Sheffield: Sheffield Academic Press, 1995.

———. "Inscribing the Covenant: Writing and the Written in Jeremiah." Pages 61-76 in Understanding Poets and Prophets: Essays in Honour of George Wishart Anderson, ed. by Graeme A. Auld (JSOTSup 152; Sheffield: JSOT, 1993).

———. *Jeremiah: A Commentary*. OTL. Philadelphia: Westminster, 1986.

Carvalho, Corrine L. "Putting the Mother Back in the Center: Metaphor and Multivalence in Ezekiel 19." Pages 208–21 in *Thus Says the Lord: Essays on the Former and Latter Prophets in Honor of Robert R. Wilson*. Edited by John J. Ahn and Stephen L. Cook. LHBOTS 502. New York: T&T Clark, 2009.

Carvalho, Corrine L. *See also* Patton, Corrine L.

Cathcart, Kevin J., and Robert P. Gordon. *The Targum of the Minor Prophets*. Aramaic Bible 14. Wilmington, Del.: Glazier, 1989.

Cavigneaux, Antoine, and Farouk N. H Al-Rawi. "Gilgameš et Taureau de Ciel (šul-mè-kam) (Textes de Tell Haddad IV)." *RA* 87 (1993): 97–129.

Chapman, Cynthia R. *The Gendered Language of Warfare in the Israelite-Assyrian Encounter*. HSM 62. Winona Lake, Ind.: Eisenbrauns, 2004.

———. "Sculpted Warriors: Sexuality and the Sacred in the Depiction of Warfare in the Assyrian Palace Reliefs and in Ezekiel 23:14–17." Pages 1–17 in *The Aesthetics of Violence in the Prophets*. Edited by Julia M. O'Brien and Chris Franke. LHBOTS 517. New York: T&T Clark, 2010.

Charlesworth, James H., ed. *The Old Testament Pseudepigrapha*. 2 vols. ABRL. New York: Doubleday, 1983–1985.

Chau, P.-L., and Jonathan Herring. "Defining, Assigning and Designing Sex." *International Journal of Law, Policy and the Family* 16 (2002): 327–67.

Chawla, Janet. "The Not-So-Subtle Body in Dais' Birth Imagery." Pages 127–41 in *Women and Indigenous Religions*. Edited by Sylvia Marcos. Women and Religion in the World. Santa Barbara, Calif.: Praeger, 2010.

Childs, Brevard. *Isaiah: A Commentary*. OTL. Louisville: Westminster John Knox, 2001.

Civil, Miguel. *The Series lú = ša and Related Texts*. MSL 12. Rome: Pontifical Biblical Institute, 1969.

Clines, David J. A. "He-Prophets: Masculinity as a Problem for the Hebrew Prophets and Their Interpreters." Pages 311–28 in *Sense and Sensitivity: Essays on Reading the Bible in Memory of Robert Carroll*. Edited by Alistair G. Hunter and Philip R. Davies. JSOTSup 348. Sheffield: Sheffield Academic Press, 2002.

———. *Interested Parties: The Ideology of Writers and Readers of the Hebrew Bible.* JSOTSup 205. GCT 1. Sheffield: Sheffield Academic Press, 1995.

Coats, George W. "Humility and Honor: A Moses Legend in Numbers 12." Pages 97–107 in *Art and Meaning: Rhetoric in Biblical Literature.* Edited by David J. A. Clines, David M. Gunn, and Alan J. Hauser. JSOTSup 19. Sheffield: JSOT Press, 1982.

Cohn, Leopold. "An Apocryphal Work Ascribed to Philo of Alexandria." *JQR* 10 (1898): 277–332.

Collins, John J. *Jewish Wisdom in the Hellenistic Age.* OTL. Louisville: Westminster John Knox, 1997.

———. *The Sibylline Oracles of Egyptian Judaism.* SBLDS 13. Missoula, Mont.: Society of Biblical Literature, 1974.

Connell, Raewyn W. *Masculinities.* 2nd ed. Berkeley: University of California Press, 2005.

Connelly, Joan Breton. "Narrative and Image in Attic Vase Painting: Ajax and Cassandra at the Trojan Palladion." Pages 88–129 in *Narrative and Event in Ancient Art.* Edited by Peter J. Holliday. Cambridge Studies in New Art History and Criticism. Cambridge: Cambridge University Press, 1993.

———. *Portrait of a Priestess: Women and Ritual in Ancient Greece.* Princeton: Princeton University Press, 2007.

Cook, Lesley A. "Body Language: Women's Rituals of Purification in the Bible and Mishnah." Pages 40–59 in *Women and Water: Menstruation in Jewish Life and Law.* Edited by Rahel R. Wasserfall. Brandeis Series on Jewish Women. Hanover, N.H.: University Press of New England for Brandeis University Press, 1999.

Cook, Stephen L. "Death, Kinship, and Community: Afterlife and the חסד Ideal in Israel." Pages 106–21 in *The Family in Life and in Death: The Family in Ancient Israel: Sociological and Archaeological Perspectives.* Edited by Patricia Dutcher-Walls. LHBOTS 504. New York: T&T Clark, 2009.

Cooke, George A. *A Critical and Exegetical Commentary on the Book of Ezekiel.* ICC. 1936. Repr., Edinburgh: T&T Clark, 1985.

Cooper, Jerrold S. *The Return of Ninurta to Nippur: An-gim dím-ma.* AnOr 52. Rome: Pontifical Biblical Institute, 1978.

Crawford, Sidnie White. "Lady Wisdom and Dame Folly at Qumran." *DSD* 5 (1998): 355–66.

———. "Traditions about Miriam in the Qumran Scrolls." *Studies in Jewish Civilization* 14 (2003): 33–44.

Creangă, Ovidiu, ed. *Men and Masculinity in the Hebrew Bible and Beyond.* BMW 33. Sheffield: Sheffield Phoenix, 2010.

Crim, Keith R., ed. *Interpreter's Dictionary of the Bible: Supplementary Volume.* Nashville: Abingdon, 1976.

Cross, Frank Moore. *Canaanite Myth and Hebrew Epic: Essays in the History of the Religion of Israel.* 1973. Repr., Cambridge: Harvard University Press, 1997.

Curtis, Adrian H. W. "Terror on Every Side!" Pages 111–18 in *The Book of Jeremiah and Its Reception.* Edited by Adrian H. W. Curtis and Thomas Römer. BETL 128. Leuven: Peeters, 1997.

Czaplicka, Marie Antoinette. *Aboriginal Siberia: A Study in Social Anthropology.* Oxford: Clarendon, 1914.

Dalley, Stephanie. *Mari and Karana: Two Old Babylonian Cities.* London: Longman, 1984.

Darr, Katheryn Pfisterer. "The Book of Ezekiel: Introduction, Commentary, and Reflections." Pages 1073–1607 in vol. 6 of *The New Interpreter's Bible.* Edited by Leander E. Keck. Nashville: Abingdon, 2001.

Davies, Philip. *Scribes and Schools: The Canonization of the Hebrew Scriptures.* Library of Ancient Israel. Louisville: Westminster John Knox, 1998.

Day, John. *Molech: A God of Human Sacrifice in the Old Testament.* Cambridge Oriental Publications 41. Cambridge: Cambridge University Press, 1989.

———, ed. *Prophecy and Prophets in Ancient Israel: Proceedings of the Oxford Old Testament Seminar.* LHBOTS 531. New York: T&T Clark, 2010.

Derrida, Jacques. *Of Grammatology.* Translated by Gayatri Chakravorty Spivak. Baltimore: Johns Hopkins University Press, 1976.

Destro, Adriana. "The Witness of Times: An Anthropological Reading of *Niddah*." Pages 124–38 in *Reading Leviticus: A Conversation with Mary Douglas.* Edited by John F. A. Sawyer. JSOTSup 227. Sheffield: Sheffield Academic Press, 1996.

Diamond, A. R. Pete. "Deceiving Hope: The Ironies of Metaphorical Beauty and Ideological Terror in Jeremiah." *SJOT* 17 (2003): 34–48.

Diamond, A. R. Pete, and Kathleen M. O'Connor. "Unfaithful Passions: Coding Women Coding Men in Jeremiah 2–3 (4:2)." *BibInt* 4 (1996): 288–310.

Dieterle, Martina. *Dodona: Religionsgeschichtliche und historische Unter-*

suchungen zur Entstehung und Entwicklung des Zeus-Heiligtums. Spudasmata 116. Hildesheim: Olms, 2007.
Dijk-Hemmes, Fokkelien van. "Laments and Rituals of Lament." Pages 83–90 in *On Gendering Texts: Female and Male Voices in the Hebrew Bible*. Edited by Athalya Brenner and Fokkelien van Dijk-Hemmes. BIS 1. Leiden: Brill, 1993.
———. "The Metaphorization of Woman in Prophetic Speech: An Analysis of Ezekiel 23." Pages 244–55 in *A Feminist Companion to the Latter Prophets*. Edited by Athalya Brenner. FCB 8. Sheffield: Sheffield Academic Press, 1995.
Dillery, John. "Chresmologues and *Manteis*: Independent Diviners and the Problem of Authority." Pages 167–231 in *Mantikê: Studies in Ancient Divination*. Edited by Sarah Iles Johnston and Peter T. Struck. RGRW 155. Leiden: Brill, 2005.
Dillmann, August. *Die Bücher Numeri, Deuteronomium und Josua*. 2nd ed. Kurzgefasstes exegetisches Handbuch zum Alten Testament 13. Leipzig: Hirzel, 1886.
Dillon, Matthew. *Girls and Women in Classical Greek Religion*. London: Routledge, 2002.
Dimant, Devorah. "The Qumran Aramaic Texts and the Qumran Community." Pages 197–205 in *Flores Florentino: Dead Sea Scrolls and Other Early Jewish Studies in Honour of Florentino García Martínez*. Edited by Anthony Hilhorst, Émile Puech, and Eibert J. C. Tigchelaar. JSJSup 122. Leiden: Brill, 2007.
Diodorus Siculus. *Diodorus of Sicily*. Translated by Charles Henry Oldfather, Charles L. Sherman, C. Bradford Welles, Russel M. Geer, and Francis R. Walton. 12 vols. LCL. Cambridge: Harvard University Press, 1933–1968.
Dörrfuss, Ernst Michael. "'Um mit ihnen zu sitzen, zu essen und zu trinken': Am 6,7; Jer 16,5 und die Bedeutung von *marze^{a}ḥ*." ZAW 111 (1999): 45–57.
Drawnel, Henryk. "The Initial Narrative of the *Visions of Amram* and Its Literary Characteristics." *RevQ* 24 (2010): 517–54.
Dreger, Alice Domurat. *Hermaphrodites and the Medical Invention of Sex*. Cambridge: Harvard University Press, 1998.
Drucker, Peter, ed. *Different Rainbows*. London: Gay Men's Press, 2000.
Dubbink, Joep. "Getting Closer to Jeremiah: The Word of Yhwh and the Literary-Theological Person of a Prophet." Pages 25–39 in *Reading the*

Book of Jeremiah: A Search for Coherence. Edited by Martin Kessler. Winona Lake, Ind.: Eisenbrauns, 2004.

Duguid, Iain M. *Ezekiel and the Leaders of Israel*. VTSup 56. Leiden: Brill, 1994.

Duke, Robert R. *The Social Location of the Visions of Amram (4Q543–547)*. StBL 135. New York: Lang, 2010.

Dunbabin, T. J. "The Oracle of Hera Akraia at Perachora." *Annual of the British School at Athens* 46 (1951): 61–71.

Dupré, Louis. *Marx's Social Critique of Culture*. New Haven: Yale University Press, 1983.

Eagleton, Terry. *Ideology: An Introduction*. London: Verso, 1991.

Ebeling, Erich, Bruno Meissner, Ernst Weidner, Wolfram von Soden, and Dietz Otto Edzard, eds. *Reallexikon der Assyriologie*. Berlin: de Gruyter, 1928–.

Edwardes, Allen. *Erotica Judaica: A Sexual History of the Jews*. New York: Julian Press, 1967.

Edzard, Dietz Otto. "ᵐNingal-gāmil, ᶠIštar-damqat: Die Genuskongruenz im akkadischen theophoren Personennamen." *ZA* 55 (1962): 113–30.

Eichrodt, Walther. *Ezekiel: A Commentary*. Translated by Cosslett Quin. OTL. Phildelphia: Westminster, 1970.

Eidinow, Esther. *Oracles, Curses, and Risk among the Ancient Greeks*. Oxford: Oxford University Press, 2007.

Eilberg-Schwartz, Howard. *God's Phallus and Other Problems for Men and Monotheism*. Boston: Beacon, 1994.

Ellis, Maria deJong. "Observations on Mesopotamian Oracles and Prophetic Texts: Literary and Historiographic Considerations." *JCS* 41 (1989): 127–86.

———. "The Goddess Kititum Speaks to King Ibalpiel: Oracle Texts from Ishchali." *MARI* 5 (1987): 235–66.

Erbele-Küster, Dorothea. "'Kann denn ein Männliches gebären?' (Jer 30,6): Noch mehr *gender trouble* im Alten Testament." Pages 39–54 in *"Du hast mich aus meiner Mutter Leib gezogen": Beiträge zur Geburt im Alten Testament*. Edited by Detlef Dieckmann and Dorothea Erbele-Küster. Biblisch-theologische Studien 75. Neukirchen-Vluyn: Neukirchener, 2006.

Euripides. *Works*. Translated by David Kovacs. 6 vols. LCL. Cambridge: Harvard University Press, 1994–2002.

Everhart, Janet S. "Jezebel: Framed by Eunuchs?" *CBQ* 72 (2010): 688–98.

Exum, J. Cheryl. "The Ethics of Biblical Violence against Women." Pages 248–71 in *The Bible in Ethics: The Second Sheffield Colloquium*. Edited by John W. Rogerson, Margaret Davies, and Mark Daniel Carroll R. JSOTSup 207. Sheffield: Sheffield Academic Press, 1995.

———. *Plotted, Shot, and Painted: Cultural Representations of Biblical Women*. JSOTSup 215. GCT 3. Sheffield: Sheffield Academic Press, 1996.

Falk, Nancy Auer, and Rita M. Gross, eds. *Unspoken Worlds: Women's Religious Lives*. 3rd ed. Belmont, Calif.: Wadsworth, 2001.

Falkenstein, Adam. "Sumerische religiöse Texte." *ZA* 52 (1957): 56–75.

Farber-Flügge, Gertrud. *Der Mythos "Inanna und Enki" unter besonderer Berücksichtigung der Liste der ME*. Studia Pohl 10. Rome: Biblical Institute Press, 1973.

Fausto-Sterling, Anne. *Sexing the Body: Gender Politics and the Construction of Sexuality*. New York: Basic Books, 2000.

Feld, Gerburgis. "'… Wie es eben Frauen ergeht' (Gen 31:35): Kulturgeschichtliche Überlegungen zum gegenwärtigen Umgang mit der Menstruation der Frau in Gesellschaft und Theologie." Pages 29–42 in *Von der Wurzel getragen: Christlich-feministische Exegese in Auseinandersetzung mit Antijudaismus*. Edited by Luise Schottroff and Marie-Theres Wacker. BIS 17. Leiden: Brill, 1996.

Feldman, Louis H. "Josephus' Jewish Antiquities and Pseudo Philo's Biblical Antiquities." Pages 59–80 in *Josephus, the Bible, and History*. Edited by Louis H. Feldman and Gohei Hata. Leiden: Brill, 1989.

Fischer, Georg. *Jeremia: Der Stand der theologischen Diskussion*. Darmstadt: Wissenschaftliche Buchgesellschaft, 2007.

Fischer, Irmtraud. "The Authority of Miriam: A Feminist Rereading of Numbers 12 Prompted by Jewish Interpretation." Translated by Barbara Rumscheidt and Martin Rumscheidt. Pages 159–73 in *Exodus to Deuteronomy*. Edited by Athalya Brenner. FCB 2/5. Sheffield: Sheffield Academic Press, 2000.

———. *Gotteskünderinnen: Zu einer geschlechterfairen Deutung des Phänomens der Prophetie und der Prophetinnen in der Hebräischen Bibel*. Stuttgart: Kohlhammer, 2002.

Fisk, Bruce Norman. *Do You Not Remember? Scripture, Story and Exegesis in the Rewritten Bible of Pseudo-Philo*. JSPSup 37. Sheffield: Sheffield Academic Press, 2001.

Flannery-Dailey, Frances. *Dreamers, Scribes, and Priests: Jewish Dreams in the Hellenistic and Roman Eras*. JSJSup 90. Leiden: Brill, 2004.

Flower, Michael Attyah. "The Iamidae: A Mantic Family and Its Public Image." Pages 187–206 in *Practitioners of the Divine: Greek Priests and Religious Officials from Homer to Heliodorus*. Edited by Beate Dignas and Kai Trampedach. HellSt 30. Washington, D.C.: Center for Hellenic Studies, 2008.

———. *The Seer in Ancient Greece*. Joan Palevsky Imprint in Classical Literature. Berkeley: University of California Press, 2008.

Flückiger-Hawker, Esther. *Urnamma of Ur in Sumerian Literary Tradition*. OBO 166. Göttingen: Vandenhoeck & Ruprecht, 1999.

Fokkelman, J. P. *The Crossing Fates*. Vol. 2 of *Narrative Art and Poetry in the Books of Samuel*. Studia semitica Neerlandica 23. Assen: Van Gorcum, 1986.

Fonrobert, Charlotte Elisheva. *Menstrual Purity: Rabbinic and Christian Reconstructions of Biblical Gender*. Contraversions. Stanford: Stanford University Press, 2000.

Fontana, Benedetto. *Hegemony and Power: On the Relation Between Gramsci and Machiavelli*. Minneapolis: University of Minnesota Press, 1993.

Fontenrose, Joseph. *The Delphic Oracle: Its Responses and Operations, with a Catalogue of Responses*. Berkeley: University of California Press, 1978.

———. *Didyma: Apollo's Oracle, Cult, and Companions*. Berkeley: University of California Press, 1988.

Freedman, David Noel, ed. *Anchor Bible Dictionary*. 6 vols. New York: Doubleday, 1992.

Freeman, James M. "The Ladies of Lord Krishna: Rituals of Middle-Aged Women in Eastern India." Pages 114–24 in *Unspoken Worlds: Women's Religious Lives*. Edited by Nancy Auer Falk and Rita M. Gross. 3rd ed. Belmont, Calif.: Wadsworth, 2001.

Frend, W. H. C. *The Rise of Christianity*. Philadelphia: Fortress, 1984.

Fretheim, Terence E. "The Character of God in Jeremiah." Pages 211–30 in *Character and Scripture: Moral Formation, Community, and Biblical Interpretation*. Edited by William P. Brown. Grand Rapids: Eerdmans, 2002.

———. "Is Anything Too Hard for God? (Jeremiah 32:27)." *CBQ* 66 (2004): 231–36.

———. *Jeremiah*. SHBC. Macon, Ga.: Smyth & Helwys, 2002.

Friebel, Kelvin G. *Jeremiah's and Ezekiel's Sign-Acts: Rhetorical Nonverbal Communication*. JSOTSup 283. Sheffield: Sheffield Academic Press, 1999.

Fuchs, Esther. "Prophecy and the Construction of Women: Inscription and Erasure." Pages 54–69 in *Prophets and Daniel*. Edited by Athalya Brenner. FCB 2/8. Sheffield: Sheffield Academic Press, 2001.
Gabbay, Uri. "The Akkadian Word for 'Third Gender': The *kalû* (gala) Once Again." Pages 49–56 in *Proceedings of the 51st Rencontre Assyriologique Internationale Held at the Oriental Institute of Chicago, July 18–22, 2005*. Edited by Robert D. Biggs, Jennie Myers, and Martha T. Roth. SAOC 62. Chicago: Oriental Institute of the University of Chicago, 2008.

———. *The Ersema Prayers of the First Millennium BCE*. Heidelberger Emesal-Studien 2. Wiesbaden: Harrassowitz, forthcoming.
Gafney, Wilda C. *Daughters of Miriam: Women Prophets in Ancient Israel*. Minneapolis: Fortress, 2008.
Galambush, Julie. "God's Land and Mine: Creation as Property in the Book of Ezekiel." Pages 91–108 in *Ezekiel's Hierarchical World: Wrestling with a Tiered Reality*. Edited by Stephen L. Cook and Corrine L. Patton. SBLSymS 31. Atlanta: Society of Biblical Literature, 2004.

———. *Jerusalem in the Book of Ezekiel: The City as Yahweh's Wife*. SBLDS 130. Atlanta: Scholars Press, 1992.
García Martínez, Florentino, and Eibert J. C. Tigchelaar, eds. *The Dead Sea Scrolls Study Edition*. 2 vols. Leiden: Brill, 1997–1998.
Gelb, I. J. "The Name of the Goddess Innin." *JNES* 19 (1960): 72–79.
Genette, Gérard. *Palimpsestes: La littérature au second degré*. Collection poétique. Paris: Seuil, 1982.
George, Andrew R. *House Most High: The Temples of Ancient Mesopotamia*. MC 5. Winona Lake, Ind.: Eisenbrauns, 1993.
Gesche, Petra D. *Schulunterricht in Babylonien im ersten Jahrtausend v.Chr.* AOAT 275. Münster: Ugarit-Verlag, 2001.
Giles, Linda L. "Possession Cults on the Swahili Coast: A Re-examination of Theories of Marginality." *Africa* 57 (1987): 234–58.
Gladd, Benjamin L. *Revealing the Mysterion: The Use of Mystery in Daniel and Second Temple Judaism and Its Bearing on First Corinthians*. BZNW 160. Berlin: de Gruyter, 2009.
Gödecken, Karin. "Bemerkungen zur Göttin Annunītum." *UF* 5 (1973): 141–63.
Goldingay, John. "Hosea 1–3, Genesis 1–4, and Masculist Interpretation." *HBT* 17 (1995): 37–44.
Goldman, Liora. "Dualism in the *Visions of Amram*." *RevQ* 24 (2010): 421–32.

Grabbe, Lester L. "The Case of the Corrupting Consensus." Pages 83–92 in *Between Evidence and Ideology: Essays on the History of Ancient Israel Read at the Joint Meeting of the Society for Old Testament Study and the Oud Testamentisch Werkgezelschap, Lincoln, July 2009*. Edited by Bob Becking and Lester L. Grabbe. OTS 59. Brill: Leiden, 2011.

———. *Priests, Prophets, Diviners, Sages: A Socio-Historical Study of Religious Specialists in Ancient Israel*. Valley Forge, Pa.: Trinity Press International, 1995.

———. "Shaman, Preacher, or Spirit Medium? The Israelite Prophet in the Light of Anthropological Models." Pages 117–32 in *Prophecy and the Prophets in Ancient Israel: Proceedings of the Oxford Old Testament Seminar*. Edited by John Day. LHBOTS 531. London: T&T Clark, 2010.

Gramsci, Antonio. *Prison Notebooks*. Edited by Joseph A. Buttigieg. Translated by Joseph A. Buttigieg and Antonio Callari. 3 vols. New York: Columbia University Press, 1992–2007.

———. *Selections from the Prison Notebooks*. Edited and translated by Quintin Hoare and Geoffrey Nowell Smith. London: Lawrence & Wishart, 1971.

Gray, George Buchanan. *A Critical and Exegetical Commentary on Numbers*. ICC. 1903. Repr., Edinburgh: T&T Clark, 1965.

Grayson, A. Kirk, and Wilfred G. Lambert. "Akkadian Prophecies." *JCS* 18 (1964): 7–30.

Greenberg, Moshe. *Ezekiel 1–20*. AB 22. Garden City, N.Y.: Doubleday, 1983.

———. *Ezekiel 21–37*. AB 22A. Garden City, N.Y.: Doubleday, 1997.

Greenfield, Jonas C., Esther Eshel, and Michael E. Stone. *Aramaic Levi Document: Edition, Translation, Commentary*. SVTP 19. Leiden: Brill, 2004.

Greenstein, Edward L. "Jeremiah as an Inspiration to the Poet of Job." Pages 98–110 in *Inspired Speech: Prophecy in the Ancient Near East: Essays in Honor of Herbert B. Huffmon*. Edited by John Kaltner and Louis Stulman. JSOTSup 378. London: T&T Clark, 2004.

Groneberg, Brigitte. *Lob der Ištar: Gebet und Ritual an die altbabylonische Venusgöttin Tanatti Ištar*. CM 8. Groningen: Styx, 1997.

———. "Namûtu ša Ištar: Das Transvestieschauspiel der Ištar." *NABU* 2 (1997): 64–66.

———. "Die sumerisch-akkadische Inanna/Ištar: Hermaphroditos." *WO* 17 (1986): 25–46.

Gross, Rita M. "Menstruation and Childbirth as Ritual and Religious Experience among Native Australians." Pages 301–10 in *Unspoken Worlds: Women's Religious Lives.* Edited by Nancy Auer Falk and Rita M. Gross. 3rd ed. Belmont, Calif.: Wadsworth, 2001.

Gruber, Mayer I. "Hebrew *qedeshah* and Her Canaanite and Akkadian Cognates." *UF* 18 (1986): 133–48.

Guest, Deryn. "From Gender Reversal to Genderfuck: Reading Jael through a Lesbian Lens." Pages 12–20 in *Bible Trouble: Queer Reading at the Boundaries of Biblical Scholarship.* Edited by Teresa J. Hornsby and Ken Stone. SemeiaSt 67. Atlanta: Society of Biblical Literature, 2011.

Gurney, O. R. *The Assyrian Tablets from Sultantepe.* Proceedings of the British Academy 41. London: Oxford University Press, 1955.

Gurney, O. R., Jacob J. Finkelstein, and Paul Hulin. *The Sultantepe Tablets.* 2 vols. Occasional Publications of the British Institute of Archaeology at Ankara 3, 7. London: British Institute of Archaeology at Ankara, 1957–1964.

Haddox, Susan E. *Metaphor and Masculinity in Hosea.* StBL 141. New York: Lang, 2011.

Hadley, Judith M. "The Queen of Heaven—Who Is She?" Pages 30–51 in *Prophets and Daniel.* Edited by Athalya Brenner. FCB 2/8. Sheffield: Sheffield Academic Press, 2001.

Hagedorn, Anselm C. *Die Anderen im Spiegel: Israels Auseinandersetzung mit den Völkern in den Büchern Nahum, Zefanja, Obdaja und Joel.* BZAW 414. Berlin: de Gruyter, 2011.

———. "Looking at Foreigners in Biblical and Greek Prophecy." *VT* 57 (2007): 432–48.

———. "'Über jedes Land der Sünder kommt einst ein Sausen': Überlegungen zu einigen Fremdvölkerworten der Sibyllinen." Pages 73–98 in *Orakel und Gebete: Interdisziplinäre Studien zur Sprache der Religion in Ägypten, Vorderasien und Griechenland in hellenistischer Zeit.* Edited by Markus Witte and Johannes F. Diehl. FAT 2/38. Tübingen: Mohr Siebeck, 2009.

Hall, Donald E. *Queer Theories.* Transitions. New York: Palgrave Macmillan, 2003.

Halperin, David J. *Seeking Ezekiel: Text and Psychology.* University Park: Pennsylvania State University Press, 1993.

Halpern-Amaru, Betsy. "Biblical Women in Josephus." *JJS* 39 (1988): 143–70.

———. "Burying the Fathers: Exegetical Strategies and Source Traditions in Jubilees 46." Pages 135–52 in *Reworking the Bible: Apocryphal and Related Texts at Qumran*. Edited by Esther G. Chazon, Devorah Dimant, and Ruth A. Clements. STDJ 58. Leiden: Brill, 2005.

———. "Portraits of Women in Pseudo-Philo's *Biblical Antiquities*." Pages 83–106 in *"Women Like This": New Perspectives on Jewish Women in the Greco-Roman World*. Edited by Amy-Jill Levine. SBLEJL 1. Atlanta: Scholars Press, 1991.

Hals, Ronald M. *Ezekiel*. FOTL 19. Grand Rapids: Eerdmans, 1989.

Hämeen-Anttila, Jaakko. *A Sketch of Neo-Assyrian Grammar*. SAAS 13. Helsinki: Neo-Assyrian Text Corpus Project, 2000.

Hamilton, Gordon J. "A Proposal to Read the Legend of a Seal-Amulet from Deir Rifa, Egypt as an Early West Semitic Alphabetic Inscription." *JSS* 54 (2009): 51–79.

Hamori, Esther J. "Gender and the Verification of Prophecy at Mari." *WO* 42 (2012): 1–22.

———. "The Prophet and the Necromancer: Women's Divination for Kings." *JBL* (2013): forthcoming.

———. *Women's Divination in Biblical Literature: Prophecy, Necromancy, and Other Arts of Knowledge*. AYBRL. New Haven: Yale University Press, forthcoming.

Hard, Robin. *The Library of Greek Mythology: Apollodorus*. Oxford World's Classics. Oxford: Oxford University Press, 1997.

Harrington, Daniel J. "A Decade of Research on Pseudo-Philo's Biblical Antiquities." *JSP* 2 (1988): 3–12.

Harris, Edward Monroe. *Aeschines and Athenian Politics*. New York: Oxford University Press, 1995.

Harvey, Youngsook Kim. "Possession Sickness and Women Shamans in Korea." Pages 59–65 in *Unspoken Worlds: Women's Religious Lives*. Edited by Nancy Auer Falk and Rita M. Gross. 3rd ed. Belmont, Calif.: Wadsworth, 2001.

Hawkins, J. David. "Inscription." Pages 11–31 in *A New Luwian Stele and the Cult of the Storm-God at Til Barsib–Masuwari*, by Guy Bunnens. Tell Ahmar 2. Publications de la Mission archéologique de l'Université de Liège en Syrie. Leuven: Peeters, 2006.

Hayes, Jarrod, Margaret R. Higonnet, and William J. Spurlin. "Comparing Queerly, Queering Comparison: Theorizing Identities Between Cultures, Histories, and Disciplines." Pages 1–19 in *Comparatively Queer: Interrogating Identities across Time and Cultures*. Edited by Jarrod

Hayes, Margaret R. Higonnet, and William J. Spurlin. New York: Palgrave Macmillan, 2010.
Heacock, Anthony. *Jonathan Loved David: Manly Love in the Bible and the Hermeneutics of Sex*. BMW 22. Sheffield: Sheffield Phoenix, 2011.
Heimpel, Wolfgang. "Catalogue of Near Eastern Venus Deities." *Syro-Mesopotamian Studies* 4 (1982): 59–72.
Heine, Ronald E. *The Montanist Oracles and Testimonia*. PMS 14. Macon, Ga.: Mercer University Press, 1989.
———. "The Role of the Gospel of John in the Montanist Controversy." *SecCent* 6 (1987/1988): 1–19.
Heinisch, Paul. *Das Buch Numeri*. Heilige Schrift des Alten Testaments 2.1. Bonn: Hanstein, 1936.
Henshaw, Richard A. *Female and Male: The Cultic Personnel: The Bible and the Rest of the Ancient Near East*. PrTMS 31. Allison Park, Pa.: Pickwick, 1994.
Herdt, Gilbert. "Mistaken Sex: Culture, Biology and the Third Sex in New Guinea." Pages 419–45 in *Third Sex, Third Gender: Beyond Sexual Dimorphism in Culture and History*. Edited by Gilbert Herdt. New York: Zone, 1994.
———. *Sambia Sexual Culture: Essays from the Field*. Worlds of Desire. Chicago: University of Chicago Press, 1999.
Hoffman, Yair. "Aetiology, Redaction and Historicity in Jeremiah XXXVI." *VT* 46 (1996): 179–89.
Holladay, William L. *Jeremiah 1: A Commentary on the Book of the Prophet Jeremiah, Chapters 1–25*. Hermeneia. Philadelphia: Fortress, 1986.
Holt, Else K. "Word of Jeremiah—Word of God: Structures of Authority in the Book of Jeremiah." Pages 172–82 in *Uprooting and Planting: Essays on Jeremiah for Leslie Allen*. Edited by John Goldingay. LHBOTS 459. New York: T&T Clark, 2007.
Homer. *The Iliad*. Translated by Augustus Taber Murray. 2 vols. LCL. Cambridge: Harvard University Press, 1924–1925.
———. *The Odyssey*. Translated by Augustus Taber Murray. Revised by George E. Dimock. 2 vols. LCL. Cambridge: Harvard University Press, 1995.
Hooper, Charlotte. *Manly States: Masculinities, International Relations, and Gender Politics*. New York: Columbia University Press, 2001.
Hornsby, Teresa. "Ezekiel." Pages 412–26 in *The Queer Bible Commentary*. Edited by Deryn Guest. London: SCM, 2006.

Horst, Pieter W. van der. "Moses' Father Speaks Out." Pages 491–98 in *Flores Florentino: Dead Sea Scrolls and Other Early Jewish Studies in Honour of Florentino García Martínez*. Edited by Anthony Hilhorst, Émile Puech and Eibert J. C. Tigchelaar. JSJSup 122. Leiden: Brill, 2007.

———. "Portraits of Biblical Women in Pseudo-Philo's Liber Antiquitatum Biblicarum." *JSP* 5 (1989): 29–46.

———. "Tamar in Pseudo-Philo's Biblical History." Pages 300–305 in *Feminist Companion to Genesis*. Edited by Athalya Brenner. FCB 2. Sheffield: Sheffield Academic Press, 1997.

Hovi, Tuija. "Sukupuoli, toimijuus ja muutos: Uuskarismaattisen liikkeen 'uutuus.'" [Gender, Actorship, and Change: "Novelty" in the Neo-Charismatic Movement] *Teologinen Aikakauskirja* 116 (2011): 195–207.

Huehnergard, John. *A Grammar of Akkadian*. 2nd ed. HSS 45. Winona Lake, Ind.: Eisenbrauns, 2005.

Huffmon, Herbert B. "The *Assinnum* as Prophet: Shamans at Mari?" Pages 241–47 in *Amurru 3: Nomades et sédentaires dans le Proche-Orient ancien. Compte rendu de la XLVIe Rencontre Assyriologique Internationale (Paris, 10–13 juillet 2000)*. Edited by Christophe Nicolle. Paris: ERC, 2004.

———. "A Company of Prophets: Mari, Assyria, Israel." Pages 47–70 in *Prophecy in Its Ancient Near Eastern Context: Mesopotamian, Biblical, and Arabian Perspectives*. Edited by Martti Nissinen. SBLSymS 13. Atlanta: Society of Biblical Literature, 2000.

———. "The Origins of Prophecy." Pages 171–86 in *Magnalia Dei, the Mighty Acts of God: Essays on the Bible and Archaeology in Memory of G. Ernest Wright*. Edited by Frank Moore Cross, Werner E. Lemke, and Patrick D. Miller. Garden City, N.Y.: Doubleday, 1976.

———. "Prophecy in the Mari Letters." *BA* 31 (1968): 101–24.

Humes, Cynthia Ann. "Becoming Male: Salvation through Gender Modification in Hinduism and Buddhism." Pages 123–37 in *Gender Reversals and Gender Cultures: Anthropological and Historical Perspectives*. Edited by Sabrina Petra Ramet. London: Routledge, 1996.

Husser, Jean-Marie. *Dreams and Dream Narratives in the Biblical World*. BiSe 63. Sheffield: Sheffield Academic Press, 1999.

Ilan, Tal. "Huldah, the Deuteronomic Prophetess in the Books of Kings." *lectio difficilior* 1 (2010): 1–16. Online: http://www.lectio.unibe.ch/10_1/ilan.html.

———. "The Torah of the Jews of Ancient Rome." *JSQ* 16 (2009): 363–95.
Jacobson, Howard. *A Commentary on Pseudo-Philo's Liber Antiquitatum Biblicarum with Latin Text and English Translation*. 2 vols. AGJU 31. Leiden: Brill, 1996.
Jagose, Annamarie. *Queer Theory: An Introduction*. New York: New York University Press, 1996.
James, M. R. *The Biblical Antiquities of Philo*. 1917. Repr., with a new prolegomenon by Louis H. Feldman. Library of Biblical Studies. New York: Ktav, 1971.
Jameson, Fredric. *The Cultural Turn: Selected Writings on the Postmodern, 1983–1998*. London: Verso, 1998.
———. *Postmodernism, or, the Cultural Logic of Late Capitalism*. Postcontemporary Interventions. Durham, N.C.: Duke University Press, 1991.
———. *Valences of the Dialectic*. London: Verso, 2009.
Jeffers, Ann. *Magic and Divination in Ancient Palestine and Syria*. SHCANE 8. Leiden: Brill, 1996.
Jensen, Anne. *God's Self-Confident Daughters: Early Christianity and the Liberation of Women*. Translated by O. C. Dean Jr. Louisville: Westminster John Knox, 1996.
Jepsen, Alfred. "Die Nebiah in Jes 8, 3." *ZAW* 72 (1960): 267–68.
Job, John Brian. *Jeremiah's Kings: A Study of the Monarchy in Jeremiah*. SOTSMS. Aldershot: Ashgate, 2006.
Johnson, Douglas H. *Nuer Prophets: A History of Prophecy from the Upper Nile in the Nineteenth and Twentieth Centuries*. Oxford Studies in Social and Cultural Anthropology. Oxford: Clarendon, 1994.
Johnston, Sarah Iles. *Ancient Greek Divination*. Blackwell Ancient Religions. Malden, Mass.: Wiley-Blackwell, 2008.
Joosten, Jan. *People and Land in the Holiness Code: An Exegetical Study of the Ideational Framework of the Law in Leviticus 17–26*. VTSup 67. Leiden: Brill, 1996.
Jost, Renate. "The Daughters of Your People Prophesy." Pages 70–76 in *Prophets and Daniel*. Edited by Athalya Brenner. FCB 2/8. Sheffield: Sheffield Academic Press, 2001.
Joyce, Paul M. *Divine Initiative and Human Response in Ezekiel*. JSOTSup 51. Sheffield: JSOT Press, 1989.
———. "Dislocation and Adaptation in the Exilic Age and After." Pages 45–58 in *After the Exile: Essays in Honour of Rex Mason*. Edited by John Barton and David J. Reimer. Macon, Ga.: Mercer University Press, 1996.

———. *Ezekiel: A Commentary*. LHBOTS 482. New York: T&T Clark, 2007.

———. "King and Messiah in Ezekiel." Pages 232–27 in *King and Messiah in Israel and the Ancient Near East: Proceedings of the Oxford Old Testament Seminar*. Edited by John Day. JSOTSup 270. Sheffield: Sheffield Academic Press, 1998.

Kaiser, Barbara Bakke. "Poet as 'Female Impersonator': The Image of Daughter Zion as Speaker in Biblical Poems of Suffering." *JR* 67 (1987): 164–82.

Kaiser, Otto. "Die Sibyllinischen Orakel und das Echo biblischer Ethik und Prophetie in ihrem dritten Buch." Pages 381–400 in *Schriftprophetie. Festschrift für Jörg Jeremias zum 65. Geburtstag*. Edited by Friedhelm Hartenstein, Jutta Krispenz, and Aaron Schart. Neukirchen-Vluyn: Neukirchener, 2004.

Kalmanofsky, Amy. "The Monstrous-Feminine in the Book of Jeremiah." Pages 190–208 in *Jeremiah (Dis)Placed: New Directions in Writing/Reading Jeremiah*. Edited by A. R. Pete Diamond and Louis Stulman. LHBOTS 529. New York: T&T Clark, 2011.

———. *Terror All Around: Horror, Monsters, and Theology in the Book of Jeremiah*. LHBOTS 390. London: T&T Clark, 2008.

Kamionkowski, S. Tamar. *Gender Reversal and Cosmic Chaos: A Study of the Book of Ezekiel*. JSOTSup 368. London: Sheffield Academic Press, 2003.

———. "Gender Reversal in Ezekiel 16." Pages 170–85 in *Prophets and Daniel*. Edited by Athalya Brenner. FCB 2/8. Sheffield: Sheffield Academic Press, 2001.

Kazen, Thomas. "Dirt and Disgust: Body and Morality in Biblical Purity Laws." Pages 43–64 in *Perspectives on Purity and Purification in the Bible*. Edited by Baruch J. Schwartz, David P. Wright, Jeffrey Stackert, and Naphtali S. Meshel. LHBOTS 474. New York: T&T Clark, 2008.

Keefe, Alice. *Woman's Body and Social Body in Hosea*. JSOTSup 338. GCT 10. Sheffield: Sheffield Academic Press, 2001.

Keller, Mary. *The Hammer and the Flute: Women, Power, and Spirit Possession*. Baltimore: Johns Hopkins University Press, 2002.

Kendall, Laurel. *Shamans, Housewives, and Other Restless Spirits: Women in Korean Ritual Life*. Studies of the East Asian Institute. Honolulu: University of Hawaii Press, 1985.

Kendall, Laurel, and Hien Thi Nguyen. "Dressing up the Spirits: Costumes, Cross-Dressing, and Incarnation in Korea and Vietnam." Pages

93–114 in *Women and Indigenous Religions*. Edited by Sylvia Marcos. Santa Barbara, Calif.: Praeger, 2010.

Kennedy, George A. *Comparative Rhetoric: An Historical and Cross-Cultural Introduction*. New York: Oxford University Press, 1998.

Kerns, Virginia. "Garífuna Women and the Work of Mourning (Central America)." Pages 125–33 in *Unspoken Worlds: Women's Religious Lives*. Edited by Nancy Auer Falk and Rita M. Gross. 3rd ed. Belmont, Calif.: Wadsworth, 2001.

Kessler, Martin, ed. *Reading the Book of Jeremiah: A Search for Coherence*. Winona Lake, Ind.: Eisenbrauns, 2004.

Kessler, Rainer. "Mirjam und die Prophetie der Perserzeit." Pages 64–72 in *Gott an den Rändern: Sozialgeschichtliche Perspektiven auf die Bibel*. Edited by Ulrike Bail und Renate Jost. Gütersloh: Kaiser, 1996.

Kessler, Suzanne J. "From Sex to Sexuality: The Medical Construction of Gender." Pages 135–57 in *Theorizing Feminism: Parallel Trends in the Humanities and Social Sciences*. Edited by Anne C. Hermann and Abigail J. Stewart. Boulder, Colo.: Westview, 1994.

———. *Lessons from the Intersexed*. New Brunswick, N.J.: Rutgers University Press, 1998.

Kilmer, Anne Draffkorn. "The First Tablet of *malku* = *šarru* together with Its Explicit Version." *JAOS* 83 (1963): 421–46.

Kipnis, Kenneth, and Milton Diamond. "Pediatric Ethics and the Surgical Assignment of Sex." *Journal of Clinical Ethics* 9 (1998): 398–410.

Kisch, Guido. *Pseudo-Philo's Liber Antiquitatum Biblicarum*. Publications in Medieval Studies 10. Notre Dame, Ind.: University of Notre Dame Press, 1949.

Knierim, Rolf P., and George W. Coats. *Numbers*. FOTL 4. Grand Rapids: Eerdmans, 2005.

Köckert, Matthias. "Zum literargeschichtlichen Ort des Prophetengesetzes Dtn 18 zwischen dem Jeremiabuch und Dtn 13." Pages 80–100 in *Liebe und Gebot: Studien zum Deuteronomium: Festschrift zum 70. Geburtstag von Lothar Perlitt*. Edited by Reinhard G. Kratz and Hermann Spieckermann. FRLANT 190. Göttingen: Vandenhoeck & Ruprecht, 2000.

Köckert, Matthias, and Marti Nissinen, eds. *Propheten in Mari, Assyrien und Israel*. FRLANT 201. Göttingen: Vandenhoeck & Ruprecht, 2003.

Koehler, Ludwig, Walter Baumgartner, and J. J. Stamm. *The Hebrew and Aramaic Lexicon of the Old Testament*. Translated by M. E. J. Richardson. 5 vols. Leiden: Brill, 1994–2000.

Konkel, Michael. *Architektonik des Heiligen: Studien zur zweiten Templevision Ezechiels (Ez 40–48)*. BBB 129. Berlin: Philo, 2001.

Korsmeyer, Carolyn, and Barry Smith. "Visceral Values: Aurel Kolnai on Disgust." Pages 1–25 in *On Disgust* by Aurel Kolnai. Edited by Carolyn Korsmeyer and Barry Smith. Chicago: Open Court, 2004.

Korte, Alexander, David Goecker, Heiko Krude, Ulrike Lehmkuhl, Annette Grüters-Kieslich, and Klaus Michael Beier. "Gender Identity Disorders in Childhood and Adolescence: Currently Debated Concepts and Treatment Strategies." *Deutsches Ärzteblatt International* 105 (2008): 834–41.

Korte, Anne-Marie. "Female Blood Rituals: Cultural-Anthropological Findings and Feminist-Theological Reflections." Pages 165–86 in *Wholly Woman, Holy Blood: A Feminist Critique of Purity and Impurity*. Edited by Kristin De Troyer, Judith A. Herbert, Judith Ann Johnson, and Anne-Marie Korte. SAC. Harrisburg: Trinity Press International, 2003.

Kowalzig, Barbara. *Singing for the Gods: Performances of Myth and Ritual in Archaic and Classical Greece*. Oxford Classical Monographs. Oxford: Oxford University Press, 2007.

Kramer, Samuel N. Review of Adam Falkenstein, *Sumerische und akkadische Hymnen und Gebete*. *BiOr* 11 (1954): 170–76.

Kron, Uta. "Priesthoods, Dedications and Euergetism: What Part Did Religion Play in the Political and Social Status of Greek Women?" Pages 139–82 in *Religion and Power in the Ancient Greek World: Proceedings of the Uppsala Symposium 1993*. Edited by Pontus Hellström and Brita Alroth. Acta Universitatis Upsaliensis: Boreas 24. Uppsala: Almquist & Wiksell, 1996.

Kruger, Paul A. "'A Woman Will 'Encompass' a Man: On Gender Reversal in Jer 31,22b." *Bib* 89 (2008): 380–88.

Kselman, John S. "A Note on Numbers 12:6–8." *VT* 26 (1976): 500–505.

Kugler, Robert. "Testaments." Pages 933–36 in vol. 2 of *The Encyclopedia of the Dead Sea Scrolls*. Edited by Lawrence H. Schiffman and James C. VanderKam. 2 vols. New York; Oxford University Press, 2000.

Labriolle, Pierre de. *Les sources de l'histoire du Montanisme: Textes grecs, latins, syriaques publiés avec une introduction critique, une traduction française des notes et des "indices."* Collectanea Friburgensia, n.s. 15. Paris: Leroux, 1913.

Lackenbacher, Sylvie. "Un nouveau fragment de la 'Fête d'Ištar.'" *RA* 71 (1977): 39–50.

Lambert, Wilfred G. "A Babylonian Prayer to Anuna." Pages 321–36 in *DUMU-E2-DUB-BA-A: Studies in Honor of Åke W. Sjöberg*. Edited by Hermann Behrens, Darlene Loding, and Martha T. Roth. Occasional Publications of the Samuel Noah Kramer Fund 11. Philadelphia: University Museum, 1989.

———. "The Problem of the Love Lyrics." Pages 98–135 in *Unity and Diversity: Essays in the History, Literature, and Religion of the Ancient Near East*. Edited by Hans Goedicke and J. J. M. Roberts. JHNES 7. Baltimore: Johns Hopkins University Press, 1975.

———. "Prostitution." Pages 127–57 in *Aussenseiter und Randgruppen: Beiträge zu einer Sozialgeschichte des Alten Orients*. Edited by Volkert Haas. Xenia 32. Konstanz: Universitätsverlag, 1992.

———. "The Qualifications of Babylonian Diviners." Pages 141–58 in *Festschrift für Rykle Borger zu seinem 65. Geburtstag am 24. Mai 1994: Tikip santakki mala basmu*. Edited by Stefan M. Maul. CM 10. Groningen: Styx, 1998.

Lan, David. *Guns and Rain: Guerrillas and Spirit Mediums in Zimbabwe*. Perspectives on South Africa 38. London: James Currey, 1985.

Land, Gary, ed. *Adventism in America: A History*. Studies in Adventist History. Grand Rapids: Eerdmans, 1986.

Lange, Armin. "Greek Seers and Israelite-Jewish Prophets." *VT* 57 (2007): 461–82.

———. "Literary Prophecy and Oracle Collection: A Comparison between Judah and Greece in Persian Times." Pages 248–75 in *Prophets, Prophecy, and Prophetic Texts in Second Temple Judaism*. Edited by Michael H. Floyd and Robert D. Haak. LHBOTS 427. New York: T&T Clark, 2006.

Lapinkivi, Pirjo. "The Sumerian Sacred Marriage and Its Aftermath in Later Sources." Pages 7–41 in *Sacred Marriages: The Divine-Human Sexual Metaphor from Sumer to Early Christianity*. Edited by Martti Nissinen and Risto Uro. Winona Lake, Ind.: Eisenbrauns, 2008.

Lapsley, Jacqueline E. "A Feeling for God: Emotions and Moral Formation in Ezekiel 24:15–27." Pages 93–102 in *Character Ethics and the Old Testament: Moral Dimensions of Scripture*. Edited by Mark Daniel Carroll R. and Jacqueline E. Lapsley. Louisville: Westminster John Knox, 2007.

———. *Can These Bones Live? The Problem of the Moral Self in the Book of Ezekiel*. BZAW 301. Berlin: de Gruyter, 2000.

———. "Shame and Self-Knowledge: The Positive Role of Shame in Ezekiel's View of the Moral Self." Pages 143–73 in *The Book of Ezekiel:*

Theological and Anthropological Perspectives. Edited by Margaret S. Odell and John T. Strong. SBLSymS 9. Atlanta: Scholars Press, 2000.

———. *Whispering the Word: Hearing Women's Stories in the Old Testament.* Louisville: Westminster John Knox, 2005.

Larrain, Jorge. "Ideology." Pages 219–23 in *A Dictionary of Marxist Thought.* Edited by Tom Bottomore. Oxford: Blackwell, 1983.

———. *Marxism and Ideology.* Contemporary Social Theory. London: Macmillan, 1983.

Launderville, Dale. *Celibacy in the Ancient World: Its Ideal and Practice in Pre-Hellenistic Israel, Mesopotamia, and Greece.* Collegeville, Minn.: Liturgical Press, 2010.

———. *Spirit and Reason: The Embodied Character of Ezekiel's Symbolic Thinking.* Waco, Tex.: Baylor University Press, 2007.

Lee, Nancy C. "Prophet and Singer in the Fray: The Book of Jeremiah." Pages 190–209 in *Uprooting and Planting: Essays on Jeremiah for Leslie Allen.* Edited by John Goldingay. LHBOTS 459. New York: T&T Clark, 2007.

———. *The Singers of Lamentations: Cities under Siege, from Ur to Jerusalem to Sarajevo.* BIS 60. Leiden: Brill, 2002.

Leene, Hendrik. "Blowing the Same Shofar: An Intertextual Comparison of Representations of the Prophetic Role in Jeremiah and Ezekiel." Pages 175–98 in *The Elusive Prophet: The Prophet as a Historical Person, Literary Character and Anonymous Artist.* Edited by Johannes C. de Moor. OTS 45. Leiden: Brill, 2001.

———. "Jeremiah 31,23–26 and the Redaction of the Book of Comfort." *ZAW* 104 (1992): 349–64.

Lefkovitz, Lori Hope. *In Scripture: The First Stories of Jewish Sexual Identities.* Landham, Md.: Rowman & Littlefield, 2010.

Leichty, Erle. *The Royal Inscriptions of Esarhaddon, King of Assyria (680–669 BC).* RINAP 4. Winona Lake, Ind.: Eisenbrauns, 2011.

Leming, Laura M. "Sociological Explorations: What Is Religious Agency?" *Sociological Quarterly* 48 (2007): 73–92.

Lemos, T. M. "Emasculation of Exile: Hypermasculinity and Feminization in the Book of Ezekiel." Pages 377–93 in *Interpreting Exile: Displacement and Deportation in Biblical and Modern Contexts.* Edited by Brad E. Kelle, Frank Ritchell Ames, and Jacob L. Wright. SBLAIL 10. Atlanta: Society of Biblical Literature, 2011.

———. "Shame and Mutilation of Enemies in the Hebrew Bible." *JBL* 125 (2006): 225–41.

———. "'They Have Become Women': Judean Diaspora and Postcolonial Theories of Gender and Migration." Pages 81–109 in *Social Theory and the Study of Israelite Religion: Essays in Retrospect and Prospect*. Edited by Saul M. Olyan. SBLRBS 71. Atlanta: Society of Biblical Literature, 2012.

Lenzi, Alan. *Secrecy and the Gods: Secret Knowledge in Ancient Mesopotamia and Biblical Israel*. SAAS 19. Helsinki: Neo-Assyrian Text Corpus Project, 2008.

Levenson, Jon D. *Theology of the Program of Restoration of Ezekiel 40–48*. HSM 10. Atlanta: Scholars Press, 1976.

Levine, Baruch A. *Leviticus*. JPSTC. Philadelphia: Jewish Publication Society of America, 1989.

———. *Numbers 1–20*. AB 4. New York: Doubldeay, 1993.

———. *Numbers 21–36*. AB 4A. New York: Doubleday, 2000.

Lévi-Strauss, Claude. *Tristes Tropiques*. Translated by John Weightman and Doreen Weightman. 1973. Repr., Picador Classics. London: Pan, 1989.

Lev-Ran, Arye. "Sex Reversal as Related to Clinical Syndromes in Human Beings." Pages 157–71 in *Genetics, Hormones and Behavior*. Vol. 2 of *Handbook of Sexology*. Edited by John Money and Herman Musaph. New York: Elsevier, 1978.

Lewis, I. M. *Ecstatic Religion: A Study of Shamanism and Spirit Possession*. 1st ed. Harmondsworth, Eng.: Penguin, 1971; 3rd ed. London: Routledge, 2003.

Lightfoot, J. L. *The Sibylline Oracles: With Introduction, Translation, and Commentary on the First and Second Books*. Oxford: Oxford University Press, 2007.

Linssen, Marc J. H. *The Cults of Uruk and Babylon: The Temple Ritual Texts as Evidence for Hellenistic Cult Practises*. CM 25. Leiden: Brill, Styx, 2004.

Lion, Brigitte. "Dame Inanna-ama-mu, scribe à Sippar." *RA* 95 (2001): 7–32.

Lipton, Diana. "Early Mourning? Petitionary Versus Posthumous Ritual in Ezekiel XXIV," *VT* 56 (2006): 185–202.

———. *Revisions of the Night: Politics and Promises in the Patriarchal Dreams of Genesis*. JSOTSup 288. Sheffield: Sheffield Academic Press, 1999.

Loader, William. *The Dead Sea Scrolls on Sexuality: Attitudes towards Sexuality in Sectarian and Related Literature at Qumran*. Grand Rapids: Eerdmans, 2009.

Lundbom, Jack R. *Jeremiah 1–20*. AB 21A. New York: Doubleday, 1999.
———. *Jeremiah 21–36*. AB 21B. New York: Doubleday, 2004.
Lust, Johan. "The Delight of Ezekiel's Eyes: Ez 24:15–24 in Hebrew and in Greek." Pages 1–26 in *X Congress of the International Organization for Septuagint and Cognate Studies, Oslo, 1998*. Edited by Bernard A. Taylor. SBLSCS 51. Atlanta: Society of Biblical Literature, 2001.
Macwilliam, Stuart. "Ideologies of Male Beauty and the Hebrew Bible." *BibInt* 17 (2009): 265–87.
———. "Queering Jeremiah." *BibInt* 10 (2002): 384–404.
Maier, Christl M. *Daughter Zion, Mother Zion: Gender, Space, and the Sacred in Ancient Israel*. Minneapolis: Fortress, 2008.
Maier, Christl, and Ernst Michael Dörrfuss. "'Um mit ihnen zu sitzen, zu essen und zu trinken': Am 6,7; Jer 16,5 und die Bedeutung von marze^{a}ḥ." *ZAW* 111 (1999): 45–57.
Malamat, Abraham. *Mari and the Bible*. SHCANE 12. Leiden: Brill, 1998.
Marcos, Sylvia, ed. *Women and Indigenous Religions*. Santa Barbara, Calif.: Praeger, 2010.
Marjanen, Antti. "Montanism: Egalitarian Ecstatic 'New Prophecy.'" Pages 185–212 in *A Companion to Second-Century Christian "Heretics."* Edited by Antti Marjanen and Petri Luomanen. VCSup 76. Leiden: Brill, 2005.
Marsman, Hennie J. *Women in Ugarit and in Israel: Their Social and Religious Position in the Context of the Ancient Near East*. OTS 49. Leiden: Brill, 2003.
Maul, Stefan M. "kurgarrû und assinnu und ihr Stand in der babylonischen Gesellschaft." Pages 159–71 in *Aussenseiter und Randgruppen: Beiträge zu einer Sozialgeschichte des Alten Orients*. Edited by Volkert Haas. Xenia 32. Konstanz: Universitätsverlag, 1992.
Maurizio, Lisa. "Delphic Oracles as Oral Performances: Authenticity and Historical Evidence." *Classical Antiquity* 16 (1997): 308–34.
Mayfield, Tyler D. *Literary Structure and Setting in Ezekiel*. FAT 2/43. Tübingen: Mohr Siebeck, 2010.
McCaffrey, Kathleen. *Changed by the Goddess: Lay and Cultic Gender Variance in the Ancient Near East*. Forthcoming.
———. "Reconsidering Gender Ambiguity in Mesopotamia: Is a Beard Just a Beard?" Pages 379–91 in *Sex and Gender in the Ancient Near East: Proceedings of the 47th Rencontre Assyriologique Internationale, Helsinki, July 2–6, 2001*. Edited by Simo Parpola and Robert M. Whiting. Helsinki: Neo-Assyrian Text Corpus Project, 2002.

———. "The Female Kings of Ur." Pages 173–215 in *Gender through Time in the Ancient Near East*. Edited by Diane Bolger. GAS. Lanham, Md.: AltaMira, 2008.

McGinn, Sheila E. "The 'Montanist' Oracles and Prophetic Theology." Pages 128–35 in *Papers Presented at the Twelfth International Conference on Patristic Studies Held in Oxford, 1995*. Vol. 3 of *Preaching, Second Century, Tertullian to Arnobius, Egypt before Nicaea*. Edited by Elizabeth A. Livingstone. StPatr 31. Leuven: Peeters, 1997.

McKane, William. *A Critical and Exegetical Commentary on Jeremiah*. Vol. 1: *Introduction and Commentary on Jeremiah I–XXV*. ICC. Edinburgh: T&T Clark, 1986.

———. "Worship of the Queen of Heaven (Jer 44)." Pages 318–24 in *"Wer ist wie du, Herr, unter den Göttern?" Studien zur Theologie und Religionsgeschichte Israels für Otto Kaiser zum 70. Geburtstag*. Edited by Ingo Kottsieper et al. Göttingen: Vandenhoeck & Ruprecht, 1994.

McLaughlin, John L. *The marzēaḥ in the Prophetic Literature: References and Allusions in Light of the Extra-Biblical Evidence*. VTSup 86. Leiden: Brill, 2001.

Meacham, Tirzah. "An Abbreviated History of the Development of the Jewish Menstrual Laws." Pages 23–39 in *Women and Water: Menstruation in Jewish Life and Law*. Edited by Rahel Wasserfall. Brandeis Series on Jewish Women. Hanover, N.H.: University Press of New England for Brandeis University Press, 1999.

Meier, Samuel A. "Women and Communication in the Ancient Near East." *JAOS* 111 (1991): 540–47.

Melville, Sarah C. "Neo-Assyrian Royal Women and Male Identity: Status as a Social Tool." *JAOS* 124 (2004): 37–57.

———. *The Role of Naqia/Zakutu in Sargonid Politics*. SAAS 9. Helsinki: Neo-Assyrian Text Corpus Project, 1999.

Menadier, Blanche. "The Sanctuary of Hera Akraia and Its Religious Connections with Corinth." Pages 85–91 in *Peloponnesian Sanctuaries and Cults: Proceedings of the Ninth International Symposium at the Swedish Institute at Athens, 11–13 June 1994*. Edited by Robin Hägg. Skrifter utgivna av Svenska institutet i Athen 4o, 48. Stockholm: Swedish Institute at Athens, 2002.

Menninghaus, Winfried. *Disgust: The Theory and History of a Strong Sensation*. Intersections. Translated by Howard Eiland and Joel Golb. Albany: State University of New York Press, 2003.

Menzel, Brigitte. *Untersuchungen zu Kult, Administration und Personal*.

Vol. 1 of *Assyrische Tempel*. StP Series Maior. 10.1. Rome: Biblical Institute Press, 1981.

Merkel, Helmut. *Sibyllinen*. JSHRZ 5.8. Gütersloh: Gütersloher Verlagshaus, 1998.

Merkelbach, Reinhold, and Josef Stauber. "Die Orakel des Apollon von Klaros." *Epigraphica Anatolica* 27 (1996): 1–53.

Meyers, Carol L. "Contesting the Notion of Patriarchy: Anthropology and the Theorizing of Gender in Ancient Israel." Pages 84–105 in *A Question of Sex? Gender and Difference in the Hebrew Bible and Beyond*. Edited by Deborah W. Rooke. HBM 14. Sheffield: Sheffield Phoenix, 2007.

———. *Exodus*. New Cambridge Bible Commentary. Cambridge: Cambridge University Press, 2005.

———. "The Family in Early Israel." Pages 1–47 in *Families in Ancient Israel*. Edited by Leo Perdue, Joseph Blenkinsopp, John J. Collins, and Carol Meyers. Family, Religion, and Culture. Louisville: Westminster John Knox, 1997.

Milgrom, Jacob. *Leviticus 1–16*. AB 3. New York: Doubleday, 1991.

———. *Leviticus: A Book of Ritual and Ethics*. CC. Minneapolis: Fortress, 2004.

———. *Numbers*. JPSTC. Philadelphia: Jewish Publication Society of America, 1990.

Miller, Andrew M. *Greek Lyric: An Anthology in Translation*. Indianapolis: Hackett, 1996.

Miller, Jay. "The 1806 Purge among the Indiana Delaware: Sorcery, Gender, Boundaries, and Legitimacy." *Ethnohistory* 41 (1994): 245–66.

Miller, William Ian. *The Anatomy of Disgust*. Cambridge: Harvard University Press, 1997.

Mills, Mary E. *Alterity, Pain, and Suffering in Isaiah, Jeremiah, and Ezekiel*. LHBOTS 479. New York: T&T Clark, 2007.

Milne, Pamela. "Labouring with Abusive Biblical Texts: Tracing Trajectories of Misogyny." Pages 267–83 in *The Labour of Reading: Desire, Alienation, and Biblical Interpretation*. Edited by Fiona C. Black, Roland Boer, and Erin Runions. SemeiaSt 36. Atlanta: Society of Biblical Literature, 1999.

Möbius, Hans. "Diotima." Pages 33–46 in *Studia varia: Aufsätze zur Kunst und Kultur der Antike mit Nachträgen*. Edited by Wolfgang Schiering. Wiesbaden: Steiner, 1967.

Mooney, James. *The Ghost-Dance Religion and the Sioux Outbreak of 1890*.

Fourteenth Annual Report of the Bureau of Ethnology, 1892–1893, part 2. 1896. Repr., Lincoln: University of Nebraska Press, 1991.
Moore, Stephen D. *God's Beauty Parlor: And Other Queer Spaces in and around the Bible*. Stanford: Stanford University Press, 2001.
Moore, Stephen D., and Janice Capel Anderson. "Taking It Like a Man: Masculinity in 4 Maccabees." *JBL* 117 (1998): 249–73.
Morgan, Catherine. "Divination and Society at Delphi and Didyma." *Hermathena* 147 (1989): 17–42.
Morgan, Janett. "Religion, Women, and the Home." Pages 297–310 in *A Companion to Greek Religion*. Edited by Daniel Ogden. Blackwell Companions to the Ancient World: Literature and Culture. Oxford: Blackwell, 2007.
Murphy, Frederick J. *Pseudo-Philo: Rewriting the Bible*. New York: Oxford University Press, 1993.
Murray, Stephen O. *Homosexualities*. Worlds of Desire. Chicago: University of Chicago Press, 2000.
Musurillo, Herbert. *The Acts of the Christian Martyrs*. Oxford Early Christian Texts. Oxford: Clarendon, 1972.
Nadeau, Randall L. "Harmonizing Family and Cosmos: Shamanic Women in Chinese Religions." Pages 66–79 in *Unspoken Worlds: Women's Religious Lives*. Edited by Nancy Auer Falk and Rita M. Gross. 3rd ed. Belmont, Calif.: Wadsworth, 2001.
Nasrallah, Laura. *An Ecstasy of Folly: Prophecy and Authority in Early Christianity*. HTS 52. Cambridge: Harvard University Press, 2003.
Neblung, Dagmar. *Die Gestalt der Kassandra in der antiken Literatur*. Beiträge zur Altertumskunde 97. Leipzig: Teubner, 1997.
Nelson, James B. *Embodiment: An Approach to Sexuality and Christian Theology*. Minneapolis: Augsburg, 1978.
Nicholson, Sarah. *Three Faces of Saul: An Intertextual Approach to Biblical Tragedy*. JSOTSup 339. Sheffield: Sheffield Academic Press, 2002.
Nickelsburg, George W. E. *1 Enoch 1: A Commentary on the Book of 1 Enoch, Chapters 1–36; 81–108*. Hermeneia. Minneapolis: Fortress, 2001.
Niessen, Christina. "Schuld, Strafe und Geschlecht: Die Auswirkungen der Genderkonstruktionen auf Schuldzuweisungen und Gerichtsankündigungen in Jer 23,9–32 und Jer 13,20–27." *BZ* 48 (2004): 86–96.
Nihan, Christophe. "Un prophète comme Moïse (Deutéronome 18:15): Genèse et relectures d'une construction Deutéronomiste." Pages 43–76 in *La construction de la figure de Moïse—The Construction of the Figure*

of Moses. Edited by Thomas C. Römer. Supplément à Transeuphratène 13. Paris: Gabalda, 2007.

Nissinen, Martti. "Akkadian Rituals and Poetry of Divine Love." Pages 93–136 in *Mythology and Mythologies: Methodological Approaches to Intercultural Influences*. Edited by Robert M. Whiting. Melammu Symposia 2. Helsinki: Neo-Assyrian Text Corpus Project, 2001.

———. "Biblical Prophecy from a Near Eastern Perspective: The Cases of Kingship and Divine Possession." Pages 441–68 in *Congress Volume Ljubljana 2007*. Edited by André Lemaire. VTSup 133. Leiden: Brill, 2010.

———. "City Lofty as Heaven: Arbela and Other Cities in Neo-Assyrian Prophecy." Pages 172–209 in *"Every City Shall Be Forsaken": Urbanism and Prophecy in Ancient Israel and the Near East*. Edited by Lester L. Grabbe and Robert D. Haak. JSOTSup 330. Sheffield: Sheffield Academic Press, 2001.

———. "Falsche Prophetie in neuassyrischer und deuteronomistischer Darstellung." Pages 172–95 in *Das Deuteronomium und seine Querbeziehungen*. Edited by Timo Veijola. Schriften der Finnischen Exegetischen Gesellschaft 62. Göttingen: Vandenhoeck & Ruprecht, 1996.

———. *Homoeroticism in the Biblical World: A Historical Perspective*. Minneapolis: Fortress, 1998.

———. "Prophecy and Omen Divination: Two Sides of the Same Coin." Pages 341–51 in *Divination and Interpretation of Signs in the Ancient World*. Edited by Amar Annus. OIS 6. Chicago: Oriental Institute of the University of Chicago, 2010.

———. "Prophecy as Construct, Ancient and Modern." In *"Thus Speaks Ishtar of Arbela": Prophecy in Israel, Assyria and Egypt in the Neo-Assyrian Period*. Edited by Robert P. Gordon and Hans M. Barstad. Winona Lake, Ind.: Eisenbrauns, forthcoming.

———. "Prophetic Madness: Prophecy and Ecstasy in the Ancient Near East and in Greece." Pages 3–29 in *Raising Up a Faithful Exegete: Essays in Honor of Richard D. Nelson*. Edited by K. L. Noll and Brooks Schramm. Winona Lake, Ind.: Eisenbrauns, 2010.

———. *Prophets and Prophecy in the Ancient Near East*. With contributions by C. L. Seow and Robert K. Ritner. SBLWAW 12. Atlanta: Society of Biblical Literature, 2003.

———. "Prophets and the Divine Council." Pages 4–19 in *Kein Land für sich allein: Studien zum Kulturkontakt in Kanaan, Israel/Palästina und*

Ebirnâri für Manfred Weippert zum 65. Geburtstag. Edited by Ulrich Hübner and Ernst Axel Knauf. OBO 186. Fribourg: Universitätsverlag, 2002.

———. *References to Prophecy in Neo-Assyrian Sources*. SAAS 7. Helsinki: Neo-Assyrian Text Corpus Project, 1998.

———. "Song of Songs and Sacred Marriage." Pages 173-218 in *Sacred Marriages: The Divine-Human Sexual Metaphor from Sumer to Early Christianity*. Edited by Martti Nissinen and Risto Uro. Winona Lake, Ind.: Eisenbrauns, 2008.

———. "Transmitting Divine Mysteries: The Prophetic Role of Wisdom Teachers in the Dead Sea Scrolls." Pages 513-33 in *Scripture in Transition: Essays on Septuagint, Hebrew Bible, and Dead Sea Scrolls in Honour of Raija Sollamo*. Edited by Anssi Voitila and Jutta Jokiranta. JSJSup 126. Leiden: Brill, 2008.

———. "What Is Prophecy?" Pages 13-37 in *Inspired Speech: Prophecy in the Ancient Near East: Essays in Honour of Herbert B. Huffmon*. Edited by John Kaltner and Louis Stulman. JSOTSup 378. London: T&T Clark, 2004.

———. "Wisdom as Mediatrix in Sirach 24: Ben Sira, Love Lyrics, and Prophecy." Pages 377-90 in *Of God(s), Trees, Kings, and Scholars: Neo-Assyrian and Related Studies in Honour of Simo Parpola*. Edited by Mikko Luukko, Saana Svärd, and Raija Mattila. StudOr 106. Helsinki: Finnish Oriental Society, 2009.

Noth, Martin. *Numbers: A Commentary*. Translated by James D. Martin. OTL. Philadelphia: Westminster, 1968.

Numbers, Ronald L. *Prophetess of Health: A Study of Ellen G. White*. 2nd ed. Knoxville: University of Tennessee Press, 1992.

Nussbaum, Martha C. *Hiding from Humanity: Disgust, Shame, and the Law*. Princeton: Princeton University Press, 2004.

O'Connor, Kathleen M. "The Book of Jeremiah: Reconstructing Community after Disaster." Pages 81-92 in *Character Ethics and the Old Testament: Moral Dimensions of Scripture*. Edited by Mark Daniel Carroll R. and Jacqueline E. Lapsley. Louisville: Westminster John Knox, 2007.

———. *The Confessions of Jeremiah: Their Interpretation and Role in Chapters 1-25*. SBLDS 94. Atlanta: Scholars Press, 1988.

———. "The Feminist Movement Meets the Old Testament: One Woman's Perspective." Pages 3-24 in *Engaging the Bible in a Gendered World: An Introduction to Feminist Biblical Interpretation in Honor of Katharine*

Doob Sakenfeld. Edited by Linda Day and Carolyn Pressler. Louisville: Westminster John Knox, 2006.

———. *Lamentations and the Tears of the World*. Maryknoll, N.Y.: Orbis, 2002.

———. "Reclaiming Jeremiah's Violence." Pages 37–49 in *The Aesthetics of Violence in the Prophets*. Edited by Julia M. O'Brien and Chris Franke. LHBOTS 517. New York: T&T Clark, 2010.

———. "The Tears of God and Divine Character in Jeremiah 2–9." Pages 172–85 in *God in the Fray: A Tribute to Walter Brueggemann*. Edited by Tod Linafelt and Timothy K. Beal. Minneapolis: Fortress, 1998.

———. "Terror All Around: Confusion as Meaning-Making." Pages 67–79 in *Jeremiah (Dis)Placed: New Directions in Writing/Reading Jeremiah*. Edited by A. R. Pete Diamond and Louis Stulman. LHBOTS 529. New York: T&T Clark, 2011.

Odell, Margaret. "An Exploratory Study of Shame and Dependence in the Bible and Selected Near Eastern Parallels." Pages 217–29 in *The Biblical Canon in Comparative Perspective*. Vol. 4 of *Scripture in Context*. Edited by K. Lawson Younger Jr., William W. Hallo, and Bernard F. Batto. Ancient Near Eastern Texts and Studies 11. Lewiston, N.Y.: Mellen, 1991.

———. *Ezekiel*. SHBC. Macon, Ga.: Smyth & Helwys, 2005.

———. "Genre and Persona in Ezekiel 24:15–24." Pages 195–219 in *The Book of Ezekiel: Theological and Anthropological Perspectives*. Edited by Margaret S. Odell and John T. Strong. SBLSymS 9. Atlanta: Society of Biblical Literature, 2000.

Oesterheld, Christian. *Göttliche Botschaften für zweifelnde Menschen: Pragmatik und Orientierungsleistung der Apollon-Orakel von Klaros und Didyma in hellenistisch-römischer Zeit*. Hypomnemata 174. Göttingen: Vandenhoeck & Ruprecht, 2008.

O'Grady, Kathleen. "The Semantics of Taboo: Menstrual Prohibitions in the Hebrew Bible." Pages 1–28 in *Wholly Woman, Holy Blood: A Feminist Critique of Purity and Impurity*. Edited by Kristin De Troyer, Judith A. Herbert, Judith Anne Johnson, and Ann-Marie Korte. SAC. Harrisburg: Trinity Press International, 2003.

Olson, Dennis T. "Untying the Knot? Masculinity, Violence, and the Creation-Fall Story of Genesis 2–4." Pages 73–86 in *Engaging the Bible in a Gendered World: An Introduction to Feminist Biblical Interpretation in Honor of Katherine Doob Sakenfeld*. Edited by Linda Day and Carolyn Pressler. Louisville: Westminster John Knox, 2006.

Olyan, Saul M. *Biblical Mourning: Ritual and Social Dimensions.* Oxford: Oxford University Press, 2004.

———. "The Biblical Prohibition of the Mourning Rites of Shaving and Laceration: Several Proposals." Pages 181–89 in *"A Wise and Discerning Mind": Essays in Honor of Burke O. Long.* Edited by Saul M. Olyan and Robert C. Culley. BJS 325. Providence: Brown Judaic Studies, 2000.

———. "The Cultic Confessions of Jer 2,27a." *ZAW* 99 (1987): 254–59.

———. "Honor, Shame, and Covenant Relations in Ancient Israel and Its Environment." *JBL* 115 (1996): 201–18.

———. *Rites and Rank: Hierarchy in Biblical Representations of Cult.* Princeton: Princeton University Press, 2000.

———. "Some Observations Concerning the Identity of the Queen of Heaven." *UF* 19 (1987): 161–74.

———. "What Do Shaving Rites Accomplish and What Do They Signal in Biblical Ritual Contexts?" *JBL* 117 (1998): 611–22.

Osborne, Michael J. "Honours for Sthorys (*IG* ii^2. 17): *IG* ii^2. 17+; Wilhelm, *Attische Urkunden* v 87–96; Meritt, *Hesperia* xxvi (1957) 51–2." *Annual of the British School at Athens* 65 (1970): 151–74.

Overholt, Thomas W. *Cultural Anthropology and the Old Testament.* GBS. Minneapolis: Fortress, 1996.

Pakkala, Juha. *Intolerant Monolatry in the Deuteronomistic History.* Publications of the Finnish Exegetical Society 76. Göttingen: Vandenhoeck & Ruprecht, 1999.

Parke, Herbert W. *The Oracles of Apollo in Asia Minor.* London: Croom Helm, 1985.

———. *Sibyls and Sibylline Prophecy in Classical Antiquity.* Edited by Brian C. McGing. Croon Helm Classical Studies. London: Routledge, 1988.

Parker, Robert. "Greek States and Greek Oracles." Pages 76–108 in *Oxford Readings in Greek Religion.* Edited by Richard G. A. Buxton. Oxford: Oxford University Press, 2000.

———. *Polytheism and Society at Athens.* Oxford: Oxford University Press, 2005.

Parker, Robert, and Dirk Obbink. "Aus der Arbeit der Inscriptiones Graecae VI. Sales of Priesthoods on Cos I." *Chiron* 30 (2000): 415–49.

Parpola, Simo. *Assyrian Prophecies.* SAA 9. Helsinki: Helsinki University Press, 1997.

———. "Monotheism in Ancient Assyria." Pages 165–209 in *One God or Many? Concepts of Divinity in the Ancient World.* Edited by Barbara

Nevling Porter. Transactions of the Casco Bay Assyriological Institute 1. Chebeague, Me.: Casco Bay Assyriological Institute, 2000.

———, ed, *The Prosopography of the Neo-Assyrian Empire*. 3 vols. Helsinki: Neo-Assyrian Text Corpus Project, 1998–2011.

Parpola, Simo, and Kazuko Watanabe. *Neo-Assyrian Treaties and Loyalty Oaths*. SAA 2. Helsinki: Helsinki University Press, 1988.

Parry, Donald W., and Emanuel Tov, eds. *Dead Sea Scrolls Reader*. 6 vols. Leiden: Brill, 2004–2005.

Patton, Corrine L. "Layers of Meaning: Priesthood in Jeremiah MT." Pages 149–76 in *The Priests in the Prophets: The Portrayal of Priests, Prophets and Other Religious Specialists in the Latter Prophets*. Edited by Lester L. Grabbe and Alice Ogden Bellis. JSOTSup 408. Sheffield: Sheffield Academic Press, 2004.

———. "Priest, Prophet, and Exile: Ezekiel as a Literary Construct." Pages 73–89 in *Ezekiel's Hierarchical World: Wrestling with a Tiered Reality*. Edited by Stephen L. Cook and Corrine L. Patton. SBLSymS 31. Atlanta: Society of Biblical Literature, 2004.

———. "'Should Our Sister Be Treated Like a Whore?': A Response to Feminist Critiques of Ezekiel 23." Pages 221–38 in *The Book of Ezekiel: Theological and Anthropological Perspectives*. Edited by Margaret S. Odell and John T. Strong. SBLSymS 9. Atlanta: Society of Biblical Literature, 2000.

Patton, Corrine L. *See also* Carvalho, Corrine.

Pausanias. *Description of Greece*. Translated by W. H. W. Jones. 5 vols. LCL. London: Heinemann, 1918–1935.

Pede, Elena di. "Jérémie et les rois de Juda, Sédécias et Joaqim." VT 56 (2006): 452–69.

Perlitt, Lothar. "Mose als Prophet." EvT 31 (1971): 588–608. Reprint, pages 1–19 in *Deuteronomium-Studien*. FAT 2/8. Tübingen: Mohr Siebeck, 1994.

Perrot, Charles, and Pierre-Maurice Bogaert. *Introduction littéraire, commentaire et index*. Vol. 2 of *Les antiquités bibliques* by Pseudo-Philo. SC 230. Paris: Cerf, 1976.

Petterson, Christina. *The Missionary, the Catechist and the Hunter: Governmentality and Masculinites in Greenland*. Leiden: Brill, forthcoming.

Philip, Tarja S. *Menstruation and Childbirth in the Bible: Fertility and Impurity*. StBL 88. New York: Lang, 2005.

Plutarch. *Plutarch's Moralia*. Translated by Frank Cole Babbitt et al. 15 vols. LCL. Cambridge: Harvard University Press, 1927–1969.

Pohlmann, Karl-Friedrich. *Das Buch des Propheten Hesekiel (Ezechiel): Kapitel 20–48*. ATD 22.2. Göttingen: Vandenhoeck & Ruprecht, 2001.
Pongratz-Leisten, Beate. "Sacred Marriage and the Transfer of Divine Knowledge: Alliances between the Gods and the King in Ancient Mesopotamia." Pages 43–73 in *Sacred Marriages: The Divine-Human Sexual Metaphor from Sumer to Early Christianity*. Edited by Martti Nissinen and Risto Uro. Winona Lake, Ind.: Eisenbrauns, 2008.
———. "When Gods Are Speaking: Toward Defining the Interface between Polytheism and Monotheism." Pages 132–68 in *Prophetie in Mari, Assyrien und Israel*. Edited by Matthias Köckert and Martti Nissinen. FRLANT 201. Göttingen: Vandenhoeck & Ruprecht, 2003.
Porten, Bezalel, and Ada Yardeni. *Textbook of Aramaic Documents from Ancient Egypt*. 4 vols. Jerusalem: Hebrew University Department of the History of the Jewish People, 1993–1999.
Potter, Jack M. "Cantonese Shamanism." Pages 321–45 in *Studies in Chinese Society*. Edited by Arthur P. Wolf. Stanford: Stanford University Press, 1978.
Pritchard, James B., ed. *Ancient Near Eastern Texts Relating to the Old Testament*. 3rd ed. Princeton: Princeton University Press, 1969.
Puech, Émile. *Qumrân Grotte 4.XXII: Textes araméens, première partie: 4Q529–549*. DJD 31. Oxford: Clarendon, 2001.
Pyysiäinen, Ilkka. *Supernatural Agents: Why We Believe in Souls, Gods, and Buddhas*. Oxford: Oxford University Press, 2009.
Raitt, Thomas M. *A Theology of Exile: Judgment/Deliverance in Jeremiah and Ezekiel*. Philadelphia: Fortress, 1977.
Ramet, Sabrina Petra, ed. *Gender Reversals and Gender Cultures: Anthropological and Historical Perspectives*. London: Routledge, 1996.
Ranger, Terence O. *Revolt in Southern Rhodesia, 1896–97: A Study in African Resistance*. 1967. Repr., London: Heinemann, 1979.
Rapp, Ursula. *Mirjam: Eine feministisch-rhetorische Lektüre der Mirjamtexte in der hebraischen Bibel*. BZAW 317. Berlin: de Gruyter, 2002.
Reisman, Daniel. "Iddin-Dagan's Sacred Marriage Hymn." *JCS* 25 (1973): 185–202.
Renz, Thomas. *The Rhetorical Function of the Book of Ezekiel*. 1999. Repr., Boston: Brill, 2002.
Roberts, Alexander, and James Donaldson, eds. *Ante-Nicene Fathers*. 10 vols. 1885–1896. Repr., Peabody, Mass.: Hendrickson, 1994.
Robinson, Bernard P. "The Jealousy of Miriam: A Note on Num 12." *ZAW* 101 (1989): 428–32.

Römer, Thomas C. "L'école deutéronomiste et la formation de la Bible hébraïque." Pages 179–93 in *The Future of the Deuteronomistic History*. Edited by Thomas Römer. BETL 147. Leuven: Leuven University Press, 2000.

Römer, Willem H. Ph. *Sumerische 'Königshymnen' der Isin-Zeit*. DMOA 13. Leiden: Brill, 1965.

Runions, Erin. "From Disgust to Humor: Rahab's Queer Affect." Pages 45–74 in *Bible Trouble: Queer Reading at the Boundaries of Biblical Scholarship*. Edited by Teresa J. Hornsby and Ken Stone. SemeiaSt 67. Atlanta: Society of Biblical Literature, 2011.

———. "Violence and the Economy of Desire in Ezekiel 16:1–45." Pages 156–69 in *Prophets and Daniel*. Edited by Athalya Brenner. FCB 2/8. Sheffield: Sheffield Academic Press, 2001.

Rüpke, Jörg. "Controllers and Professionals: Analyzing Religious Specialists." *Numen* 43 (1996): 241–62.

Šašková, Katerina. "Esarhaddon's Accession to the Assyrian Throne." Pages 147–79 in *Shepherds of the Black-Headed People: The Royal Office vis-à-vis Godhead in Ancient Mesopotamia*. Edited by Kateřina Šašková, Lukáš Pecha, and Petra Charvát. Plzeň: Západočeská univerzita, 2010.

Sasson, Jack M., ed. *Civilizations of the Ancient Near East*. 4 vols. New York: Scribner, 1995.

Sawyer, Deborah F. "Gender-Play and Sacred Text: A Scene from Jeremiah." *JSOT* 83 (1999): 99–111.

Sawyer, John F. A. "A Note on the Etymology of ṣāraʿat." *VT* 26 (1976): 241–45.

Sax, Leonard. "How Common Is Intersex? A Response to Anne Fausto-Sterling." *Journal of Sex Research* 39 (2002): 174–78.

Schachter, Albert. "The Seer Tisamenos and the Klytiadai." *CQ* 50 (2000): 292–95.

Schaper, Joachim. "Exilic and Post-Exilic Prophecy and the Orality/Literacy Problem." *VT* 55 (2005): 324–42.

Schein, Seth L. "The Cassandra Scene in Aeschylus' Agamemnon." *Greece and Rome* 29 (1982): 11–16.

Schepelern, Wilhelm. *Der Montanismus und die phrygischen Kulte: Eine religionsgeschichtliche Untersuchung*. Tübingen: Mohr Siebeck, 1929.

Schiffman, Lawrence H., and James C. VanderKam, eds. *Encyclopedia of the Dead Sea Scrolls*. 2 vols. New York: Oxford University Press, 2000.

Schipper, Bernd U. *Die Erzählung des Wenamun: Ein Literaturwerk im*

Spannungsfeld von Politik, Geschichte und Religion. OBO 209. Fribourg: Academic Press, 2005.

Schorch, Stefan. "Die Propheten und der Karneval: Marzeach—Maioumas—Maimuna." *VT* 53 (2003): 397–415.

Schroeder, Otto. *Keilschrifttexte aus Assur verschiedenen Inhalts: Autographiert, mit Inhaltsübersicht und Namenliste versehen.* WVDOG 35. Ausgrabungen der Deutschen Orient-Gesellschaft in Assur. E, Inschriften 3. Leipzig: Hinrichs, 1920.

Schroer, Silvia. *Wisdom Has Built Her House: Studies on the Figure of Sophia in the Bible.* Translated by Linda M. Maloney and William McDonough. Collegeville, Minn.: Liturgical Press, 2000.

Schwartz, Baruch J. "Ezekiel's Dim View of Israel's Restoration." Pages 43–67 in *The Book of Ezekiel: Theological and Anthropological Perspectives.* Edited by Margaret S. Odell and John T. Strong. SBLSymS 9. Atlanta: Society of Biblical Literature, 2000.

Seebass, Horst. *Numeri.* BKAT 4.2. Neukirchen-Vluyn: Neukirchener, 2003.

Seim, Turid Karlsen. "Johannine Echoes in Early Montanism." Pages 345–64 in *The Legacy of John: Second-Century Reception of the Fourth Gospel.* Edited by Tuomas Rasimus. NovTSup 132. Leiden: Brill, 2010.

Selz, Gerbhard J. "Five Divine Ladies: Fragments to Inana(k), Ištar, In(n) in(a), Annunītum, and Anat, and the Origin of the Title 'Queen of Heaven.'" *Nin* 1 (2000): 29–62.

Sered, Susan Starr. *Priestess, Mother, Sacred Sister: Religions Dominated by Women.* Oxford: Oxford University Press, 1994.

Sharp, Carolyn J. *Prophecy and Ideology in Jeremiah: Struggles for Authority in the Deutero-Jeremianic Prose.* OTS. London: T&T Clark, 2003.

Sharp, Lesley A. *The Possessed and the Dispossessed: Spirits, Identity, and Power in a Madagascar Migrant Town.* Comparative Studies of Health Systems and Medical Care. Berkeley: University of California Press, 1993.

———. "The Power of Possession in Northwest Madagascar: Contesting Colonial and National Hegemonies." Pages 3–21 in *Spirit Possession: Modernity and Power in Africa.* Edited by Heike Behrend and Ute Luig. Oxford: James Currey, 1999.

Shields, Mary E. "Circumcision of the Prostitute: Gender, Sexuality, and the Call to Repentance in Jeremiah 3:1–4:4." *BibInt* 3 (1995): 61–74.

Siquans, Agnethe. *Die alttestamentlichen Prophetinnen in der patristischen Rezeption: Texte—Kontexte—Hermeneutik.* HBS 65. Freiburg: Herder, 2011.
Sissa, Giulia. *Greek Virginity.* Revealing Antiquity 3. Cambridge: Harvard University Press, 1990.
Sjöberg, Åke W. "A Hymn to Inanna and Her Self-Praise." *JCS* 40 (1988): 165–86.
———. "in-nin šà-gur₄-ra: A Hymn to the Goddess Inanna by the en-Priestess Enḫeduanna." *ZA* 65 (1975): 161–253.
Sladek, William R. "Inanna's Descent to the Nether World." Ph.D. diss. Johns Hopkins University, 1974.
Smith, Mark S. *The Laments of Jeremiah and Their Contexts: A Literary and Redactional Study of Jeremiah 11–20.* SBLMS 42. Atlanta: Scholars Press, 1990.
Sourvinou-Inwood, Christiane. "What Is Polis Religion?" Pages 13–37 in *Oxford Readings in Greek Religion.* Edited by Richard G. A. Buxton. Oxford: Oxford University Press, 2000.
Sperling, S. David. "Miriam, Aaron and Moses: Sibling Rivalry." *HUCA* 70–71 (1999–2000): 39–55.
Stein, Elissa, and Susan Kim. *Flow: The Cultural Story of Menstruation.* New York: St. Martin's Griffin, 2009.
Stiebert, Johanna. *The Construction of Shame in the Hebrew Bible: The Prophetic Contribution.* JSOTSup 346. Sheffield: Sheffield Academic Press, 2002.
Stipp, Hermann-Josef. "Zedekiah in the Book of Jeremiah: On the Formation of a Biblical Character." *CBQ* 58 (1996): 627–48.
Stökl, Jonathan. "Female Prophets in the Ancient Near East." Pages 47–61 in *Prophecy and the Prophets in Ancient Israel: Proceedings of the Oxford Old Testament Seminar.* Edited by John Day. LHBOTS 531. London: T&T Clark, 2010.
———. "Ištar's Women, YHWH's Men? A Curious Gender-Bias in Neo-Assyrian and Biblical Prophecy." *ZAW* 121 (2009): 87–100.
———. "The מתנבאות of Ezekiel 13 Reconsidered." *JBL* 132 (2013): forthcoming.
———. *Prophecy in the Ancient Near East: A Philological and Sociological Comparison.* CHANE 56. Leiden: Brill, 2012.
———. "The Role of Women in the Prophetical Process in Mari: A Critique of Mary Keller's Theory of Agency." Pages 173–88 in *Thinking towards New Horizons: Collected Communications to the XIXth Congress of*

the *International Organization for the Study of the Old Testament, Ljubljana 2007*. Edited by Matthias Augustin and Hermann Michael Niemann. BEATAJ 55. Frankfurt am Main: Lang, 2008.

Stone, Ken. "Gender and Homosexuality in Judges 19: Subject-Honor, Object-Shame?" *JSOT* 67 (1995): 87–107.

———. "Gender Criticism: The Un-Manning of Abimelech." Pages 183–201 in *Judges and Method: New Approaches in Biblical Studies*. Edited by Gale A. Yee. Minneapolis: Fortress, 2007.

———. "Homosexuality and the Bible or Queer Reading? A Response to Martti Nissinen." *Theology and Sexuality* 14 (2001): 107–18.

———. *Practicing Safer Texts: Food, Sex and Bible in Queer Perspective*. Queering Theology. London: T&T Clark, 2005.

———. "Queer Commentary and Biblical Interpretation: An Introduction." Pages 11–34 in *Queer Commentary and the Hebrew Bible*. Edited by Ken Stone. JSOTSup 334. Sheffield: Sheffield Academic Press, 2001.

———. "Queer Reading between Bible and Film: *Paris Is Burning* and the 'Legendary Houses' of David and Saul." Pages 75–98 in *Bible Trouble: Queer Reading at the Boundaries of Biblical Scholarship*. Edited by Teresa J. Hornsby and Ken Stone. SemeiaSt 67. Atlanta: Society of Biblical Literature, 2011.

———. *Sex, Honor, and Power in the Deuteronomistic History*. JSOTSup 234. Sheffield: Sheffield Academic Press, 1996.

Stott, Katie M. *Why Did They Write This Way? Reflections on References to Written Documents in the Hebrew Bible and Ancient Literature*. LHBOTS 492. London: T&T Clark, 2008.

Strawn, Brent A. "Jeremiah's In/Effective Plea: Another Look at נער in Jeremiah I 6." *VT* 55 (2005): 366–77.

Stulman, Louis. *Jeremiah*. Abingdon Old Testament Commentaries. Nashville: Abingdon, 2005.

———. "Jeremiah as a Polyphonic Response to Suffering." Pages 302–18 in *Inspired Speech: Prophecy in the Ancient Near East: Essays in Honor of Herbert B. Huffmon*. Edited by John Kaltner and Louis Stulman. JSOTSup 378. London: T&T Clark, 2004.

———. "Jeremiah the Prophet: Astride Two Worlds." Pages 41–56 in *Reading the Book of Jeremiah: A Search for Coherence*. Edited by Martin Kessler. Winona Lake, Ind.: Eisenbrauns, 2004.

———. *Order amid Chaos: Jeremiah as Symbolic Tapestry*. BiSe 57. Sheffield: Sheffield Academic Press, 1998.

Sugden, John. *Tecumseh: A Life of America's Greatest Indian Leader.* New York: Random House, 1997.
Svärd, Saana. *Women's Roles in the Neo-Assyrian Era: Female Agency in the Empire.* Saarbrücken: VDM, 2008.
———. See also Teppo, Saana.
Tabbernee, William. *Fake Prophecy and Polluted Sacraments: Ecclesiastical and Imperial Reactions to Montanism.* VCSup 84. Leiden: Brill, 2007.
———. *Montanist Inscriptions and Testimonia: Epigraphic Sources Illustrating the History of Montanism.* PMS 16. Macon, Ga.: Mercer University Press, 1997.
Taylor, Jonathan. "Babylonian Lists of Words and Signs." Pages 432–46 in *The Babylonian World.* Edited by Gwendolyn Leick. Routledge Worlds. New York: Routledge, 2007.
Teppo, Saana. "Agency and the Neo-Assyrian Women of the Palace." *StudOr* 101 (2007): 381–420.
———. "The Role and the Duties of the Neo-Assyrian *šakintu* in the Light of Archival Evidence." *SAAB* 16 (2007): 257–72.
———. "Sacred Marriage and the Devotees of Ištar." Pages 75–92 in *Sacred Marriages: The Divine-Human Sexual Metaphor from Sumer to Early Christianity.* Edited by Martti Nissinen and Risto Uro. Winona Lake, Ind.: Eisenbrauns, 2008.
———. See also Svärd, Saana.
Tervanotko, Hanna. "Miriam's Mistake: Numbers 12 Renarrated in Demetrius the Chronographer, 4Q377 (*Apocryphal Pentateuch b*), Legum allegoriae and the Pentateuchal Targumim." Pages 131–48 in *Embroidered Garments: Priests and Gender in Biblical Israel.* Edited by Deborah W. Rooke. HBM 25. King's College London Studies in the Bible and Gender 2. Sheffield: Sheffield Phoenix, 2009.
Thomas, Peter. *The Gramscian Moment: Philosophy, Hegemony and Marxism.* HM 24. Leiden: Brill, 2009.
Thomas, Samuel I. *The "Mysteries" of Qumran: Mystery, Secrecy, and Esotericism in the Dead Sea Scrolls.* SBLEJL 25. Atlanta: Society of Biblical Literature, 2009.
———. "'Riddled' with Guilt: The Mysteries of Transgression, Sealed Vision, and the Art of Interpretation in 4Q300 and Related Texts." *DSD* 15 (2008): 155–71.
Toorn, Karel van der. *From Her Cradle to Her Grave: The Role of Religion in the Life of the Israelite and the Babylonian Woman.* Translated by Sara J. Denning-Bolle. BiSe 23. Sheffield: JSOT Press, 1994.

———. "From the Mouth of the Prophet: The Literary Fixation of Jeremiah's Prophecies in the Ancient Near East." Pages 191–202 in *Inspired Speech: Prophecy in the Ancient Near East: Essays in Honor of Herbert B. Huffmon*. Edited by John Kaltner and Louis Stulman. JSOTSup 378. London: T&T Clark, 2004.

———. *Scribal Culture and the Making of the Hebrew Bible*. Cambridge: Harvard University Press, 2007.

Torjesen, Karen Jo. "Martyrs, Ascetics, and Gnostics: Gender-Crossing in Early Christianity." Pages 79–91 in *Gender Reversals and Gender Cultures: Anthropological and Historical Perspectives*. Edited by Sabrina Petra Ramet. London: Routledge, 1996.

Trevett, Christine. *Montanism: Gender, Authority and the New Prophecy*. Cambridge: Cambridge University Press, 1996.

Trible, Phyllis. "Bringing Miriam out of the Shadows." *BRev* 5 (1989): 14–25.

Tuell, Stephen S. *The Law of the Temple in Ezekiel 40–48*. HSM 49. Atlanta: Scholars Press, 1992.

———. "Should Ezekiel Go to Rehab? The Method to Ezekiel's 'Madness.'" *PRSt* 36 (2009): 289–302.

Ugolini, Gherhardo. *Untersuchungen zur Figur des Sehers Teiresias*. Classica Monacensia 12. Tübingen: Narr, 1995.

Ustinova, Yulia. *Caves and the Ancient Greek Mind: Descending Underground in the Search for Ultimate Truth*. Oxford: Oxford University Press, 2009.

VanderKam, James C. *An Introduction to Early Judaism*. Grand Rapids: Eerdmans, 2001.

Varughese, Alex. "The Royal Family in the Jeremiah Tradition." Pages 319–28 in *Inspired Speech: Prophecy in the Ancient Near East: Essays in Honor of Herbert B. Huffmon*. Edited by John Kaltner and Louis Stulman. JSOTSup 378. London: T&T Clark, 2004.

Veldhuis, Niek. "Continuity and Change in the Mesopotamian Lexical Tradition." Pages 101–18 in *Aspects of Genre and Type in Pre-Modern Literary Cultures*. Edited by Bert Roest and Herman L. J. Vanstiphout. COMERS/ICOG Communications 1. Groningen: Styx, 1999.

———. "How Did They Learn Cuneiform? 'Tribute/Word List C' as an Elementary Exercise." Pages 181–200 in *Approaches to Sumerian Literature in Honour of Stip (H. L. J. Vanstiphout)*. Edited by Piotr Michalowski and Niek Veldhuis. CM 35. Leiden: Brill, 2006.

Vieweger, Dieter. *Die literarischen Beziehungen zwischen den Büchern Jeremia und Ezechiel*. BEATAJ 26. Frankfurt: Lang, 1993.

Viviano, Pauline A. "Characterizing Jeremiah." *WW* 22 (2002): 361–68.
Washington, Harold C. "Violence and the Construction of Gender in the Hebrew Bible: A New Historicist Approach." *BibInt* 5 (1997): 324–63.
Wasserfall, Rahel. "Introduction: Menstrual Blood into Jewish Blood." Pages 1–18 in *Women and Water: Menstruation in Jewish Life and Law*. Edited by Rahel Wasserfall. Brandeis Series on Jewish Women. Hanover, N.H.: University Press of New England for Brandeis University Press, 1999.
Watson, Wilfred G. E. "Symmetry of Stanza in Jeremiah 2,2b–3." *JSOT* 19 (1981): 107–10.
Watts, John D. W. *Isaiah 1–33*. WBC. Waco, Tex.: Word, 1985.
———. "Two Studies in Isaiah." Pages 135–46 in *Biblical Studies in Honor of Simon John De Vries*. Vol. 1 of *God's Word for Our World*. Edited by J. Harold Ellens, Deborah L. Ellens, Rolf P. Knierim, and Isaac Kalimi. JSOTSup 388. London: T&T Clark, 2004.
Weinfeld, Moshe. *Deuteronomy and the Deuteronomic School*. Oxford: Clarendon, 1972.
Weippert, Manfred. " 'König, fürchte dich nicht!': Assyrische Prophetie im 7. Jahrhundert v. Chr." *Or* 71 (2002): 1–54.
Welch, J. L. "Cross-Dressing and Cross-Purposes: Gender Possibilities in the Acts of Thecla." Pages 66–78 in *Gender Reversals and Gender Cultures: Anthropological and Historical Perspectives*. Edited by Sabrina Petra Ramet. London: Routledge, 1996.
Wenham, Gordon. *The Book of Leviticus*. NICOT. Grand Rapids: Eerdmans, 1979.
West, Martin L. *Greek Epic Fragments: From the Seventh to the Fifth Centuries BC*. LCL. Cambridge: Harvard University Press, 2003.
Wiesemann, Claudia, Susanne Ude-Koeller, Gernot H. G. Sinnecker, and Ute Thyen. "Ethical Principles and Recommendations for the Medical Managements of Differences of Sex Development (DSD)/Intersex in Children and Adolescents." *European Journal of Pediatrics* 169 (2010): 671–79.
Wildberger, Hans. *Isaiah 1–12*. Translated by Thomas H. Trapp. CC. Minneapolis: Fortress, 1991.
———. *Jesaja 1–12*. BKAT 10.1. Neukirchen-Vluyn: Neukirchener, 1972.
Williams, Frank, trans. *The Panarion of Epiphanius of Salamis: Books II and III (Sects 47–80, De Fide)*. Nag Hammadi and Manichaean Studies 36. Leiden: Brill, 1994.

Williams, Walter L. *The Spirit and the Flesh: Sexual Diversity in American Indian Culture*. 2nd ed. Boston: Beacon, 1992.
Williamson, Hugh G. M. "Prophetesses in the Hebrew Bible." Pages 65–80 in *Prophets and Prophecy: Proceedings of the Oxford Old Testament Seminar*. Edited by John Day. LHBOTS 531. London: T&T Clark, 2010.
Wilson, Brian. "The Korean Shaman: Image and Reality." Pages 113–28 in *Korean Women: View from the Inner Room*. Edited by Laurel Kendall and Mark Peterson. New Haven: East Rock Press, 1983.
Wilson, Robert R. "Early Israelite Prophecy." *Int* 32 (1978): 3–16.
———. "Poetry and Prose in the Book of Jeremiah." Pages 413–27 in *Ki Baruch Hu: Ancient Near Eastern, Biblical, and Judaic Studies in Honor of Baruch A. Levine*. Edited by Robert Chazan, William W. Hallo, and Lawrence H. Schiffman. Winona Lake, Ind.: Eisenbrauns, 1999.
———. *Sociological Approaches to the Old Testament*. GBS. Philadelphia: Fortress, 1984.
Winslow, Karen Strand. "'For Moses Had Indeed Married a Cushite Woman': The LORD's Prophet Married Well." *lectio difficilior* 1/2011: 1–18. Online: http://www.lectio.unibe.ch/11_1/inhalt_e.htm.
Wright, Benjamin G. "Conflicted Boundaries: Ben Sira, Sage and Seer." Pages 229–53 in *Congress Volume Helsinki 2010*. Edited by Martti Nissinen. VTSup 148. Leiden: Brill, 2012.
Wright, David P. "The Spectrum of Priestly Impurity." Pages 150–81 in *Priesthood and Cult in Ancient Israel*. Edited by Gary A. Anderson and Saul M. Olyan. JSOTSup 125. Sheffield: JSOT Press, 1991.
Yates, Gary E. "Narrative Parallelism and the 'Jehoiakim Frame': A Reading Strategy for Jeremiah 26–45." *JETS* 48 (2005): 263–81.
Yee, Gale. *Poor Banished Children of Eve: Woman as Evil in the Hebrew Bible*. Minneapolis: Fortress, 2003.
Zeitlin, Froma I. "Cultic Models of the Female: Rites of Dionysios and Demeter." *Arethusa* 15 (1982): 129–57.
Zgoll, Annette. *Traum und Welterleben im antiken Mesopotamien: Traumtheorie und Traumpraxis im 3.–1. Jahrtausend v. Chr. als Horizont einer Kulturgeschichte des Träumens*. AOAT 333. Münster: Ugarit-Verlag, 2006.
Zimmerli, Walther. *Ezechiel 1, I. Teilband*. BKAT 13.1. Neukirchen-Vluyn: Neukirchener, 1979.
———. *Ezekiel 1: A Commentary on the Book of Ezekiel, Chapters 1–24*. Translated by Ronald E. Clements. Hermeneia. Philadelphia: Fortress, 1979.

———. *Ezekiel 2: A Commentary on the Book of Ezekiel, Chapters 25–48.* Translated by James D. Martin. Hermeneia. Philadelphia: Fortress, 1983.

Zimmermann, Ruben. "The Love Triangle of Lady Wisdom: Sacred Marriage in Jewish Wisdom Literature?" Pages 243–58 in *Sacred Marriages: The Divine-Human Sexual Metaphor from Sumer to Early Christianity.* Edited by Martti Nissinen and Risto Uro. Winona Lake, Ind.: Eisenbrauns, 2008.

Zipor, Moshe A. "'Scenes from a Marriage'—According to Jeremiah." *JSOT* 65 (1995): 83–91.

Žižek, Slavoj, ed. *Mapping Ideology.* London: Verso, 1994.

Zsolnay, Ilona. "Do Divine Structures of Gender Mirror Mortal Structures of Gender?" Pages 103–20 in *In the Wake of Tikva Frymer-Kensky.* Edited by Steven Holloway, Jo Ann Scurlock, and Richard Beal. Gorgias Précis Portfolios 4. Piscataway, N.J.; Gorgias, 2009.

———. "The Function of Ištar in the Assyrian Royal Inscriptions: A Contextual Analysis of the Actions Attributed to Ištar in the Inscriptions of Ititi through Šalmaneser III." Ph.D. diss. Brandeis University, 2009.

———. "Ištar, 'Goddess of War, Pacifier of Kings': An Analysis of Ištar's Martial Role in the Maledictory Sections of the Assyrian Royal Inscriptions." Pages 389–402 in *Language in the Ancient Near East.* Vol. 1 of *Proceedings of the 53e Rencontre Assyriologique Internationale.* Edited by Leonid Kogan, N. Koslova, S. Loesov, and S. Tishchenko. Orientalia et Classica 30/1. Babel und Bibel 4/1. Winona Lake, Ind.: Eisenbrauns, 2010.

CONTRIBUTORS

Roland Boer is Distinguished Professor of Liberal Arts at Remnin (People's) University of China, Beijing, and research professor at the University of Newcastle, Australia. His research passions are in Marxism, religion, and biblical economics and culture. His most recent books are *In the Vale of Tears* (Brill, 2013) and *Lenin, Religion, and Theology* (Palgrave Macmillan, 2013).

Corrine (Patton) Carvalho is a Professor at the University of St. Thomas in St. Paul, Minnesota. Research interests include exilic prophets, especially Ezekiel and Jeremiah. Her publications include *Encountering Ancient Voices: A Guide to Reading the Old Testament* (2nd ed., Anselm Academic, 2009), *The Book of Ezekiel: Question by Question* (Paulist, 2010), and *Ezekiel and Daniel*, co-authored with Paul Niskanen (New Collegeville Bible Commentary; Liturgical Press, 2012).

Lester L. Grabbe is Professor Emeritus in the Department of Religion and Theology at the University of Hull (England). He has a PhD from Claremont Graduate University and an earned DD from the University of Hull. Recent publications include *Ancient Israel: What Do We Know and How Do We Know It?*, *History of the Jews and Judaism in the Second Temple Period*: Volume 1—*Persian Period*; Volume 2—*Early Greek Period* (volumes 3 and 4 in preparation).

Anselm C. Hagedorn, MLitt (St. Andrews), M.A. (Notre Dame), DPhil, habil. (Berlin) is Privatdozent for Hebrew Bible/Old Testament at the Humboldt-Universität zu Berlin/Germany. His main areas of research are biblical and Greek legal history, Song of Songs, and the Minor Prophets. He is the author of *Between Moses and Plato: Individual and Society in Deuteronomy and Ancient Greek Law* (FRLANT 204; Göttingen, 2004) and

Die Anderen im Spiegel: Israels Auseinandersetzung mit den Völkern in den Büchern Nahum, Zefanja, Obadja und Joel (BZAW 414; Berlin, 2011).

Esther J. Hamori is an Associate Professor of Hebrew Bible at Union Theological Seminary in New York. Her book, *Women's Divination in Biblical Literature: Prophecy, Necromancy, and Other Arts of Knowledge*, is forthcoming from Yale University Press. She is also the author of *"When Gods Were Men": The Embodied God in Biblical and Near Eastern Literature* (BZAW 384; Berlin: de Gruyter, 2008). Hamori holds a PhD from New York University.

Dale Launderville (Ph.D., The Catholic University of America) is professor of theology at Saint John's University School of Theology/Seminary, Collegeville, Minnesota. He is the author of *Piety and Politics: The Dynamics of Royal Authority in Homeric Greece, Biblical Israel, and Old Babylonian Mesopotamia* (Eerdmans, 2003); *Spirit and Reason: The Embodied Character of Ezekiel's Symbolic Thinking* (Baylor University Press, 2007); and *Celibacy in the Ancient World: Its Ideal and Practice in Pre-Hellenistic Israel, Mesopotamia, and Greece* (Liturgical Press, 2010).

Antti Marjanen, Professor of Gnostic Studies at the University of Helsinki, earned his ThD from the University of Helsinki (1996). His main research interests are Gnosticism, Montanism, and early Christian women. His publications include *The Woman Jesus Loved: Mary Magdalene in the Nag Hammadi Library and Related Documents* (Brill, 1996), *A Companion to Second-Century Christian "Heretics"* (ed. with P. Luomanen; Brill, 2005), *Was There a Gnostic Religion?* (ed.; Vandenhoeck & Ruprecht, 2005).

Martti Nissinen, Doctor of Theology (University of Helsinki), is Professor of Old Testament Studies at the University of Helsinki. Research interests include history of religion in the ancient Eastern Mediterranean, especially prophecy and gender-related issues. His publications include *Prophets and Prophecy in the Ancient Near East* (Society of Biblical Literature, 2003); *References to Prophecy in Neo-Assyrian Sources* (Neo-Assyrian Text Corpus Project, 1998); and *Homoeroticism in the Biblical World* (Fortress, 1998).

Jonathan Stökl, DPhil (Oxford), is a postdoctoral researcher at Leiden University. His research interests include the religions of ancient Israel and Judah in their ancient Near Eastern contexts, especially prophecy and priestly religion, as well as Classical Hebrew and Northwest Semitic epigraphy. He recently published *Prophecy in the Ancient Near East: A Philological and Sociological Comparison* (Brill, 2012).

Hanna Tervanotko (PhD, University of Helsinki and University of Vienna) is a researcher at the Department of Biblical Studies of the University of Helsinki. She teaches at the Protestant Theological Faculty of Brussels. She is the author of *Denying Her Voice: The Figure of Miriam in Ancient Jewish Literature* (Journal of Ancient Judaism Supplement Series; Vandenhoeck & Ruprecht, forthcoming).

Index of Primary Sources

Hebrew Bible/Old Testament

Genesis
1:26–28	198
15:1	150 n. 8
15:4	150 n. 8
15:12	150
16:7–12	150
20:7	150 n. 8
25:23	150
26:24	150
28:12–15	150
28:16	150
37:7	150
37:9	150
38	163 n. 54
40:8	150
40:12–13	150
40:18–19	150
41:8	173
41:16	150
41:25–36	150

Exodus
1:21	170, 178
2	164
7:1	176 n. 8
15	170
15:20	11, 24, 30 n. 16, 139, 142, 170
15:20–21	147–48, 148 n. 2, 152 n. 13, 156
34:1	230
34:27	230

Leviticus
10:10	197
12:4–5	205
12–15	193, 199, 200
13–14	156
14:3–8	199
15	197, 198, 200, 202, 203, 205
15:2–15	198
15:13	198
15:14–15	198
15:16–18	198
15:17	199
15:18	198, 200
15:19	199
15:19–24	198
15:20–23	199
15:24	200
15:25–30	198
15:28	198
15:29–30	198
18–20	202
18:6–29	200
18:19	199, 200, 202
18:22	210
18:25–30	204
18:26	210
18:27	210
18:28–29	202
18:29	210
18:30	210
20:5	202
20:13	210
20:18	196, 199, 201, 202
20:22	202

Numbers		1 Samuel	
12	5, 148 n. 3, 149, 152–56, 165–67, 170, 171	5:12	174
		9:9	151
12:1	153, 155, 156 n. 27	10:5	148 n. 42
12:1–2	153, 154	12:11	156 n. 29
12:1–15	153–56, 153 n. 15	25:3	174
12:2	148, 153, 154, 165, 166, 167	25:32	156 n. 29
12:2–9	165 n. 61	28	25, 36
12:4–5	154	28:6	151
12:5	155	28:15	151
12:6–8	148, 153, 154, 154 n. 155, 165, 166, 167	2 Samuel	
12:6	154	2	245
12:10–15	154, 156, 156 n. 27, 167	3:16	245
12:13–14	154, 156 n. 27, 167	11:26	245
26:58–60	170	12:16	245
26:59	164	12:16–17	259
		12:21	245
Deuteronomy		12:21–22	245
12:31	210	14	173
12:32b-13:5	151	14:7	174
13:1–5	142	18:33	245
13:15	210	20	173
14:3	210	20:18	171
18	102 n. 5	20:19	174
18:9–20	102 n. 4	23:36	177
18:21–22	142		
34:10	155	1 Kings	
		4:5	177
Joshua		11	177 n.11
24:5	156 n. 29	11:41	228
		12:22	177
Judges		13	176
4–5	152 n. 13, 163 n. 54	14:19–20	228
4:4	24, 30 n. 16, 139, 142, 171	16:7	176
4:14	11	20	177
5:7	171, 174		
13:8	156 n. 29	2 Kings	
		22	44
Ruth		22:13–20	152 n. 13
4:16–17	170	22:14	11, 139, 142, 171
		22:14–20	30 n. 16, 44

INDEX OF PRIMARY SOURCES

1 Chronicles		11:5	221
5:29 [Eng. 6:3]	164, 170	19:11–12	173
25:1–8	176	30:8	230
25:5	176 n. 9	44:25	173
35:15	176 n. 9	64:10	244
2 Chronicles		Jeremiah	
9:29	177, 228	1	262, 262 n. 93
11:2	177	1–10	251, 257
12:5	177	1–20	262
12:15	177	1:6	257
15:1–8	177	1:11	257
15:12	177	1:13	257
16:7	176	2	247 n. 37
19:2	176	2–3	263
25:15–16	177	2:1–4:2	251
29:13–14	176 n. 9	2:2–4:2	238
29:30	176 n. 9	2:20	254
34:22	11	2:26–28	255
34:22–28	30 n. 16, 152 n. 13	3:1–10	254
36:19	244	3:9	255
		4	261–62 n. 89
Job		4:3–31	256 n. 74
31:9	261	4:8	256
		4:9–21	261–62 n. 89
Psalms		4:10	257
51:13	203	4:19–22	256
		4:31	254
Proverbs		5:7–8	254
4:5–8	55 n. 141	5:8	232
8:22–31	55, 56	6	262 n. 96, 263
8:35	55	6:2	254
18:22	55	6:23–26	254
		6:26	256
Song of Songs		7:18	254
5:16	244	8:11	254
		8:18–21	256
Isaiah		8:22–9:1 [Eng. 2]	256, 256 n. 74
4:3	230	9:6	254
8	24, 172	9:10–11	256
8:1	221, 230	9:16	254
8:3	11, 30 n. 16, 169, 175, 191	9:17–22	256, 258
10:1	230	10:17–25	256 n. 74

Jeremiah (cont.)

10:19–21	256	20:17	262
11	257	22:30	230
11–20	257	23:14	255
11:5	260	23:25–28	151
11:14	258	24:7	238
11:15	254	25:13	230
12:7	254	26	255 n. 65
13	263	26–45	265 n. 104
13:1–11	260	26–52	265
13:20–27	238, 255	26:20	176
13:27	254	27:9	151
14	258	28	176
14–15	258	29:31	176
14:7–9	258	30:2	230
14:9	258	30:6	155, 164
14:11	258	31	264
14:11–12	260	31:15–17	254
14:12	258	31:21–22	254
14:13–16	260	31:22	264
14:17	254	31:29	238
14:9–22	258	31:33	230
15:1	258	32:2–12	263
15:1–2	260	32:27	267
15:10	254	32:29	238
15:18	258	35:15	156 n. 29
15:19	260	36	6, 227, 229, 230
15:20	260	36–45	251, 265 n. 106
16:1	237	36:12	176
16:1–2	260	37:13	176
16:2	253	40:8	232 n. 34
16:3–4	254	41:4	255
16:5	260	42:1	232 n. 34
16:5–9	254	44	265, 265 n. 105
17:1	221, 230	44:15–19	254
17:13	230	46:11	254 n. 62
19:8–9	262	46:19	254 n. 62
20	6, 261, 262 nn. 90 and 93	46:24	254 n. 62
20:4–5	261	48:18	254 n. 62
20:7	261–62 n. 89	49:2	254 n. 62
20:9	137	49:3	254 n. 62
20:14–18	254	49:4	254 n. 62
20:15	262	50:37	255
		50:42	254 n. 62

51:30	255	16:36	207
51:33	254 n. 62	16:37–41	208
		16:39–41	193
Lamentations		16:41	208 n. 64
1:10	244	16:44–45	211
1:17	196 n.10	16:52	211
		16:63	211
Ezekiel		18:2	238
2	6	18:21–32	208, 209
2–3	232, 233 n. 36	19:17–23	242
2:8–3:3	233	20:1	196
2:9	233	20:7	210
2:10	233, 234	20:7–39	210
3:3	234	20:8	210, 211
3:16–21	207	20:13	211
7:19–20	196, 196 n. 10	20:16	211
8	222	20:19–20	203
8–11	247, 249	20:21	211
8:6	210	20:24	211
8:9	210	20:30	210
8:13	210	20:30–31	203
8:14	242	20:31	203
8:15	210	20:42–44	211
8:17	210, 233	22–23	220
9	6, 219, 220, 221–23, 226, 227, 229, 233	22:6–12	204
		22:10	202
9:1	222	22:10–11	203
9:2	222	22:15	202
9:2–3	219	22:17–22	204
9:11	219	22:26	197, 204
11:16	202, 204	23	6, 194, 231, 238, 242, 247, 248
11:19	238	23–24	247 n. 37
13	25, 36, 175, 242, 242 n. 21	23:6	247
13:17–23	169	23:8	193
14:12–20	177 n. 13	23:12	231, 247
14:13–23	175	23:20	193, 231, 232
16	6, 194, 207, 211, 220, 238, 242, 247, 248	23:23	247
		23:37	175
16:9	207	23:43–48	203
16:15–53	207	23:45	194, 207
16:20–21	175	23:45–47	247
16:25	193	23:48	194, 207, 208 n. 64
16:35–43	208, 209	24	242 n. 20, 243, 246–49

324 PROPHETS MALE AND FEMALE

Ezekiel (cont.)		Joel	
24:2	230	2:28	139
24:15–27	238 n. 4, 243	2:28–29	152 n. 14
24:16	237	3:1	169
24:18	243, 244	3:1–2	175
24:19–23	243	4:5	244
24:21	244, 246, 248		
24:23	247	Micah	
33:1–9	207	6:4	156
33:30–33	196		
36	194	Zechariah	
36:16–20	202	10:2	151
36:16	203		
36:16–38	203	Malachi	
36:17	6, 193, 195, 207	3:23	156 n. 29
36:17–18	200, 202		
36:18	203	**DEUTEROCANONICAL WORKS**	
36:22–23	203		
36:23	204	Wisdom of Solomon	
36:24–25	204	6:12–25	55
36:25–31	211	7:7–14	55
36:26–27	203, 211	8:2–21	55
36:28	204	8:3–4	55
36:31	211	8:4	55 n. 140
36:32	203	9:4	55
37:16	233		
43:11	230	Ben Sira	
44	242 n. 21	4:14	55
44:23	201	4:17–18 [Heb.]	55
45:18–24	201	24	27
46:3	201	24:2	56–7
46:9	201	24:13–22	57
		24:23	57
Daniel		24:33	57
2	173	50:27	122
2:19	160	51:13–30	55
2:48	160 n. 45		
4	173	**PSEUDEPIGRAPHA**	
5	173, 231		
8:14	21	1 Enoch	
		93:3	123 n. 72
Hosea			
9:6	244		

INDEX OF PRIMARY SOURCES

Aramaic Levi	
4	160
11	160
11:5–6	160
11:6	160
12:4	160

Sibylline Oracles	
3:4–6	120
3:162–164	120 n. 62
3:194–195	125
3:297–299	120 n. 62
3:490–491	120 n. 62
3:582	119 n. 57
3:781	119 n. 57
3:809–812	122
3:813–818	123
3:818	119 n. 57
3:823–827	121
4:14	120 n. 62
5:52	120 n. 62
5:111	120 n. 62
5:286	120 n. 62

Testament of Levi	
2:6–12	160 n. 46
8	160 n. 46

Dead Sea Scrolls

1Q20 (Genesis Apocryphon)	159 n. 41

1Q20 (Genesis Apocryphon)	
V, 20	159
V, 20–21	159
V, 25	159
VI, 12	159

4Q76 (Twelve Prophets)	102 n. 5
4Q174 (4QFlorilegium)	160 n. 45

4Q185	
2:8–15	55 n. 141

4Q201 (1 Enoch)	
1 IV, 5	159 n. 41

4Q203 (1 Enoch)	
9 3	159 n. 41

4Q204 (1 Enoch)	
5 II, 26	159 n. 41

4Q213 (Aramaic Levi)	
1 I 5	160

4Q491 (War Scroll)	56

4Q534 (Elect of God)	
1 I 7–8	159 n. 41

4Q536 (Elect of God)	
2i + 3 9, 12	159 n. 41

4Q543–549 (Visions of Amram[a-g])	157
4Q543 (Visions of Amram[a])	157
4Q544 (Visions of Amram[b])	157

4Q544 (Visions of Amram[b])	
I, 1	158
I, 5	164
I, 7	164
I, 8	164
I, 10–11	160

4Q545 (Visions of Amram[c])	
3 2–4	160
4 15–16	160
4 16	159 n. 41

4Q546 (Visions of Amram^d)	149, 161 n. 51	1 Corinthians	
9 2	160	7:15	135 n.27
12	161 n.51	11:1–16	139
2 4	159 n. 41, 161 n. 50	14:36	138–39
12 6	158	Revelation	
14 5	160	1:4	135 n. 25
		1:11	135 n. 25
4Q547 (Visions of Amram^e)	157	1:20	135 n. 25
		2:20	139
4Q547 (Visions of Amram^e)		11:19	21
9 8	160		

West-Semitic

4Q548 (Visions of Amram^f) 158 n. 38	
	Amman Citadel Inscription 47
4Q549 (Visions of Amram^g) 158 n. 38	
	Deir 'Allā 28, 29
4QInstruction 159	
	Lachish
4QMysteries 159	Ostracon 3 29, 29, 30, 31, 47
	Ostracon 16 29, 30, 31, 47
11QPs^a	
XXI 11–17 55	*TAD* C 1.1:79 (Ahiqar) 56

New Testament

	KTU 1.23: 30–39 226–227
Matthew	UC 51354 29
2:1–2 173 n. 7	
	Zakkur Stele 29, 30, 47
Luke	
2:36 139	### Rabbinic Literature
John	b. Megillah
16:12–13 127, 140, 142	14a 152 n. 13, 165 n. 60
Acts	b. Soṭah
2:17–18 139	12b–13a 165 n. 60
10:10 142	
21:9 142	Exodus Mekhilta de Rabbi Shimon
21:10 139	ben Yoḥa 165 n. 60
Galatians	
3:28 134	

INDEX OF PRIMARY SOURCES

Jewish Authors

Josephus, *Antiquitates Iudaicae*
10.263-281   160 n. 45

Philo, *De ebrietate*
30-36   55

Philo, *Quis rerum divinarum heres sit*
263-265   142 n. 42

Pseudo-Philo, *Liber antiquitatum biblicarum*
4:6   160 n. 45
4:8   160 n. 45
9:5   162-163 n. 54, 164
9:9   164
9:10   162-164
9:12   164
20:8   162
30-33   162-163 n. 54

Cuneiform Texts

A.2484 7'   73-74 n. 39

A.3796   28, 30, 31, 47

A.4676   28, 30, 31, 47

AD 3 -132 B: rev.25-u.e.5   28, 31, 47

Agušaya   93

Angim   89
  Angim III 32 = 140   90 n. 36

AO. 7439+ r. 25'   70 n. 28

ARM
9 22   28
21 333   28, 30, 31, 47
22 167   28, 30, 31, 47
22 326   28, 30, 31, 47
23 446   28, 30, 31, 47
25 15   28, 30, 31, 47
25 142   29, 30, 31, 47
26 194   29, 30, 31, 47, 49
26 195   28, 29, 30, 31, 47, 49
26 197   29, 30, 30, 31, 41, 47, 49, 69, 72
26 198   29, 30, 45, 47, 69, 72
26 199   28, 29, 30, 31, 41, 47, 49
26 200   28, 30, 31, 45, 47
26 201   29, 45
26 202   29, 30, 31, 47
26 203   29, 41, 45
26 204   28, 29, 45
26 205   30, 47
26 206   29, 30, 31, 47
26 207   29, 95 n. 57
26 208   28, 30, 31, 47, 49
26 209   29, 30, 31, 47, 49
26 210   29, 30, 31, 39, 47, 82
26 211   30, 47, 49
26 212   29, 30, 47, 49, 69, 72, 95
26 213   29, 30, 45, 47, 69, 72, 95
26 214   28, 30, 31, 45, 47, 82, 95
26 214: 7-18   96
26 215   29, 30, 31, 45, 47, 49
26 216   29, 45
26 217   29, 45
26 219   29, 30, 31, 45, 47, 49
26 220   29, 30, 31, 47, 49
26 221   29, 30, 31, 47, 49
26 221bis   29
26 222   28, 95 n. 57
26 223   29, 30, 31, 47
26 226   41 n. 87
26 227   28
26 229   28
26 232   28, 30, 31, 41, 47
26 233   29, 30, 31, 47, 49
26 234   29, 30, 31, 45, 47
26 235   29
26 236   28, 30, 31, 47

ARM (cont.)
26 237   29, 30, 31, 41, 45, 47
26 238   28, 30, 31, 47
26 239   28, 41
26 240   28, 30, 31, 47
26 243   29, 30, 47
26 371   29, 30, 31, 47, 49
26 414   28, 30, 31, 47
27 32   29, 30, 47

Ass A i 31–ii 26   29

BM 41005 obv. col iii 16–17   93

CT
    24 41: 84 [An=Anum]   94 n. 52
    39 45: 32   70 n. 30

Death of Ur-Namma: see ETCSL 2.4.1.1

The Debate between Ewe and Grain: see ETCSL 5.3.2

El Amarna 23   47

Enmerkar and the Lord of Aratta: see ETCSL 1.8.2.3

Epic of Tukulti-Ninurta
    col iii 40–53   93

Epic of Zimri-Lim   29

Erra iv 55–56   70

Erimhuš III 172ff.   86 n. 21

ETCSL
    1.3.1 (Inana and Enki): segment I,
        16–27   91–92
    1.3.2 (Inana and Ebih)   88–91
    1.4.3 (Inana's Descent to the Underworld)   91–92, 179
    1.8.1.2 (Gilgamesh and the Bull of Heaven): rev. I 94   89
    1.8.2.3 (Enermrkar and the lord of Aratta)   93
    2.1.7 (The Building of Ningirsu's Temple – Gudea Cylinders A and B)   87, 89
    2.4.1.1 (The Death of Ur-Namma / Ur-Namma A)   87, 89 n. 32
    2.4.1.3 (A Praise Poem of Ur-Namma / Ur Namma C)   87
    2.4.2.01 (Self-Praise of Šulgi / Šulgi A)   92 n. 45
    2.4.2.05 (Praise for Šulgi / Šulgi E)   92
    2.4.2.16 (Praise of Šulgi / Šulgi P)   89 n. 32
    2.5.3.1 (Inana and Iddin-Dagan / Iddin-Dagan A)   88–91
    5.3.2 (The Debate between Ewe and Grain)   87, 88, 90, 93

Farber 1977 A II a: 1–33   29, 30, 47

FLP
    1674   47
    1674: 1–8   53
    2064   47

FM
    3 2   29, 30, 47
    3 3   29, 30, 47
    3 152   29, 30, 47
    6 1   29, 30, 31, 47
    6 45   28
    7 38   28, 30, 31, 45, 47, 49
    7 39   29, 30, 31, 47, 49

Gilgamesh and the Bull of Heaven: see ETCSL 1.8.1.2

Gudea Cylinder AB: see ETCSL 2.1.7

INDEX OF PRIMARY SOURCES

ḪAR-gud B 133	70
Iddin-Dagan A: *see* ETCSL 2.5.3.1	
Inana and Ebiḫ: *see* ETCSL 1.3.2	
Inana and Enki: *see* ETCSL 1.3.1	
Inana's Descent to the Underworld: *see* ETCSL 1.4.3	
Innin-šagura	89 n. 30
Ištar's Decent into the Underworld	71, 84
K.3438a+9912	69 n. 26
KAV 121 5	73
M.11436	28, 30, 31, 47
Malku=šarru	
134–135	86 n. 21
135	70 n. 30
MDP	
22 73: 23	75 n. 45
22 230: 10	75 n. 45
24 353: 30	75 n. 45
24 382: 29	75 n. 45
28 414: rev. 2ff.	75 n. 45
MSL	
12 6.22: 133	70 n. 29
Nin A i 1–ii 11	29, 30, 47
OECT 1 20–21	29, 41
Prism A (Assurbanipal)	
ii 126–iii 26	30, 47, 49, 51
Prism B (Assurbanipal)	
v 16–vi 16	30, 47, 49, 51, 52
v 44	50 n. 107
Prism T (Assurbanipal)	
ii 7–24	29, 30, 47, 49
RIME	
1 4.6	95
2 1.4	95
3 1.1.7.StB: IV 1–16	87
4 3.7.7: 36b–42	96
4 3.7.7: 71–75	97
4 34.1.1: 16–18	97
4 34.1.1: 19–20	97
SAA	
2 6 455	90
3 3 10	52 n. 124
3 3 13, rev. 14	50
3 13	54 n. 136
3 13 rev. 6–8	52
4 321	36 n. 53
4 322	36 n. 53
7 9	28
7 24 rev. 2	38 n. 59
7 145 7	73–74 n. 39
9 1	61, 73, 76
9 1.1	29, 30, 42, 47, 49, 51, 76
9 1.1 i 28–29	42, 47
9 1.2	28, 30, 31, 47, 49, 51
9 1.3	28, 30, 31, 47, 51
9 1.4	29, 30, 47, 47, 49, 51, 75–76
9 1.4 ii 40'	42, 75
9 1.5	29, 30, 47
9 1.5 iii 5–6	42, 73
9 1.5 iii 15–18	50 n. 116
9 1.6	30, 47, 49, 52
9 1.6 iv 2, 21	50 n. 112
9 1.7	28, 30, 31, 41, 49
9 1.8	28, 30, 31, 47, 49, 51
9 1.9	30, 30, 47
9 1.10	28, 30, 31, 47, 49, 51

SAA (cont.)		STT 406 rev. 10	75
9 2.1	28, 30, 31, 47		
9 2.2	29, 30, 49, 51, 75–76	Šulgi P: *see* ETCSL 2.4.2.16	
9 2.3	28, 30, 31, 47, 49		
9 2.4	28, 30, 31, 47, 49, 51	T.82 ix: 2–4	28, 30, 31, 47
9 2.5	28, 30, 31, 49, 52		
9 2.5 iii 26–27	50 n. 114	TCL 15 12: *see* ETCSL 2.4.1.3	
9 2.6	30, 47, 51		
9 3.1	30, 47	TCS 1 369	29, 31, 41, 47
9 3.2	30, 47, 49		
9 3.3	30, 47, 49	Ugaritica 5 162: 2–12	29
9 3.4	30, 47		
9 3.5	28, 30, 31, 47, 49, 51	Ur-Namma C 84: *see* ETCSL 2.4.1.3	
9 5	30, 47		
9 6	28, 30, 31, 47, 51	Uru-Amirabi	88, 90, 91
9 7	28, 30, 31, 47, 49, 52		
9 7 rev. 6	50 n. 113	VAT 1339 = VAS 2 29	88
9 7 rev. 7–10	50 n. 116		
9 8	28	VS 19 1: i 37'–39'	29, 41, 47
9 9	28, 30, 31, 47, 49, 51, 54		
9 9 5, rev. 2	50 n. 111	**Hittite/Luwian**	
9 10	28, 30, 31		
10 109	29	Tell Ahmar 6 §§21–23	30 n. 22
10 111	30, 47, 49		
10 284	30, 47, 49	**Egyptian**	
10 294	29		
10 352	29	Wenamon	29, 30, 31, 47
12 10 7'	73–74 n. 39		
12 13 9'	73–74 n. 39	**Greek and Latin Texts**	
12 40 13'	73–74 n. 39		
12 69	29, 41	Aelius Aristides, *In Defense of*	
13 37	28, 49	*Oratory*	34–35
13 139	30, 47		
13 140	51–52	Aeschylus, *Agamemnon*	
13 141	51–52	810	109
13 144	29, 30, 31, 47, 49, 51	950ff.	109
13 148	29, 30, 31, 41, 47	1072	109
16 59	29, 30, 31, 39, 47, 49	1072–1340	34
19 17 8	73–74 n. 39	1073	109
19 49 74	73–74 n. 39	1084	110 n. 33
		1098	110 n. 33
SBH 65 13	75 n. 45	1099	110 n. 33
		1140	110 n. 33

INDEX OF PRIMARY SOURCES

1161	110 n. 33	Cyprian, *Epistula*	
1195	110 n. 33	75.10	132
1200–1212	181		
1202–1214	110	Cyril of Jerusalem, *Cathecheses illuminandorum*	
1203	34		
1209	110 n. 33	16.8	128 n. 3
1210	110 n. 33		
1212	110	Didymos, *De Trinitate*	
1213	110 n. 33	3.41	127–28 n. 2, 131, 138 n. 33
1215	110 n. 33		
1241	110 n. 33	Diodorus Siculus, *Bibliotheca historica*	
1264–1276	111	4.66.6	34, 115–116
1275	110 n. 33		
1295	110 n. 33	Ephoros, *FGH* 70 F 119	32

Eumenides

Epiphanius, *Panarion* (*Adversus haereses*)

1–10	116		
614–619	34	48.1.3	129
		48.2.1–2	129
Alcaeus		48.2.4	131
fr. S262	113	48.2.6	142
fr. 298.20	107 n. 24	38.3.1	142
		48.3.11–4.2	142
Anticlides		48.7.3	142
FGH 140, fr. 17	34 n. 44, 108	48.9.7	136 n. 29
		48.10.3–11.10	130
Apollodoros: see Pseudo-Apollodorus		48.11.1	131 n. 13
		48.11.5–8	127 n. 2
Aristides, *In Defence of Oratory*		48.13.1	136
34–35	45 n. 88	48.14.1–2	133–134
		49.1.1–3.4	133
Aristophanes, *Birds*		49.1.3	133
521.988	103 n. 8	49.2.2	134
		49.2.3–4	135
Aristophanes, *Peace*		49.2.5	134
1095, 1116	122	51.33.8–9	139

Basil of Caesarea, *Epistula*

Epigonoi, fr. 3 = Scholium ad Apollonius Rhod. 1.308b

188	127 n. 2		117

Clement of Alexandria, *Stromata*

Epiphanius of Salamis, *Panarion* 133, 139

1.21.108   121 n. 63

Euripides, *Alcmaeon in Corinth*	
fr. 73a	117–118 n. 52
Euripides, *Bacchae*	
32–36	105
298–301	103
Euripides, *Hecuba*	
676–677	111 n. 37
Euripides, *Melanippe Desmotis*	
fr. 494	34, 104–105
Euripides, *Phoenissae*	
834–835	115
Euripides, *Trojan Women*	
41–44	111, 112
69–70	112
Euripides, *Trojan Women* (cont.)	
253	112 n. 39
Eusebius, *Dialogue of a Montanist and an Orthodox*	130 n. 10
Eusebius, *Historia ecclesiastica*	
5.1.9–10	127 n. 2
5.3.4	133
5.14	127–128 n. 2
5.15.5	141
5.16.3	133
5.16.7	130
5.16.9	129
5.16.13	129
5.16.16	130, 131
5.16.17	133
5.17.1–14	141
5.17.3–4	138
5.18.2	129, 133
5.18.3	129, 130, 135, 136
5.18.3–4	135
5.18.4	134 n. 21
5.18.5	133
5.18.13	130
5.19.3	130, 131
6.20.3	130 n. 10, 133
Eusebius, *Life of Constantine*	
3.66	130 n. 10
Herodotus, *Historiae*	
1.46	33 n. 40
1.62–63	33–34 n. 41
1.92	33 n. 40
1.141	33 n. 40
1.157	33 n. 40
2.55	33 n. 39
2.159	33 n. 40
4.67	41
5.36	33 n. 40
6.19	33 n. 40
Heraclitus, fr. B92 DK	120
Hippolytus, *Refutatio omnium haeresium* (*Philosophoumena*)	
8.19	129
8.19.1	127 n. 2, 129 n. 7, 130
8.19.2	143
Homer, *Hymn to Apollo*	
1.40	118 n. 55
Homer, *Hymn to Artemis* (9)	
5	118 n. 55
Homer, *Iliad*	
1.72	119
3.121	107
3.124	106
6.252	106
7.44–53	33 n. 41
13.173	107
13.363–368	107
16.234	33 n. 38

INDEX OF PRIMARY SOURCES

19.282	107
24.697–701	107
24.697–706	108
24.699	108

Homer, *Odyssey*

10.490–495	115
10.494–495	33–34 n. 41
11.150–151	33–34 n. 41
17.160–161	33–34 n. 41
20.350–357	33–34 n. 41

Iamblichus, *De mysteriis*

3.11	33

Ibycus, fr. 303 (a)   107 n. 24

Irenaeus, *Adversus haereses*

3.11.9	127 n. 2

Jerome, *Epistula*

41.3	136 n. 29
41.4	127 n. 2, 138 n. 33

Lactantius, *Epitome*

68.1	119 n. 58

Martyrdom of Saints Perpetua and Felicitas   140 n. 38

Michael the Syrian, *Chronicle* 130 n. 10

Origen, *Fragmenta ex commentariis in epistulam i ad Corinthios*

1 Cor. 14:36	138, 141

Origen, *Fragmenta ex commentariis in epistulam ii ad Corinthios*

2 Cor 5:12	142

Origen, *De principiis*

2.7.3	127 n. 2

Ovid, *Metamorphoses*

3.316–350	114 n. 46
14.131–146	120–121

Pausanias, *Graeciae descriptio*

1.34	48 n. 95
1.40.6	48 n. 98
3.19.6	114
10.12.1	121
10.33	48 n. 95

Pherecydes of Athens

FGH 3, fr. 92	114–115 n. 46

Photius, *Bibliotheca*

239.321b–322a	32 n. 34

Pindar, *Paean*

8a (fr. 52i [A] M)

Pindar, *Pythionikai*

11.33	34 n. 44, 108

Plato, *Phaedrus*

244b	122

Pliny, *Naturalis historia*

2.232	33 n. 37
10.137	109 n. 29
28.147	48

Plutarch, *Agis et Cleomenes*

9.2	114 n. 44

Plutarch, *Moralia*

434c	48 n. 95
397a	120 n. 61

Plutarch, *Pericles*

6.2	103 n. 8

Pseudo-Apollodoros, *Epitome*

3.7.7	117–118 n. 5

Pseudo-Apollodoros, Epitome (cont.)
6.2–6   117–118
6.4   118

Pseudo-Dionysius of Tell Mahrē, *Zuqnin Chronicle*   127–128 n. 2

Pseudo-Hesiod
fr. 275 W-M   114 n. 46
fr. 276 W-M   114 n. 46

Pseudo-Tertullian, *Adversus omnes haereses*
7   127 n. 2

Sophocles, *Antigone*
998–1014   33–34 n. 41
1087   115 n. 48

Sophocles, *Odysseus Akanthlopes*
456   33 n. 39

Sophocles, *Oedipus tyrannus*
297–299   33–34 n. 41
300–304   33–34 n. 41
444   115 n. 48

Sophocles, *Trachiniae*
1164–72   33 n. 39

Strabo, *Geography*
7.7.12   33
8.6.22   48
9.2.4   32
14.1.27   118 n. 55

Tacitus, *Annales*
2.54   33

Tertullian, *Adversus Marcionem*
1.29   136 n. 29
4.22.5   142 n. 42
5.8   132, 139, 140

Tertullian, *Adversus Praxean*
1   127 n. 2, 132

Tertullian, *De anima*
9.4   131–132
45.3   142 n. 42

Tertullian, *De culta feminarum*
2.12   132

Tertullian, *De fuga in persecutione*
9   136

Tertullian, *De jejunio adversus psychicos*
1   127 n. 2, 129, 132

Tertullian, *De monogamia*
1   136 n. 29
2   127 n. 2
3   127 n. 2
14   136 n. 29
15   136 n. 29

Tertullian, *De praescriptione haereticorum*
41   132

Tertullian, *De pudicitia*
1   136 n. 29
21   127 n. 2

Tertullian, *De resurrectione carnis*
11   127 n. 2

Tertullian, *De virginibus velandis*
1   127 n. 2, 140–141
9   132

Thucydides, *History*
3.33   118 n. 55

Greek Epigraphy

IG i^2 76:47–48	103 n. 8
IG ii^2.17	103 n. 7
IGR IV 1540	122
SEG 26.524	48 n. 95
SEG 35.626	31 n. 28, 124 n. 74

Index of Modern Authors

Abrahami, Philippe 74 n. 41
Ackerman, Susan 30 n. 16, 147 n. 1, 171, 172
Acosta-Hughes, Benjamin 131 n. 29
Aland, Kurt 130 n. 9,
Albright, William Foxwell 154 n. 20
Alexander, Philip 157 n. 31
Allen, Leslie C. 208 n. 64, 209 n. 70
Al-Rawi, Farouk N. H. 89 n. 33
Alsop, Rachel 63 n. 10
Althusser, Louis 218
Anderson, Gary A. 199 n. 29, 244 n. 28
Ansom, John 182 n. 22
Asher-Greve, Julia M. 36 n. 52, 67 n. 22, 67–68 n. 22, 75 n. 44
Ashley, Timothy R. 156 n. 28
Assante, Julia 42 n. 75, 70 n. 31, 72 n. 36, 84–85, n. 12
Bach, Alice 231
Bacigalupo, Ana Mariella 189
Bahrani, Zainab 43 n. 83, 50 n. 109, 61 n. 4.
Balzer, Marjorie Mandelstam 184 n. 31, 185 n. 32
Barrett, Michèle 216 n. 1
Batto, Bernard F. 40 n. 65
Bauer/Bauer-Levesque, Angela 250 n. 48, 251–52 n. 52, 253 n. 60, 256 n. 73, 257 n. 77, 261, 262 n. 94, 264 nn. 101, 103
Baumann, Gerlinde 238 n. 6, 242 n. 20, 250–51 n. 48, 256 n. 73
Baumbach, Manuel 131 n. 29
Becking, Bob 264 n. 101

Beentjes, Pancratius C. 55 n. 142
Behr, Charles Allison 106 n. 18
Behrend, Heike 12 n. 3, 14 n. 4
Bellis, Alice Ogden 264 n. 101
Bergman, Jan 149 n. 5
Bergmann, Claudia 255 n. 66
Berquist, Jon L. 207 n. 62
Beuken, Willem A. 221 n. 16
Beyer, Klaus 161 n. 51
Biddle, Mark E. 253 n. 58, 256 n. 72, 257 n. 78
Bird, Phyllis A. 70 n. 31
Black, Jeremy 179 n. 14
Blenkinsopp, Joseph 81 n. 2, 240 n. 11
Block, Daniel I. 200 n. 34, 203 nn. 44, 46, 210 n. 74, 240 n. 11, 242–43 n. 21
Boadt, Lawrence E. 237–38 n. 3
Böck, Barbara 84 n. 9
Bodi, Daniel 203 n. 43
Boer, Roland 1, 2, 5, 6, 217 n. 7, 227 n. 25, 229 n. 27, 239 n. 7, 242 n. 17
Bogaert, Pierre-Maurice 162 nn. 52 and 54
Böhl, F. M. Th. de Liagre 90 n. 40
Borger, Rykle 51 n. 123
Botterweck, Johannes 149 n. 5
Bowden, Hugh 32 n. 32, 106 n. 19
Bowen, Nancy R. 36 n. 54, 242 n. 18
Brenner, Athalya 148 n. 3, 152 n. 13, 249 n. 46, 250 n. 48, 252–253 n. 56
Bright, John 232 n. 34
Brinkman, J. A. 67–68 n. 22, 74
Brisson, Luc 41 n. 74, 114 n. 46
Bronner, Leila Leah 173 n. 6

INDEX OF MODERN AUTHORS

Brown, John Pairman 184 n. 30
Brown-Gutoff, Susan E. 254 n. 63
Brueggeman, Walter 264 n. 100
Budin, Stephanie Lynn 70 n. 31
Buitenwerf, Rieuwerd 34 n. 46
Bullough, Vern L. 181 n. 21
Bullough, Bonnie 181 n. 21
Burkert, Walter 38
Burns, John Barclay 67 n. 19
Burns, Rita 147 n. 1, 148 n. 2, 152 n. 13, 153 nn. 15, 17, 154 nn. 18, 20, 165 n. 61
Busine, Aude 33 n. 37
Butler, Judith 62, 65 n. 15, 185 n. 33, 217
Butler, Sally A. L. 149 nn. 5, 6, 177 n. 12
Cagni, Luigi 70 n. 28
Calame, Claude 112 n. 40
Callaway, Mary Chilton 257 n. 78, 258 n. 79
Camp, Claudia V. 171
Carroll, Robert P. 230 n. 29, 232 n. 34, 250–51 n. 48, 266
Carvalho, Corrine 3, 6, 27, 229 n. 28, 242 n. 19
Cathcart, Kevin J. 102 n. 5
Cavigneaux, Antoine 89 n. 33
Chapman, Cynthia R. 240, 255 n. 69
Chau, P.-L. 63 n. 11
Chawla, Janet 188 n. 47
Childs, Brevard 221 n. 16
Civil, Miguel 70 n. 29, 86 n. 19
Clines, David J. A. 78 n. 54, 239 n. 7, 262 n. 92
Coats, George W. 153 n. 15, 154 n. 21
Cohn, Leopold 162 n. 52
Collins, John J. 120 n. 62, 121 n. 65, 122 n. 70, 123 nn. 71, 73, 159 n. 42
Connell, Raewyn W. 216 n. 4, 217 n. 5
Connelly, Joan Breton 104, 113 n. 42
Cook, Edward 161 n. 48
Cook, Lesley A. 206 n. 58

Cook, Stephen L. 244–45 n. 28
Cooke, George A. 219 n. 11, 220 n. 13, 233 n. 36
Cooper, Jerrold S. 90 n. 36
Crawford, Sidnie White 55 n. 141, 147 n. 1
Creangă, Ovidiu 239 n. 7
Cross, Frank Moore 154 n. 20
Cunningham, Graham 179 n. 14
Curtis, Adrian H. W. 262 n. 96
Czaplicka, Marie Antoinett 184
Dalley, Stephanie 40 n. 65
Darr, Katheryn Pfisterer 240 n. 11, 244 n. 25, 249 n. 45
Davies, Philip 230 n. 30
Day, John 203 n. 44
Derrida, Jacques 224
Destro, Adriana 197 n. 19, 205 nn. 55, 57, 206 n. 61
Diamond, A. R. Pete 250 n. 48, 251 n. 49
Diamond, Milton 64 n. 14
Dieterle, Martina 32 n. 35
Dijk-Hemmes, Fokkelien van 194, 205 n. 54, 231 n. 33, 256 n. 73
Dillery, John 103 n. 8, 106 n. 19
Dillmann, August 153 n. 15
Dillon, Matthew 104 n. 12, 105 n. 15
Dimant, Devorah 157 n. 33
Donaldson, James 141 n. 39
Dörrfuss, Ernst Michael 260 n. 84
Drawnel, Henryk 158 n. 35, 161 n. 49
Dreger, Alice Domurat 64 n. 13
Drucker, Peter 65 n. 15
Dubbink, Joep 253 n. 58, 259 n. 80
Duguid, Iain M. 242–43 n. 21
Duke, Robert R. 157 n. 33, 158 n. 38, 161 n. 51
Dunbabin, T. J. 48 n. 96
Dupré, Louis 216 n. 1
Eagleton, Terry 216 n. 2
Edwardes, Allen 231 n. 33, 232 n. 34, 234

Edzard, Dietz Otto 76
Eichrodt, Walther 219 n. 11, 233 n. 36, 240 n. 11
Eidinow, Esther 32 n. 35
Eilberg-Schwartz, Howard 277 n. 24, 247 n. 37
Ellis, Maria deJong 54 n. 133, 82 n. 2
Erbele-Küster, Dorothea 264 n. 101
Eshel, Esther 158 n. 37
Everhart, Janet S. 253 n. 59
Exum, J. Cheryl 195, 206 n. 59, 250 n. 48
Falkenstein, Adam 85
Farber-Flügge, Gertrud 85 n. 17
Fausto-Sterling, Anne 64 n. 14
Feld, Gerburgis 201 n. 36
Feldman, Louis H. 162 n. 52
Finkelstein, Jacob J. 75 n. 43
Fischer, Georg 263 n. 98
Fischer, Irmtraud 30 n. 16, 44 n. 85, 147 n. 1, 148 n. 3, 154 n. 22, 155 n. 23, 156 n. 28
Fisk, Bruce Norman 162 n. 52
Fitzsimons, Annette 63 n. 10
Flannery-Dailey, Frances 152 n. 11, 163 n. 56
Flower, Michael Attyah 31 n. 27, 31–32 n. 30, 32 n. 32, 40 n. 68, 101 n. 1, 104 nn. 13 and 14, 110 n. 34, 114 n. 45, 118 n. 54, 119 n. 57, 176 n. 10, 180 n. 17
Flückiger-Hawker, Esther 87 n. 23
Fokkelman, J. P. 173 . 6
Fonrobert, Charlotte Elisheva 197 n. 19, 199 n. 25, 200 n. 30, 205 n. 56, 206 n. 58
Fontana, Benedetto 217 n. 7
Fontenrose, Joseph 32 nn. 32 and 33, 34 n. 42
Freeman, James M. 188
Frend, W. H. C. 138 n. 33
Fretheim, Terence E. 240 n. 10, 259 n. 80, 261 nn. 86, 87, 264 n. 102, 267

Friebel, Kelvin G. 237–38 n. 3, 240 n. 10, 244 n. 24, 245 n. 31, 246 n. 34, 257 n. 76, 260 n. 84
Fuchs, Esther 242 n. 18
Gabbay, Uri 42 n. 75, 60 n. 3, 91 n. 43
Gafney, Wilda 30 n. 16, 62 n. 7, 148 n. 3, 152 nn. 13, 14, 154 n. 22
Galambush, Julie 201 n. 36, 207 n. 63, 208 n. 66, 209 n. 69, 241, 244 n. 25
García Martínez, Florentino 157 n. 31, 161 n. 48
Gelb, Ignace J. 94 n. 55
Genette, Gérard 157 n. 31
George, Andrew R. 51 n. 122
Gesche, Petra D. 38 n. 60
Giles, Linda L. 15–16
Gladd, Benjamin L. 160 n. 45
Gödecken, Karin 94 n. 54
Goldingay, John 239 n. 7
Goldman, Liora 158 nn. 36, 38
Gordon, Robert P. 102 n. 5
Grabbe, Lester L. 1, 2, 3, 4, 5, 7, 12 n. 2, 35 n. 50, 59, 60, 183 n. 26
Gramsci, Antonio 217, 218
Gray, George Buchanan 153 n. 15
Grayson, A. Kirk 81–82 n. 2
Greenberg, Moshe 193 n. 1, 202 n. 42, 203 n. 44, 204 n. 49, 209 n. 69, 213 n. 86, 219 n. 11, 220 n. 13, 233 n. 36, 238 n. 4, 240 n. 11, 244 n. 26
Greenfield, Jonas C. 158 n. 37
Greenstein, Edward L. 261 n. 88
Groneberg, Brigitte 50 n. 108, 84 n. 9, 93 n. 48
Gross, Rita M. 190 n. 53
Gruber, Mayer I. 70 n. 31
Guest, Deryn 252 n. 56, 262 n. 90
Gurney, O. R. 75 n. 43
Haddox, Susan E. 239 n. 7
Hadley, Judith M. 265 n. 105
Hagedorn, Anselm C. 2, 3, 31 n. 26, 34, 101 n. 1, 102 n. 5, 123–24 n. 73
Hall, Donald E. 67 n. 20

INDEX OF MODERN AUTHORS

Halperin, David J. 231 n. 33, 233 n. 36
Halpern-Amaru, Betsy 162 n. 54, 164 n. 57
Hals, Ronald M. 240 n. 11
Hämeen-Anttila, Jaakko 73–74 n. 39, 74
Hamilton, Gordon J. 29 n. 13
Hamori, Esther J. 1, 2, 5, 6, 11 n. 1, 27, 30 n. 16, 36 n. 54, 45, 169 n. 1, 173 n. 5, 180 n. 15, 237 n. 2
Hard, Robin 118 n. 53
Harrington, Daniel J. 162 n. 53
Harris, Edward Monroe 102 n. 3, 103 n. 6, 114 n. 45
Harvey, Youngsook Kim 185 n. 33, 186 n. 34
Hawkins, J. David 30–31 n. 22
Hayes, Jarrod 67 n. 20
Heacock, Anthony 43 n. 81, 252–53 n. 56
Heimpel, Wolfgang 88 n. 28
Heine, Ronald E. 127 n. 2, 129 n. 4, 130 n. 9, 131 n. 13
Heinisch, Paul 153 n. 15
Henshaw, Richard A. 69 n. 24, 84 n. 8, 94 n. 52
Herdt, Gilbert 64–65 n. 14, 65 n. 15
Herring, Jonathan 63 n. 11
Higonnet, Margaret R. 67 n. 20
Hoffman, Yair 267 n. 109
Holladay, William L. 232 n. 34, 240 n. 10
Holt, Else K. 256 n. 72, 260 n. 83
Hooper, Charlotte 216 n. 4, 217 n. 5
Hornsby, Teresa 43 n. 81, 231 n. 32, 249 n. 46, 252 nn. 55, 56, 253 n. 57, 262 n. 91
Horst, Pieter W. van der 160 n. 47, 162 n. 54
Hovi, Tuija 37 n. 57
Huehnergard, John 73 n. 39
Huffmon, Herbert B. 71 n. 32, 72, 77, 82 n. 3, 148 n. 4, 251 n. 50

Humes, Cynthia Ann 188, 189 n. 48
Husser, Jean-Marie 150 n. 7
Ilan, Tal 44 n. 86, 152 n. 13, 162 n. 53
Jacobson, Howard 162 n. 52, 162–63 n. 54, 163 n. 55
Jagose, Annamarie 43 n. 81
James, M. R. 162 n. 52
Jameson, Fredric 216 nn. 2, 3
Jeffers, Ann 173 n. 7
Jensen, Anne 130, 132–33 n. 17
Jepsen, Alfred 24 n. 21, 172 n. 4
Job, John Brian 254 n. 64
Johnson, Douglas H. 19 n. 13, 23 n. 20
Johnston, Sarah Iles 32 nn. 32, 35, 38 n. 58, 40 n. 68, 180 nn. 16, 18, 181
Joosten, Jan 202 n. 40
Jost, Renate 242 n. 18
Joyce, Paul M. 202 n. 38, 240 n. 11, 242–43 n. 21, 248 nn. 39, 40, 249 nn. 44, 45
Kaiser, Barbara B. 257 n. 77
Kaiser, Otto 123–24 n. 73
Kalmanofsky, Amy 255 n. 66, 262 n. 96
Kamionkowski, S. Tamar 193 n. 2, 208 nn. 66, 67, 209 n. 69, 247 n. 38, 248 n. 42, 249 n. 46
Kazen, Thomas 199 n. 27, 209 nn. 70–72, 210 n. 75
Keefe, Alice 194–95 n. 5
Keller, Mary 17 n. 10, 39 n. 62, 44 n. 84, 182–83 n. 25, 183 n. 26, 183–84 n. 29, 190 n. 53
Kendall, Laurel 183 n. 27, 185 n. 33, 186
Kennedy, George A. 204 n. 51
Kerns, Virginia 190 n. 53
Kessler, Martin 251 n. 51, 253 n. 58
Kessler, Rainer 147 n. 1, 156 nn. 28, 30
Kessler, Suzanne J. 63 n. 10, 64 n. 13
Kilmer, Anne Draffkorn 70 n. 30
Kim, Susan 212 n. 83

Kipnis, Kenneth 64 n. 14
Kisch, Guido 162 n. 52
Knierim, Rolf P. 153 n. 15
Köckert, Matthias 81–82 n. 2, 102 n. 4
Konkel, Michael 242–43 n. 21
Korsmeyer, Carolyn 210 n. 77
Korte, Alexander 64–65 n. 14
Korte, Anne-Marie 197 nn. 16 and 20, 201 n. 36, 206 n. 61
Kosmetatou, Elizabeth 131 n. 29
Kovacs, David 103 n. 10, 112 n. 38, 112 n. 41
Kowalzig, Barbara 32 n. 35, 33 n. 39
Kramer, Samuel N. 85 n. 14
Kron, Uta 103 n. 9
Kruger, Paul 264 n. 101
Kselman, John S. 154 n. 20
Kugler, Robert 158 n. 36
Labriolle, Pierre de 128 n. 2, 129 n. 4, 130 n. 10, 131 n. 13, 138 n. 33, 139 nn. 34 and 35 and 37, 141 n. 41, 142 n. 42, 143 n. 43
Lackenbacher, Sylvie 70 n. 28
Lambert, Wilfred G. 81–82 n. 2, 85, 85 n. 15, 93–94 n. 51, 94 n. 55, 176 n. 10
Lan, David 17 n. 10, 190 n. 53
Land, Gary 20 n. 16
Lange, Armin 33, 33 n. 41, 41 n. 74, 101 n. 1, 124 n. 75, 157 n. 31
Lapinkivi, Pirjo 53 n. 129, 263 n. 99
Lapsley, Jacqueline E. 194–95 n. 5, 195–96 n. 8, 208 n. 65, 211 nn. 79–81, 213 n. 86, 246 n. 35, 248 nn. 39 and 41, 259 n. 80
Larrain, Jorge 216 n. 1
Launderville, Dale 2, 3, 200 n. 33, 203 n. 48, 207 n. 62, 213 n. 86, 239–40 n. 9, 246 n. 33, 247 n. 36, 260 n. 82
Lee, Nancy C. 256 nn. 72 and 74
Leene, Hendrik 264 n. 101, 237–38 n. 3
Lefkovitz, Lori Hope 239 n. 7
Leichty, Erle 51 n. 123
Leming, Laura M. 37, 37 n. 55
Lemos, T. M. 239 n. 7, 241 n. 14, 255 n. 67
Lennon, Kathleen 63 n. 10
Lenzi, Alan 53 n. 131, 54 n. 134, 56, 56 n. 144
Levenson, Jon D. 242–43 n. 21
Levine, Baruch A. 153 nn. 15 and 17, 154 n. 21, 155 n. 24, 156 nn. 27–28, 197, 197 nn. 14–15, 199 n. 27
Lévi-Strauss, Claude 223–26, 223 n. 17, 224 n. 20
Lev-Ran, Arye 64 n 14
Lewis, I. M. 16, 16 n. 9, 23 n. 5, 77 n. 51, 137 n. 31, 190, 190 n. 54
Lightfoot, J. L. 123 n. 72, 123–24 n. 73
Linssen, Marc J. H. 70 n. 28
Lion, Brigitte 38 n. 59
Lipton, Diana 150 n. 8, 238 n. 4, 245 n. 31
Loader, William 164 n. 57
Lundbom, Jack R. 240 n. 10
Lust, Johan 243 n. 22
Macwilliam, Stuart 239 n. 7, 247 n. 37, 252 n. 54
Maier, Christl M. 160 n. 84, 250–51 n. 48, 260 n. 84, 263 n. 97
Malamat, Abraham 40 n. 65
Marjanen, Antti 2, 3, 127 n.1, 133 n. 19, 143 n. 42
Marsman, Hennie J. 149 n. 6
Maul, Stefan M. 70 n. 31, 71 n. 32, 84 n. 9, 85 n. 17, 176 n. 10
Maurizio, Lisa 32 n. 32
Mayfield, Tyler D. 240 n. 11
McCaffrey, Kathleen 59, 61 n. 4, 64 nn. 13–14, 14, 66, 66 nn. 16–17, 67 n. 21
McGinn, Sheila E. 130 n. 9
McKane, William 232 n. 34, 265 n. 105
McLaughlin, John L. 260 n. 84

INDEX OF MODERN AUTHORS 341

Meacham, Tirzah 206 n. 58
Meier, Samuel A. 38 n. 59
Melville, Sarah C. 40 nn. 64 and 66, 52, 52 nn. 126 and 127
Menadier, Blanche 48 n. 96
Menninghaus, Winfried 196 n. 11
Menzel, Brigitte 51 n. 122
Merkel, Helmut 120 n. 60
Merkelbach, Reinhold 33 n. 37
Meyers, Carol L. 148 n. 2, 183–84 n. 29, 206 n. 60
Milgrom, Jacob 153 n. 16, 154 n. 18, 156 n. 28, 196 nn. 10 and 12, 198, 198 nn. 22–24, 199 n. 26, 200 nn. 31 and 33, 201 n. 37, 202 nn. 40 and 42, 204 n. 50, 205 n. 52
Miller, Andrew M. 113 n. 43
Miller, Jay 18 nn. 11 and 12
Miller, William Ian 21, 209 n. 71, 212 n. 84
Mills, Mary E. 253 n. 59, 259 n. 81
Milne, Pamela 194 n. 5
Möbius, Hans 31 n. 30
Mooney, James 18 n. 11
Moore, Stephen D. 252 n. 55
Morgan, Catherine 32 nn. 32 and 33, 33 n. 40
Morgan, Janett 103–4 n. 11
Murphy, Frederick J. 162 n. 52, 162–63 n. 54
Murray, A. T. 107 nn. 21, 22
Murray, Stephen O. 77 nn. 51 and 52
Musurillo, Herbert 140 n. 38
Nadeau, Randall L. 186–87, 186 n. 36, 187 nn. 40–41
Nasrallah, Laura 129 n. 5, 142–43 n. 42
Neblung, Dagmar 111 n. 36
Nelson, James B. 203 n. 45
Nguyen, Hien Thi 185 n. 33, 186
Nicholson, Sarah 173 n. 6
Nickelsburg, George W. E. 123 n. 72
Niessen, Christina 255 n. 68

Nihan, Christophe 155 n. 26
Nissinen, Martti 2–5, 28 nn. 2–3, 32 n. 31, 36 n. 51, 39 n. 63, 40 n. 67, 42 n. 75, 46 n. 89, 51 n. 118, 52 n. 126, 53 nn. 129 and 131, 56 n. 146, 57 n. 148, 59*, 69 n. 23, 73 n. 38, 73–74 n. 39, 75 n. 42, 76 nn. 46–47, 78 n. 54, 81 n. 1, 81–82 nn. 2–3, 84 n. 10, 95 n. 58, 101 n. 1, 104 n. 14, 147*, 148 n. 2, 148 n. 4, 149 n. 6, 151 n. 10, 159 n. 39, 252 nn. 54–55, 263 n. 99
Noth, Martin 153 n. 15, 154 n. 19, 155 n. 26, 156 n. 28
Numbers, Ronald L. 20 n. 16, 21 n. 17
Nussbaum, Martha C. 200 n. 30, 205 n. 54, 208 n. 68, 210 n. 73 and 76, 212 nn. 83–84, 213 n. 85
Obbink, Dirk 103 n. 9
O'Connor, Kathleen M. 250, 250 n. 48, 259 n. 80, 267
Odell, Margaret 211 n. 80, 243 n. 23, 244 n. 27, 245 n. 29, 246 n. 34
Oesterheld, Christian 32 n. 33, 33 n. 37, 118 n. 56
O'Grady, Kathleen 197 n. 18, 210 n. 77
Oldfather, C. H. 116 n. 49
Olson, Dennis T. 239 n. 7
Olyan, Saul M. 206 n. 60, 242 n. 16, 244–45 n. 28, 246 n. 32, 255 n. 70, 260 n. 85, 265 n. 105
Osborne, Michael J. 103 n. 7
Ottoson, Magnus 149 n. 5
Overholt, Thomas W. 183 n. 28
Pakkala, Juha 151 n. 10
Parke, Herbert W. 34 n. 46, 118 nn. 54 and 56, 122 n. 69
Parker, Robert 103 n. 9, 104 n. 14, 124 n. 74
Parpola, Simo 42 n. 80, 50 n. 110, 51 n. 117, 52, 52 n. 125, 73, 73 nn. 38–39, 75 n. 43, 76, 76 n. 47, 77, 77 n. 49, 81–82 n. 2, 84, 84 n. 11, 90 n. 39, 149 n. 6

Patton, Corrine L.   241–42 n. 15, 242 n. 17, 253 n. 58
Pede, Elena di   254 n. 64
Perlitt, Lothar   155 n. 26
Perrot, Charles   162 nn. 52 and 54
Petterson, Christina   223, 225–26, 225 n. 22
Philip, Tarja S.   196 nn. 9 and 12, 197 nn. 19–20, 198 nn. 21–22, 200 nn. 30 and 32 and 35, 202 nn. 39 and 41, 205 n. 55, 206 n. 58, 212 n. 83
Pillinger, Renate   157 n. 31
Pohlmann, Karl-Friedrich   240 n. 11
Pongratz-Leisten, Beate   52, 52–53 n. 128, 53 n. 129–30, 56 n. 143, 263 n. 99
Porten, Bezalel   56 n. 145
Potter, Jack M.   187, 187 n. 40
Pritchard, James B.   234 n. 37
Puech, Émile   157, 157 n. 32, 158, 159 n. 43, 160 n. 47, 161 nn. 50–51
Pyysiäinen, Ilkka   46 n. 90
Raitt, Thomas M.   237 n. 3
Ramet, Sabrina Petra   181 n. 21
Ranger, Terence O.   17 n. 10
Rapp, Ursula   147 n. 1, 153 n. 15, 154 n. 22, 155 n. 23, 156 n. 28
Reisman, Daniel   89 n. 30, 91. 41
Renz, Thomas   244 n. 27
Ringgren, Helmer   149 n. 5
Robinson, Bernard P.   153 n. 15
Robson, Eleanor   179 n. 14
Römer, Thomas C.   155 n. 26, 156 nn. 27–28
Römer, Willem H. Ph.   89 n. 30
Runions, Erin   231 n. 33, 262 n. 91
Rupke, Jorg   101 nn. 1–2
Šašková, Katerina   40 n. 66
Sawyer, Deborah F.   264 nn. 101 and 103
Sawyer, John F. A.   154 n. 18
Sax, Leonard   64 n. 14
Schachter, Albert   114 n. 45
Schaper, Joachim   266–67 n. 109
Schein, Seth L.   34 n. 44
Schepelern, Wilhelm   137 n. 32
Schipper, Bernd U.   29 n. 15
Schorch Stefan   260–61 n. 85
Schroeder, Otto   73 n. 38
Schroer, Silvia   55 n. 137
Schwartz, Baruch J.   249 n. 45
Seebass, Horst   153 n. 15
Seim, Turid Karlsen   127 n. 2
Selz, Gerbhard J.   94 n. 55
Sered, Susan Starr   182–83 n. 25
Sharp, Carolyn J.   151 n. 10
Sharp, Lesley A.   14 n. 4
Shields, Mary E.   250 n. 48
Sinnecker, Gernot H. G.   63–64 n. 12
Siquans, Agnethe   147 n. 1
Sissa, Giulia   40 n. 68
Sjöberg, Åke W.   85 n. 14, 90 n. 38
Sladek, William R.   91 n. 42
Smith, Barry   210 n. 77
Smith, Mark S.   257 n. 78
Sourvinou-Inwood, Christiane   101 n. 2
Spurlin. William J.   67 n. 20
Stauber, Josef   33 n. 37
Stein, Elissa   212 n. 83
Stiebert, Johanna   266 n. 108
Stipp, Hermann-Josef   254 n. 64
Stökl, Jonathan   3–4, 8, 24 n. 21, 27*, 31 n. 23, 36 n. 54, 39 n. 62, 42 n. 79, 44 n. 85, 47 n. 91, 61 n. 5, 71 n. 34, 73 n. 37, 81*, 81 n. 1, 82 n. 4, 149 n. 6, 226 n. 23, 252 n. 53
Stone, Ken   43 n. 81, 239 nn. 7–8, 246 n. 32, 252 nn. 53–54, 253, 253 nn. 57, 262 n. 90–91
Stone, Michael E.   158 n. 37
Stott, Katie M.   228 n. 26
Strawn, Brent A.   257 n. 75, 262 n. 93
Stulman, Louis   240 n. 10, 251 nn. 50–51, 253 n. 58, 259 n. 80, 260 n. 82, 261 n. 87, 262 nn. 93–94, 265 n. 106

Sugden, John 18 n.11
Svärd, Saana 41 n. 72, 27*, 36 n. 53, 40 nn. 64 and 66
Tabbernee, William 128 n. 2, 129 n. 4, 130 n. 10, 131 n. 13, 131–32 n. 14, 134 nn. 20 and 22, 135 n. 25, 136, 136 n. 28, 141 n. 40
Taylor, Jonathan 86 n. 19
Teppo, Saana 39–40 n. 64, 42 n. 75, 43 n. 82, 59, 59 n. 1, 60 n. 3, 61 n. 6, 77, 77 n. 50
Tervanotko, Hanna 2, 5, 153 n. 16, 158 n. 38
Thomas, Peter 217 n. 7
Thomas, Samuel I. 159 nn. 40 and 42 and 44
Thyen, Ute 63–64 n. 12
Tigchelaar, Eibert J.C. 157 n. 31, 161 n. 48
Toorn, Karel van der 38 n. 60, 196 n. 9, 199 n. 27, 200 n. 33, 266–67 n. 109
Torjesen, Karen Jo 182, 182 n. 24
Tov, Emanuel 157 n. 31
Trevett, Christine 127 nn. 1–2, 131 n. 12, 132 n. 15
Trible, Phyllis 147 n. 1
Tuell, Stephen S. 242–43 n. 21, 246 n. 34
Ude-Koeller, Susanne 63–64 n. 12
Ugolini, Gherhardo 41 n. 74, 114 n. 46
Ustinova, Yulia 48 n. 97
VanderKam, James C. 120 n. 59
Varughese, Alex 254 n. 64
Veldhuis, Niek 86 nn. 19–20
Vieweger, Dieter 237 n. 3
Viviano, Pauline A. 253 n. 58
Washington, Harold C. 239 n. 7
Wasserfall, Rahel 199 n. 28
Watanabe, Kazuko 90 n. 39
Watson, Wilford G. E. 255 n. 70
Weinfeld, Moshe 155 n. 25
Weippert, Manfred 42 n. 79, 73 n. 39, 76, 76 n. 47

Welch, J. L. 182 n. 23
Wenham, Gordon 198, 198 n. 21 and 23
West, Martin L. 117 n. 51
Wiesemann, Claudia 63–64 n. 12
Wildberger, Hans 221 n. 16
Williams, Walter L. 185 n. 32
Williamson, Hugh G. M. 11 n. 1, 30 n. 16
Wilson, Brian 183 n 27
Wilson, Robert R. 151 n. 10, 154 n. 21, 155 n. 26, 265 n. 104
Winslow, Karen Strand 153 n. 16
Wright, Benjamin G. 55 n. 142, 57, 57 n. 147
Wright, David P. 199 n. 29
Yardeni, Ada 56 n. 145
Yates, Gary E. 265 n. 104
Yee, Gale 195 n. 7, 242 n. 17, 247 n. 38
Youngsook Kim Harvey 185 n. 33
Zeitlin, Froma I. 103–4 n. 11
Zgoll, Annette 177 n. 12
Zimmerli, Walther 194, 194 n. 4, 201 n. 37, 203 n. 44, 204 n. 50, 210 n. 78, 219 n. 11, 220 n. 13, 233 n. 36, 238 n. 4, 240 n. 11
Zimmermann, Ruben 55 n. 138
Zipor, Moshe A. 253 n. 61
Žižek, Slavoj 216 n. 2
Zólyomi, Gábor 179 n. 14
Zsolnay, Ilona 3–4, 36 n. 52, 61 n. 5, 69 n. 24, 71, 72 n. 36, 96 n. 60, 97 n. 61

Concordance of Text Numbers

Concordance of text numbers in Nissinen, *Prophets and Prophecy in the Ancient Near East* (SBLWAW 12; Atlanta: Society of Biblical Literature, 2003) (= WAW), Florilegium Marianum (= FM), Les Archives royales de Mari (= ARM), and the State Archives of Assyria (= SAA).

WAW	FM / ARM / SAA		
1	FM 7 39	28	ARM 26 218
2	FM 7 38	29	ARM 26 219
3	FM 6 1	30	ARM 26 220
4	ARM 26 194	31	ARM 26 221
5	ARM 26 195	32	ARM 26 221bis
6	ARM 26 196	33	ARM 26 222
7	ARM 26 197	34	ARM 26 223
8	ARM 26 198		ARM 26 224–226
9	ARM 26 199	35	ARM 26 227
10	ARM 26 200		ARM 26 228
11	ARM 26 201	36	ARM 26 229
12	ARM 26 202		ARM 26 230–231
13	ARM 26 203	37	ARM 26 232
14	ARM 26 204	38	ARM 26 233
15	ARM 26 205	39	ARM 26 234
16	ARM 26 206	40	ARM 26 235
17	ARM 26 207	41	ARM 26 236
18	ARM 26 208	42	ARM 26 237
19	ARM 26 209	43	ARM 26 238
20	ARM 26 210	44	ARM 26 239
21	ARM 26 211	45	ARM 26 240
22	ARM 26 212		ARM 26 241–242
23	ARM 26 213	46	ARM 26 243
24	ARM 26 214	47	ARM 26 371
25	ARM 26 215	48	ARM 26 414
26	ARM 26 216	49	ARM 27 32
27	ARM 26 217	50	FM 3 152
		51	FM 3 2

CONCORDANCE OF TEXT NUMBERS

52	FM 3 3	95	SAA 9 10
53	A.3796	96	SAA 9 11
54	ARM 9 22	97	Nin A i 1–ii 11
55	ARM 21 333	98	Ass A i 31–ii 26
56	ARM 22 167	99	Prim T ii 7–24
57	A.4676	100	Prism A ii 126–iii 26
58	ARM 22 326	101	Prism B v 16–vi 16
59	ARM 23 446	102	SAA 2 6, §10 (108–122)
60	ARM 25 15	103	SAA 3 34/35
61	ARM 25 142	104	SAA 7 9
62	M.11436	105	SAA 10 109
63	T.82 ix: 2–4	106	SAA 10 111
64	Epic of Zimri-Lim, 137–142	107	SAA 10 284
65	FM 6 45	108	SAA 10 294
66	FLP 1674	109	SAA 10 352
67	FLP 2064	110	SAA 12 69
68	SAA 9 1.1	111	SAA 13 37
69	SAA 9 1.2	112	SAA 13 139
70	SAA 9 1.3	113	SAA 13 144
71	SAA 9 1.4	114	SAA 13 148
72	SAA 9 1.5	115	SAA 16 59
73	SAA 9 1.6	116	SAA 16 60
74	SAA 9 1.7	117	SAA 16 61
75	SAA 9 1.8	118	Farber 1977 A II a: 1–33
76	SAA 9 1.9	119	TCS 1 369
77	SAA 9 1.10	120	MSL 12 5.22: 20–32
78	SAA 9 2.1	121	EA 23
79	SAA 9 2.2	122	*Ugaritica* 5 162: 2–12
80	SAA 9 2.3	123	VS 19 1: i 37'–39'
81	SAA 9 2.4	124	MSL 12 4.212: 193–217
82	SAA 9 2.5	125	MSL 12 4.222: 116–123
83	SAA 9 2.6	126	MSL 12 6.2: 129–149
84	SAA 9 3.1	127	*Šumma izbu* xi: 7–8
85	SAA 9 3.2	128	K 1913: 365d-e
86	SAA 9 3.3	129	*Šumma ālu* i: 85–117
87	SAA 9 3.4	130	OECT 1 20–21: rev. 35–46
88	SAA 9 3.5	131	YOS 6 18
89	SAA 9 4	132	YOS 7 135
90	SAA 9 5	133	ABRT I 1, 434–452
91	SAA 9 6	134	AD 3 -132 B: rev. 25–u.e. 5
92	SAA 9 7	135	AD 3 -132 C: 26–33
93	SAA 9 8		
94	SAA 9 9	136	Amman Citadel Inscription

137	Zakkur Stela	ARM 26 216	26
138	Deir 'Allā	ARM 26 217	27
139	Lachish 3	ARM 26 218	28
140	Lachish 6	ARM 26 219	29
141	Lachish 16	ARM 26 220	30
142	Wenamon	ARM 26 221	31
		ARM 26 221bis	32
		ARM 26 222	33
FM / ARM / SAA	**WAW**	ARM 26 223	34
A.3796	53	ARM 26 224–226	/
A.4676	57	ARM 26 227	35
ABRT I 1, 434–452	133	ARM 26 228	/
AD 3 -132 B: rev. 25–u.e. 5	134	ARM 26 229	36
AD 3 -132 C: 26–33	135	ARM 26 230–231	/
ARM 9 22	54	ARM 26 232	37
ARM 21 333	55	ARM 26 233	38
ARM 22 167	56	ARM 26 234	39
ARM 22 326	58	ARM 26 235	40
ARM 23 446	59	ARM 26 236	41
ARM 25 15	60	ARM 26 237	42
ARM 25 142	61	ARM 26 238	43
ARM 26 194	4	ARM 26 239	44
ARM 26 195	5	ARM 26 240	45
ARM 26 196	6	ARM 26 241–242	/
ARM 26 197	7	ARM 26 243	46
ARM 26 198	8	ARM 26 371	47
ARM 26 199	9	ARM 26 414	48
ARM 26 200	10	ARM 27 32	49
ARM 26 201	11	Ass A i 31–ii 26	98
ARM 26 202	12	EA 23	121
ARM 26 203	13	Epic of Zimri-Lim, 137–142	64
ARM 26 204	14	Farber 1977 A II a: 1–33	118
ARM 26 205	15	FLP 1674	66
ARM 26 206	16	FLP 2064	67
ARM 26 207	17	FM 3 2	51
ARM 26 208	18	FM 3 3	52
ARM 26 209	19	FM 3 152	50
ARM 26 210	20	FM 6 1	3
ARM 26 211	21	FM 6 45	65
ARM 26 212	22	FM 7 39	1
ARM 26 213	23	FM 7 38	2
ARM 26 214	24	K 1913: 365d-e	128
ARM 26 215	25	M.11436	62

CONCORDANCE OF TEXT NUMBERS

MSL 12 5.22: 20–32	120
MSL 12 4.212: 193–217	124
MSL 12 4.222: 116–123	125
MSL 12 6.2: 129–149	126
OECT 1 20–21: rev. 35–46	130
Nin A i 1–ii 11	97
Prism T ii 7–24	99
Prism A ii 126–iii 26	100
Prism B v 16–vi 16	101
SAA 2 6, §10 (108–122)	102
SAA 3 34/35	103
SAA 7 9	104
SAA 9 1.1	68
SAA 9 1.2	69
SAA 9 1.3	70
SAA 9 1.4	71
SAA 9 1.5	71
SAA 9 1.6	73
SAA 9 1.7	74
SAA 9 1.8	75
SAA 9 1.9	76
SAA 9 1.10	77
SAA 9 2.1	78
SAA 9 2.2	79
SAA 9 2.3	80
SAA 9 2.4	81
SAA 9 2.5	82
SAA 9 2.6	83
SAA 9 3.1	84
SAA 9 3.2	85
SAA 9 3.3	86
SAA 9 3.4	87
SAA 9 3.5	88
SAA 9 4	89
SAA 9 5	90
SAA 9 6	91
SAA 9 7	92
SAA 9 8	93
SAA 9 9	94
SAA 9 10	95
SAA 9 11	96
SAA 10 109	105
SAA 10 111	106

SAA 10 284	107
SAA 10 294	108
SAA 10 352	109
SAA 12 69	110
SAA 13 37	111
SAA 13 139	112
SAA 13 144	113
SAA 13 148	114
SAA 16 59	115
SAA 16 60	116
SAA 16 61	117
Šumma ālu i: 85–117	129
Šumma izbu xi: 7–8	127
T.82 ix: 2–4	63
TCS 1 369	119
Ugaritica 5 162: 2–12	122
VS 19 1: i 37'–39'	123
YOS 6 18	131
YOS 7 135	132
Amman Citadel Inscription	136
Deir 'Allā	138
Lachish 3	139
Lachish 6	140
Lachish 16	141
Wenamon	142
Zakkur Stela	137

www.ingramcontent.com/pod-product-compliance
Lightning Source LLC
Chambersburg PA
CBHW022008300426
44117CB00005B/86